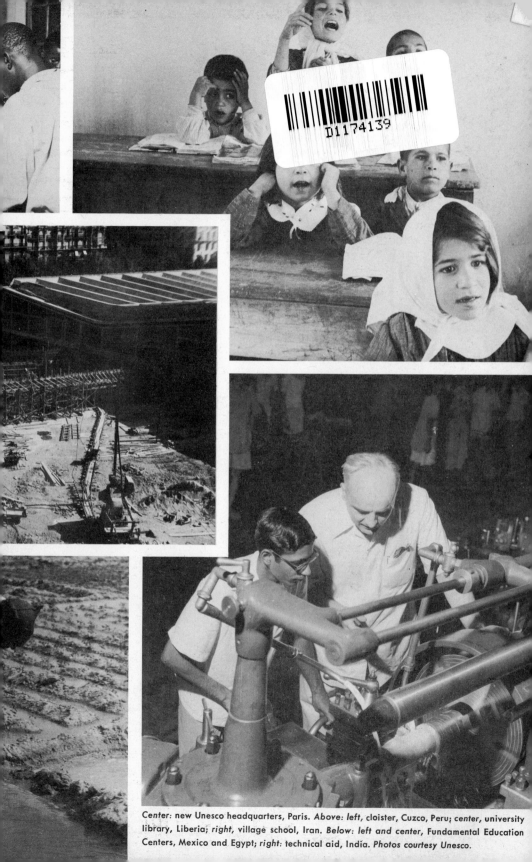

Center: new Unesco headquarters, Paris. Above: *left, cloister, Cuzco, Peru; center, university library, Liberia; right, village school, Iran. Below: left and center, Fundamental Education Centers, Mexico and Egypt; right: technical aid, India. Photos courtesy Unesco.*

U
N
E
S
C
O

Purpose
Progress
Prospects

U N E S C O

Purpose
Progress
Prospects

WALTER H. C. LAVES
CHARLES A. THOMSON

INDIANA UNIVERSITY PRESS
BLOOMINGTON 1957

SECOND PRINTING

Copyright © 1957 by Indiana University Press
All Rights Reserved

MANUFACTURED IN THE UNITED STATES OF AMERICA

Library of Congress Catalog Card Number: 57-10728

20040

To the Memory

of

Grayson N. Kefauver
Pioneer, 1942-1946,
in the Planning of Unesco

and

William Hodson, Jr.
Pioneer, 1947-1954,
in the Administration of Unesco

PREFACE

WRITTEN by two Americans who have observed closely the work of the United Nations Educational, Scientific and Cultural Organization (Unesco) during most of its first decade, this book is intended for citizens of all countries in the United Nations family.

The idea of doing jointly a volume on Unesco came to both of the authors separately and almost simultaneously. They have collaborated closely in the planning and writing of the book. Mr. Thomson, who came to Indiana University under a research grant early in 1955, carried major responsibility for the basic research and the initial drafting of most of the program chapters. However, the final manuscript is a joint product of the two authors in its organization, content, and style.

The earlier activities of the two authors in relation to Unesco have complemented each other. From 1947 to 1950, Mr. Laves served at Paris as Deputy Director General of Unesco. Mr. Thomson was in Washington during this period, as Director of the Unesco Relations Staff in the Department of State—the governmental focus for relations with Unesco—and as Executive Secretary of the United States National Commission for Unesco, a body of one hundred members set up by Act of Congress. From 1950 to 1954, the geographic locations of the authors were reversed. Mr. Laves returned to the United States, playing a leading part in the U. S. National Commission for Unesco, and serving for a time as its Chairman. During these years Mr. Thomson was in Paris as Counselor for Unesco Affairs of the American Embassy, and as United States representative at Unesco. While Mr. Laves' academic experience has been primarily in political science, Mr. Thomson's major academic interest has been in the field of sociology. Both Mr. Laves and Mr. Thomson have had many years of administrative experience with the Federal government.

Because of the range and complexity of Unesco's work, the authors have consulted many persons in various fields of study and in a large number of countries. They wish to express gratitude for reading the manuscript, in whole or in part, and making comments and criticisms, and for other counsel, to Sir Ronald Adam, Robert C. Angell, Bunthin Attagara, Charles S. Ascher, John W. Ashton, Wallace W. Atwood, Jr., Willard W. Beatty, Jaime Benítez, William Benton, Mrs. Esther C. Brunauer, Edward H. Buehrig, William G. Carr, Ben M. Cherrington, Brock Chisholm, Verner W. Clapp, Ralph E. Cleland, Frederick S. Dunn, H. Lionel Elvin, A. Peter Fraenkel, Ralph W. Hardy, Merrill F. Hartshorn, Richard H. Heindel, Monsignor Frederick G. Hochwalt, Henry Hope, John Howe, Henry Kellerman, Otto Klineberg, L. C. Larson, Waldo Leland, Richard P. McKeon, James Marshall, Guy S. Métraux, Mrs. Grace L. McCann Morley, Mrs. Alva Myrdal, W. Albert Noyes, Jr., Charles E. Odegaard, William R. Parker, Mrs. Henry Potter Russell, Howland H. Sargeant, Herbert W. Schneider, Paul H. Sheats, Robert S. Smith, Harold W. Spivacke, Elvin C. Stakman, Murray Stedman, George D. Stoddard, Donald F. Sullivan, John W. Taylor, Ralph E. Turner, Gerald Wendt, Gilbert F. White, Miss Helen C. White, Howard E. Wilson, and Mrs. Louise Leonard Wright.

For responding helpfully to special questions regarding Unesco, they are indebted to Mohammed Awad (Egypt), Clarence E. Beeby (New Zealand), Frans Bender (Netherlands), Paulo E. de Berrêdo Carneiro (Brazil), F. R. Cowell (United Kingdom), Gardner Davies (Australia), Toru Hagiwara (Japan), David Hardman (United Kingdom), Humayun Kabir (India), Henri Laugier (France), Monsignor Jean Maroun (Lebanon), Nathaniel V. Massaquoi (Liberia), Jakob Nielsen (Denmark), Mrs. Gerónima Pecson (Philippines), C. Parra-Pérez (Venezuela), Alexandre Photiades (deceased) (Greece), G. A. Raadi (Iran), A. Adrian Roberts (Union of South Africa), Alf Sommerfelt (Norway), Robert Valeur (France), Louis Verniers (Belgium), E. Ronald Walker (Australia), Chen Yuan (China), Kuo Yu-shou (China), Constantin K. Zurayk (Syria).

A word of particular appreciation goes to Luther H. Evans, Director General of Unesco, and numerous past and present members of the secretariat in Paris; and to Max McCullough and his colleagues on the Unesco Relations Staff of the Department of State.

This study could not have been undertaken without the encouragement, financial and otherwise, of Indiana University, its President, Herman B Wells, and many members of the faculty, to whom we wish here to express our deep gratitude. The volume has profited from the editorial assistance of Bernard B. Perry and his colleagues of the Indiana University Press. The Columbia Foundation of San Francisco and the New World Foundation of Chicago have generously made grants for the completion and wider distribution of the volume.

A special word of thanks is due Miss Dorothy Lazarus, whose service in the Paris office of the Counselor for Unesco Affairs of the American Embassy, and as a member of the United States Delegation at several sessions of the Unesco General Conference, gave her a unique and detailed knowledge of Unesco documents, publications, and other material. Her help as research assistant throughout the preparation of the book was invaluable. She contributed continually to the progress of the manuscript and made many positive suggestions for the improvement of its content and clarity.

Without the help of Mrs. Harry Buchler and members of the secretarial staff of the Department of Government, the volume could not have been completed.

The authors alone are responsible for the content of the book, and for whatever errors of fact or interpretation it may contain. One of them happily acknowledges the many contributions made to the development of Unesco as well as to the writing of this book by Ruth, Ruthie, and Peggy in Paris, in Washington, and in Bloomington. The other bears witness to the devotion to Unesco and the unfailing support and sympathy of his wife, who embarked on the "great exploration" before the end of her service in Paris; and to the continuing and sustaining understanding of his daughter.

Contents

Mass Communication

Libraries

Bibliography, Documentation, and Abstracting—Exchange of Publications

Museums

Monuments and Historic Sites

Removal of Barriers to Free Flow of Information

Unesco and the Advancement of Knowledge

Subventions to Nongovernmental Organizations—Attitude of Governments and Specialists

Fundamental Education

The Marbial Valley Project—War on Ignorance and Illiteracy —UN Technical Assistance Program—Finding the Best Methods and Media—Applying Methods and Media—Preparing Workers and Materials—Appraisal of the Fundamental Education Centers

Adult Education

Extension of Free and Compulsory Education

The Size and Nature of the Task—Recommendations and Regional Conferences—Access of Girls and Women to Education—International Institute of Child Study at Bangkok

Secondary and Higher Education

The Curriculum

Natural Sciences—Social Sciences—Philosophy and Humanities—The Arts

Braille for the Blind

Unesco and World Educational Needs

Policies of Individual States toward Unesco

France—United Kingdom and Commonwealth of Nations—
United States—USSR—India—Arab States—Latin American
Republics—Germany and Japan

Unesco in National Policies

Where Has Unesco Been Most Effective?

Advancement of Knowledge—Promotion of Human Welfare
—Development of International Understanding

Unesco in the Perspective of History

A New Kind of World Influence—Emphasis on the Individual—Help to New States

What Are Unesco's Prospects for the Future?

INTRODUCTION

THE PURPOSE of this book is to review the first ten years of a relatively new kind of international agency: the United Nations Educational, Scientific and Cultural Organization (Unesco). In this period the words of its Constitution concerning objectives and methods were translated into a program whose impact has been felt on every continent and in almost every country. It was a period of uncertainty and trial and error regarding what Unesco should do and how it should do it. Only gradually did the practical importance of Unesco become clear to member states, to many public groups, and to specialists in education, science, and culture.

The creation of the United Nations system with its specialized agencies was an endeavor to provide an institutional framework for organized international cooperation. The need for it derived in general from the growing interdependence of nations, and in particular from the human suffering and the material destruction caused by World War II. But with this motivation was combined a new realization, based on the experience of inter-Allied cooperation during the war, that it was practical to organize international relations on a clear and more logical basis.

Such wartime experiments in international collaboration as the Raw Materials Control Board, the Inter-Allied Commodities Control Board, the Inter-Allied Shipping Board, and the combined Chiefs of Staff had gone far beyond inter-Allied cooperation in the first World War and anything attempted under the League of Nations. These experiments had indicated that, when survival was at stake, concepts of national sovereignty could in some cases be modified and the emotions associated with nationalism disciplined to permit effective cooperation among sovereign states.

The United Nations system represented an effort to apply the liberal democratic doctrines underlying a number of national governments to world-wide institutions of international cooperation. The role of force in the maintenance of peace was not disregarded but increased recognition was given to the significant role of persuasion and agreement in attaining united action. The creation of the United Nations served, as it were, to provide an international capstone for the structure of responsible democratic governmental institutions which had gradually been taking form within various nations. The move to establish the United Nations was evidence of pragmatic faith in man's ability to organize his world-wide relationships in such a way as to reduce the risk of war and increase the use of productive energy for the constructive advancement of human welfare. The most extensive application of liberal democratic ideas was found in the provisions for economic, social, and humanitarian cooperation written into the Charter of the United Nations and the constitutions of its specialized agencies.

Undoubtedly, individuals and nations were in part motivated in their support of the United Nations by considerations other than the extension of democratic ideas or the achievement of peace. But the background for the development of the United Nations system is to be found in the long history of liberalism and democracy. That is why that system has been widely considered by free peoples as mankind's best hope for peace. And that is why the UN was intended to have a place in the power structure of postwar international relations.

Read by Americans or by citizens of other democratic countries, the language of the basic documents of the United Nations agencies recalls familiar faiths: in man, in truth, and in the possibility of achieving a peaceful world through international understanding and cooperation. Faith in man was stated in terms of the dignity and worth of the individual, and of the capacity of man for education, for freedom, and for cooperation. Human rights and fundamental freedoms were values which must be respected and encouraged. Faith in truth was reflected in the emphases on the free exchange of knowledge and ideas and on "the unrestricted pursuit of objective truth."[1] Faith in the attainment of world peace through international understanding and cooperation was mirrored in declarations that the United Nations could "save succeeding generations from the scourge of war" and that the resources of education, science, and culture could con-tribute to peace and security and foster the intellectual and moral solidarity of mankind.

Unesco was established on the assumption that the resources of education, science, and culture could usefully contribute to interna-tional peace and security by complementing the work of the United Nations.

Thus the creation of Unesco in 1945 was a natural part of this post-war effort to build a democratic framework for organized interna-tional cooperation. It was in a sense a practical application of the long tradition of human speculation concerning the relation of edu-cation, science, and culture to politics and the problems of the com-munity—a tradition which includes in its history the Roman con-ception of philosophy, the Renaissance idea of a republic of letters, and the academies and scientific interchange of the seventeenth century. To attack the world's educational and cultural problems and to mobilize the world's resources in these areas toward the achieve-ment of a peaceful United Nations community seemed both logical and necessary.

Léon Blum perhaps best expressed the prevailing attitude at the 1945 London Conference where the Unesco Constitution was written, when he urged the importance of steering Unesco's future activities "in the direction of that 'ideology' of democracy and progress which is the psychological condition, the psychological basis of international solidarity and peace."[2]

The current mood at the time of the 1945 Unesco Conference at London was one of hope as well as faith. The war was over. Victory over the Fascist dictatorships had been complete. The democratic nations had reached, in the military collaboration that brought vic-tory, a new peak in international cooperation and solidarity. Surely, it was believed, if the highly organized and powerful forces of Fascist aggression had been turned back and the opportunity for democratic life again restored, then means and a will could now be found to ensure a peace among genuinely peaceful people.

This faith and hope that something could and would be done were reinforced by a special sense of urgency. Something must be done. The operations of the Fascist system which had led to the capturing of men's minds first within the dictatorships themselves, and then to a

lesser extent in the occupied territories, had given new emphasis to
the importance of human attitudes and particularly to freedom of
thought as a condition for a lasting peace.

A further element in the optimistic outlook of the London Conference of 1945 was the general expectation that the world was to be
blessed by a prolonged period of peace—a positive peace and not
merely the absence of war—which would provide opportunity to build
securely a world community, to serve as a foundation for the work
of the United Nations. Much of the history of Unesco is therefore
the story of the effort to realize the high hopes of its creators despite
the fact that this fundamental assumption had proved to be illusory.

An international agency, a specialized agency of the United Nations, seemed to some statesmen and scholars as well as to many members of the general public an appropriate means of helping nations
to organize themselves and their relationships toward achieving the
goal which appeared almost within man's grasp. The purpose of
Unesco would be to contribute to peace and security by strengthening
the educational, scientific, and cultural resources of the world and by
stimulating the use of these resources in the maintenance of peace
and the promotion of human welfare. Its task would thus be central
to that of the entire United Nations system, and the degree of
Unesco's success would be an evidence of man's will and ability to
apply rational democratic doctrine in the area of this particular organization's jurisdiction. It would go far beyond the necessarily timid
beginnings of intellectual cooperation developed under the League
of Nations. It would try actually to come to grips with one of the
central problems of peace: the attitudes of peoples toward each other
and their understanding of the role of international cooperation in
the promotion of human welfare.

Unesco has functioned for a full decade, carrying on a wide variety
of tasks and providing assistance in response to demands from its
eighty member states. Coupled with the many responsibilities relating to its program activities has been the task of setting up the organization and developing it into an effective administrative agency.
For over ten years the headquarters have been in the former Hotel
Majestic in Paris. A new building is under construction, to be finished
in 1958. In addition, offices have been established and maintained in
Cairo, New Delhi, Jakarta, Montevideo, Havana, and at United
Nations headquarters in New York City. A secretariat of 1,100 per-

sons has been recruited, including citizens of more than fifty member states.

The number of member states increased from thirty in December 1946 to eighty in December 1956. The composition of the membership has been materially altered, reflecting the changes in the family of nations resulting from the rise of new states, the decline of colonialism, and the wave of nationalism that has swept over the world.

During the first ten years the General Conference, made up of delegations of member states, has held nine regular sessions, four in Paris, the others in Mexico City, Beirut, Florence, Montevideo, and New Delhi.[3] The Executive Board has held forty-six sessions, an average of four to five a year, mostly at Paris headquarters. Within the decade, Unesco has had three Directors General—an Englishman, a Mexican, and most recently a citizen of the United States.

Unesco's program has been focused upon three principal objectives: the advancement of knowledge by strengthening the educational, scientific, and cultural resources of individual countries and of mankind as a whole; the promotion of human welfare through a cooperative attack on major world problems; and the development of international understanding by a variety of means both direct and indirect. All three objectives were believed to be essential parts of Unesco's function to contribute to peace and security. The scope and structure of the program, initially overloaded and confused, are gradually becoming clarified. With the acquisition of experience, Unesco activities have grown in efficiency and usefulness.

Although Unesco is basically an intergovernmental organization, it has sought to develop contacts through National Commissions with the people in more than seventy of its member states and with a multitude of nongovernmental organizations.

Public support for and response to Unesco's efforts have not been uniform. They have varied with circumstances and the climate of international politics. Following fairly general enthusiasm in 1945 and 1946 for the ideas underlying the organization and the work it was to perform, interest declined in some countries and increased in others. This paralleled growing disappointment that none of the United Nations agencies seemed able to guarantee lasting peace. Only in the United States and the countries of the Soviet bloc was there at any time systematic opposition to the work of Unesco. The opposition in the Soviet countries, prior to the USSR's joining Unesco in

1954, came from those who controlled the governments. In the United States the opposition has centered in a number of "professional" patriotic groups. The attacks by these groups upon Unesco have been more vitriolic than those on any other international agency.

Response among specialist groups within the area of Unesco's responsibility has varied. Among scientists, educators, and cultural leaders there has been growing interest over the years in individual projects, but probably general regret at the small appropriations governments have provided for the work of Unesco. Among the public at large, in spite of an almost instinctive appreciation of Unesco's work, there has been a noticeable lack of knowledge of what Unesco was attempting to do, paralleled by disappointment that the organization was having only a limited impact outside the technical field of education, science, and culture.

Governments, with the exception for a time of the Soviet bloc, have given formal support to the organization, but none of the principal member states has yet appeared to consider Unesco of major concern in its foreign policy or in the broader frame of United Nations affairs. None has consistently accorded it top-level governmental support. Response has been slow in terms of domestic legislation and administrative action to carry out obligations deriving from the Constitution or from General Conference resolutions.

Neither Unesco nor its member states have lived up to the expectations of those who pressed for its creation in 1945. Even so, as one of the leading specialized agencies of the United Nations system and as the first international agency of its scope, Unesco appears not only to hold promise but actually to be growing into a position of importance in the public affairs of mankind.

The present volume will review what Unesco has done from 1946 to 1956. It gives primary attention to the Unesco program and discusses such matters as budget, administration, and personnel, only as they bear on the program. The book is therefore not a general history of the organization but rather an explanation and analysis of its program. The omission of an analysis of the secretariat as a branch of the new postwar international civil service has been dictated only by considerations of space and organization. This the authors regret, particularly because of the dedication and high quality of service evidenced throughout the decade by this particular group of pioneers in international administration.

There is also no separate discussion of the technical assistance program. Since so much of Unesco's "normal" program involves the providing of technical assistance, no good purpose would be served by such separate treatment. This is not to belittle the tremendous importance of the administrative device developed under the United Nations Expanded Program of Technical Assistance. Its impact upon Unesco's other activities is discussed in Chapter III.

The book tries to explain for the general reader what Unesco has done and why, and, to the extent that judgment may be possible, how useful Unesco has been. The introductory part of the book, made up of three chapters, reviews briefly the institutions and activities which served as forerunners to Unesco; the issues faced in drafting its Constitution; and the stages through which the program has developed. The main part of the book, composed of nine chapters, outlines the character and scope of the Unesco program, listing the activities undertaken to serve its central purpose of contributing to peace and security.

The final section of the book consists of three chapters. One discusses the factors which have shaped the Unesco program—the influence of member states, the role of the Executive Board and of the first three Directors General, and the impact of such factors as special interest groups and the cold war. Another chapter deals with Unesco and member states, giving special attention to National Commissions. The final chapter attempts to present a summary and appraisal of the organization's work during its first decade.

The authors have attempted to maintain an objective approach to the purpose and program of Unesco and one that recognizes the complexity of its task. Yet it is inevitable that they express a point of view that is influenced by the fact that they are citizens of the United States.

LIST OF ABBREVIATIONS

ACC	United Nations Administrative Committee on Coordination
AFL	American Federation of Labor
ASFEC	Arab States Fundamental Education Center
CAME	Conference of Allied Ministers of Education
CERN	European Organization for Nuclear Research
CIO	Congress of Industrial Organizations
CIOMS	Council of International Organizations of Medical Science
CIPHS	See ICPHS
CREFAL	Regional Fundamental Education Training Center for Latin America
ECOSOC	United Nations Economic and Social Council
FAO	Food and Agricultural Organization of the United Nations
GATT	General Agreement on Tariffs and Trade
IBE	International Bureau of Education
ICOM	International Council of Museums
ICPHS	International Council for Philosophy and Humanistic Studies (sometimes CIPHS from initials of title in French)
ICSU	International Council of Scientific Unions
ILO	International Labor Organization
NGO	An international nongovernmental organization
OAS	Organization of American States
P.E.N. Club	International Poets, Editors and Novelists Club
SUNFED	Special United Nations Fund for Economic Development
TAB	United Nations Technical Assistance Board
TAC	United Nations Technical Assistance Committee
TICER	Temporary International Council for Educational Reconstruction
UN	United Nations

Unesco	United Nations Educational, Scientific and Cultural Organization
UNETAP	United Nations Expanded Technical Assistance Program
UNKRA	United Nations Korean Reconstruction Agency
UNRRA	United Nations Relief and Rehabilitation Administration
UNRWA	United Nations Relief and Works Agency
URS	Unesco Relations Staff, U.S. Department of State
U.S.	United States of America
USSR	Union of Soviet Socialist Republics
WCOTP	World Confederation of Organizations of the Teaching Profession
WHO	World Health Organization
WMO	World Meteorological Organization

PART 1

UNESCO'S ORIGINS, ITS CHARACTER,
AND THE EVOLUTION OF
ITS PROGRAM

CHAPTER I

WHY WAS UNESCO CREATED?

In the gray days of November 1945, with the second World War scarcely over, representatives of forty-four nations met at London, in the Institute of Civil Engineers on Great George Street not far from Westminster Abbey, to write the constitution for the United Nations Educational, Scientific and Cultural Organization (Unesco). War had cruelly marred the British capital. There were bombed-out buildings, and gaping pits where homes once stood. At the conference were delegates still in uniform, fighters in the Allied forces and the underground resistance movements, recent prisoners of war returned to freedom.

These government delegates met in an atmosphere of bitter memories but of renewed hope. The war's destructiveness had surpassed anything previously known to man. The atomic bomb had been dropped on Hiroshima. With such a weapon of absolute destruction, civilization could survive only if a climate of mutual understanding and mutual trust were created.[1] This universal longing for a better world had already brought adoption of the United Nations Charter at San Francisco. According to a French philosopher, that charter had created the United Nations as a body; and now Unesco's constitution would "give that body a soul."[2]

At this meeting in London in November 1945 were Prime Minister Clement Attlee of Great Britain, and Ellen Wilkinson, his Minister of Education. Léon Blum, former French Premier, with his charity, urbanity, and faith uncorroded by four long years in a German concentration camp, led the French delegation. Among China's representatives was Hu Shih, the philosopher. Archibald MacLeish, poet and scholar, formerly Librarian of Congress and Assistant Secretary of State, spoke for the United States. Gilbert Murray of Oxford, long

3

prominent in the League of Nations, and Sir Alfred Zimmern, a keen student of international relations, represented earlier efforts to link internationally the intellectual forces of the world; as did Henri Bonnet, who had directed for many years the Institute of Intellectual Cooperation at Paris; Jean Piaget, Director of the International Bureau of Education at Geneva; and Concha Romero James of the Pan American Union.

Present also were three men who later headed successively the new organization. First, Julian Huxley of England, Director General of Unesco from 1946 to 1948, a man of wit, intellectual eagerness, and an enormous range of knowledge. He was not a member of the British delegation but was in and out of the conference. Second, Jaime Torres Bodet of Mexico, Director General from 1948 to 1952, poet and diplomat of distinction, who as Mexico's Minister of Education had won international renown for his campaign against illiteracy. Luther Evans from the United States, successor to MacLeish as Librarian of Congress, unassuming, forthright, genial, was chosen Director General in 1953. Present also was an American Lieutenant Colonel, John W. Taylor, then working on educational plans for the United States military government in Germany. He served Unesco as Deputy Director General from 1951 to 1952, and as Acting Director General from the latter date until July 1953.

Of the fifty-one states signing the United Nations Charter at San Francisco, all were represented at the London Conference except seven: Ethiopia; Costa Rica, Honduras, and Paraguay; the USSR, Byelorussia, and the Ukraine.

What Needs Was Unesco to Meet?

Why did this large number of nations join to establish an international organization for education, science, and culture? What were the needs which they were trying to meet? The answers lie only in part in the discussions at San Francisco and in the diplomatic exchanges that preceded the meeting in the British capital. The real needs that gave rise to the demand for Unesco, voiced in the debates at the London Conference, were the outgrowth not only of the war but of many decades of earlier experience.

Reconstruction

Most obvious was the need for educational and cultural reconstruction of war-damaged countries, among which Poland, Greece, China, and the Philippines had perhaps suffered most grievously. School and university buildings had to be repaired or rebuilt; textbooks and furnishings replaced; libraries and laboratories restocked and equipped. Serious losses among teachers, directors, and other educational personnel demanded new programs of recruitment and training. Educational methods needed revision and improvement. Many countries required both material and technical aid from the outside if their schools were again to start training children and youth, and if such countries were to contribute effectively to Unesco's future activities.

Delegates at London had in mind, of course, more than the material ravages of war. They were also deeply concerned with the devastation in moral and spiritual values, by both war and totalitarianism, and with the need for international understanding in preserving peace. The Turkish delegate referred to the scorn of human values implanted by the Axis powers. The Belgian representative commented on the prominence in World War II of a propaganda of lies and hate and stressed the need for what he described as "moral disintoxication." Léon Blum emphasized the distortion of education and culture by the totalitarian regimes. Prime Minister Attlee denounced "the totalitarian practice of drawing a curtain around the minds of the people"—the indoctrination that throttled mental freedom and independent judgment.[3]

Building for Peace through Understanding

The climate of opinion at the time of the London Conference revealed a horror of German Nazism and a resolve that such a system should never rise again. Nazism, everyone agreed, was the chief enemy, with its aggressive nationalism, racism, and brutality, rather than the basically similar Italian fascism or Japanese militarism. It was Nazism that had raised havoc with the nations whose delegations were most vocal at London in 1945. These nations determined to create an agency to make education an instrument for peace rather than war, curb the destructive force of exaggerated nationalism, throw the beam of truth on the claims of racism, and establish the human rights of every man.[4]

Participants at London thus identified in unequivocal terms the educational and moral causes of war. But the positive role of international understanding in a secure peace was also in their minds. Attlee said once again what many individuals had said in the 1930's— that "wars begin in the minds of men. And we are to live," he added, "in a world of democracies, where the mind of the common man will be all important."[5] The New Zealand delegate stressed the ties linking peace, democracy, and education. "A peace-loving democracy cannot live and breathe freely except in a world of peace-loving democracies; and we know further that education, in the broad sense of that word, is the only means whereby peace-loving democracies can be created and renewed."[6]

The constructive task of the new organization was outlined by Léon Blum, who asked Unesco to "establish the spirit of peace in the world," a spirit which called for courage, resolution, and sacrifice. The Peruvian delegate said that education must recognize the unity of the human race. The Yugoslav representative urged re-education both of the people of the Axis countries and of "ourselves." The Indian delegate argued that education must refashion itself to reshape the world.[7] In short, the delegates at London called for better education to fashion better men for a new life in a democratic society.[8] Such comments reveal something of the sense of urgency which men showed in creating Unesco, and indicate even more clearly than the words of Unesco's constitution the needs which the organization was created to meet.

Exchange of Useful Knowledge

A third need, less dramatic but no less fundamental than the two mentioned above, was for exchange of knowledge among educational leaders and scholars. A "clearing house" could accomplish this—an international instrument through which any country might gain access to knowledge and ideas from other parts of the world. A "clearing house" had a demonstrable practical value. Thus Mr. Attlee asked at London what the new organization would do for the man in the

street and "the children in the street?" He answered that every country could learn from efforts of other countries to fit education to the
needs of a changing world.[9]

The French and certain other Europeans were concerned with exchange of knowledge and ideas among scholars and "intellectuals"—
among what they called the "élite." Through such leaders knowledge
and ideas would exert, they believed, influence on the masses of people. For some, intellectual cooperation was an end in itself. For others
it was a means to a larger end. Torres Bodet viewed it as "the cooperation of men of brain . . . to prevent the reproduction of the monstrous
errors which have led nations to settle their problems by violence."[10]

Other delegates at London emphasized that Unesco's role must not
stop with the élite. Intellectual cooperation was not unimportant,
but rather too limited an approach. The Norwegian delegate urged
the new organization to "plough much deeper than to the strata of
the intellectual professions. . . ."[11] Leaders at London sensed the gulf
in the modern world between specialists, on whose help Unesco must
depend, and the mass public to which it wished to appeal.

At London both camps agreed that there was need for an international organization which would open channels for all peoples to
the world's body of knowledge. The only question involved was that
of relative importance. Unesco must seek to reach both the masses
and the leaders. It could not stop with intellectual groups but must
try to influence the broadest possible audience. This everyone admitted. Yet the larger part of the public can most effectively be
reached through leadership groups such as teachers, writers, scholars,
and others.

Aid to Economically Less Developed Countries

A fourth need mentioned at London concerned the economically
less developed countries. Their spokesmen pleaded for all possible
assistance in improving the economic and social lot of their people.
(This was an early expression of the later more articulate demand
for technical assistance.) Torres Bodet reminded the delegates that
they were concerned not only with the "mis-shaping of education,
but also with its inadequacy—the latter in a very high degree." The
Colombian representative declared that one of the purposes of the
new organization should be a world crusade against illiteracy. The
Egyptian delegate spoke of illiteracy in his country, the shortage of

technicians, the consequent rudimentary stage of production. "No country today," he said, "can afford to live next door to poverty or ignorance."[12]

Unesco, therefore, was not created in a vacuum, nor dreamed up in an ivory tower. It was the creature of the specific needs of multitudes of people throughout the world.

How Did Past Experience Shape the Unesco Idea?

Unesco was also the creature of much history. Countless efforts at international cooperation in the fields of education, science, and culture had preceded the London meeting of 1945. In broad terms, Unesco's roots extended to ancient times, to the translation of Greek philosophy and science into Latin and Arabic, to the spread of Buddhism, Christianity, and Islam. For many centuries sailors and soldiers, explorers and traders, had served as agents of cultural exchange. Customs and ideas had been carried from one people to another, sometimes imposed, sometimes welcomed and accepted. Individual scholars and artists had sought to broaden their knowledge and experience by correspondence and by travel. Medieval universities served this process. Missionaries had promoted expansion of their national customs as well as of their religion. Traditionally cultural interchange had been "unsystematic, often unconscious of itself, casual, slow-moving, individualistic."[13]

Private International Organizations

During the second half of the nineteenth century such interchange took form in international congresses and continuing organizations.[14] These were of a private, nongovernmental character, such as the International Congress of Anthropology and Pre-History, which first met in 1866; the Congress of Orientalists in 1873; the International Congress of Psychology in 1899; and the Congress of Historical Sciences in 1898. Similar meetings took place in the natural sciences. International congresses, at first occasional and later periodic, led to the formation of continuing international bodies. Early in the present century there was an array of periodic meetings and congresses, of committees functioning between congresses, of associations in specific fields, of international federations of scholarly groups in related fields.[15]

After World War I there was a marked increase of international scholarly organizations. The International Research Council, now known as the International Council of Scientific Unions, appeared in 1919. It includes scientific organizations in such fields as mathematics, astronomy, physics, chemistry, and biology. At the same time a similar movement in the humanities created the International Academic Union, as successor to the defunct International Association of Academies. In the United States the National Academy of Sciences–National Research Council and the American Council of Learned Societies served as the national components of these international associations.

Linked with this movement was a growing recognition by educational leaders of the need for educational cooperation across national frontiers. Education in Europe during the Middle Ages had been under the influence of the Church and was therefore transnational, but in the latter part of the eighteenth century the rise of nationalism and demands of the national state to control education had raised paradoxically the question of international cooperation in education. New national ministries of public instruction sought information about educational methods used in other countries. Marc-Antoine Jullien of Paris in 1817 urged the comparative study of education in European countries. But for more than half a century the idea slumbered. It revived with a nongovernmental international conference on education at Philadelphia in 1876 and another on primary instruction at Brussels in 1880. The subject attracted increasing interest during the early years of the twentieth century.[16]

On the initiative of the National Education Association of the United States, the World Federation of Education Associations was established in 1923. It met biennially until World War II, and following that conflict was succeeded by the World Organization of the Teaching Profession.[17] All these bodies and others which had their start in the period between the two world wars were, as already noted, private rather than government organizations. They were not based on intergovernmental agreements, nor did they often receive financial support from governments. Their membership was mainly European and North American, and they were therefore more regional than world-wide in character.

Intergovernmental Organizations

National governments began in the latter half of the nineteenth century to develop international cultural and educational relationships. New rapid means of communication together with increased economic interdependence drew nations into more intimate contact. The growth of democracy and the extension of public education created a broad public opinion whose importance in international relations governments gradually came to recognize and whose support they began to cultivate. Governments came to organize and regulate, sometimes to limit and sometimes to expand, what had previously been done by private individuals and groups.

All this ultimately led to the formation of intergovernmental organizations, whose activities provided important precedents for the work eventually assigned to Unesco.

It may be helpful to sketch here the patterns laid down by these institutions. The first initiative proved vain. In September, 1914, largely because of the efforts of Fannie Fern Andrews of the United States, an International Conference on Education was to meet at The Hague with delegations from sixteen countries. The outbreak of the World War forced abandonment of the plan.[18] It was only after the war that intergovernmental action began in the educational, scientific, and cultural fields. The Covenant of the League of Nations was silent about activities in the intellectual sphere,[19] and at the First Assembly of the League in December 1920 intellectual matters were termed "either the exclusive province of each government or of private initiative . . . the League could have nothing to do with them." League activities in education were opposed as amounting "almost to interference with freedom of thought and religion." The First Assembly of the League, however, asked the Council to give attention to international organization of intellectual activities. After consideration by the Second Assembly in September, 1921, of a report by the French delegate, Léon Bourgeois, an International Committee on Intellectual Cooperation was approved.[20]

The League of Nations Precedent

Here was one of the chief forerunners of Unesco. The Committee was made up originally of twelve distinguished leaders of thought, scholars in the sciences and humanities, and men of letters. Its first chairman was Henri Bergson, and among its early members were Marie Curie, Gilbert Murray, and Robert A. Millikan. Individual Americans, notably James T. Shotwell, were active in the organization, although the United States government had no part in its support or program. The Committee functioned as a consultative body to the League of Nations, meeting annually at Geneva and reporting to the Council and the Assembly.

Its inadequate staff and facilities later expanded as a result of an offer from the French government to establish at Paris an International Institute of Intellectual Cooperation.[21] The Committee became the governing body of the Institute, and the Institute served as its secretariat—although the Committee retained its tiny staff at League headquarters in Geneva. Activities of the secretariat at Paris supplemented those of advisory committees and other related bodies. National Committees on Intellectual Cooperation were organized in some forty countries, and these served to fashion a network of relations with private groups as well as government agencies. The United States had a nongovernmental National Committee which conducted a study on improvement of domestic copyright legislation, published an extensive survey of the *Study of International Relations in the United States,* and served in a liaison capacity with the Paris Institute.

It was not until 1926 that the League Assembly in a special resolution recognized the existence of the International Organization for Intellectual Cooperation as a technical body, similar to other technical organs of the League. The Organization was made up of the Committee, of the Institute, and of the National Committees on Intellectual Cooperation. There was an effort made in 1936 to broaden membership and strengthen financial support of this movement.[22] An International Act concerning intellectual cooperation was drafted, providing an autonomous basis for the International Organization for Intellectual Cooperation while keeping it within the League system. This Act became effective in January 1940 with ratification of the necessary eight governments, and by June four additional governments had signed it. By then the outbreak of World War II had forced suspension of the Organization's work except in the Western Hemisphere.

This International Organization for Intellectual Cooperation merits examination. It sponsored collaboration among intellectual leaders on problems of common concern.[23] It provided a kind of clearing house for government departments dealing with intellectual matters and for its own National Committees on Intellectual Cooperation, as well as for such private organizations as learned societies and organizations of educators or writers. It furnished a number of useful technical services. It exchanged information on museums and archives; it published lists of translations and bibliographies; it studied problems of copyright; it issued reports on employment of intellectuals. Scholars and men of letters from many countries came together through conferences and symposia which sought the psychological causes of war and solutions for world tensions.

Although the original responsibility of the League of Nations' intellectual cooperation system did not extend into the field of education,[24] it was soon working actively on educational questions. The Organization investigated the structure of higher education throughout the world and became a center for studies of secondary education. It explored the desirability of textbook revision. The League Assembly adopted a declaration on teaching history. At its request, the Organization prepared a convention in 1931 to govern broadcasting in the interests of peace. It worked on problems relating to use of radio and films in schools, and drew up an international convention on free circulation of educational films.

In response to a request from the Chinese government in 1931, it sent an educational mission to that country to advise on reorganization of the Chinese school system. At the invitation of the International Labor Office it fostered an international inquiry into popular libraries and the arts in relation to the leisure time of workers. It encouraged instruction in the schools about aims of the League of Nations and methods of international cooperation. In its later years the Institute served as a secretariat for the International Council of Scientific Unions and for the International Studies Conference, which brought together scholars in various fields for an examination of problems such as reconstruction of world trade, population, raw materials, and colonies, and procedures for peaceful change.[25]

Two things stand out in the brief history of the Organization. First, its origin was not provided for in the Covenant of the League, but came later from the efforts of a few individuals to include an agency of this kind within the League system. Second, its effect was substantially limited to small groups of individuals,[26] partly because of its modest budget. But from the start its focus was largely on the interests and potentialities of educated people, and its program was largely made up of specialized projects, often unrelated to government policies, of little concern to government officials, and little understood by the ordinary citizen. Over the years its program did move toward broader activities. With the disappearance of the League of Nations following World War II, the Institute of Intellectual Cooperation went out of existence. Unesco took over its assets, functions, and activities.

One result of the League of Nations' hesitancy to encourage an official international educational agency was the founding in 1925 of the International Bureau of Education at Geneva. The IBE began as a private agency for exchange of information and research in education, chiefly on the primary and secondary level, but in 1929 it received a quasi-official status, with governments, public institutions, and international organizations eligible for membership. Its membership in 1946 included fifteen governments and two nongovernmental organizations. Neither the United Kingdom nor the United States was a member. Still, official delegates of forty to fifty governments participated in the Bureau's annual International Conference on Public Instruction. The Bureau was primarily an information center on education, but it also gave attention to methods of education for international understanding and cooperation.[27] Although Unesco's future program as outlined at the London Conference included the Bureau's field of activities, the influence of Switzerland, where the Bureau is located, helped to assure its continuance as a separate organization and it has maintained a complementary relationship with Unesco.

Beginning with the First International Conference of American States at Washington in 1889-90, questions of cultural cooperation have been considered at successive inter-American conferences. In response to recommendations made at these conferences, the Pan American Union established a section on education in 1917. This office became in 1928 the Division of Intellectual Cooperation, and in 1948 was renamed the Department of Cultural Affairs. The Department includes the Columbus Memorial Library, Divisions of Education and of Philosophy, Letters, and Sciences, and sections on

Music and Visual Arts. It has tried to develop a broad program: conferences on education, preparation of materials on fundamental education, exchange of persons, bibliographic information, cultural agreements, lectures, concerts, art exhibits, publication of books, pamphlets, and reviews.

National Cultural Relations Programs

Unesco thus inherited from earlier international organizations a legacy of theory and practice, relating primarily to the collaboration of scholars and intellectuals, but extending to some degree into broader reaches of primary and secondary education. Another part of Unesco's heritage came from government programs of cultural relations.[28] As in the international field, where pioneering efforts of private individuals and organizations preceded government action under the League of Nations, national efforts at cultural relations with other countries were first begun by voluntary groups, and it was only later that government entered the picture.[29]

France was the first modern nation to embark on an official program of cultural relations. It was originally focused on the Middle East and Asia, where, during the second half of the nineteenth century, Catholic educational missionaries, aided by subsidies from the French government, built schools and orphanages, hospitals and dispensaries. In 1906 France initiated cultural activities in Europe and the Americas with assistance to French primary and secondary schools and a few scholarly institutes. The Alliance Française, a private agency enjoying government subsidy, furthered knowledge of the French language abroad. Following the close of the First World War the French program of "intellectual expansion" was enlarged. "Of all our products for exportation," M. Raiberti, rapporteur for the Commission on the Budget of the Ministry of Foreign Affairs, declared in 1919, "the finest product and that best fitted to make French genius known, admired and loved, is French thought." Earlier a supporter of the program had commented, "If commerce follows the flag, it follows for even stronger reasons the national language."[30]

One reason for expansion in 1920 of the French program was the need to combat the German propaganda developed before and during the World War. The official German cultural program recognized the importance of the German schools set up by emigrant German communities in Asia, South Africa, and Latin America, as well as in Southeast Europe. These schools served to expand German influence among the nationals of such areas. While supported by private contributions, some began as early as 1875 to receive modest government subsidies. It was argued that the world would be poorer if the German language and culture lost ground in relation to other languages and cultures. After Germany's defeat in World War I and loss of territory inhabited by considerable numbers of Germans, the program for expansion of German culture abroad took on new importance. Germany, its military and economic power reduced, sought to win prestige by "a friendly cultural offensive in the outside world."[31]

The Soviet Union had no organized cultural relations with other countries until the avowed abandonment of immediate efforts for world revolution. In 1925 there was established the All Union Society for Cultural Relations with Foreign Countries (known as Voks from the initial letters of the first four words in its Russian title), with propaganda for the Soviet system as its object. Voks was to seek "the world union of intellectual forces for the triumph of genuine world culture" and to "demonstrate to foreign countries a general outline of Soviet culture in its totality." Intellectuals were to "fight the war danger, agitate for peace." Bilateral institutes such as the American-Russian Institute in the United States were set up. The Vice President of Voks, E. Lerner, stated in 1931, "Our foreign societies would however be entirely wrong in limiting their work to disseminating neutral information which often hides a desire to efface our victories. . . . These societies must create a ring of trust, sympathy and friendship around the USSR, through which all plans of intervention will be unable to penetrate."[32]

Not until 1934 did the United Kingdom initiate its official program, with establishment of the British Council for Relations with Other Countries. Diplomats abroad and members of British trade missions had for some time reported that British interests were suffering from propaganda activities of other countries, and recommended that the United Kingdom counteract such propaganda. The British Council was an agency of "national interpretation" abroad. At the start it was hoped that financial support would come largely from such private agencies as chambers of commerce and other trade organizations, but this expectation was soon disappointed and the government through the Foreign Office assumed responsibility for major support.[33] Nonetheless, the Council considers itself a nongovernmental body.

The United States was one of the last of the major powers to initiate an official program of cultural relations, although numerous private organizations had long been active in this field. Two important moves were made in 1938, with the creation of an Inter-departmental Committee on Scientific and Cultural Cooperation with the Other American Republics and, in the Department of State, a Division of Cultural Relations, also to focus on relations with Latin America. The purpose of the Division was to "make friends for the United States abroad through the development of a greater understanding and appreciation of the best contribution which this country may exchange with other nations."[34]

Various other countries had such programs but they cannot be reviewed here. All these programs had numerous common elements. They were all concerned with "exchanges of persons," encouragement of contacts between members of one national community and those of another; exchange of books and periodicals; lectures, concerts, and theatrical productions; art and science exhibits; broadcasts and motion pictures. They usually encouraged "cultural institutes," to foster knowledge of the language, literature, and life of the sponsoring country. Some programs included sports and festivals. There has been a growing tendency to formalize such programs by "cultural agreements" which outline how cultural relations are to be carried on and often stress the importance of reciprocity. Most of these are bilateral, although a few are multilateral. The number of bilateral agreements, especially, has expanded rapidly in recent years.[35]

There is some similarity in purpose, as well as content, among the national programs, although their aims are variously described. While the French emphasized "intellectual expansion," the Germans focused largely on preservation of German culture among the large groups of Germans abroad. The Soviet Union fostered propaganda for Soviet culture. The British talked of "national interpretation." The Americans engaged in making "friends for the United States." But common to all or almost all of these national activities is the intent of governments "to use certain aspects of their national cultures for the purposes of their foreign relations."[36] Although in theory cultural relations are often viewed as reciprocal, in practice most national programs have emphasized understanding of their national life among other peoples and have neglected education of their own people as to the character of foreign peoples.

Private international organizations had viewed knowledge and understanding as good per se, irrespective of political or economic consequences. By contrast the official programs of cultural relations looked beyond the educational and cultural results of their activities to some useful contribution to the political and economic aspects of foreign policy.

After the National Socialists took control of Germany in 1933, the German cultural relations program, with its emphasis on unity of all Germans without as well as within the Fatherland, was used to compel every German citizen abroad to participate in the Nazi program. During World War II all these activities were regimented to serve Nazi purposes. Italy and Japan followed suit.[37] Compulsions of the war strengthened in all countries the element of nationalistic propaganda.

In summary, private international programs, intergovernmental programs both regional and world-wide in character, and national government programs—all these were part of Unesco's ancestry. Scholarly interests, international interests, and national interests, all influenced the new agency within the framework of the United Nations system.

Varied lessons had come from the different types of experience. Private programs had revealed resources that could link different peoples, as well as advance knowledge. League experience had revealed both the weakness and the strength of cooperation through an intergovernmental agency. National experience had tested methods that might serve an international body. Particularly in the United States and the United Kingdom, where voluntary groups are a factor of immense importance in national life, many activities of a cultural relations nature were carried on by nongovernmental organizations, often without government subsidy. Thus cooperation of private agencies in government programs, together with the League of Nations National Committees on Intellectual Cooperation, prefigured the emphasis in Unesco's constitution on national commissions and on cooperation with nongovernmental organizations.

Unesco was to profit from this experience. Its program was destined to do old things in new ways, on an international rather than a national plane. But much of its activity would be linked to national action, and public and private efforts would be mingled.

Immediate Origins of Unesco Idea

Conference of Allied Ministers of Education

The most direct official stimulus for creation of an international organization in the field of education, science, and culture came from a body established three years before the London Conference of 1945. In the autumn of 1942, with the war still in mid-course, a Conference of Allied Ministers of Education (CAME) was set up in London. It met on invitation of the chairman of the British Council and on the initiative of the British Foreign Office and of R. A. Butler, President of the Board of Education, who presided over its sessions. In attendance were Ministers of Education or their representatives from the governments in exile in London: Belgium, Czechoslovakia, Greece, Holland, Luxembourg, Norway, Poland, Yugoslavia, and the French National Committee of Liberation. The meeting considered "what help would be needed and could be given to the occupied countries of Europe in the restoration of their educational systems."[38] It resulted in a continuing body which met bi-monthly and carried on most of its work through committees and commissions. CAME did not concern itself with reform of education in the Axis countries, nor did it seek primarily to influence educational systems in its member states. Nonetheless, the problems of postwar educational reconstruction which it faced were staggering.[39]

It soon became evident that educational reconstruction concerned non-European as well as European countries. Help was needed from Allied countries other than Great Britain and those under enemy occupation. Observers from the United States and Soviet embassies in London were invited to the meeting on May 25, 1943. Subsequently observers from China, India, Australia, Canada, New Zealand, and South Africa further broadened the base. A meeting in December 1943 invited all governments with observers to appoint regular representatives, in connection with a plan to create an inter-Allied bureau of education which might become a permanent international agency in that field.

In the meantime private groups in Great Britain and the United States were concerned with problems of educational reconstruction and of postwar cultural cooperation. In Great Britain as early as January, 1941, educators from the Allied countries had met in unofficial conferences. In November 1941 the London International Assembly and the Council for Education in World Citizenship (established by the League of Nations Union in Great Britain) agreed to a joint commission, under the chairmanship of Professor Gilbert Murray, to prepare a report on "the place of education, science and learning in postwar reconstruction." This report, published in March 1943,[40] outlined proposals for educational reconstruction of the war-devastated countries, re-education of the peoples of the Axis countries, and establishment of a permanent international organization to advance equal educational opportunities for all peoples and to encourage education for international understanding.

While British groups were interested primarily in an agency for educational reconstruction, American groups emphasized a broad, continuing organization, and their view eventually prevailed. Included among American organizations were the American Association for an International Office for Education, the Liaison Committee for International Education led by Grayson N. Kefauver, and the National Education Association. Many of their efforts displayed dedication, enthusiasm, and drive. The National Education Association raised a War and Peace Fund totaling almost half a million dollars; organized a series of nation-wide conferences; prepared material for parent-teacher, church, and labor organizations; and used pamphlets, magazine articles, broadcasts, public opinion surveys, and conversations with government officials to call attention to the contribution of education to world peace. Its pamphlet, *Education and the People's Peace,* was the most widely circulated document issued by the Association.[41]

The idea of a permanent organization to be concerned with matters going beyond immediate postwar reconstruction had also begun to win support in the Conference of Allied Ministers of Education. In the summer of 1943 the Chinese observer at the Conference reported in conversation that the Chinese Ambassador in London favored an international organization for education and had so informed the Chinese government in Chungking. The USSR observer in private conversation in December 1943 indicated that the Soviet

Union might participate in an educational organization whose activities were confined to exchange of purely technical information, but would hesitate to take part in an international agency concerned with national curricula.[42]

In the fall of 1943, CAME therefore requested its Executive Committee to consider the creation of a permanent United Nations Bureau of Education. Proposals for such an agency by various voluntary organizations in Great Britain and the United States were studied. The burden of these plans was that the future organization should serve temporarily as an agency of educational reconstruction to repair the damage and devastation suffered by the enemy-occupied countries; that it should function permanently as a clearing house of information and a research center; that the organization should foster "an international spirit" for maintenance of peace; that it should define teaching standards and assist individual countries in attaining them. They clearly recognized that an international organization should not intervene in domestic education activities, nor should it have mandatory power. The plans agreed further that the annual conference of the proposed organization should be composed of representatives of both governments and private groups. They called for creation of a national commission in each country to support the work of the international organization.

Consideration in the United States of problems of educational reconstruction and postwar organization was stimulated by public statements of educational leaders and the organizations mentioned above; the cultural relations program of the Department of State; and the planning for a general international organization. The communication from CAME in December 1943, inviting the United States to be represented by a regular representative rather than by an observer, led the Department of State to consider whether it should recommend CAME's transformation into a United Nations agency. It finally decided that it would be unwise to become involved in negotiations on a specialized agency in the educational and cultural field before the plan for the general United Nations organization had been clearly formed. It therefore proposed that the United States agree to a "provisional commission on educational and cultural reconstruction." The provisional organization was to "pave the way for the permanent international organization for educational and cultural relations."[43]

The Department of State on March 31, 1944, issued a statement of policy announcing the willingness of the United States government to take part in an international program for the educational and cultural reconstruction of the war-torn countries. To help these countries to help themselves, the Department would collaborate with the Conference of Allied Ministers of Education in London to set up at the earliest practicable moment a United Nations organization for educational and cultural reconstruction.[44] Secretary of State Cordell Hull meanwhile had announced that the United States would send a delegation to the Ninth Meeting of CAME to open at London on April 5, 1944. The delegation was headed by Congressman (later Senator) J. William Fulbright, former President of the University of Arkansas. Its members included Archibald MacLeish, Librarian of Congress; Grayson N. Kefauver, Dean of Education at Stanford University;[45] John W. Studebaker, United States Commissioner of Education; Dean C. Mildred Thompson of Vassar College; and Ralph E. Turner of the Department of State.

Following meetings with the United States delegation, the Conference of Allied Ministers produced a draft for an interim United Nations organization for educational and cultural reconstruction, whose work might provide the basis for cooperation in education and culture. This document was transmitted to the governments of the United Nations.[46]

During the latter half of 1944 both government and private opinion became more favorable to a possible permanent agency for educational and cultural cooperation. Proposals for a general United Nations organization were being formulated for consideration at Dumbarton Oaks. They included specialized agencies. During the second phase of the discussions (September 29–October 7, 1944), China won support of the United Kingdom and the United States for its proposal that, in connection with the Economic and Social Council and the specialized agencies, there should be provision for educational and other forms of cultural cooperation. The Soviet government agreed to sponsor the Chinese proposal to the San Francisco Conference.

There was another reason for the shift in the attitude of the United States toward reconstruction. It was becoming doubtful that Congress, with the United Nations Relief and Rehabilitation Administration (UNRRA) already undertaking the general task of reconstruction,[47] would approve the sums needed for educational rehabilitation of devastated countries. If support were not forthcoming from the United States, an international agency of reconstruction would not only be futile, but might threaten the prospects for creation of a permanent agency at a later date. Belief was growing in the United States that the American contribution to educational reconstruction could be more effective through direct gifts than through an international fund, since private organizations would be responsible for a large share of the American contribution.

With the announcement of plans for the San Francisco Conference to draft the United Nations Charter, it was clear that creation of an educational and cultural agency would have to yield to establishment of the central United Nations organization, and that separate initiative would be necessary for a permanent educational and cultural agency. The Department of State began preparation of a draft constitution for a permanent agency. The United States notified China, Great Britain, and the Soviet Union that the changing international picture, and particularly progress in plans for a general United Nations organization, might require new thinking about an educational and cultural agency.

A parallel development was unfolding at London, questioning the idea that reconstruction could well serve as the starting point for educational and cultural activities of the United Nations. A representative of the International Labor Organization, sitting with the CAME Drafting Committee established when the Fulbright Mission visited London, opposed linking the aims of the proposed organization to the immediate job of reconstruction. He suggested that plans for the latter should be incorporated in a separate document. The Drafting Committee ultimately decided on February 14, 1945, to recommend omission of "reconstruction" from the title of the organization and to place the proposal for an Emergency Rehabilitation Fund in a protocol annexed to the Constitution.[48] CAME agreed to redraft the Constitution along these lines. The United States draft for the Constitution of a permanent agency was presented to CAME in April.

Such support had developed for a permanent educational and cultural organization, as distinguished from a temporary reconstruction agency, that the American proposal was accepted. It was the only comprehensive document before the Drafting Committee, and inevitably became the principal source for the Draft Constitution, which was made public jointly by CAME and the United States government on July 31, 1945, as a basis for discussions at the London Conference the following November. The final version omitted the protocol on the Emergency Rehabilitation Fund earlier suggested by the Drafting Committee.

The American proposal did not mention educational and cultural reconstruction, which had first stirred the hope of the war-damaged countries. A Committee statement explained, however, why earlier drafts were restudied in the light of new realities, and why new proposals were developed in cooperation with the United States government. Meanwhile the Inter-American Conference at Mexico City in February and March 1945 recommended an international agency to promote "intellectual and moral cooperation between nations."[49]

San Francisco Conference

On the eve of the opening day of the San Francisco Conference, Secretary of State Edward R. Stettinius announced inclusion in the agenda of a proposal that the Economic and Social Council should provide for educational and other forms of cultural cooperation. Several other delegations stressed the same note.[50]

While the United States delegation supported inclusion of the phrase "cultural cooperation," some members opposed use of the term "education." The influential group of consultants to the delegation, particularly those representing agriculture, labor, business, and education, pressed for inclusion of educational as well as cultural cooperation among the objectives and activities of the United Nations Organization. Approval at Washington on May 22 and 24, respectively, of the Mundt resolution in the House and the Fulbright-Taft resolution in the Senate, calling for an international education agency, revealed that the word "education" could be included in the Charter without antagonizing Congress.[51] The American Association for an International Office for Education, together with the National Education Association and the American Federation of Teachers, was active in support of these resolutions. The United States delegation at San Francisco agreed, and the Conference voted to incorporate appropriate language in the Charter.[52]

This language provided that "the United Nations shall promote...

international cultural and educational cooperation," member states cooperating to achieve the purposes outlined in the Charter. Further "specialized agencies established by intergovernmental agreement and having wide international responsibilities . . . in economic, social, cultural, educational, health, and related fields, shall be brought into relationship with the United Nations" through agreements with the Economic and Social Council. The International Trusteeship System was to promote education in trust territories.[53]

In an address to the closing plenary session of the Conference, President Truman stated that: "The world has learned again that nations, like individuals, must know the truth if they would be free— must read and hear the truth, learn and teach the truth. We must set up an effective agency for constant and thorough interchange of thought and ideas. For there lies the road to a better and more tolerant understanding among nations and among peoples."[54]

The idea of an international educational and cultural agency thus had grown in the process of planning and negotiation, and had won wide support in official and unofficial circles. The French government associated itself with the British government in its invitation for the London Conference. The French proposed as an alternative to the CAME draft a document which sought to build the new organization around the Institute of Intellectual Cooperation. The Soviet government did not attend the London Conference on the ground that the Economic and Social Council rather than the United Kingdom and France should have called the conference. Suggestions were made that the conference be postponed, in the hope that further negotiation would alter the Soviet attitude. The British government insisted that the meeting be held without delay, and the conference opened on November 1, 1945. What it did, and what kind of agency it created, is the subject of the next chapter.

CHAPTER II

WHAT SHOULD BE UNESCO'S CHARACTER? FIVE CRITICAL ISSUES

The preliminary design for Unesco had been sketched out by midsummer of 1945. It had been drawn in the light of previous experience of member states and of earlier international organizations. Drafts of a constitution had been worked out at London and Washington. The San Francisco Conference, meeting from April to June, outlined the place of Unesco in the United Nations system. It remained for the London Conference of November 1945 to decide on the final design.

In slightly more than two weeks (November 1-16), the delegates to the Conference for the Establishment of the United Nations Educational, Scientific and Cultural Organization drafted and signed a constitution. Official delegations were present from forty-three countries.[1] Miss Ellen Wilkinson, British Minister of Education, was elected President of the Conference, and Léon Blum, head of the French delegation, was chosen as Associate-President.

At the outset the Conference had before it two drafts of a constitution.[2] The first, prepared by CAME and closely following the United States draft, proposed a structure for the new organization consisting of a General Conference, meeting annually with equal representation of all member states; an Executive Board of fifteen members; and a Director General and secretariat. The second was a French counter-proposal with certain differences from the CAME draft as outlined below.

Many important decisions had to be taken at the London meeting, and the constitution and other essential documents put in writing, before nations could commit themselves to the obligations of membership. Five outstanding issues faced the Conference. The manner in which they were dealt with affected Unesco's record during its first ten years, and will influence Unesco's work far into the future. These issues were: (1) Unesco's program: its content and range; (2) Unesco's purpose: single or multiple; (3) Unesco's character: governmental or nongovernmental; (4) Unesco's relation to the United Nations; (5) Unesco's role: how should the organization be used?

Program: Content and Range

It was clear from the start that Unesco, like other international agencies, would have none of the initiative and authority usually found in sovereign national governments. Unesco's functions would affect citizens of member states only through decisions by their own governments. Unesco was not to intervene in member states on matters "essentially within their domestic jurisdiction."[3] This indirect approach appeared in such words in Article I of the Constitution as "encouraging," "recommending," and "suggesting." The breadth of Unesco's activities was indicated by references to education, for adults as well as for children; books, works of art, monuments of history and science; press, radio, and film; indeed "all branches of intellectual activity," including exchange of persons, publications, and objects of artistic and scientific interest. It was evident that Unesco would have a far more difficult task in developing a coherent and integrated program than such sister agencies as the Food and Agriculture Organization and the World Health Organization, which dealt with more limited areas and more tangible activities.[4]

The only program issue on which a clash of views appeared at London was educational reconstruction. Reference was made earlier to the discussions in CAME, where the proposal for an agency dedicated to educational and cultural reconstruction was sidetracked for an organization with more long-term aims. The French draft in its preamble made specific reference to the need for educational reconstruction, and thus reopened a question on which the CAME preamble was silent. In early sessions of the Conference the representatives of Greece, Poland, and other countries[5] sounded an eloquent plea for help. Delegates of the war-torn countries argued forcefully for mention in the Constitution's preamble of the need of reconstruction. Others, specifically the Indian delegate, said that reconstruction was a temporary function and therefore should not take an unduly prominent place among objectives of the organization.[6]

The United States delegation pointed out that the new organization could not become a relief agency, receiving and distributing relief funds—a task for which UNRRA already had responsibility. This position presented for the United States delegation a dilemma later outlined in its report to the Secretary of State, the chairman stating that "in combination, the United States policies on education and relief seemed to certain of our colleagues at the Conference to lack consistency with previous declarations of our policy. To channel American relief through UNRRA, while at the same time limiting narrowly the authority of UNRRA to deal with educational and cultural needs, seemed . . . to amount in effect to a refusal of American assistance in the rehabilitation of educational and cultural facilities. To refuse such assistance in fact while declaring the desire of the American people to participate in a common labor of understanding in which education in all countries would play a most important part, seemed . . . further, to involve a basic contradiction in American aims. This opinion the United States Delegation was not altogether successful in dispelling."[7]

In this baffling situation, with the position of the United States as the largest contributor to UNRRA the determining factor, the Conference agreed that the Preparatory Commission should serve as a clearing house, to help put potential givers in touch with needs of war-devastated countries and to coordinate offers of assistance. With the aid of a technical subcommittee, the Commission was to study problems of devastated countries and report in 1946 to the first session of the General Conference. More immediately, it was to bring practical measures for reconstruction to the attention of governments, organizations, and individuals.[8]

The Conference approved this limited plan with one dissenting voice, that of Bernard Drzewieski of Poland, who said, "You have to help us not tomorrow or after tomorrow; you have to help us today, immediately, presently, without delay . . . our needs are tremendous. Our schools are roofless. Our teachers faint because they are starving and exhausted." Despite this crucial need, the Conference, he declared, had postponed relief for at least a year.[9]

The London Conference restricted Unesco's activities in educational reconstruction to collection and circulation of information. But it greatly broadened the role of the organization by incorporating science and mass communication in its program. Science was included also in the title of the organization. Almost all of a series of titles previously suggested had contained the words "educational" and "cultural."[10] The latter was inadequate if used in its narrow sense, referring to creative expressions of the human spirit. It was too broad if interpreted as a people's way of living, which would have covered education as well. Educators, who had played such an active part in preliminary planning for Unesco, insisted on "educational" in the title, since otherwise the organization might be limited to intellectual cooperation among scholars. CAME, in the draft constitution submitted to the London Conference, proposed as a title "Educational and Cultural Organization of the United Nations." The French, borrowing from the League of Nations, suggested "United Nations Organization of Intellectual Cooperation."

Six months earlier, in April 1945, the Science Commission of CAME had suggested inclusion of the word "scientific" in the title of the new organization. Scientific exchanges were already better organized internationally than those in any other intellectual field. Hope had been widely expressed by scientists for creation in the United Nations system of a separate science organization. In the end they agreed to merge their field in Unesco, the word "scientific" to appear in the name of the organization. The explosion of the first atomic bomb in August 1945 had emphasized the urgent need for international cooperation in development and application of scientific knowledge. Ellen Wilkinson, British Minister of Education, therefore announced at the London Conference that the British delegation favored inclusion of "scientific" in the title—which would then read United Nations Educational, Scientific and Cultural Organization.[11] The Conference agreed to this proposal without serious opposition. However, the question of Unesco's competence in the field of science, and particularly its ability to play a leading role with regard to the peaceful use of atomic energy, came up in 1955 during United Nations discussions of this subject. Unesco's title and program should be viewed not as examples of pure logic, but rather as the result of historical circumstance.

The influence of the United States was largely responsible for specific reference in the Unesco Constitution to mass communication. The United States also secured approval at London of a resolution urging the Preparatory Commission to give attention to press, radio, and film.[12] Here, it was believed, was the channel through which Unesco might become a positive influence for peace in the United Nations by reaching directly the peoples of the world. This approach was new. The idea was controversial; many considered it even dangerous. It excited both great hope and intense fear; neither extreme was justified by later experience.[13]

Purpose: Single or Multiple?

Unesco was established to further peace through international understanding, to forward human welfare through aid both to war-devastated and to underdeveloped countries, to expand and circulate knowledge. It was therefore natural to find these needs mirrored in the objectives laid down in the Constitution.

The task of incorporating in the Preamble and Article I of the Constitution ideas advanced in documents and discussions of the Conference was delegated to a drafting committee of the First Commission. Actually the resulting statement was primarily the work of Archibald MacLeish of the United States delegation, and Etienne Gilson of the French delegation. Here one finds Attlee's reference to "the minds of men";[14] stress on such factors as ignorance, denial of democratic principles, and Nazi racial doctrines as causes of World War II; a call for a new education; the emphasis of Mexico's Torres Bodet on "the intellectual and moral solidarity of mankind" as basic to peace.

Unesco's precise purpose has been debated since its earliest days. Discussion has turned on certain phrases in the Constitution, but involves also a fundamental difference in viewpoint as to what Unesco should do. This difference results in part from the different stages of development characterizing Unesco's member states, their diverse educational and cultural traditions and political, economic, and social systems. In part it turns upon whether Unesco should serve broad political objectives or limited technical purposes.

One may say, in an oversimplified analysis, that there are two approaches. The first argues that Unesco's purpose is to contribute directly to peace and security. The other contends that Unesco's approach to peace should be indirect, by furthering the welfare of mankind through education, science, and culture. The first view would have Unesco choose each activity consciously in terms of direct contribution to peace. It emphasizes coordination between Unesco's activities and those of the United Nations. The second view adopts a long-range approach, and argues that strengthening education, science, and culture will promote human welfare and that this is the surest and soundest approach to peace.

The first view appears to be influenced by the immediacy of threats to peace and the need to mobilize every resource to strengthen peace. It reflects a conviction that Unesco's program in education, science, and culture can have an immediate, or at least something more than a remote, effect on world affairs. It assumes frankly that Unesco is a political organization and part of a world political system. If Unesco does not act politically, in this view, it is doomed to a secondary, unimportant role.

By contrast the second view assumes that maintaining peace in contemporary international relations is a task for the United Nations Security Council and the United Nations General Assembly. Unesco's task is to lay foundations for future peace. The projects of Unesco cannot by their nature have an immediate effect upon peace. They must be long-range.[15]

This analysis is oversimplified, but it will serve to describe the two poles between which the rationale for Unesco's program has tended to fluctuate. Neither view has ever completely captured the program-making process. Neither has been consistently held by the General Conference, the Executive Board, or the secretariat. Undoubtedly the conviction that Unesco should stay away from contemporary political struggles discouraged government support during the difficult years of the cold war.

Both in considering what Unesco should do and in evaluating what it has done, it is desirable to note what Unesco was intended to do. The London Conference did not find constitutional language that was clear and unequivocal. This was particularly true with regard to terms used in the Preamble and Article I. Although the title for Article I, "Purposes and Functions," suggests a multiple purpose, the body of the Article states a single purpose, that of contributing to "peace and security." This language was inserted by deliberate decision, after protracted discussion at London. The text of Article I, Section 1 reads:

The purpose of the Organization is to contribute to peace and security by promoting collaboration among the nations through education, science and culture in order to further universal respect for justice, for the rule of law and for the human rights and fundamental freedoms which are affirmed for the peoples of the world, without distinction of race, sex, language or religion, by the Charter of the United Nations.

Section 2 then outlines how this purpose will be carried out:

(a) Collaborate in the work of advancing the mutual knowledge and understanding of peoples, through all means of mass communication and to that end recommend such international agreements as may be necessary to promote the free flow of ideas by word and image;

(b) Give fresh impulse to popular education and to the spread of culture;

by collaborating with Members, at their request, in the development of educational activities;

by instituting collaboration among the nations to advance the ideal of equality of educational opportunity without regard to race, sex or any distinctions, economic or social;

by suggesting educational methods best suited to prepare the children of the world for the responsibilities of freedom;

(c) Maintain, increase and diffuse knowledge;

by assuring the conservation and protection of the world's inheritance of books, works of art and monuments of history and science, and recommending to the nations concerned the necessary international conventions;

by encouraging cooperation among the nations in all branches of intellectual activity, including the international exchange of persons active in the fields of education, science and culture and the exchange of publications, objects of artistic and scientific interest and other materials of information;

by initiating methods of international cooperation calculated to give the people of all countries access to the printed and published material produced by any of them.

The Preamble of the Constitution, in contrast to Article I, introduces in its final paragraph broader language concerning Unesco's purpose. This language has frequently been mentioned in support of the longer-range view of Unesco's purpose. The Preamble declares that States parties to the Constitution "do hereby create the United Nations Educational, Scientific and Cultural Organization for the purpose of advancing, through the educational, scientific and cultural relations of the peoples of the world, the objectives of international peace *and of the common welfare of mankind* for which the United Nations Organization was established and which its Charter proclaims." (Italics added.) The phrase "common welfare of mankind" is not in the body of the Constitution, and it is often argued that a preamble does not possess operative force. This phrase nonetheless has been cited many times as one of Unesco's major objectives. Many delegates in General Conferences, and influential members of the Unesco secretariat, including Unesco's first Director General, Julian Huxley, have maintained that Unesco was designed to serve the common welfare of mankind as well as to promote peace and security and that in fact improvement of economic and social conditions was a direct if slow-moving contribution to peace.[16]

An important statement bearing on this discussion was that found in the Report of the Program Commission, adopted by the First Session of the General Conference in 1946. This report mentioned, as the first criterion to be applied in choosing program proposals, their contribution to peace and security. As regards this criterion recognition had been accorded to the language in the Preamble to the Constitution which cited the "common welfare of mankind." The report continued, "we assume it is the view of the General Conference, that the stated purpose of Unesco to contribute to peace and security must be read in the light of this phrase, and that the 'peace' to which reference is made must be interpreted in a positive rather than a negative sense. 'Peace' in this context, in other words, means something more than a mere absence of overt hostilities. It means a condition of solidarity, harmony of purpose and co-ordination of activities in which free men and women can live a secure and satisfactory life—a condition in which war is affirmatively prevented by the dynamic and purposeful creation of a decent and human relationship between the peoples of the world—a condition in which the incentives to war are neutralized by the social, spiritual and economic advances created and achieved."[17]

Earlier in a statement of the same tenor to the Program Commission of the First Session, Archibald MacLeish had said that it was not enough "merely to demand of a given proposal whether it contributes directly to the construction of a positive and living peace. The directness of the relationship between the means and the end will vary fróm project to project, depending upon the role which Unesco plays." He noted three roles which Unesco might assume. First, it could function as a stimulating agency for other organizations. Second, it could act as a service agency providing member states with information, bibliographies, liaison centers, and communication. Finally, it could function as an operating agency by undertaking specific projects.

In each case, MacLeish said, "the role of Unesco would be different and the relation of the project to the objective of the support of peace would therefore vary." Unesco's activities as a stimulating agency would not necessarily be immediately related to achievement of a positive peace. Nor would its service activities. But in its operating function, the relation should be direct and precise.[18] Thus, this interpretation of "peace" approved by Unesco's first General Conference seems to have been designed as a compromise to blend rather than to distinguish the two ideas of Unesco's purpose. It is not easy to see how an activity which contributes to "positive peace" in this sense differs substantially from one which advances "the common welfare of mankind."

The legislative history of the Unesco Constitution points to the blending of still another objective, "advancement of knowledge," with the goals of peace and security and common welfare. Supporters of the "common welfare" objective of Unesco have usually supported "advancement of knowledge," including "intellectual cooperation" among scientists and other scholars. Proponents of peace and security as the goal of Unesco have recognized the importance of advancing knowledge and enhancing human welfare, but have stressed that such activities were valid for Unesco only if clearly employed to promote international understanding and peace.

The two drafts before the London Conference reflected different approaches to the issue of purpose. The CAME draft listed two purposes for the organization: development of mutual understanding as basic to peace; and extension to all peoples, for service of human needs, of the world's body of knowledge. The French draft outlined four purposes: diffusion of the spirit of peace; spread of popular education and of culture among peoples; advance of knowledge and expansion of culture; protection of the rights of intellectuals.

The language approved in substance by the First Commission actually listed five purposes: maintenance of international peace and security; promotion of universal respect for and observance of human rights and fundamental freedoms; development of the sciences and arts; diffusion of knowledge and culture to all peoples for the service of human needs; preservation of the world's inheritance of art and monuments of history. All these points were included in the more condensed draft adopted by the Conference. The language of this draft on Article I made contribution to peace and security the major goal of Unesco, listing other purposes as avenues of activity pointing toward attainment of the ultimate purpose.[19]

Aside from the question of educational reconstruction, decisions at London were made on a "both—and" rather than an "either—or" basis. The meeting favored recognition of all worthy undertakings in education, science, and culture and their inclusion in Unesco's purpose and program. Reaction to the end of World War II had been almost unlimited enthusiasm and willingness to work for every means which promised to maintain peace. In part the eclectic attitude was a result of the Conference's focus on general rather than specific proposals. In part it was owing to the different cultural backgrounds and lack of much common international experience in the Unesco field. In part it stemmed from lack of serious attention by foreign offices to Unesco's place in the United Nations. Important also was absence of any immediate need to consider budgets.

It is apparent that the Constitution of Unesco, like that of many other public agencies, was sometimes a compromise, deliberately vague, that its language is not a clear guide for determining in any simple way the kind of activity Unesco should properly carry on, that the record of the debate during the London Conference reveals diversity rather than unity in the intentions of the fathers of the Constitution. During the First Session of the General Conference at Paris in 1946, and throughout program discussions in subsequent years, lack of clarity in constitutional language permitted a variety of activities by Unesco that reflected nearly every idea and interpretation found at London.[20]

The deteriorating world situation even during the earliest years of Unesco's life, and the rapid intensification of the cold war, provided new reason for thought about Unesco's purpose. In March 1947 the Truman doctrine was proclaimed to save Greece and Turkey from international Communism. In May, Communist pressure forced Ferenc Nagy to resign as Hungarian premier. In July 1947 the Soviets withdrew from the three-power conference at Paris considering Marshall plan assistance. The Cominform was established in October. Belief was spreading that a new war was inevitable. The year 1948 saw the Communist *coup d'état* in Czechoslovakia, and Soviet blockade of West Berlin. Tito broke with Stalin. The Middle East was torn by Arab-Israeli conflict. Cooperation within all United Nations agencies seemed threatened.

Mounting tension was reflected in demands that Unesco focus not only on building the foundations of long-term peace but on helping to preserve the "precarious peace that now exists."[21] Yet there was no effort to reduce Unesco's preoccupation with advancement of knowledge and promotion of the general welfare of mankind, in favor of more intense activities to counter immediate threats to peace. This was in part because a large number of new states, not yet aware of the threat to their freedom and independence, appeared in the family of nations, bringing into international relations new expressions of self-determination and nationalism, pressing for help to combat poverty, malnutrition, disease, and illiteracy of their peoples. It was mostly due, however, to lack of willingness among Unesco's original member states to take it seriously as an instrument for peace, that Unesco's contribution did not come more into focus.

The General Conference in 1950 did adopt a resolution recommending that the future program of the organization should "tend more directly . . . towards the maintenance and consolidation of peace." But this was largely verbiage, for the same session approved a document on the continuing Basic Program of Unesco, the preamble of which listed Unesco's objectives as both international peace and the common welfare of mankind.[22]

Integration of three approaches to peace was suggested by the Director General, Torres Bodet,[23] in *Report to the United Nations for 1949-50*. He noted that the fundamental ideas underlying the Unesco program were (1) advancement of knowledge through exchange of information and cooperation among specialists; (2) promotion of human welfare through popular participation in the benefits of economic and social progress; (3) development of international understanding as a contribution to peace.[24]

In summary, the London Conference foreshadowed the lack of

clarity concerning Unesco's basic purpose which was to characterize succeeding conferences. Experience has shown that while the single purpose of Unesco to contribute to peace and security has not been deliberately ignored, member states have shown a marked preference for activities that contribute indirectly rather than directly. Hence the immediate objective of Unesco tends to be seen as the advancement of knowledge, promotion of human welfare, and development of international understanding. In practice this has meant the acceptance of a multiple purpose which justifies a wider range of activities than would have been possible had it been required that each activity should make a direct contribution to peace and security. How this interpretation of the Constitution has affected the scope of Unesco's program will be noted in greater detail in the following chapter.

Governmental or Nongovernmental?

The third critical issue arising at London was the kind of organization Unesco should be. Should it be governmental or nongovernmental? Should it have a mixed character? If nongovernmental, should its constituency be scholars and intellectuals with their international professional organizations, or should it be an agency where "peoples speak to peoples"? The International Committee on Intellectual Cooperation of the League of Nations had been a group of distinguished individuals sitting in a personal capacity. Unesco's most immediate predecessor, the Conference of Allied Ministers of Education, had been solely intergovernmental in character. Cooperation of governments was viewed as essential to assure authority and financial support for the organization, but in matters dealing with "the life of the mind" the hand of government might be deadening. This issue underlay such questions as composition of the General Conference and the Executive Board, as well as of National Commissions. It also concerned the relations of international nongovernmental organizations to Unesco.

The French draft for the Constitution proposed that the annual conference should be a tripartite body of governments, National Commissions, and leading nongovernmental "world associations." But the London Conference resolved that only governments could be members of the organization with a right to vote in the annual conference. This decision was coupled with a provision that Unesco might consult and cooperate with nongovernmental international organizations, inviting them to undertake specific tasks and to participate in advisory committees. Representatives of these organizations might sit as observers in the General Conference.[25] The relation of these organizations to Unesco is discussed in later chapters.

Choice of members of the Executive Board was another question which occasioned debate on the matter of government versus private influence. Both the CAME and the French draft provided for election to the Executive Board of persons (not states) from among delegates to the General Conference.[26] The CAME draft stipulated that: "The members of the Executive Board shall exercise the powers delegated to them by the Conference on behalf of the whole Conference and not as representatives of their respective governments." At issue was whether members of the Executive Board should be chosen as distinguished individuals in the educational, scientific, and cultural fields, or as representatives of member states. Some tradition lay behind the theory that the Board should be made up of distinguished individuals. Earlier discussions of a possible international educational agency as well as of agencies in other fields had often stressed the guidance that such persons might provide to governments. The Committee on Intellectual Cooperation of the League of Nations offered a precedent. Those who favored making Unesco a technical and "nonpolitical" agency favored a Board composed of individuals.[27] They found attractive the view that in such an agency neither nationalism nor governmental bureaucracy would deter the worldwide and creative interests of education, science, and culture. They appeared unconcerned that this view might deny the representative and responsible character of democratic government. They saw no danger that government support might thereby be weakened.

After considering various proposals, the Conference agreed that members of the Board should be chosen by the General Conference from among the government delegates in that body. After election these members should serve, not as representatives of their respective governments, but on behalf of the Conference as a whole.[28] In relation to their own governments the members were to function as free individuals, relying upon their own wisdom and responsible to no one but the General Conference. This provision, it was later argued, made the members actually irresponsible. Experience did not support the view that Board members would necessarily be of outstanding quality. As the result of a proposal urged principally by the United Kingdom and the United States, the 1954 session of the General Conference approved an amendment to the Constitution changing the status of Board members to that of government representatives.[29] This decision was related to approval by the 1952 General Conference of a constitutional amendment making its sessions biennial rather than annual. The argument ran that with the Conference meeting every two years responsibilities of the Executive Board would broaden and therefore members of the Board should be responsible representatives of governments. The real reason was dissatisfaction with the role the Board had played. At the New Delhi General Conference in 1956, inability to organize the unwieldy number of delegations present seemed likely to lead to a more important role for the Board on program matters, especially since its members are now government representatives. The wisdom of such development would depend on much more serious government control over Board members, in keeping with declared government policies, and also upon more clearly recognized leadership by the Director General.

The question of national cooperating bodies or of National Commissions also involved the role of governments and that of private bodies. As noted in the preceding chapter, various private organizations in Great Britain and the United States, which during World War II put forward plans for an international educational organization, had stressed the importance of national commissions in each member country. These bodies, patterned somewhat after the National Committees of the League of Nations Intellectual Cooperation Organization but of broader and more democratic character, were to link private educational, scientific, and cultural agencies with the government in carrying out Unesco activities.

A compromise was worked out at London on the character and functions of these bodies. National Commissions were to include representatives of both governments and private bodies. They were not to be represented per se in the General Conference, but national delegations were to be chosen after consultation with National Commissions. National Commissions were also to advise their respective governments and General Conference delegations, and were to act as "agencies of liaison."[30]

Thus the Constitution adopted at London makes Unesco primarily an intergovernmental organization,[31] with the limitation, later removed, that the Executive Board should be composed of individuals representing the General Conference as a whole rather than individual governments. The roles of national governments and private agencies were foreshadowed in the first sentence of the Constitution: "The governments of the States parties to this Constitution on behalf of their peoples declared. . . ." Unesco was in the first place an organization of governments, but governments functioned "on behalf of their peoples."

As noted above,[32] the word "peoples" was interpreted in two senses. The French and other Europeans held that the important element for Unesco in any national group was not the ordinary citizen but the élite of intellectuals. The French had urged a place in the new organization for scholars and their international associations. The Americans and others maintained that the word meant the whole people, in the broadest democratic sense; Unesco's major object was the "common understanding of the masses of the people in this world."[33] Therefore the United States, and particularly William Benton, Assistant Secretary of State, pressed for mass communication as the most effective channel for reaching great masses of people. In practice Unesco's approach to people in the broad sense and its employment of press, radio, and film as media of mass communication has been largely through projects directed toward the "masses of people" rather than through activities which would enlist widespread popular participation.[34]

There were those who believed that Unesco must seek to approach both leaders and masses. Speaking at the London Conference, Torres Bodet said, "Our purpose is to find a *modus vivendi,* whereby the training of strong personalities shall not presuppose the neglect of the masses, and the expansion of the masses shall not imply the stifling of the individual."[35] Later at the Sixth Session of the General Conference in 1951 he emphasized that Unesco has all the complexity and richness of a "synthetic organization. By its administrative structure," he continued, "Unesco is linked with governments; by its National Commissions it is more directly linked with peoples; by the international non-governmental organizations it is linked with experts. All these resources must converge if Unesco is to succeed."[36]

In the United States, the United Kingdom, Canada, and certain other nations of the British Commonwealth, as well as in some of the European countries, the intellectual and professional élite includes a large group. Reaching such an élite borders on a mass operation, where personal contact needs to be supplemented to some degree by mass communication.

Unesco's Relation to the United Nations

A fourth basic question that faced the delegates at London was Unesco's relationship to the United Nations. The San Francisco Conference had written into the United Nations Charter the framework into which Unesco could fit as a specialized agency. How much or how little autonomy would it have? Among the principal organs of the United Nations—General Assembly, Security Council, Economic and Social Council (ECOSOC), Trusteeship Council, International Court of Justice, Secretariat—ECOSOC is the one with which Unesco and other specialized agencies are most closely linked. The specialized agencies are administratively independent, but each has an agreement with the United Nations.[37] Each must present an annual report to ECOSOC. The latter may coordinate the activities of specialized agencies through consultation and recommendation. It may review and discuss their programs. National states, through common membership in these agencies, can make for better coordination by greater consistency toward the same issues as they arise in ECOSOC and the various specialized agencies.

The London Conference decided that in accordance with Article 63 of the United Nations Charter, a general agreement on the relationship between the United Nations and Unesco was to be worked out. This agreement should ensure cooperation and at the same time recognize the autonomy of Unesco within the fields of its competence. Further, the agreement might "provide for the approval and financing of the budget of the Organization by the General Assembly of the United Nations."[38] This last provision was never put into practice. Unesco's budget is approved by the General Conference of Unesco, although the UN Advisory Committee on Budget and Financial Questions regularly "examines" and may comment on the Unesco and other specialized agency budgets.

The London Conference agreed that the Constitution should become effective when accepted by twenty signatory nations, with no action required by the General Assembly of the United Nations.

Constitutional amendments would require approval only of the General Conference, by a two-thirds majority, except in a limited number of cases when acceptance by two-thirds of the member states would also be necessary.[39]

Unesco thus became a planet in the United Nations solar system. It was to have its own orbit, but was subject to forces exerted by other members of the system. Time would make clear the precise role Unesco should play in the United Nations system. Should it be primarily a technical institution, complementing the concern of the United Nations for international peace and security with an effort to strengthen the bases of a world community; or should it seek directly a better understanding of and more vigorous support for the United Nations?[40]

George V. Allen, head of the United States delegation at the Fourth Session of the General Conference in 1949, urged that Unesco "integrate itself more closely into the general United Nations structure. . . . Unesco's specific assignment in the general United Nations structure is to try to create enough understanding and friendship in the international sphere, among all the peoples of the world, to give the rest of the United Nations a chance to succeed. . . . Unesco, then, must contribute its part to a world system strong enough to keep the peace."[41]

This point of view was challenged by Georges Bidault, the head of the French delegation, who said: "It is, I think, permissible to state from this platform that the United Nations has not entirely lived up to the hopes we reposed in it . . . it would be unreasonable, I think, to make our advance dependent upon the way being cleared by organizations which are hampered more than we are by difficulties of a political character. Let us therefore act by ourselves, in conformity with the main principles of the United Nations, as an organ dependent upon, and related to that Organization, but having nevertheless its own life, its own aims and intentions; its own desires, and, I maintain, its own duties."[42]

In less political matters, Unesco's first decade witnessed integration of many of its activities into those of the United Nations system. The UN Administrative Committee on Coordination, made up of the Secretary General of the United Nations and the Directors General of the specialized agencies, has proved useful. Further, as activities have grown in such areas as fundamental education and application of scientific findings to problems of the arid and humid tropical zones, and as the value of a "team" approach to the needs of the economically less developed countries has been increasingly recognized, closer cooperation between Unesco, the other specialized agencies, and the United Nations has become indispensable.

How Should Unesco Be Used?

The varying views expressed at London concerning Unesco's purpose and character naturally had an effect upon the question of how nations should use the new organization once it was established. The vast scope of Unesco's responsibilities when linked to its small budget presented a perplexing problem. Should Unesco limit its activities to those of a clearing house and liaison center—to preserve, share, and extend the educational, scientific, and cultural resources of the world? Should it undertake leadership in fostering peace and social progress? Should governments be satisfied with Unesco as a means to diffuse existing knowledge and encourage new knowledge and insight? Or should Unesco be used as an action agency promoting a peaceful and prosperous world through meeting the needs of member states and helping solve major problems of the present day?

In many cases Europeans who have emphasized the "common welfare" purpose of Unesco and have favored the indirect approach to peace and security have viewed the exchange of information and "intellectual cooperation" among scholars as Unesco's basic task. Exchange and intellectual contact have as a rule been the earliest and most important function of international organizations working in education, science, and culture. This was true of the array of congresses, bureaus, and unions which developed in the last part of the nineteenth century and the early years of the twentieth. It was largely true of the Paris Institute of Intellectual Cooperation, although that agency did assume initiative in launching certain new projects, such as free circulation of educational films.

Thus it is not surprising that Unesco's role was early pictured as that of a telephone exchange, to connect and coordinate lines of communication which—particularly in Europe and North America—already existed. Members of this school of thought were not primarily concerned with the object of such communication, whether it be expansion of knowledge, fostering common welfare, or promotion of peace and security.

Countries of South and Southeast Asia, the Middle East and Latin America felt otherwise. Their problems were urgent ones of poverty, ill health, and illiteracy. They were not equipped as a rule with long-established scientific and learned societies or with libraries and museums which would enable them to profit from Unesco if it functioned only as a clearing house. They wanted much more—a world crusade against illiteracy. They demanded direct services from Unesco. They viewed education and technical assistance as aids for pressing needs and solutions for major problems.

The issue of how Unesco should be used came up in other ways. William Benton had called in 1946 for a world-wide radio network. He urged active Unesco prosecution of the campaign for freedom of information. At the 1950 session of the General Conference he argued that "The political struggle raging in the world was an intellectual, moral and educational struggle; Unesco could not remain indifferent to the pressures from which the minds of men were assailed from all sides. . . . Unesco must find a way to tap all the resources of the free world, and to learn to use every means of mass communication to tell the glorious story of freedom."[43]

The 1945 London Conference before adjourning had embodied its conclusions in three documents: the Final Act, the Constitution, and the Instrument Establishing a Preparatory Commission.[44] This Commission was to guide the process which would translate Unesco from a paper to a living organization. The Conference, through its work in drafting the Unesco Constitution, determined that the approach of the organization would be basically indirect, as a service agency to member states and as a stimulus to governments and private organizations. As an operating agency, in educational reconstruction as well as in other activities, it would have certain limits. The scope of the Unesco program would be broad, covering the field of education from pre-school to university and adult education; the whole range of the natural[45] and social sciences; the arts together with philosophy and the humanities; such agencies of information and communication as libraries and museums, press, film, radio, television.

These activities were to be carried on in implementing what came to be accepted as the triple purpose of the organization: promotion of international understanding and of human welfare, and advancement of knowledge. The consequences of this triple purpose were unfavorable to program concentration, but favorable perhaps to wider support from private groups, member states, and nongovernmental international organizations.

As the needs which Unesco was set up to meet molded its purpose, so its inheritance from national programs of cultural relations, and from earlier international organizations both private and governmental, shaped its character. Unesco was to be an intergovernmental organization, but through international nongovernmental organizations and through its National Commissions it was to be linked to scholars and experts as well as to peoples.

As a specialized agency it would be a member of the United Nations family, while still enjoying substantial autonomy. It was left to the future to define Unesco's place in the United Nations system, whether it should serve as a technical institution with a task similar to that of the Food and Agriculture Organization and the World Health Organization, or become "political" and support the efforts of the United Nations for peace.[46] As to what Unesco should do, the tradition of previous international cooperation in this field suggested a modest role as a clearing house and center for intellectual cooperation. The more positive and aggressive objectives of national programs of cultural relations and the critical world problems associated with the cold war urged Unesco toward the role of an action agency exercising such leadership as member states would permit.

CHAPTER III

Evolution of the Program

During Unesco's first ten years, its program underwent many changes, reflecting uncertainties in the Constitution, varied interests of member states, and changing world conditions. By the end of the decade, notably at the conclusion of the Ninth Session of the General Conference at New Delhi in 1956, the program had gained in both clarity and coherence. There was reason to hope that Unesco's next ten years would show greater stability than its first decade. In this chapter we shall review the main lines of development. Succeeding chapters will discuss specific activities undertaken by Unesco in various fields.

The Unesco program is usually presented by chapters or departments, of which there are now six: education, natural sciences, social sciences, cultural activities, mass communication, and technical assistance. By a series of resolutions approved by the General Conference, the Director General carries out specified activities which together constitute the program.

In the field of education, the most important emphasis has been on fundamental education, extension of primary education, and education for international understanding. In the natural sciences the program has focused on international scientific cooperation, encouragement of research for the improvement of the economic and social conditions of mankind (such as the arid zone project), and teaching about science. The emphasis in the social sciences has been on international development of those sciences and on their application to social tensions, human rights, and international understanding. The program in the field of cultural activities has stressed international contacts in the arts, better understanding of the cultural history of mankind, in-

45

ternational cooperation in the humanities and philosophy, and services rendered by libraries and museums. Finally, use of press, radio, film, and television for international understanding has been explored, an attempt has been made to help member states improve their facilities in such channels of mass communication, and steps have been taken to reduce obstacles to the free flow of information among nations.

For an idea of the evolution that took place from 1946 to 1956, it may be useful to divide the history of Unesco's program development into three stages: 1947-49, a period of exploration and uncertainty in which the optimism of member states seemed unlimited as to the number and variety of activities that the organization could carry on; 1950-52, a period of acute dissatisfaction with the scattered and ineffective character of Unesco's program and of mounting internal struggles and tensions, culminating in resignation of the second Director General; and 1953-56, a period marked by growing interest in the organization on the part of member states and by increasing effort toward program concentration, clearer structure, and more effective administration. One result of the struggles over purpose and program during Unesco's first decade was a sense of frustration. But out of these struggles also gradually emerged a total program that went beyond what might have been anticipated from any single interpretation of Unesco's purpose. This program promised to permit the organization to function more consistently, even under rapidly changing world conditions.

Early leaders of Unesco recognized that the organization would have to experiment. These leaders apparently believed that in the face of the bewildering complexity of human life the spirit of man should have opportunity to reach out and adventure in new fields, even if success were doubtful. The encyclopedic interests of the Preparatory Commission's Executive Secretary,[1] Julian Huxley, were a further spur toward a far-spreading program. The Commission, many of whose members were drawn from academic life, organized program proposals along the lines of a university faculty. It set up seven committees which worked with seven planning divisions of the temporary secretariat to deal respectively with education, natural sciences, libraries and museums, social sciences, mass media of communication, fine and applied arts, letters and philosophy.

The 1947-49 Period

The setting for the period 1947-49 therefore is provided by the work of this Commission, which had received program suggestions from many sources—governments, organizations national and international, its own members and secretariat, and specialists in many fields. The mass of suggestions was pruned and organized, but the tendency of the Commission was to approve rather than reject program proposals. Experience had made evident the value of exchange of persons and of clearing house services. Outside of these areas, no one knew what activities would be effective.

When the Commission reviewed the range of proposed activities in July 1946, it found them so numerous and broad that a scheme of priorities was suggested: first, those projects which should be attacked immediately; second, those which should be considered by the First Session of the General Conference for operation in 1947-48; third, those to be studied for action later; fourth, long-term projects approved in principle only.[2] The Commission also adopted a three-fold classification of program activities, according to their objectives: (1) those which would promote peace and security directly; (2) those which would advance human welfare directly; and (3) those that would indirectly serve these objectives by developing the resources of education, science, and culture.[3]

These efforts of the Preparatory Commission failed to cut back the proposed program. Its report to the First Session of the General Conference (1946) putting forward some 150 proposals was called a "parade of hobby-horses." On the other hand, the Commission staked out a number of paths for development. Some confusion about program was inevitable at the start of Unesco and in the world that it faced. The year 1946, it was contended, was not the time for a narrow program. Had such a course been followed, Unesco might have become an educational UNRRA and nothing more.

The Preparatory Commission's proposals presented for the first General Conference the question of criteria to be followed if the program were to show coherence and to fit within the resources of budget and staff. Several approaches to this problem were attempted. The Program Commission of the General Conference adopted a list of criteria, prominent among which was the qualitative one of contribution to peace and security, with attention also to cost, available staff, and timing. Unfortunately these criteria were not applied. Most discussion took place in subcommissions of specialists in the seven program areas, whose primary interest was in their own individual fields rather than in the total program.

Final decision of the General Conference was to list for first attention the projects of greatest significance, classified into those contributing to preservation, increase, and dissemination of man's knowledge. This list of priority subjects was not mandatory on the Director General, who "as the responsible officer of the Organization, must, in the last analysis, make the selection and produce the program in consultation with the Executive Board."[4] Responsibility for bringing the program within a budget of $6,500,000 was left to the Director General and the Executive Board.[5] The Conference went little further than the Preparatory Commission in clarifying Unesco's objectives and the content of its program.

A proposal by the United States delegation at this same session sought to avoid subdividing the secretariat into rigid compartments. It urged a few "crucially important" undertakings to be carried out by "task-forces," including specialists from all the program areas, and involving substantial assistance from at least a number of member states. This suggestion led to the formulation by the Executive Board of a program organized not under subject-matter departments but under four general themes or objectives in which all departments might cooperate.[6] At the Second Session of the General Conference at Mexico City, this proposal was successfully opposed by natural scientists and educators, who secured separate programs for those fields. Subsequently the social scientists did the same. Thus the subject matter approach became the basis for organization of both program and secretariat. The idea, however, of focusing Unesco's efforts on a few major enterprises was revived in 1954, in connection with a basic "remodelling" of the Unesco program.[7]

A Unesco "Philosophy"

Another attempt at the First Session of the General Conference to develop unity among the multiplicity of Unesco's activities deserves special attention. Julian Huxley, as Executive Secretary of the Preparatory Commission, outlined a basic Unesco "philosophy" which he hoped might serve as a general frame for the program. He presented it in a pamphlet entitled *Unesco: Its Purpose and Its Philosophy,*[8] from which, however, the Preparatory Commission withheld its sponsorship. It was circulated as the personal statement of the Executive Secretary. Huxley argued that the organization needed "a working hypothesis" more precise than that set forth in the general language of the Constitution. Such a statement could not be based on "sectarian" theologies, competing politico-economic doctrines, or special points of view. He consequently offered a philosophy which he called "world scientific humanism": "humanism" because Unesco was concerned with peace and human welfare; "world" because Unesco had to do with all the peoples of the world and with all individuals on a basis of equality for all; "scientific" because science provided "most of the material basis for human culture" and because science needed to be integrated with intellectual and spiritual values. Further, this philosophy must be evolutionary, in his view, because the theory of evolution had indicated man's place in nature and his relations to the rest of the universe.

The Huxley approach was almost immediately challenged by the late Vladislav Ribnikar, the Yugoslav observer, who questioned whether Unesco, if it were true to its pledge of cultural diversity, could reject "the scientific character of dialectical materialism." Adoption of an international official philosophy, Ribnikar argued, would "lead to the enslavement of thought and of the spirit of creation and would form an arbitrary obstacle to the spread of culture." He dubbed such an approach "a kind of philosophic esperanto."[9]

The debate on Huxley's proposal was continued by William Benton, head of the United States delegation, who argued that world peace could not rest on any single political philosophy or religious faith. Unesco was pledged to cultural democracy, "a democracy of mind and spirit in which every culture shall be free to live and develop in itself and in the great community of common culture. . . . Free men do not fear ideas; free men are not afraid of thought; free men are eager to confront the differences and rich varieties that life presents, and to determine for themselves the things they take as true. This, from the beginning, has been the path of freedom."[10]

The General Conference eventually took the attitude, as had the Preparatory Commission, that the Huxley statement represented solely his personal views and not those of the Conference.

At the Second Session of the General Conference a year later, Jacques Maritain, France's eminent Catholic philosopher, continued discussion of theoretical principles as a possible guide for program selection. In a thoughtful address, he noted the paradoxical character of Unesco's task, "since it implies intellectual agreement between men whose views of the world, of culture and even of knowledge are different and even opposed." How then is it possible to secure agreement in the Babel of modern thought? He discarded the possibility that Unesco should give up all effort to achieve a declaration of common ideas; and equally so, that Unesco should attempt to establish an artificial conformity of minds. He found the solution in a third direction. Since "the goal of Unesco is a practical goal, agreement between minds can be reached spontaneously, not on the basis of common speculative ideas, but on common practical ideas," which could serve for guidance in action. He pointed out that such practical ideas as, for example, the importance of human rights, were already embodied in the Unesco Constitution on which Unesco's member states had agreed.[11]

The attempt to outline a Unesco philosophy, which would serve as a guide in forming a program, had led back to ideas outlined in the Constitution, ideas perhaps purposely left vague to win wider acceptance. It was argued therefore that to the degree that Unesco had a philosophy, it was one of "respect for diversity, a conscious pluralism." Implicit rejection of fascist doctrines in the Constitution's Preamble, and explicit rejection of the doctrine of the inequality of men and races, gave "a positive content to Unesco's tolerance and pluralism."[12] Viewed in retrospect, one of Unesco's greatest contributions may have been recognition of a pluralistic world and of the possibility of cooperation among peoples whose different approaches were accepted and respected.

It is improbable that the last word has been said on Unesco's philosophy. Historically speaking, the assumptions underlying the organization were those of Western democratic liberalism.[13] Unesco has proceeded on the premise that education, information, and personal contact will help international understanding, and that understanding will contribute to peace. The sufficiency of these means and the relation of understanding to peace have been questioned.[14] Entry into Unesco of the USSR with its authoritarian Communist ideology may threaten the quasi-monopoly of the liberal democratic countries and face Unesco with the need of reappraising the assumptions on which it at first proceeded.[15]

Search for Criteria of Selection

During the first two years of operation, no notable progress was made in reaching criteria for selection of projects or areas of concentration. Instructions of the 1946 General Conference required examination of the program in detail by the Director General and the Executive Board if it was to be fitted in any way within the 6½ million dollar budget. The staff immediately available in the secretariat had mostly served in the Preparatory Commission, and were at least emotionally committed to its original program. The Board took seriously the special assignment of supervising closely the work of the Director General,[16] but lacked agreement on either purpose or program. Many Board members had been members of specialist groups at the First Session of the General Conference and continued their support for projects representing those interests. The Board rejected flatly the effort of the Acting Director General to achieve program concentration by application of criteria drawn from the Constitution.

A variety of other factors involved in this initial stage of Unesco's development barred progress toward program clarification. Recruitment of new staff members was a pressing and time-consuming problem, since selection had to be made with regard to nationality as well as competence. Efforts to organize the secretariat on functional rather than on academic lines met with resistance from the Board and from every organized intellectual discipline. The secretariat had to function in unsatisfactory quarters amid the unsettled conditions in postwar Paris. Within three months from the adjournment of the First Session, member countries which had shifted to the shoulders of the Director General and the Executive Board the task of making a program began to demand knowledge of proposals to the Second Session of the General Conference scheduled to meet at Mexico City in November 1947. Governments, facing legislative bodies reluctant to appropriate funds for the vague if admirable objectives of Unesco, asked for quick and tangible results from the new organization.

The program presented to the Mexico City Conference in 1947 was in all important respects a replica of the Paris program, except for certain new proposals and a request for more money. The same was true of proposals which emerged a year later for the Third Session of the General Conference held at Beirut.

Torres Bodet was elected Director General at this latter session. He referred in his initial speech to program concentration. Early in his term—in a speech at Cleveland in April, 1949, before the Second National Conference convened by the United States National Commission for Unesco—he proposed three yardsticks to govern the selection of Unesco activities: (1) Will the project promote mass welfare? (2) Will it enlist cooperation of intellectual leaders everywhere to work for humanity? (3) Will it produce tangible results quickly? He presented these criteria to the Fourth Session of the General Conference in somewhat modified form.[17] When he employed them in program discussions with the Executive Board he was reversed on several points, and he apparently came to believe that no system of priorities could withstand pressure for favorite projects by member states and Board Members, as well as certain members of the secretariat.[18] It may be said that through its third year Unesco held to the pattern of the program as conceived by the Preparatory Commission. Sentiment continued to mount, however, in favor of clearer logic for determining program content.

Technical Assistance

It was at this stage in Unesco's history that the United Nations Expanded Technical Assistance Program was launched. It was to be increasingly important in Unesco's program. No single factor has so influenced the direction of the program as has technical assistance.

In the autumn of 1948, the United Nations General Assembly embarked on a major program to provide technical knowledge and aid for economic development of the less industrialized countries of the world. This was a logical outgrowth of Articles 55-60 of the United Nations Charter. It was even more an obvious response to the need for promoting the peaceful integration of these states, many of them newly independent, in the world community, by helping to raise their standards of living and furthering their economic and social progress. These countries were located principally in South and

Southeast Asia, the Middle East, Africa, and some parts of Latin America.

In January, 1949, President Truman in his inaugural address called for a program of technical assistance both by the United States (later called the "Point IV" program) and "as a cooperative enterprise in which all nations work together through the United Nations and its specialized agencies wherever possible."[19] In the following month the Economic and Social Council approved a resolution introduced by the United States, and later that year the Secretary General of the United Nations and the Directors General of the specialized agencies outlined a comprehensive program of technical assistance. This program was approved by ECOSOC in August, 1949.[20] During the first six years of this enterprise almost eighty countries pledged it 142 million dollars. Through its activities, 131 countries and territories have been helped.[21] Between 1950 and 1956, more than 5,000 experts were sent out and 8,000 training fellowships awarded. Development of the program is supervised by a Technical Assistance Committee (TAC) of ECOSOC and by a Technical Assistance Board (TAB) of representatives of the various United Nations agencies which administer the program.

The technical assistance program made available to Unesco additional funds beyond the regular budget of the organization. These were initially allocated to Unesco in accordance with a formula approved by ECOSOC for distributing funds received for the Expanded Technical Assistance Program (UNETAP). Projects under the program are planned and undertaken only at the request of governments of the recipient countries, which themselves contribute part of the costs payable in local currency. By 1956 Unesco had sent out in response to these requests 500 scientists and educators and provided 600 fellowships. It should be noted that in practically all the less economically developed countries, Unesco's efforts to provide technical assistance have been overshadowed by the larger and more generously financed activities of the U. S. technical assistance (Point IV) programs, in lesser degree by the Colombo Plan, and in some parts of Asia by those of the Soviet Union and the People's Republic of China.

Unesco's contributions to the technical assistance program have been primarily in the fields of education and the natural sciences. In education it has helped member states in expansion and improve-

ment of primary and secondary education, fundamental education, and technical education. In the natural sciences it has provided assistance for scientific research, science teaching, and scientific and technical documentation. Activities in the above fields have been considered as directly related to economic development, in contrast to other parts of Unesco's program such as the social sciences and cultural activities. However, experience has increasingly demonstrated that social and economic development are inevitably linked, and therefore that the social sciences have an essential contribution to make.

Aside from the benefits it brought to member states, the United Nations Expanded Technical Assistance Program had a major effect on Unesco's program operation. It enabled Unesco to carry out a larger program, and thus Unesco's importance may have been enhanced in the eyes of member states. In 1950 the allotment from UN funds was approximately 2½ million dollars.[22] In 1956 this figure had increased to almost 5 million dollars. This growing enterprise demonstrated the effect which an effort with precise goals (i.e., specific projects in specific countries toward a specific objective—economic development) can have in the country of operation. It introduced a faster tempo in activities of the secretariat, as a result of additional funds and a specially organized staff. It helped recipient countries identify their most fundamental and pressing needs, and gave a stronger focus within Unesco's regular program to aid for member states. It indicated the need and usefulness of coordination between Unesco and other United Nations agencies on problems of human welfare and world peace. In some projects this coordination illustrated the effectiveness of the "task-force" approach, that is, bringing specialists from various fields to work together on one enterprise.

The 1950-52 Period

The Fourth Session of the General Conference held at Paris in September–October 1949 gave special expression to the demand for clearer logic in program formulation by requesting that the Director General and the Executive Board in preparing the draft program for 1951 include "a statement of the Basic Programme of the Organization . . . and the purposes stated in the Constitution which they are designed to serve."[23] A simple and cogent statement for the intelligent citizen was needed if public understanding of Unesco's purpose and program was to be achieved. More important, the Basic Program was conceived as a long-term plan from which the annual General Conference would for a given year select items to be pushed actively to completion.

The Fifth Session at Florence consequently had before it, in addition to the regular 1951 program, a draft of a Basic Program, organized under seven main heads: education, natural sciences, social sciences, cultural activities, exchange of persons, mass communication, and relief services. Following explanatory preambles, the principal continuing activities of Unesco were listed under ninety-six propositions.[24] While this draft compressed the lines of activity into a number of general resolutions, it failed to point toward tasks of major importance, nor did it change the "university faculty" structure set up by the Preparatory Commission.

To develop sharper focus, the United States delegation at Florence prevailed on the Conference to include in the exposition of the Basic Program a listing of ten main tasks, such as fundamental education, education in support of human rights, free flow of ideas and knowledge, progress and use of science, attack on social tensions, demonstration of world cultural interdependence, use of mass media to advance the cause of truth, freedom, and peace, and development of better international understanding and of more loyal cooperation in the framework of the United Nations.[25] The effect of this Decalogue, so-called, was to arouse resistance from those already committed to pet projects. Confusing as the Decalogue seemed to many, as adding merely a further classification of Unesco's projects, it and other efforts kept alive the idea of program concentration and the need for more careful selection of projects.

Allied to the American delegation's emphasis on "major tasks," as outlined in the Decalogue, was stress on the idea of "major projects" as a means for concentration. It was recognized that Unesco's technical and professional services, such as interchange of knowledge on educational, scientific, and cultural developments, international cooperation among scientists and other scholars, expert guidance for education, and development of mass communication, were useful and should be continued. These services, it was argued, should be related to a small number of major projects. Two examples of such "skyscraper" projects—so-called because they were expected to rise above the prevailing level of Unesco program activities—were promotion of international understanding, including support of the Universal Declaration of Human Rights, and intensified efforts to assist the German people in re-entering the world of international cooperation.

The United States delegation argued that Unesco should present to the world appealing and dramatic plans for outstanding projects. Such an approach might attract additional financial support from outside the regular budget, as had already happened with the United Nations Expanded Program of Technical Assistance.[26] This hope for outside support was later disappointed even though specific major projects were proposed.

The United Nations also at this stage debated the importance of setting priorities as a guide in selection of program projects. In a series of discussions, criteria for program selection were urged upon all the specialized agencies as well as upon the United Nations itself.[27] It may be noted, however, that the United Nations presented to Unesco a wide range of requests (hardly conducive to program concentration), calling for translation of the classics, international research laboratories, exchange of workers, a training center for public administration, and teaching about the United Nations.

Conflicting pressures for concentration or expansion were part of the background for the 1950 crisis at Florence which arose in program discussions and which led to the resignation of Torres Bodet, later withdrawn. This was the first major crisis within Unesco of conflicting interpretations of the purpose of the organization, of attempts to put a budget ceiling on an expanding program, and of the deteriorating world climate of opinion caused by the cold war.

Another approach to concentration was brought forward by the Director General in the draft program presented to the 1951 session of the General Conference. These proposals were related to major themes or objects such as fundamental education and human rights.[28] This functional approach was not translated into administrative terms. Subject matter remained the basis for both program and secretariat.

The United States at the General Conference in 1952 sought, in line with the pattern laid down by the United Nations, to develop and apply priorities to the Unesco program. A special Working Party on Future Program and Development was appointed. Its report with comments received from member states was to be used by the Director

General and the Executive Board as a guide in preparing the 1955-56 draft program. When after successive postponements it came before the Executive Board in March–April 1954, its examination was eclipsed by a proposal for a fundamental remodeling of Unesco's future program with which the Board had become engrossed.[29]

The 1953-56 Period

Here we move to the third stage in the evolution of the Unesco program, where a new approach was to be taken toward program formulation and concentration. The most recent and important effort to concentrate Unesco's program took its origin from a proposal to the Executive Board in July 1953 by Vittorino Veronese, member from Italy. This move was initiated after election of the third Director General, Luther H. Evans. At the suggestion of Dr. Veronese, the Board met informally in November to discuss Unesco's program, its methods of work, and organization of the secretariat. Discussions focused in large part on four points: (1) Unesco's failure to obtain the full support of member states, creative thinkers, and peoples; (2) greater use of a regional approach in Unesco activities; (3) need for more effective National Commissions; (4) means of further concentrating the program.[30]

Out of these conversations emerged a long memorandum whose emphasis on the needs of member states was reinforced by mounting requests for Unesco assistance coming from the countries of Asia. This emphasis received expression in a conference of the Indian National Commission held at New Delhi, January 9-14, 1954, and attended by the Director General; Sir Ronald Adam, Chairman of the Executive Board; and Oscar Secco Ellauri, member of the Board from Uruguay. The Conference had something of a regional character because of the presence of guests from Afghanistan, Ceylon, Egypt, Indonesia, Iran, Iraq, Japan, Lebanon, Nepal, and Syria, and an observer from Turkey.

The President of the Indian National Commission, Minister of Education Maulana Abul Kalam Azad, called attention to the feeling in Asia and Africa that the needs of those areas were not accorded adequate consideration by the United Nations or Unesco. He pointed out that while Unesco could help to bring to the East the advances of the West in education and the natural sciences, it should also make available to the West "the abiding values of Eastern culture."[31]

In the view of the Asians, Unesco could channel to the West the traditional riches of Asia's ancestral cultures and acquaint the East with Western methods for preservation and diffusion of cultural resources. The Asian countries desired technical assistance from Unesco in preserving and publicizing historical monuments and archaeological sites, fostering the cultural development of their peoples through traditional arts, setting up public libraries and museums as educational instruments, establishing publishing houses and producing good, simple, cheap books for the growing school population and for the newly literate adults, and developing national motion pictures to counteract the often lurid and violent imports from the West. This expression of Asian views affected the Board's deliberations the more because of the growing influence of this region in United Nations affairs.

The memorandum mentioned above noted the paradox in Unesco's position after eight years of work. While the organization had to its credit a record of achievement, it had failed to win wide support in public opinion or full support of governments. Structure and content of its program were shaped in terms of ideas, rather than practical problems. It was not in touch "with the real interests of governments and peoples." The program needed to recognize the requirements of member states, and to turn to "concrete tasks related to the cares and aspirations of Member States."

The memorandum proposed division of the program into two major categories: (a) permanent activities, such as technical services and campaigns and measures intended to have a universal effect; and (b) activities limited in space and time bearing on clearly specified problems. Certain of these proposals already had been put forward on several occasions. Their relevance had been strengthened by initiation of the technical assistance program. The time apparently was ripe for a change.

The first category, termed "the continuing universal program," would include clearing-house services in which Unesco functions as an international fund of knowledge and ideas for the collection and distribution of information; assistance to the international cooperation of specialists, scientists and other scholars; technical advice to the United Nations; development of international standards or regulations in such fields as copyright, protection of cultural property, and free importation of educational, scientific, and cultural material; a continuing campaign for promotion of human rights, education about the United Nations, and education for living in a world community.

The second main category, "a program of action," included two types of activities: (a) an enlarged service of technical assistance (not limited as that of the United Nations to "economic development") for meeting specific requests from member states; and (b) major projects, few in number, to lead to achievement within a fixed period and in a definite area, carried out by "task forces" including representatives of pertinent fields and with large-scale cooperation, financial and otherwise, from interested member states.

Consideration of the ideas embodied in the memorandum at the March 1954 session of the Executive Board was conditioned by the Board's review at the same time of the draft program and budget for 1955-56, submitted by the Director General. This program encountered criticism in the Board, and the view gained ground among its members that the 1955-56 program should be reworked to make it a step toward a new program. The Director General agreed, once the Board had made clear its preference. The new draft, after Board review in July, was presented to the General Conference at Montevideo in November 1954, together with proposals for remodeling the future program of Unesco substantially along lines recommended in the memorandum referred to above.[32]

Discussion in the Executive Board had brought out that European member countries of Unesco feared that emphasis on aid to member states (e.g., for fundamental education) would reduce funds available for intellectual cooperation. The latter activity was viewed as a scholarly and relatively disinterested pursuit. The former was regarded as involving a political and propaganda element. Need for such aid had been stressed by the countries of Asia. It was supported by the United States—in the view of some European countries largely for political motives. This support was interpreted as motivated by fear that, if aid of this kind were not provided to the economically less developed countries, Soviet Communism would gain ground there. This European point of view, while agreeing that Unesco must meet the needs of member states, urged that the organization should not become an instrument of political action, which might ultimately vitiate its program and throttle general activities.

The Eighth Session of the General Conference at Montevideo approved the proposals of the Executive Board for the remodeled future program and authorized the Director General to proceed with its preparation, in accordance with definitions and procedures outlined by the Conference. It adopted two major categories for the program, general and special. It defined general activities as the "continuing functions of the Organization" of interest to all member states, which provide the basis of the program. It defined special activities, including both aid to individual states and major projects to assist a group of states, as calculated to provide a practical solution to concrete problems.

The Conference listed the distinguishing features of such special activities as clear aims, definite limits for stages of execution, and definition in advance of full financial implications and methods. Through the major projects it was hoped to link bilateral activities by many governments with multilateral activities of Unesco. The Advisory Committee on Program and Budget declared that "Unesco may also act as a co-ordinator of the bilateral and multilateral relations between States," a proposal which may have far-reaching implications.[33]

With regard to the division between general and specific activities, the Conference stated: "This distinction must not be such as to endanger the fundamental unity of the programme, for the two types of activity are essentially interdependent." They were to be viewed as aspects of a single program. They had common aims which were "to develop education, science and culture; to promote the growth of an international community of minds; to develop better mutual understanding among the peoples of the world." Despite efforts at definition mentioned above, the distinction between general and special activities became confused in the minds of many delegates, who tended to oversimplify the division as one between clearing-house work at Unesco headquarters and "activities" carried out with Unesco help in member states—a distinction which ignored the inevitable intermeshing in practice of general and special activities.[34]

The program of aid to member states, which has come to be called the Aid program to distinguish it from the UN Technical Assistance Program, was initiated following the Montevideo Conference in the 1955-56 biennium. The former, in contrast to the latter, is not limited to economic development, nor to less economically developed countries. It was designed as a cooperative enterprise with member states, the latter providing part of the cost, particularly those items which could be met in local currency. Aid would take various forms such as specialists, fellowships, documentary material, and national or regional seminars. This type of activity excited during and after the Montevideo Conference wider and more immediate interest than the proposal for major projects. The Director General drew up for information of member states a statement of principles and conditions governing grants in the Aid program. Requests were received from almost sixty countries totaling $4,000,000, although only $1,100,000 had been allotted in the 1955-56 budget for that activity. These requests involved services of 160 experts and grants of 265 training fellowships. Some requests supplemented activities already under way in the program of technical assistance for economic development, while others fell outside that program, such as preservation of monuments, development of museums, and expansion of mass media.

By the middle of February 1956, grants covering almost all of the $1,100,000 allocation had been approved. These grants provided for aid in free and compulsory education, teaching of both natural and social sciences, protection of cultural property, national and public libraries and museums, and communication services.[35] Allotment of $1,634,500, representing a fifty per cent increase, was requested by the Director General in the 1957-58 program submitted to the New Delhi Conference.

It was expected that a number of Unesco activities already initiated would be carried forward in the future by this type of assistance, including national fundamental education centers in India and Korea; a project for rural teacher training in Thailand; training of personnel for research on the peaceful uses of atomic energy; pilot projects for public libraries in Colombia and Nigeria; and a center in Egypt for photographic documentation on ancient monuments. Most of these projects will be mentioned in later chapters.

With regard to major projects for 1957-58, the Director General originally suggested four undertakings: training of normal school staff and educational administrators in Latin America; scientific research on arid lands; mutual appreciation of Eastern and Western cultural values; and reading materials for new literates. With approval of the Executive Board, the first three were presented to the

New Delhi Conference and approved by it.[36] Beginning in the latter
part of 1956 and particularly at the New Delhi General Conference,
a surge of enthusiasm was evident for the major projects. The Conference substantially increased the budgetary allocations for all three,
and authorized establishment of an intergovernmental advisory
committee for each, to aid the Director General in launching and developing the projects.

Growth of Unesco's Membership

As noted earlier, the increase in Unesco's member states was an important factor affecting evolution of the program. Before the end of
the First Session of the General Conference in 1946, twenty-eight of
the forty-four countries represented at the London Conference a year
earlier had joined the organization. Seven member states were from
the European continent: Belgium, Czechoslovakia, Denmark, France,
Greece, Norway, and Poland. Six were from the British Commonwealth: Australia, Canada, India, New Zealand, Union of South
Africa, and United Kingdom. Five were from the Middle East: Egypt,
Lebanon, Saudi Arabia, Syria, and Turkey. Two were from East Asia:
China and the Philippines. Eight were from the Americas: Bolivia,
Brazil, Dominican Republic, Haiti, Mexico, Peru, Venezuela, and
the United States. Succeeding years saw a steady increase particularly
of non-European nations as members of Unesco.

Five additional Latin American countries adhered to the organization in 1947: Colombia, Cuba, Ecuador, Honduras, and Uruguay.
The governments of Liberia, Luxembourg, and the Netherlands also
deposited their instruments of acceptance. Membership was further
increased in 1948 with admission of eight countries: Afghanistan,
Argentina, Austria, El Salvador, Hungary, Iran, Iraq, and Italy.
From South Asia, Thailand as well as the newly independent countries of Burma, Ceylon, and Pakistan came into Unesco in 1949, in
addition to Israel, Monaco, and Switzerland.

Following admission in 1950 of Costa Rica, Guatemala, Indonesia,
Jordan, the Republic of Korea, Panama, Sweden, and Yugoslavia, the
organization's membership totaled fifty-nine. The Sixth Session of
the General Conference voted in 1951 to admit Japan and the Federal Republic of Germany, and also Cambodia, Laos, and Vietnam.
Nicaragua was the only new member during 1952. Chile, Libya,

Nepal, and Spain became members in 1953. Unesco's progress toward universality continued in 1954, with entrance of the USSR, Byelorussia, and the Ukraine.[37] Accession of Paraguay and Ethiopia in 1955, and of Bulgaria, Finland, Morocco, Rumania, the Sudan, and Tunisia in 1956, brought the total member states to eighty. South Africa, however, announced on April 5, 1955, that it would end its participation in Unesco as of December 31, 1956, because of the latter's "interference in South Africa's racial problems."[38]

Of Unesco's 1956 membership, five states were not members of the United Nations: the Federal Republic of Germany, the Republic of Korea, Monaco, Switzerland, and Vietnam. Only five countries members of the United Nations had not joined Unesco: Albania, Iceland, Ireland, Portugal, and Yemen.

The category of Associate Members of Unesco was created by adoption at the 1951 session of the General Conference of an amendment to the Constitution proposed by the United Kingdom which extended such membership to "territories or groups of territories which are not responsible for the conduct of their international relations." Such members were entitled to participate in deliberations of the General Conference, without the right to vote.[39] In consequence, the 1954 session of the General Conference approved, at the request of the United Kingdom, admission as Associate Members of four British territories or groups of territories.[40] These were from Africa, Southeast Asia, and the Caribbean. Nigeria was admitted in 1956 as an Associate Member.

Progress through Compromise

Shaping the Unesco program thus has been a complex process. It began during World War II with stock-taking by the Conference of Allied Ministers of Education of the need for a world organization in this field. At the London Conference in 1945 the constitutional language was written down, involving numerous compromises and providing not entirely clear answers to questions concerning Unesco's purpose, character, and function, and the division of power for program formulation and execution between the Director General and the Executive Board. The task of working out a solid and coherent program was made more difficult by the need to obtain action by nations of widely different needs and conditions, by the immense area of

Unesco's responsibility in the fields of education, science, and culture, and the multifarious professional interests of its constituency.

Various attempts were made to introduce order and unity into a program which at first had threatened to become a catchall of almost chaotic character. "The need of a central theme, of a focus in a universe so rich in ideas haunted the staff, the Executive Board and the delegates to the General Conference."[41] The effort of Julian Huxley to provide a Unesco philosophy failed to give, as he had hoped, an acceptable frame for organization of the program. Efforts to establish criteria of selection and to set priorities met the centrifugal forces of professional, national, and regional interests. Neither the Director General, nor the Executive Board, nor even the General Conference of governmental delegates could designate major fields of program activity as outside Unesco's purpose and therefore worthy of elimination. Every such attempt met resistance from important groups or important countries.

Despite all the difficulties progress has been made. As a result of trial and error over a period of ten years and political adjustment during review of projects at sessions of the General Conference, a considerable concentration has been achieved—as evidenced by approval of three major projects at New Delhi. The program in 1956 was more sharply focused than earlier ones. Approval by the Montevideo Conference of the "remodelled future program" indicated not only willingness to compromise but a degree of mutual recognition and agreement among respective schools of thought concerning Unesco's purpose and program. Advancement of knowledge through clearing-house activities and intellectual cooperation was accepted by proponents of projects to advance human welfare and to further understanding as the essential foundation for activities toward those ends. Here the sharpest issue to remain lay between those who supported Unesco's grants to international scholarly organizations, on the ground that Unesco in its program should maintain activities that were international and world-wide in character (not merely assistance to individual states or groups of states), and those who questioned the wisdom of large subsidies to private organizations.

Member states most insistent on forwarding the welfare of their people through education and science, in particular the countries of Asia, had recognized the importance of international understanding—particularly for the West to understand the cultures of the East.

Countries which emphasized Unesco's function of promoting peace through understanding had seen that fostering human welfare was often a preliminary to international understanding. They had also begun to realize that the best service they could render to their cause was to bring forward practical activities whose contribution to international understanding could be demonstrated. Finally, the issue which had loomed large immediately after the London Conference, whether all activities should make a direct contribution to peace and security, largely receded as member states showed preference for indirect contributions by advancing knowledge, promoting human welfare, and furthering international understanding.

Greater emphasis in the program upon specific needs of individual states and upon major projects was paralleled by a shift in the locale of program planning. In the early period of exploration, of trial and error, planning was mainly carried out at headquarters. Much was done by the international secretariat, and specialists from different countries were brought together in meetings, seminars, and conferences at Paris to help identify problems and define terms. It was only with time that individual countries could take stock of their needs and develop ideas of their own on what Unesco should do. The United Nations program of technical assistance was an important stimulus in this direction. Progressively, member states have assumed a larger function in determining what the program should be. In turn, the change and growth in Unesco's membership, reducing the initial European concentration, and increasing the influence of non-Western countries in Asia, the Middle East, and Africa, brought a corresponding change in Unesco's program to reflect more directly the interests of the economically less developed countries.

A detailed consideration of the development of Unesco's budget as a reflection of changes in the program is not within the scope of this volume. However, the reader will find in Appendix E data showing the changing amounts of the budget and the allocations of funds among major program areas, and in Appendix D the current scale of contributions by member states.

PART 2

UNESCO'S WORK:
HOW IT HAS BEEN USED
BY MEMBER STATES

CHAPTER IV

Emergency and Special Aid

The preceding chapters have outlined the variety of ideas that led to the creation of Unesco, and sketched the efforts made during its first ten years to clarify and concentrate the program. Against this background we can now look at the specific jobs Unesco has been asked to do.

Our grouping of Unesco's activities in the following chapters differs from the official classification by program departments (education, natural sciences, social sciences, etc.), but makes clearer, we think, the way in which member governments have utilized Unesco. Our discussion will center upon the four major kinds of activities which Unesco has been asked to perform, each of which reflects needs of member states:

(1) Meeting immediate or emergency needs, such as postwar educational reconstruction and aid to Arab refugees (Chapter IV).

(2) Advancing knowledge and fostering wider sharing of the cultural heritage of mankind (Chapters V and VI).

(3) Promoting human welfare through education and science (Chapters VII, VIII, and IX).

(4) Forwarding international understanding among the peoples of the world and support for the United Nations (Chapters X, XI, and XII).

Each of these types of activity will be examined in the following chapters. Not all Unesco projects can be discussed in the context of this volume; we have selected examples illustrating each category.[1]

We shall then review the factors shaping development of Unesco's program (Chapter XIII) and the part played by member governments and National Commissions (Chapter XIV). Lastly, we shall offer certain conclusions about the kinds of activity which Unesco can most usefully carry on and the significance of the organization in the context of postwar international affairs and in the perspective of history (Chapter XV).

The projects described in this chapter were undertaken to meet the special needs of certain member states. Unesco was asked to engage in these projects because the problems were urgent and their solution required international help. These activities, which involve various kinds of professional assistance, fall into three main groups: (1) postwar aid to devastated countries; (2) aid to Arab refugees; and (3) aid in Korean reconstruction.

Postwar Aid to Devastated Countries

The end of World War II found the educational, scientific, and cultural resources of many countries seriously damaged. If people who had suffered from devastation were again to play an active part in human progress, outside assistance was needed. Unesco was looked to as the logical international agency to help them rebuild and restock these resources.

Countries which had suffered most were those in the path of the German, Italian, and Japanese onslaught: Poland, Czechoslovakia, and Hungary; Belgium, Holland, Luxembourg and France; Denmark and Norway; the United Kingdom; Greece; Burma, China, Indochina, Malaya, Indonesia, and the Philippines. Warfare had destroyed scientific materials, books, and other supplies in schools, universities, libraries, and museums. The number of teachers had been reduced, national exchequers drained, and currencies depreciated to the point where purchases abroad for educational purposes were almost impossible. The situation varied, of course, in different countries, as did prospects for economic recovery and for self-help.

Not all countries which suffered heavy losses asked for help from Unesco. Some had other means of repairing the damage to their educational, scientific, and cultural resources, and of promoting economic recovery. Some were moved by national pride to figure as donors rather than recipients and of these, some contributed more than token payments when special funds were raised.

The plight of the war-devastated countries had a special human appeal and attracted considerable public attention during the first three years, 1947-49, when help was most needed. Starving children huddled in bombed-out schoolrooms, sitting on the ground for want of chairs and desks, doing their arithmetic on tablets of sand or in the dirt, had an irresistible appeal. The response was generous and widespread. It involved organizing the energies of thousands of dedicated persons, to many of whom reconstruction work was a happy relief after years of military mobilization. The upsurge of human sympathy and generous giving was in many respects like that which had followed World War I.

Unesco's part in this great humanitarian effort was a modest one. Enthusiastic as were delegates to the London Conference in 1945 and the General Conference in 1946, the role of the organization was limited by certain basic considerations. UNRRA had been at work on a reconstruction program covering many fronts of human suffering: health, lodging, clothing, as well as the problem of displaced persons.[2] It had huge sums of money, an immense administrative organization, enormous supplies, and a large field staff. Never had there been such a world effort to relieve human suffering. UNRRA was not permitted to engage directly in educational reconstruction. Moreover, its operations were tapering off just as the scope of Unesco's work was being determined and it became apparent that nothing on the UNRRA scale could be undertaken by Unesco in education, although the needs were stupendous.

It was clear that, however appealing the call for help to restore educational, scientific, and cultural facilities, real and lasting progress depended upon economic rehabilitation of a kind that only large capital investment and extensive development of industry and trade could bring about. Relief efforts for school buildings, school supplies, scientific equipment, and repairs to national cultural monuments, such as Unesco might make, could be no more than temporary palliatives. Finally, basic to all discussions of Unesco's function was the conviction that its task should be primarily to stimulate action by governments, private agencies, and individuals. It was not to become an operating agency such as UNRRA.

Out of these considerations emerged the pattern for what member states asked Unesco to do: to help get the facts about needs in war-devastated countries; to publicize the facts and stimulate contributions; to encourage voluntary coordination on the part of private and governmental agencies which in many parts of the world were already engaged, or willing to engage, in reconstruction work. Unesco itself was not to collect money and materials. Such a program did not call for a big administrative and field staff, for extensive funds, or for large shipments of supplies that could be identified as coming from Unesco.

Unesco's Six-fold Task

The scope of Unesco's task was fairly well defined in the decisions of the 1946 General Conference and varied little during the years of Unesco's primary effort.[3] This program called for a six-fold approach:

(1) Unesco was to stimulate, and provide information for, an international campaign to identify needs and to collect funds and supplies.

(2) Unesco was to publish pamphlets and materials that would aid teachers and describe temporary means by which devastated countries could meet immediate problems. For example, it was to compile suggestions on alleviating the shortage of teaching equipment, including elementary scientific apparatus, while new equipment was being manufactured or procured.

(3) Following upon the UNRRA fellowship program, Unesco was to encourage the granting of fellowships to teachers and other educational leaders for foreign study and rapid retraining for their post-war jobs.

(4) It was to assist in recruiting qualified educational specialists for field assignments, to work with war-devastated countries in meeting critical educational problems.

(5) Youth service camps were to be promoted in order to marshal young people from many lands in cooperative projects of physical reconstruction. The camps were to provide suitable educational training.

(6) Unesco would give a small amount of financial assistance. The General Conference favored the purchase of limited quantities of surplus war property for educational and scientific use. A special fund would be immediately established for such purposes, while surplus property was still available at reasonable prices. The fund would assume most of the transportation costs for surplus materials, after UNRRA funds for this purpose had been exhausted. From 1947

through 1949 Unesco provided almost $900,000 from its own budget for emergency aid.[4]

Such was the task laid down for Unesco by delegates at the 1946 General Conference. For about three years the organization actively applied these methods to the needs of member states. By 1949 the crisis of postwar reconstruction had passed, and the long-term forces of economic development had taken over.

The First Session of the General Conference in 1946 instructed the Director General to develop at Unesco headquarters a world center of information for an international campaign to raise funds and collect supplies for the educational, scientific, and cultural needs of devastated countries. The organization of such a campaign proved much more difficult than had been anticipated. The governments of needy states were not organized to ascertain detailed requirements or to identify precisely where and how supplies and funds would be used. Many delayed interminably their replies to Unesco's request for precise statements of their needs. Data submitted had to be re-evaluated and screened in terms of reliability, suitability, and relative importance. Meantime, large numbers of voluntary organizations and individuals in many countries were collecting funds and supplies for specific institutions and groups in particular devastated lands. Unesco had no way of telling which of the needs stated by any government were already being met. Shipping problems were augmented by shortages of rail, ship, and truck transportation, border formalities and regulations, the absence of coordinated points of consignment, and above all by unstable and disorganized government services.

Unesco attempted to short-cut correspondence and questionnaires by using field workers or survey teams. By the end of 1947 data had been collected, with the help of UNRRA, from sixteen war-devastated countries. These data related to the needs of schools, colleges, universities, libraries, and museums, and covered such specific items as books, pencils, and other supplies. The surveys were later extended to include the remaining countries entitled to help from Unesco.

These data were made available in three directions: to the United Nations Economic Commissions for Europe and for Asia, to be taken into account in plans for economic development; to a series of voluntary international organizations interested in relief work in education and related fields which were brought together by Unesco in a

Temporary International Council for Educational Reconstruction (TICER); and to national bodies such as the American Commission for International Educational Reconstruction, the British Council for Education in World Citizenship, the Canadian Council for Reconstruction through Unesco,[5] and similar groups in many other countries, as well as to Unesco National Commissions.

During the period from 1947 to 1949, Unesco sought to keep its information current on various types of needs and to maintain a steady flow of information to the many national and international organizations interested in raising funds and supplying materials. To focus attention of donor groups and organizations on the most urgent needs, its publications listed the requirements of individual countries. A *Book of Needs* (two volumes) was published, outlining the situation from country to country, and also a separate series of illustrated pamphlets on children as war victims, and on war-devastated laboratories, art galleries, museums, and libraries.[6]

Special newsletters were issued in English, French, and Spanish. Efforts were made to bring information to the attention of the press and radio in member states, to stimulate support for collections of money and educational material. The dynamic director of Unesco's reconstruction service, the late Dr. Bernard Drzewieski, gave unstintingly of his energy both in direction of the staff and in speaking tours in donor countries.

One of the immediate needs of the war-devastated countries was to re-establish basic scientific instruction. Unesco's funds could go only a little way in purchasing scientific equipment. The organization therefore invested part of its resources in fifty large boxes of workshop apparatus—simple machines, hand tools, and raw materials needed to build the physics, chemistry, and other scientific equipment required for teaching elementary science. These boxes were sent out to scientific institutions in the war-devastated countries. The Philippines, for example, received five workshops for making basic apparatus for high schools, colleges, and universities. Thus science teaching could get started again. People were helped to help themselves.

Unesco was able to do much more indirectly. Information given to the Commission for International Educational Reconstruction in the United States enabled that body to serve as a clearing house for approximately 400 private organizations whose contributions of materials and services from 1946 through 1948 were valued at 214 million dollars.[7] The National Education Association raised an Overseas Teacher Relief Fund ultimately of almost $500,000. Another organization sent overseas 2,500 teachers' kits containing school supplies and personal articles. The Junior Red Cross sent many hundreds of thousands of kits for school children abroad. Numerous schools in the United States adopted foreign schools and provided them with needed material. Other countries made substantial contributions, such as one million dollars from Canada, $200,000 from London's Lord Mayor's Fund, and $100,000 from Norway.[8] Aid provided for the devastated countries exceeded many times what Unesco could have achieved with its own resources.

War-devastated countries needed to restore their personnel as well as their physical resources; they needed above all to train new leaders, since the Nazis had deliberately destroyed leadership in the occupied countries. Here again the direct assistance which Unesco could supply was limited. Its funds provided some ninety fellowships granted (1947-49) to the war-torn countries, but indirect efforts went farther. It published the first edition of *Study Abroad,* listing 15,000 fellowship opportunities in foreign countries.[9] Canada in 1948 gave sixty-two Unesco fellowships. Australia provided twenty-six fellowships to train young leaders from the countries of Southeast Asia—Burma, Ceylon, China, Indonesia, Pakistan, the Philippines, and Thailand. New Zealand offered eight fellowships to countries of the same area including India. India offered seven fellowships to Indonesia and eleven to Iran. Iran itself provided in its own university eleven fellowships for foreign students. Norway, occupied during the war, gave fellowships to the European countries which had been overrun by the Nazis.

In the United States the response was generous. Colleges and universities offered thousands of fellowships. Students at Massachusetts Institute of Technology raised $18,000 to bring eighty advanced engineering and scientific students from seventeen different European countries to the Institute for three-month refresher courses. National organizations assisted. The American Association of University Women gave study grants to sixty women from Europe and seven from the Far East, to do advanced work in the United States before returning to their own countries to work on reconstruction. The National Council of Jewish Women started a fellowship program to train young women in social work to rebuild Jewish life in their home communities. Sixty Rotary Clubs in California sponsored fellowships for forty foreign students.

A comprehensive investigation was undertaken of the technical needs of the war-devastated countries in the field of mass communication. This survey was originally conceived as a basis for efforts to build or rebuild such resources as radio receiving and sending sets and facilities for gathering and disseminating news, and to provide training facilities for technical personnel, but it gradually became the basis for a series of Unesco publications that today provide the only comprehensive survey of the world's resources for mass communication. The *Unesco Bulletin for Libraries,* designed originally to exchange information on gaps in library collections of war-devastated countries and the availability of duplicates elsewhere, became a regular publication of Unesco, aiming to keep librarians up to date not only on book exchanges but on developments in library science. From 1947 to 1949 the Unesco clearing house for publications distributed directly more than 250,000 books and periodicals. Its indirect contribution was even greater. The *Bulletin for Libraries* advertised publications offered by individual libraries or by national book centers set up after the war. Between 1947 and 1950 more than 1,200 libraries offered gifts and more than 2,500 libraries benefited.

In addition, a comprehensive plan was inaugurated for international exchange of duplicate medical and scientific periodicals and other publications. More than 400 libraries prepared lists of publications which they needed or had in surplus. Unesco circulated these lists to 1,600 needy institutions. Donors were able to send their publications directly to libraries which needed them most. Unesco supplied advice on allocation of materials. By these and other means, and in cooperation with the national book exchange services in France, Denmark, the Netherlands, Canada, the United Kingdom, the United States, and other countries, Unesco's clearing house helped distribute an estimated 3,500,000 books and periodicals.[10]

This campaign was not a planned or fully organized undertaking. Each needy member state saw only its own problem. Unesco itself was not equipped to collect funds. It had no authority to coordinate efforts or to determine priorities. No plans to help any individual country could be precisely formulated because needs were rapidly changing, owing to economic reconstruction and to relief from various groups whose activities were not necessarily reported to Unesco.

Finally, the role of Unesco's reconstruction service was never clarified in relation to the work of the organization as a whole, hence this service suffered continually from the confusion, already described, concerning the over-all program.

Unesco's activities defy any statistical appraisal. It is impossible to determine to what extent the raising or the allocation of funds by voluntary organizations was influenced by Unesco's fact-gathering and publicity, or by its efforts to bring the international nongovernmental organizations together through TICER. It seems reasonable to assume that all these efforts must have had some effect, if only in repeatedly drawing attention to the critical conditions prevailing after the war in certain countries. These countries could hardly have found means comparable to those provided by Unesco—publications, advice of expert committees, meetings of TICER, visits by secretariat survey teams, and regular discussions at each meeting of the Executive Board and of the General Conference—for publicizing their plight and the kind of help they needed.

Book and Gift Coupon Schemes

One of the worst effects of World War II in many countries was the intellectual blackout. New ideas could no longer travel across frontiers and progress in many fields slowed down or stopped. One of the most pressing needs was to help teachers, scientists, professional people, and others in war-devastated lands to obtain needed periodicals, textbooks, and reference books from other countries. These people had money for domestic purchases, but lacked foreign exchange, particularly the so-called "hard currencies" of such countries as Canada, Switzerland, and the United States.

So Unesco's Book Coupon Scheme was invented and launched at the end of 1948. An Italian physician, say, needed an American medical book. He bought a book coupon with his own currency. The coupon was then sent to the American Booksellers' Association, which placed the order with the American publisher. The publisher forwarded the book to the overseas purchaser and billed the American Booksellers' Association in the usual manner. The Association paid the publisher's bill in U. S. dollars and forwarded the book coupons to Unesco in Paris for redemption. With this novel device Unesco could help books and information to cross frontiers.

Unesco was able to furnish this service because it received more dollars and other hard currencies than it needed to finance its own personnel and program. Since its headquarters was in Paris, a large part of its expenditures was in French francs.

This scheme supplemented what Unesco had been able to do through the *Bulletin for Libraries* in encouraging gifts and exchanges of publications. It made possible a more sustained, long-range build-up of the educational, scientific, and cultural resources of the less-favored countries as well as those devastated by war. Individual students and research workers, as well as libraries and universities, could buy in their own currency the foreign literature they needed and could not otherwise have obtained. Their purchases ranged from astronomy to agriculture, from electronics to comparative religion, art, music, law and medicine.

In 1950 the Book Coupon Scheme was expanded to include educational and cultural films, as well as scientific material. By the end of 1956 the number of participating countries had increased from five to more than thirty. During the same period the value of coupons redeemed annually grew from $72,000 to almost $3,000,000. The total value of coupons redeemed from 1949 to 1956 was approximately $9,000,000.

In 1954 the scheme was further extended by the issuance of Unesco Travel Coupons, which made it possible for students, teachers, and research workers to cover the cost of foreign travel in their own currency. At the end of 1956 fifteen countries were participating in this program.

At the New Delhi General Conference in 1956 the Director General raised the question whether the coupon schemes for books, films, scientific material, and travel should be continued after the end of 1957. He reported that it was now possible throughout the world to import such materials without the aid of Unesco's special facilities. The Conference decided against liquidating the scheme, but provided for a separate and self-financing Coupon Fund which would continue the project without cost to Unesco.[11]

The New Delhi Conference approved also continuance of another and somewhat different coupon activity. This was the Gift Coupon Scheme started in 1951, to enable private individuals and groups to participate directly in United Nations activities and, by making useful gifts, to establish personal contact with educational institutions and educators in many parts of the world. The recipients not only obtained needed equipment and supplies, but were cheered by expressions of sympathy and support from unknown friends abroad. The project helped to provide an answer to the many queries from people in the more privileged countries who asked, "What can we do to help?"

Under this plan Unesco gathers information on the educational needs of the economically less developed countries, including detailed lists of what individual schools, colleges, and laboratories require most urgently. This is made available to individuals and groups in the more highly developed countries, who can purchase in their own currency Unesco gift coupons and send them directly to the person or institution they wish to help. Under this plan British schools paid for carpentry tools for a boys' home in Burma; a women's organization in the American Middle West provided radio sets for schools and villages in India; South African children contributed to the establishment of a kindergarten in Libya. School children in Utrecht helped a school for the blind on the Gold Coast in Africa, and students of secondary schools at Haarlem sent gift coupons to a high school in the north of India. Gift coupons have been used to furnish audio-visual aids for the training of clerks and artisans in Libya and to aid in the education of illiterates in Bombay and Delhi. The Junior Red Cross in Germany and the Italian Red Cross sent gifts to Arab refugees in the Middle East, the young Germans dispatching first-aid and sewing kits, while the Italians sent food and clothing.

Through Unesco gift coupons, some 500 war-damaged schools and institutions have received $77,000 worth of educational and recreational equipment. Rivaling in importance the gifts themselves was the exchange of letters and photographs which built up friendly contacts. A group of children in Canada sold candy and ran errands to buy pencils and notebooks for Korean children. The pupils in an American school for the handicapped helped to raise funds to furnish Korean blind children with their first Braille plates. Gift coupons provided equipment to the Sam Yook Disabled Children's Home at Seoul, founded in 1952 for disabled orphans who were begging for food on the streets, stealing, and sleeping wherever they could find shelter. At the time of the Special Session of the United Nations General Assembly at San Francisco in June 1955, the Northern California

Council of the American Association for the United Nations organized a series of special events, the income from which exceeded $10,000 and was sent in gift coupons to Korea. More recently the Amalgamated Clothing Workers, a leading trade-union in the United States, decided to participate in the project.[12]

Thus the Gift Coupon Scheme has served many countries. It had enlisted by 1956 the cooperation of twenty donor countries, and institutions benefiting from the project were located in more than thirty countries and territories. While the dollar amounts involved are not impressive, they increased from $13,000 in 1951 to approximately $100,000 in 1956.

Educational Aid to Arab Refugees

The 1948 General Conference in Beirut adopted a policy declaration forecasting a gradual transition from aid for war-devastated areas to improving educational facilities in all needy countries. The same session authorized the Director General to extend educational aid to the Arab refugees who during the Arab-Israeli conflict had fled from their homes in Palestine.[13] These refugees, numbering some 900,000, had found a haven in surrounding Arab states—Egypt, Jordan, Lebanon, and Syria. The vast majority were living in former army barracks, sheds, tents, and caves. Many delegates at Beirut visited the nearby camps to find hundreds of children, half-naked, barefoot, and shivering, with nothing to do and no school to attend.

Unesco's participation in the United Nations program to aid Arab refugees began as an immediate and presumably short-term emergency action, but it has become a continuing responsibility likely to last as long as the unsettled issue of the future of the Palestine refugees.

Following a series of inspection trips to ascertain the extent of the problem, Unesco provided an initial amount of $15,000 from its Emergency Fund. Activities were to be carried out in cooperation with agencies already engaged in relief activities among the refugees —the United Nations Relief for Palestine Refugees, which was succeeded in 1950 by the United Nations Relief and Works Agency (UNRWA), the International Red Cross Committee, the League of Red Cross Societies, and the American Friends Service Committee.

The project began with temporary schools housed in tents, in a few of the camps. By the end of 1949 the schools had 21,000 pupils and more than 500 teachers. By 1956, some 350 schools were caring for approximately 100,000 primary pupils and 10,000 secondary pupils. In addition, some 60,000 pupils had been placed in national schools, both public and private, of the host countries. The annual budget had increased to 7 million dollars, and an educational five-year plan had been set up to run from 1955 to 1960, when UNRWA's mandate expires. The schools were entirely financed by UNRWA but were under the technical direction of Unesco, which selected the teachers and supervised the educational program, providing $85,000 annually for staff salaries. Over the intervening years improvement has taken place in the housing for the people as well as for the schools. Only one third of the refugees now live in camps. Huts and tents are disappearing. The rest live in villages. Most schools are now housed in buildings.

The UNRWA-Unesco schools are located in Jordan, Lebanon, Syria, and also in the Gaza strip. The curriculum is the same as that of the country in which the refugee schools are located. Six years of primary schooling are followed by two years of secondary. In the latter there is emphasis on vocational training and handicrafts such as woodwork and metalwork. Two technical schools, one in Jordan near Jerusalem and the other in the Gaza region, provide training in plumbing, carpentry, radio, electronics, and motor mechanics. These are open to students who have finished the eight years of primary and secondary education. Plans adopted early in 1956 called for considerable expansion in vocational and agricultural education and in teacher-training. Construction was scheduled of nine training schools of various sorts including two teacher-training colleges.

At the start the main problem had been a shortage of qualified teachers; all teachers were recruited from among the refugees themselves. Only a few of them had an adequate basic education and even fewer had received teacher-training. Special teacher-training courses were started for pupils who had completed the two years of secondary school, and fellowships were given to others to attend teacher-training courses abroad. Refresher courses were held during the summer. At present there are two experimental teacher-training centers in Jordan, one for women at Nablous, the other for men near

Jerusalem. The purpose of these centers is to develop a curriculum for the projected normal schools and to prepare Arab instructors for them. Unesco specialists serve as advisers in the two centers.

Provision of higher education has begun through the grant of fellowships for university training abroad. Students on these fellowships attend the University of Cairo in Egypt, American University and St. Joseph's University at Beirut, and the Syrian University at Damascus. This program has now graduated thirty persons in the fields of medicine, law, engineering, agriculture, and science. A smaller number of fellowships is planned to permit advanced study by these university graduates in Europe and the United States.

While the efficiency of the UNRWA-Unesco system has been criticized at times in the host countries, it is reported that when pupils from the refugee schools compete in government examinations with pupils from government or private schools, the former almost always receive higher marks.[14] Along with the schools for children and young people, fundamental education centers to attack adult illiteracy have been set up among the refugees in some forty localities, with 44,000 in attendance.

Except for the fundamental education training centers in Egypt and Mexico (see Chapter VII), this educational program for Arab refugees is the only educational effort now conducted directly by Unesco anywhere in the world. Even here Unesco's responsibility is limited to technical direction. It works within the framework of UNRWA, established by the United Nations General Assembly. It was started as a temporary, emergency undertaking in response to pleas from Arab countries, but has been maintained to meet a continuing need. This enterprise well illustrates the flexibility of Unesco's program, which must be continually changing in response to new needs and world conditions.

Korean Educational Reconstruction

A third area of emergency action by Unesco was related to the Korean reconstruction program. Here we are concerned with only one section of the program of the United Nations Korean Reconstruction Agency (UNKRA), that dealing with education. A later chapter will outline what Unesco was asked to do in the Korean crisis to strengthen public understanding and support of the principles of collective security.

In August 1950 Unesco's Executive Board authorized the Director General to despatch to Korea, on the request of the UN Secretary General, a mission to investigate the needs of the civilian population and to determine how Unesco could most effectively assist in educational, scientific, and cultural aid to Korea.

Unlike its experience in the education program for Arab refugees, Unesco found difficulty in making a contribution to educational reconstruction in Korea. This was due to the continuation of hostilities, uncertain prospects for peaceful settlement, and the consequent domination of the reconstruction program by the military.

It was not until the second part of 1952 that the way was clear for Unesco to despatch to Korea a small educational mission. Following its survey, this mission presented two reports, published by Unesco as *Rebuilding Education in the Republic of Korea*.[15] The second report included recommendations for a five-year program by United Nations agencies to assist Korea in the rehabilitation of education. The war had destroyed half the schools and four-fifths of the teaching materials. The Unesco report made a major contribution to the plan for educational reconstruction which was carried out by the Republic of Korea in cooperation with UNKRA. UNKRA asked only for modest assistance from Unesco, requesting in 1953 a general educational adviser. Four months later it requested, instead, a director for a fundamental education training center at Suwon.

It was not until 1955 that the $100,000 voted by the Unesco Executive Board was used to install a press in a printing plant constructed by UNKRA. This press now produces 20 million textbooks per year for the Korean schools. As of January 1, 1957, Unesco took over from UNKRA responsibility for aiding the Korean government in support of the Suwon fundamental education center as well as for the Foreign Language Institute at Seoul.

The three undertakings outlined in this chapter were initially launched to repair damage wrought by armed conflict although later events in some cases changed their aim and character. In all three the effectiveness of Unesco's aid depended on the political and economic situation.

Intergovernmental assistance to the devastated countries in educational rebuilding after World War II was limited by the decision of the wealthier nations, particularly the United States, not to supplement the sums supplied to UNRRA for economic reconstruction with additional funds to Unesco for educational reconstruction. In the case of the Palestine refugees it was the policy of the United Nations which established bounds to, and in addition assigned necessary funds for, Unesco's participation in that broad endeavor. And it was failure to achieve any political solution of the Arab-Israeli struggle which prolonged the need for "emergency" aid. In the case of Korea the role of Unesco was determined by United Nations policy, as expressed through the military authorities of the United Nations Unified Command and through UNKRA.

Unesco's participation in educational reconstruction after World War II and in Korean reconstruction was restricted primarily to information and other services, and to stimulating other organizations. In contrast, in the Middle East Unesco was assigned direct responsibility for selecting and supervising teachers and other educational personnel.

The activities outlined in this chapter illustrate how Unesco can meet emergency and short-term needs. In educational reconstruction after World War II, Unesco faced a chaotic and shifting situation. Much floundering resulted. But the organization did succeed in collecting and circulating needed information and in stimulating a considerable amount of activity. Here, as well as in the Palestine situation, there was general recognition of the need and substantial agreement among member states on what Unesco should do. After the initial period no serious conflicts over policy developed among member states.

In Korea also the need for educational reconstruction was clear. The differences in viewpoint were not so much over what action should be taken as over how and by whom it should be carried out. Unesco played a relatively small role. UNKRA was more inclined for practical reasons to work with United States agencies which had available substantial funds for bilateral assistance.

Unesco's ability to provide a modest degree of emergency educational assistance was again recognized by the 1956 General Conference at New Delhi, which voted $200,000 to aid the schools of Hungary and the Middle East.

CHAPTER V

THE ADVANCEMENT OF KNOWLEDGE: EDUCATION, NATURAL AND SOCIAL SCIENCES

In October 1955 six leading Yugoslav educators arrived in New York City to study education in the United States. They spent some time in Tennessee, where schools for children living in the Great Smoky Mountains faced problems similar to those in the mountainous areas of Yugoslavia. They were interested in what Illinois and New York were doing in training teachers, in vocational education, and in testing educational methods. They visited the U. S. Office of Education in Washington, whose principal function is to advise and assist local and state authorities. Yugoslavia with its six republics also has a federal system of education.

This group of educators was one of ten Yugoslav teams sent abroad on Unesco fellowships. The other teams visited Belgium, France, the German Federal Republic, the Netherlands, Switzerland, the Scandinavian countries, and the United Kingdom. The task of these fifty educational leaders was to obtain information to aid in a fundamental reform of Yugoslav education.

Since the end of World War II the Yugoslav school system had been greatly expanded. The number of primary schools had increased from 9,000 in 1939 to almost 13,500 in 1953. Attendance at secondary and vocational schools had tripled. Yet the basic scheme of education in Yugoslavia was outmoded, with a curriculum inadequate for the needs of the modern world. The government therefore decided on a complete renovation of the country's educational program.[1]

It was recognized that the fact-finding missions would be much more fruitful if, before setting forth, their members had done some preparatory study. But information and publications available in

Yugoslav libraries were insufficient and out of date. Nor did educators have adequate bibliographies showing what existed outside the country and where it might be found. Yugoslavia therefore requested Unesco to supply such information, particularly on the ten countries to be visited, as would help the Yugoslav teams to derive the greatest benefit from their visits. This kind of data was readily available because Unesco had started early to collect and circulate information on educational developments throughout the world.

The Unesco secretariat prepared bibliographies in English, French, and German, designed to provide an over-all view of the educational systems of the countries chosen, in the light of the interests of the Yugoslav teams. Next, 200 volumes from Unesco's own stock of material were despatched to Belgrade. Meanwhile letters went out to Unesco National Commissions in the ten countries, listing materials still lacking and requesting these Commissions to get in direct touch with Belgrade. The Yugoslav director of the proposed operation spent two months at Unesco headquarters in Paris, studying materials in the education clearing house and receiving suggestions on how to brief the teams and how to circulate information inside Yugoslavia among its member republics. As a result, six documentation centers were set up, one in each of the capitals of the country, to facilitate the use of the materials from abroad. When, in March 1955, the teams began to pass through Paris, they were further briefed by the staff of Unesco's education clearing house. Thus in addition to assisting the immediate project under way, the secretariat cooperated in establishing services within Yugoslavia to be carried on long after that project was completed.

The Yugoslav case illustrates one way in which Unesco has helped to advance knowledge—through what are called clearing-house activities. Unesco's Constitution pledged the organization to "maintain, increase and diffuse knowledge" and to "promote the free flow of ideas by word and image." Nations signatory to the Constitution were "agreed and determined to develop and to increase the means of communication between their peoples and to employ these means for the purposes of mutual understanding and a truer and more perfect knowledge of each other's lives."[2] Further, the Universal Declaration of Human Rights stipulates that everyone may "seek, receive and impart information and ideas through any media and regardless of frontiers."[3]

"Advancement of knowledge" is therefore interpreted in this volume to include more than discovery of new knowledge through research. It also covers exchange of information on the development of education, science, and culture throughout the world. It includes cooperation to improve communication among teachers, scholars, and artists, and to help remove barriers.

No clear-cut list of methods whereby Unesco could promote advancement of knowledge in this sense was ever agreed upon.[4] But over the years a wide variety of activities was undertaken in each of the major fields of Unesco's work: education, natural and social sciences, the arts, philosophy and humanities, and mass communication. These included clearing-house activities, surveys, meetings, publications, regional offices, and cooperation with international nongovernmental agencies.

Special Role of Nongovernmental Organizations

Before examining the work for the advancement of knowledge in each major subject field, special note should be taken of the network of international nongovernmental organizations already at work in the fields of education, science, and culture. When the London Conference decided that Unesco should be basically an intergovernmental organization, it provided in the Constitution that the new agency would consult and cooperate with international nongovernmental organizations and would call on them to carry out specific tasks.[5]

More than any other specialized agency of the United Nations, Unesco has relied on these organizations for help in planning and executing its activities. By June 1956 Unesco had established relations with some 400 such groups. These are in general of two kinds: either they are composed of specialists in various branches of knowledge, or they represent important sectors of public opinion, such as trade unions, associations of women and youth, and religious bodies. From the first group Unesco receives expert information, advice, and technical help, and from the second group it receives help rather more specifically in developing cooperation and understanding among peoples.[6]

To qualify for cooperation with Unesco, these organizations are expected to be truly international in character and to be in accord with Unesco's purposes. In some cases Unesco has entered into special financial arrangements with nongovernmental organizations. Subventions are granted to a limited number which are in a position to contribute significantly to Unesco's work. In 1955 thirty-nine such organizations received subventions totaling $632,400. Unesco also concludes contracts with organizations that are equipped to carry out specific tasks. In 1955 seventy-three contracts were made with forty-four organizations totaling $257,810. Contracts were for collecting information, preparing publications, and organizing symposia, seminars, or exhibitions.

Unesco also sponsored the creation of a number of nongovernmental international organizations, particularly in the social sciences, humanities, and arts. These new associations were not always established to meet the needs of scholars and specialists. They often reflected the desire of the Unesco secretariat for a comprehensive pattern of voluntary international organizations to carry on projects for which Unesco lacked resources, or which member governments did not want the secretariat to carry on. To some degree, the establishment of these organizations represented a forced, or at least premature, rather than a natural development.

Education

Here we shall limit ourselves to a discussion of activities designed generally to take stock on the state of education throughout the world and to increase opportunities for communication among educational specialists. We shall leave for a later chapter those activities which represented an effort to help solve major problems of a worldwide character.

Education Clearing House

Stock-taking or fact-finding was fundamental to the entire Unesco program of education. When Unesco came into being in 1946, in spite of the efforts of the International Bureau of Education, huge gaps existed in knowledge about the schools of the world. These gaps concerned, for example, the extent and nature of preschool, primary, secondary, adult, and advanced education, the distribution and trends in school populations by age-groups and levels of education, and the extent of illiteracy. Many countries did not publish educational records and those that did used different methods of reporting and analysis, so that comparison was difficult or impossible.

Yet such data were essential to planning Unesco's program. They were also needed by member states in order to prepare sound plans for national education and to make intelligent requests for outside aid. Much of Unesco's effort during the first decade went into compilation of data through questionnaires and meetings of specialists, and into dissemination of this information to governments, private institutions, and individuals.

The clearing house through which data were collected from member states was used to provide information generally to member states, and also to make available specific information needed by one member state for a project, as in the case of Yugoslavia mentioned earlier.

One measure of the value of the clearing house may be found in the cooperation it has enlisted from national authorities. A British educational specialist has remarked, "If all else in Unesco's programme were to be abandoned, the education clearing house would have to be kept alive. The United Kingdom and France have paid the sincerest form of flattery by starting clearing-houses of their own."[7] In the United States the Office of Education in Washington performs a similar function. By 1955, Canada, Egypt, Haiti, Israel, Japan, Norway, the Philippines, Turkey, Yugoslavia, the Central American Republics, and the Caribbean Commission were all considering or taking steps toward establishing national or regional education clearing houses.

In Central America, following a meeting of Ministers of Education in 1955, Unesco's help was asked for an international clearing house in that area. Unesco awarded fellowships to an educational official from each of the six republics, and they received intensive training at Unesco House in Paris and at various European centers in the preparation of bibliographies and the conduct of surveys. This Central American undertaking is a regional application of the methods used in the Yugoslav project. It was expected that the establishment of national clearing houses would be further stimulated by a resolution adopted at the New Delhi General Conference inviting member states to create such centers and to strengthen existing agencies for exchange of educational information both within and between countries.[8]

In many cases the most urgent pressure for national education clearing houses has stemmed from the new urge for economic development, which obviously requires improvements in education. Countries like Indonesia, Pakistan, and Thailand must have reliable statistics upon which to estimate the number of children of school age in future years, the number of schools and teachers needed, how many technical and higher institutions are required, and how much these things will cost. The more economically developed countries have also benefited from this work. Many of them have some kind of agency for educational statistics, but these agencies need closer contact with similar centers in other countries.[9]

In one sense the clearest tangible result of Unesco's clearing-house effort was the publication in 1955 of the *World Survey of Education,* to be reissued every third year. This handbook of educational organization and statistics is a monumental work of approximately 1,000 pages, presenting information on the educational systems of almost 200 countries and territories.[10] Among other publications is the monthly *Education Abstracts,* each issue of which is devoted to recent articles and books on a single subject. Individual numbers have featured education of youth for international understanding, teaching about the United Nations, the primary school curriculum, education in Czechoslovakia, Poland, and the USSR,[11] and a comparative survey of history teaching. *Fundamental and Adult Education* is a quarterly which reports experiments and important projects in countries around the world. A series of pamphlets entitled *Towards World Understanding* grew out of international meetings of teachers to compare methods of teaching geography, history, and languages so as to increase international understanding and knowledge of world affairs.

Nongovernmental Organizations in Education

In the field of higher education, Unesco has delegated most of its clearing-house responsibility to a nongovernmental organization which it sponsored, the International Association of Universities. Regular lines of communication have been lacking among the universities of the world. There has been insufficient knowledge concerning differences in educational principles, standards, and ideals. These divergencies have been reflected in different ideas of the role and responsibility of universities in relation to such critical questions as technological change and industrialization, the economic interdependence of nations, and the maintenance of peace. Definition of the part universities may play in the solution of these and other problems calls for closer relations among universities. Growing recognition of the need for such cooperation resulted in pressure on Unesco by national educational groups, as well as by governments, to help create a channel of systematic communication among universities. The International Association of Universities was founded in 1950 and now counts among its members about 250 universities and other institutions of higher education from fifty-five countries. Three smaller associations are joined to it as associate members: the Association of Universities of the British Commonwealth, the Federation of Catholic Universities, and the Union of Latin American Universities.

The Association has a central administrative office in Paris at Unesco headquarters. Its documentation and information service brings together both published and unpublished materials concerning universities and similar institutions in all parts of the world. It provides Unesco with a clearing house in the field of higher education. It publishes every two years an *International List of Universities,* whose 1955 edition included 732 universities and university colleges and 633 technical and professional institutions. At the request of the World Health Organization it prepared a *World Directory of Medical Schools,* published in 1953, with information on conditions of admission, courses of study, tuition fees, and other matters relating to 566 faculties, colleges, and medical schools in 71 countries. The Food and Agriculture Organization requested a similar *World Directory of Institutions of Higher Agricultural Education.*[12]

The Association has a research service which, in cooperation with the International Association of University Professors and Lecturers, has focused on "equivalence" of university degrees and credits in different countries. This question affects international exchange of students, and frequently causes difficulty both for university authorities and for the student himself.

The Association has collected information on student migration and has compiled *A List of Equivalences* now recognized among certain universities in countries receiving the largest number of foreign students.[13]

Unesco's relations with nongovernmental organizations in primary and secondary education have been more complex and apparently less satisfactory than those in higher education.

Among earlier organizations was the New Education Fellowship founded in 1915 as an international body of progressive educators. At present the largest international teachers' organizations are the World Federation of Teachers' Unions, which claims more than 5½ million members in thirty countries, eighty-five per cent of whom are reported to be in Communist countries, and the World Confederation of the Teaching Profession (WCOTP), which represents more than 2¼ million teachers and has member associations in over forty countries and territories. It was formed in 1952 as the result of an agreement among the International Federation of Teachers' Associations, the International Federation of Secondary Teachers, and the World Organization of the Teaching Profession (WOTP). The first two were mainly European in membership; the third, set up largely on the initiative of the National Education Association in the United States, was world-wide. While the WOTP voted to dissolve when the WCOTP was formed, the other two continued as members of the Confederation. They were also linked through the Joint Committee of International Teachers Federations (Comité d'Entente) with the World Federation of Teachers' Unions.[14]

The WCOTP at its Manila meeting in August 1956 called upon the two European federations to withdraw from the Joint Committee, ending their association with the Communist federation, on the ground that the "external relations" of members of the Confederation with outside bodies were the concern of the Confederation as a whole rather than of its constituent units.[15] The two organizations were scheduled to consider the WCOTP recommendation at their assemblies in August 1957.

The American Federation of Teachers in the United States is affiliated nationally with the AFL-CIO, and internationally has membership in the WCOTP, the two European federations, and a fourth organization, the International Federation of Free Teachers' Unions, one of the professional departments of the International Confederation of Free Trade Unions. Almost all members of this fourth organization are also members of WCOTP.

The purposes of WCOTP are to foster international understanding; improve teaching methods, educational organization, and training of teachers; facilitate contacts between teachers of different countries and protect their rights and their material and moral interests.[16] The Confederation has received much less financial support from Unesco than has the International Association of Universities.[17]

The fourth conference of the WCOTP at Istanbul in 1955 considered "The Status of the Teaching Profession," and approved a resolution calling for raising its social and economic status. To this end, it recommended establishment of high standards of professional training. It proposed that teacher training colleges have the same entrance requirements as universities, and urged that teachers' salaries be in line with those of other professions.[18]

The WCOTP also sought greater international recognition of teachers. Its 1954 Assembly of Delegates urged in a communication to Unesco, ILO, and the International Bureau of Education that teachers' organizations be represented in discussions of educational questions and requested these international organizations to suggest to governments that national delegations in the future should include representatives of teachers' organizations.[19]

Teachers were among Unesco's most enthusiastic supporters during the early years of the organization. In some countries, however, including the United States, certain teachers' organizations have charged that Unesco has systematically neglected them, and that sizable grants given to organizations in natural and social science, humanities and arts have not been matched by comparable assistance to international associations of teachers. Hence, some national teachers' organizations have felt that they have no important place in Unesco's program. The WCOTP at its 1956 meeting in Manila appointed a committee to explore with members of the Unesco secretariat ways in which teachers might cooperate more actively in the Unesco program; and it was hoped this move would result in better collaboration.[20]

Exchanges of Persons

One of the most successful of Unesco's ventures of the clearinghouse type relates to facilitating exchanges of teachers, students, and others. Its importance is illustrated by the publication *Study Abroad*, an international handbook on fellowships, scholarships, and other educational exchange activities. This publication now comes close to being a complete annual compilation of opportunities throughout the world. The first edition in 1948 reported 15,000 opportunities; the eighth edition for 1956-57, almost 75,000 granted by governments, universities, foundations, international organizations, and other agencies in more than one hundred countries and territories. The increase in the total, it should be noted, is not all due to increase in number of fellowships offered; some of it is due to greater efficiency in reporting fellowships already existing. This work is the only international reference book in its field. It is widely consulted by thousands of students, teachers, university officials, and others who need information about opportunities for study in foreign countries.[21]

Supplementary publications are *Vacations Abroad: Courses, Study Tours, Work Camps; Travel Abroad, Frontier Formalities,* containing information on such matters as passports, visas, customs, health, and currency regulations; *Workers Abroad,* covering programs of workers' exchange; and *Teaching Abroad,* on opportunities for professors and lecturers in foreign universities.

The significance of Unesco's clearing-house activities in all fields is made clear in these publications. Only an international agency could have collected from over one hundred countries and territories information of this range and put it into a shape almost universally useful and in several languages.

These publications, each an essential tool in stimulating exchange of individuals, were the result of extensive correspondence, exchange of reports and questionnaires, and consultations. The publications constitute an important factor in establishing increased contact and cooperation among governments, foundations, and other agencies, and among individuals concerned with student and scholar exchanges. The collection of data has resulted in a major international documentation center on exchange programs. This is available to all member states and agencies. It is a valuable resource in planning Unesco's technical services designed to increase the flow of knowledge. Unesco's efforts to promote the exchange of persons have been useful in more ways than one, as will be seen in succeeding chapters. Their special role in helping to foster international understanding will be discussed in Chapter X.[22]

Natural Sciences

Unesco's activities directed toward advancement of knowledge in the natural sciences have been similar to those in education. The approaches employed have included activities of a clearing-house type, assistance to private international organizations, and publications. But in the natural sciences international contacts have in the past been more numerous and better organized than in education. Unesco's assistance has therefore taken a different form.

Science Cooperation Offices

Clearing-house activities have included a new and unique development: geographical decentralization. The First Session of the General Conference in 1946 voted to set up Science Cooperation Offices to serve regions "remote from the main centres of science and technology"—East Asia, South Asia, the Middle East, and Latin America.[23] The idea for these offices developed from experience during World War II, as a result of the establishment by the Allied nations of science cooperation offices in one another's capitals, particularly the British office in China.[24] Through these offices Unesco can be in close touch with universities, local scientific organizations, and individual scientists as well as with government agencies. This mechanism has made possible a much more intensive program than could have been operated from a Paris base.

The centers, each with a small staff, are located in Jakarta, New Delhi, Cairo, and Montevideo. In some cases the local government has supplemented the Unesco contribution in men and money. The purpose of the centers has been to channel scientific knowledge from the most advanced countries to less advanced areas, enlisting scientists in these latter regions in the "international teamwork leading to scientific progress."[25] It is in these areas that the need is greatest for the aid of science against ignorance, poverty, and disease. Social scientists were added in 1951 to the staff of the offices at Cairo, Montevideo, and New Delhi.

Numerous requests for information flow into these offices, that at Montevideo receiving an estimated 12,000 requests over a six-year period. Scientists in the region ask for names and addresses of scholars in other parts of the world engaged in specific research on a common problem, such as, for example, breeding and cultivation of silkworms. Many requests relate to immediate practical problems. Black stem rust of wheat had caused losses running into millions of dollars in the Middle East, and the Cairo office was asked to help. With the assistance of the Food and Agriculture Organization, a meeting of plant pathologists was held on Cyprus in 1952. A few months later the FAO called together a regional meeting at Istanbul on wheat and barley breeding for resistance to rust. Egypt and Pakistan had given a good deal of attention to the same problem, and through the Cairo office an exchange of information was arranged between Egyptian plant pathologists and plant breeders and research workers in Pakistan. Thanks in some degree to the research and remedial measures stimulated through this cooperative effort on a highly important regional problem, there has since been no serious outbreak of black stem rust in the Eastern Mediterranean.

Knowledge available in one country is often of particular relevance to another. In Indonesia streams were clogged by a fast-growing plant—a kind of water hyacinth—which made navigation difficult and obstructed the movement of fish. Unesco's Field Science Office helped identify an effective exterminator. This raised a new question: What was to be done with the mass of decaying hyacinth plants? Through the Unesco office, word was received of a discovery in Western Bengal. Farmers there had found that dead hyacinth weeds were a first-rate fertilizer in restoring exhausted soil.[26]

Scientists also request help in developing programs of research comparable to those carried on in the scientifically more advanced countries. The Middle East Office arranged a refresher course in physics at Damascus and another on plant ecology at Cairo. The Montevideo office organized similar courses on mathematics and physics for university professors in Argentina and Mexico. Regional training courses have been held on scientific documentation, scientific apparatus, methods of using radioisotopes, and science teaching in secondary and primary schools.

The Science Cooperation offices have organized a series of symposia on highly technical subjects, which have brought together twelve or fifteen scholars from the region and a few specialists from outside. These symposia have included such topics as new research techniques in physics (Brazil), medicinal plants (Philippines), cell biology

(Uruguay), typhoons (Japan), scientific aspects of land utilization (Pakistan), and application of scientific principles in the design and construction of tropical buildings (India). Numerous other symposia related to Unesco projects—on arid zones, humid tropical zones, and oceanography—will be described in a later chapter.[27]

One symposium deserving mention was that on high altitude biology held at Lima, Peru, in 1949. Dating from the last part of the nineteenth century, laboratories for high altitude research have been set up in various countries including Italy, France, Switzerland, the United States, Peru, and the USSR. This type of research is of value to astronomy, physics, meteorology, and biology, and is of special importance to aviation. The biological aspect of this problem, affecting reproduction and other physiological functions of animals, as well as human beings, was of special interest to the host country of Peru, since 5 million of its citizens are estimated to live 10,000 feet above sea level. Eighteen countries were represented at the symposium. The United States delegation was headed by the Deputy Surgeon General of the Air Force.[28]

One of the most useful services of the Science Cooperation Offices has been to persuade eminent scientists passing through the less economically developed countries to give lectures to students and scholars, who often are largely cut off from the main currents of scientific thought. All offices have also helped to develop basic scientific documentation in their regions. They have prepared bibliographies on special subjects—indispensable tools for scientists—and have collected much basic information in such reports and directories as *A Who's Who of Men of Science in Latin America.* Surveys have been made of scientific institutions, and lists have been prepared of scientific papers published in the region, including news of research projects.

A wider public has been reached by traveling scientific exhibitions routed by the offices through their respective regions. A popular exhibition on physics and astronomy, circulated in Latin America from 1950 to 1952, was seen by almost 500,000 people; another on "Our Senses and the Knowledge of the World" toured Eastern and Southern Asia; a third on new materials, including plastics, circulated in the Mediterranean countries and Latin America, attracting large audiences. The regional offices' records of accomplishment have of course been far from uniform. Scientific progress already achieved, existing contacts between scientists within and outside the region, the attitude of national governments, and the competence and imagination of Unesco personnel have varied from area to area. Political conditions have been unstable in some regions. In some cases the offices may not have come up to original expectations because the local program had not been adequately thought out. Each office has covered too wide a territory. Some offices have not done as much as they might in broadening the usefulness of experts sent to the region under technical assistance programs. The offices have, however, fostered appreciation for international technical aid provided by United Nations agencies, and have helped to make remote peoples conscious of the United Nations.

Nongovernmental Organizations in Natural Sciences

It was in the field of the natural sciences that, prior to the creation of Unesco, nongovernmental international organizations developed most rapidly. The leading organization in this field is the International Council of Scientific Unions (ICSU). The London Conference in 1945 recommended that, in view of the urgency of restoring and expanding the exchange of information among scientists, interrupted by the war, Unesco's Preparatory Commission initiate without delay consultation and cooperation with ICSU.[29]

The International Council of Scientific Unions came into existence in 1919 to coordinate the activities of the individual scientific unions representing various specialized fields.[30] Its budget was meager, its officers usually could not contribute more than their spare time, and its activities were therefore modest. Aid from Unesco greatly expanded its resources. During the ten-year period, 1946-56, Unesco granted subsidies to ICSU and its constituent unions totaling two million dollars.[31]

These grants were used to finance a variety of activities, such as symposia, conferences, travel by scientists, research and documentation, publications of various types, international laboratories, and to a minor extent administration. The Council and its Unions have cooperated in such Unesco projects as scientific abstracting, the Science Cooperation Offices, the development of clear and uniform scientific terminology, research on arid and humid tropical zones and on oceanography and marine biology, the popularization of science, and the History of the Scientific and Cultural Development of Mankind.

One striking example of the role of the International Council of Scientific Unions has been its sponsorship of the so-called International Geophysical Year. This is the most extensive international scientific project ever undertaken.[32] Unesco helped get this project under way through grants to the Council and Unions concerned for a central secretariat and for international meetings to plan the enterprise. The World Meteorological Organization has cooperated in the project from the start.

The plan called for an army of scientists from more than fifty-five nations throughout the world who, from July 1957 to the end of 1958, would seek answers to some of the basic questions about the surface and atmosphere of our planet: the causes of weather and climate, the conditions of the little-known upper atmosphere extending 800 miles into space, the relation of solar activity (sunspots and flares) to magnetic storms in the earth's atmosphere (which affect marine and air navigation and radio and television broadcasting), the impact of cosmic rays, the character of the earth's crust, and the prediction and charting of earthquakes. Many such problems can be solved only if numerous coordinated observations, using uniform methods, are made at the same time in various parts of the world.

Scientists were to man almost 2,000 special observation stations, some fifty of them in the Antarctic continent, including one on the barren wastes of the South Pole. Rockets loaded with scientific instruments would be fired into the upper atmosphere from widely separated points on land and sea. During the year the United States and the USSR planned to launch several instrument-equipped earth satellites.

Preparation for this vast enterprise, whose total cost was estimated at a quarter of a billion dollars (mostly financed by direct government contributions), involved the labor of thousands of specialists and the organization of national committees in all participating countries. This project illustrates how international cooperation may accomplish results which would be impossible if attempted by individual countries. Such cooperation, it is hoped, may lead to new discoveries. The participating nations agreed to share the information obtained.[33]

In addition to cooperating with the International Council of Scientific Unions, Unesco has assisted in the establishment of two

other scientific federations: the Council of International Organizations of Medical Sciences (CIOMS) and the Union of International
Engineering Organizations. In the medical and health field there
exist more than one hundred private international organizations, of
which fifty are now affiliated with the Council. These were set up in
recognition of the fact that such age-old maladies as tuberculosis,
cancer, malaria, and venereal disease can be fought successfully only if
modern science and medicine are mobilized against them on an international scale. To achieve such mobilization, knowledge must be
freely and frequently interchanged among scholars and physicians of
all countries.

The growing specialization in medicine has led to a marked increase in the number of international meetings. An agency was
needed, however, to assure that meetings would be brought to the attention of all interested specialists, and that meetings involving similar or related interests would be coordinated as to time and place. To
meet these and other difficulties, Unesco cooperated with the World
Health Organization in setting up in 1949 the Council for International Organizations of Medical Sciences. This agency furnishes essential services, such as interpretation and translation, publication of
the discussions, and suggestions on procedure. In some cases it provides subsidies to permit the attendance of younger scientists or those
living in remote areas.[34] It suggests appropriate dates and places for
international medical meetings.

The Union of International Engineering Organizations offers
analogous services to private international organizations in such
fields as roadbuilding, bridge construction, irrigation and drainage,
large electric systems, testing of materials and structures, hydraulic
research, and navigation. It has aided in the compilation of technical
dictionaries, to assure, for example, that a technical term in navigation has the same meaning in different languages.

Social Sciences

Unesco's efforts to advance knowledge in the social sciences have
differed significantly from those in education and natural science.
There was almost no tradition of international cooperation in the
social sciences. Except for international law and statistics, the social
sciences, particularly anthropology, political science, sociology, and

social psychology—even economics and psychology—were of much more recent development than the natural sciences or educational studies. Development of the social sciences has been highly uneven throughout the world. Outside the United States, a few countries of Western Europe, and even fewer nations of Latin America and Asia, social sciences are not taught and scholarly resources are not applied in analyzing such contemporary problems as standards of living, economic booms and depressions, the role of political parties, population movements, the influence of society on the development of the individual, crime and delinquency, and race relations—to mention only a few.

Thus in the twentieth century the natural sciences with their gift of awesome power have far outrun the sciences of human behavior. Unesco itself is in a sense a vast experiment in social science, for it seeks an answer to the crucial question of the present-day world: How can the peoples of the world learn to live in peace? The social sciences are the area in which international cooperation "is at once the least advanced and the most necessary."[35]

In carrying out its mandate to help advance knowledge, Unesco had to begin at a much more elementary level in the social than in the natural sciences. Member states therefore asked it to begin by encouraging social science teaching in all countries, the training of more social scientists, and international exchange of information and ideas.[36] Only after laying such a foundation could Unesco tackle its second task, that of encouraging research on problems relating to international understanding, human welfare, and peace, and stimulating wider knowledge and discussion of the results of research. Unesco's efforts to stimulate wider teaching of social sciences and their application to international problems will be discussed in Chapters VIII, IX, and XI.

Nongovernmental Organizations in Social Sciences

Projects for exchange of knowledge in the social sciences included the establishment of nongovernmental international organizations. Within three years, from 1949 to 1951, five such organizations were set up, bringing together economists, political scientists, sociologists, psychologists, and students of comparative law.[37] World congresses held by these organizations have in some cases assumed impressive importance and have stimulated a wide exchange of knowledge. In 1952 Unesco sponsored the International Social Science Council, a group of distinguished specialists in the different social sciences representing the main regions of the world. Its main object is "advancement of the social sciences throughout the world and their application to the major problems of the present day."[38]

As noted earlier, these new organizations were viewed as a forced growth in certain countries, including the United States. They were created when the social sciences in many nations were, at best, in a rudimentary stage. They lacked the solid support which Unions in the natural sciences had earlier achieved.

In linking together social scientists of the world through professional organizations, international congresses and other meetings, and information and documentation, Unesco has helped these sciences to hasten their development throughout the world; to encourage international cooperation, both within a particular field and among different fields; to apply social science to social problems; and to create professional aids, such as bibliographies and improved teaching methods.[39]

Unesco has provided these private organizations with financial support and with assistance in holding their conferences, symposia, and other meetings. Many of their activities carried forward Unesco's projects, as in improving documentation and abstracting (see Chapter VI), and in circulating information about research in progress. The organizations have helped investigate social science teaching. They have set up research committees which have examined problems identified by Unesco's General Conference as part of the social science program.

The most effective service of these organizations of social scientists has been to make accessible materials previously unobtainable by scientists working in different countries, and to provide personal contacts among scientists. This leads to cooperation in research and particularly in research using comparable techniques. Thus creative emulation, which has long been a stimulus in art and natural science, has become possible in the social sciences as the result of Unesco's efforts.

The exchange of knowledge has been furthered also through the publication, since 1947, of the *International Social Science Bulletin,* a quarterly bulletin with international circulation. It features major subjects of interest to social scientists and solicits contributions on a world-wide basis.[40]

One special effort to advance knowledge has been made by the creation of the Unesco International Social Science Research Institute at Cologne, Germany. Since it was established as part of a special program in relation to Germany as an ex-enemy country, it is discussed with that program in Chapter X. However, its principal importance today is as an international research agency to develop and apply techniques of social science.

Evaluating Unesco's Program

The development of applied social science has received some encouragement from Unesco in its effort to secure objective evaluations of its own projects. This involves a relatively new field of research which in recent years has found application, for example, in some aspects of U.S. foreign operations such as exchanges of students and technical assistance of various kinds.

From the very start of Unesco some members of the secretariat thought that whenever a new project was adopted clear objectives and criteria of performance should be laid down to permit periodic evaluation of its effectiveness. Obviously it would be useful for Unesco to have procedures for determining why some activities succeed and others fail. This need is acute because of Unesco's limited resources in relation to the magnitude of its task. While social scientists have been working to develop evaluation techniques their application is still difficult in projects whose objectives are as general as those of Unesco.[41]

Unesco sought aid on the problem of evaluation from the International Social Science Council. The Council, with the help of a number of social scientists, undertook a review of Unesco's work in fundamental education, adult education, exchange of persons, mass media, the impact of industry on less developed countries, and relations between different racial and social groups. On the basis of this review, the Council prepared a series of proposals on methods of evaluating such activities.[42]

A joint UN-Unesco conference met at Geneva in 1954 to discuss methods of evaluating technical assistance activities. One result of this meeting was a draft manual listing practical methods of evaluation.[43] The following year Unesco's pilot public library project at Delhi in India was studied, with particular attention to working out a scheme for evaluating library work.[44] An analogous effort is under way to study the long-term effects of international seminars.

Public opinion surveys may be used as a tool for evaluation. The World Association for Public Opinion Research was asked to organize a two-year study beginning in 1954 of the various methods used in public opinion polling throughout the world and how to make their results comparable on an international basis. Comparative social research employing intensive interviews was made the subject of a study by the Organization for Comparative Social Research at Oslo, Norway.

A major purpose of Unesco in promoting evaluation studies has been to stimulate research methods, thus helping advance knowledge, and to help member states understand what Unesco can and cannot do well. The results, it is hoped, will help the secretariat in planning and operations, and in working out methods of evaluation to be used by people who are not trained social scientists. There has, however, been only partial support by states for this phase of Unesco's work, because of preoccupation with getting new projects started rather than with attaining results, or because governments are unaware of the possibilities and importance of evaluation through the use of social science methods. Such attitudes limit the chance of improving Unesco's techniques and the prospects for Unesco to fulfill its defined purpose.

It will be noted that with the exception of evaluation Unesco's activities in the advancement of knowledge in the social sciences have reflected the rudimentary character of the social sciences in most countries. It has gone relatively farther, however, in attempts to apply the knowledge of social science in some fields as discussed in later chapters.

CHAPTER VI

THE ADVANCEMENT OF KNOWLEDGE: ARTS, HUMANITIES, MASS MEDIA, LIBRARIES

Cultural Activities: The Arts

The International Conference of Artists sponsored by Unesco at Venice in 1952 was the first international meeting ever to bring together painters, sculptors, architects, composers, writers, and creative workers in the theater and cinema. The two hundred participants came from more than forty countries. Among writers, to mention only a few, there were Taha Hussein, Gabriela Mistral, Jules Romains, Ignazio Silone, Stephen Spender, and Thornton Wilder; among painters, Gino Severini, Giuseppe Ungaretti, Graham Sutherland, and Jacques Villon; among sculptors, Marino Marini and Henry Moore; among composers, Arthur Honegger, Jacques Ibert, Francesco Malipiero, and William Schuman; among architects, Lucio Costa and Le Corbusier; and among creative workers in the theater and film, Marc Connelly, Alessandro Blasetti, and Roberto Rossellini.

Thornton Wilder, who served as rapporteur of the Venice Conference, pointed out the role of Unesco in linking together the artists of the world, remarking that the discussions had "revealed wide differences in the extent to which delegates . . . placed confidence in their governments as competent to regulate in matters of art. A striking fact emerges, however: committee after committee exhibited an unquestioning confidence in the competence of Unesco to collect and allocate funds, to select committees for their distribution, to supervise a wide variety of projects. Is it not a gratifying aspect of this conference that we feel that if an authority is international in character, its judgment in matters of art tends to inspire a greater confidence? Cannot we say that in an international organization of artists . . . artists have found an external and concrete expression of the function of universality which has been attributed to them in all times?"[1]

Through such international meetings, through exhibitions, and through encouragement of international organizations, Unesco has facilitated communication among creative artists and thinkers of the world. Their works will portray for future generations the character, spirit, and aspirations of the present age. Unesco has endeavored to carry out this task in a way which is in full accord with freedom of thought and creation, thus helping to maintain these values in the future society for which free men are fighting in the contemporary world.

Similarly in the applied arts, Unesco has encouraged international communication, in order to conserve and enrich the world's heritage of folk arts and handicrafts. At Unesco's fundamental education training center for the Arab States, at Sirs-el-Layyan, Egypt, a small museum was established. Here a visitor may find, together with a collection of handicrafts from Arab countries, examples of the folk arts of Mexico, Indonesia, and West Africa. The museum houses a stove devised for Egyptian villagers, more efficient than the type generally used; and a beehive modeled in clay, not in the traditional form of a hollow log which had to be broken to yield its sweets, but in the box pattern from which honey can be removed without breaking the container. To illustrate a practical manual issued by the Food and Agriculture Organization, *Small Farm Implements,* the museum prepared an exhibit in which implements commonly used in the region were shown side by side with improved implements designed for conditions in the Arab countries.[2]

Unesco has encountered more difficulty in finding its proper role in the arts than in any other area. As used here, the term "arts" includes painting and sculpture, architecture, literature and poetry, music, theater, opera, and ballet. Experience has indicated that Unesco should not seek directly to promote creative expression, but rather to facilitate communication by artists and creative writers across frontiers. A resolution at the 1946 General Conference stressed the importance of freedom for the artist, and pledged Unesco "to protect and defend the freedom of the artist wherever it is put in danger."[3] Two years later the Director General was instructed to inquire into the social, economic, and political factors which might hinder the artist's function and into contributions which creative artists might make to the purposes of Unesco.[4]

Activities of the Unesco secretariat in the area of the arts were designed principally to broaden public knowledge of masterworks produced in the past, and particularly to spread this knowledge across cultural and political boundaries. In encouraging artists and writers to develop international communication, Unesco has worked largely through private organizations—despite the fact that an organization of artists is often viewed as a contradiction in terms. Organization implies discipline and cooperation, but artists are individualists. Thornton Wilder, speaking of the artists gathered at Venice, observed that, in spite of initial anxiety, "we have shown that we can think internationally and that—extreme individualists though we are—we can think and plan and act cooperatively."[5]

Various international associations related to the arts existed prior to Unesco, or came into being independently of it—such as the International Union of Architects and the International Congresses of Modern Architecture, the International Council of Museums, and for writers the International P.E.N. Club (the initials stand for poets, editors, and novelists). Unesco, at the request of interested groups and individuals, has assisted in the establishment of such additional organizations as the International Music Council, International Theater Institute, International Association of Art Critics, and more recently the International Association of Plastic Arts. To encourage closer contact among those organizations, Unesco sponsored the creation in 1955 of a Liaison Committee of International Organizations in the Field of Arts and Letters.

Painting

The world's masterpieces of painting are normally too valuable to travel, and their distribution in various parts of the world is highly uneven. How then is it possible to enable the people of all countries, small and large, distant and near to centers of art, to come to know them? Unesco has sought to achieve this goal through increasing information about available color reproductions. From reproductions published in various countries a group of experts chose the most important and the most faithful, and these have been published in two catalogues, one of paintings prior to 1860, and the second of works from 1860 to the present. Using these catalogues, an art teacher in Australia, Bolivia, or Jordan can order reproductions to illustrate a course in the history of art, or to round out a collection for the local museum.

Traveling exhibitions of color reproductions, both old masters and modern art, have been sent by Unesco to many countries in Latin America, Southeast Asia, the Middle East, and the British Dominions as well as to many European nations. The exhibitions have been housed in varied settings—at Geneva in a large department store, at Belgrade in shop windows along the main thoroughfare, in France at a large trade fair at Limoges. In some cases the collections have been bought for permanent possession by institutions such as the London County Council, the Egyptian government, the National Library at Rio de Janeiro, the government of Israel, San Marcos University in Peru, and the New South Wales Museum in Australia. The Lebanese government set up at Beirut a permanent collection of color reproductions. More recently Unesco has organized traveling exhibitions of Japanese colored woodcuts dating from the seventeenth to the nineteenth century, of "Two Thousand Years of Chinese Painting," and of Persian miniatures.[6] Japan booked the Chinese exhibition for two years and a half, to permit its showing in many parts of the country. By 1956 almost 150 Unesco exhibitions of art reproductions were on tour throughout the world. An exhibition of reproductions of water colors of the nineteenth and twentieth centuries is now being prepared.

To widen knowledge of contemporary paintings, a collection of photographs covering the works of artists of member states is maintained at Unesco House in Paris, for examination by publishers concerned with reproduction in color of outstanding paintings. In addition Unesco has requested judges of the biennial international exhibitions of painting and sculpture held at São Paulo and Venice to select a small number of outstanding works by contemporary artists who should be better known internationally. Reproductions of these works are distributed to member states.

An interesting enterprise has been Unesco's encouragement of the careful reproduction of works to which access has been limited for geographic or other reasons. Through the *Unesco World Art Series* a number of albums have been published, reproducing in color such

varied treasures as the paintings in the Ajanta caves of India, paintings in the tombs and temples of Egypt, aboriginal paintings from
Arnhem Land in Australia, medieval frescoes in Yugoslavia, Persian
miniatures in the Imperial Library of Gulistan at Teheran, and
paintings from the Stave Churches in Norway. Plans from 1956 on
include volumes on Romanesque paintings in Spain, ancient Buddhist paintings in Ceylon and Japan, icons and frescoes in Russia,
and pre-Columbian art in Mexico.[7] The significance of this project
is dramatized when one discovers in a bookshop in Peru the volume
on Egyptian paintings, that on Persian miniatures in Nairobi, the
capital of Kenya, and a complete set in Bombay.

The International Association of Plastic Arts, organized in 1954,
has cooperated with Unesco in this field. At the end of 1956 it had
thirty-five national committees representing all continents. The
United States committee, composed of representatives of thirteen
leading art societies, prepared in 1956 an exhibition of the work of
contemporary American artists to be shown in various European
countries. In connection with its Second Congress, scheduled to meet
in Yugoslavia in 1957, the Association planned an exhibition of
photographs of works carried out in common by painters, sculptors,
and architects.[8]

Literature

In the field of literature the International P.E.N. Club, an association of groups of writers founded shortly after World War I, encourages personal contact among writers of different countries. Its
monthly bulletin in French and English, issued with Unesco's assistance, carries sketches of contemporary literature and reviews of
literary work throughout the world. Among the leaders in the association have been John Galsworthy, Benedetto Croce, Ignazio Silone,
Somerset Maugham, Thomas Mann, André Maurois, and Pearl Buck.

The P.E.N. Club seeks to encourage young writers who find themselves "on the edge" of the main literary currents. It proposes to
Unesco each year the names of authors whose work is of high quality
but has not yet been translated into widely spoken languages. Such
works are then translated, into several languages if possible, and
issued by commercial publishers. In 1954 the choice fell on two books
from Japan and one from Iran. The selections for 1955-56 came from

Norway and Sweden. Unesco is giving traveling fellowships to young writers, as well as to painters, sculptors, and musicians, who are in a position to choose freely the country or countries they wish to visit.[9]

The great works of literature have been given wider circulation through Unesco. As early as 1946 the United Nations General Assembly requested Unesco to encourage translation of literary masterpieces of different peoples into languages of wide circulation. Works have been chosen from five areas: Arabic and Persian literature, the literature of India, of the Far East, of Italy, and finally of Latin America (in which the Organization of American States has co-operated).[10]

As a first step in translation of Asian classics, *An Anthology of Japanese Literature* up to the mid-nineteenth century was published. Thirty volumes have already appeared in this project, and seventy others are in process. In addition to the classics of India, Iran, and the Arabic-speaking countries, translations will be made of the masterpieces of China, Japan, Pakistan, and Thailand. The project includes novels, plays, poetry, philosophy, and scientific works.[11]

A recent project has been the translation into English of the *Adi Granth*, containing sacred writings or scriptures venerated by the 5 million Sikhs of India. These have never been translated adequately into any language. The Sikhs consider their sacred writings to contain both the finest poetry of northern India and the best doctrines of the Hindu and Muslim religions, together with the words of saintly leaders of other creeds including some "untouchables." The volume is a compilation of poetic verses written in the sixteenth and seventeenth centuries, at a time when fiery hostility between Hinduism and Islam had cooled and movements were under way among both Muslims and Hindus to fuse the teachings of both faiths.[12]

Since, in the first stage of the program, books to be translated were chosen by national committees, national pride at times prevented a realistic appraisal of interest abroad in the writer or subject. Since December 1953, however, a committee of specialists named by the International Council for Philosophy and Humanistic Studies has reviewed and modified these national recommendations, naming works whose translation was considered urgent. The bulk of the publishing cost has been borne by the country of origin or the individual publisher, and Unesco's contribution has been limited to payment of the translator, in return for which it receives some copies for general distribution.

Unesco has also tried to persuade publishers of large, low-priced editions of the world's literary masterpieces to include in their lists more from the Orient.

A broader contribution has been the compilation and annual publication of *Index Translationum,* a world list of books in translation. Publication of this volume, issued before World War II by the Institute of Intellectual Cooperation, was resumed by Unesco in 1950. It is a valuable aid to librarians, publishers, and translators. The content of the annual edition has increased from 8,750 translations representing 30 countries listed in Volume 1 to more than 24,000 translations from 51 countries listed in Volume 8.[13]

Music

In the field of music Unesco delegated responsibility for international exchange and cooperation to the International Music Council set up in 1949,[14] whose officers have included Samuel Barber of the United States and the late Arthur Honegger of Switzerland. The council's activities from the start have emphasized contemporary music and folk music. A series of albums of recordings have been issued, dealing with the folk music of more than a score of peoples including the Eskimo, Irish, Turkish, Hindu, Formosan, and Russian. As for contemporary music, concerts, broadcasts, and recordings have been sponsored and young composers have been aided by fellowships and by the copying of "parts" or scores for the use of performers.

As a result of requests to member states for lists of national composers and works, exchange of contemporary music between Norway and the United States began in 1956. Several symphony orchestras in the United States agreed to present the works of living Norwegian composers, while the works of modern American composers were featured at Norwegian concerts.[15] The Council has also sponsored recordings of Oriental music, and in 1955 an *Anthology of Indian Classical Music* was published.

As a further stimulus to the international diffusion of contemporary music, the Council has transmitted commissions to composers, either to musicians of established reputation for easy scores which may be performed by orchestras or choirs of young people or amateurs, or to young composers not yet internationally known. Paul Hindemith, at the request of the International Music Council, composed a *Cantique de l'Espérance* using the words of a poem by Paul Claudel, which was performed for the first time at the Unesco Conference on Music in Education at Brussels in 1953. The Council has begun the compilation of an international catalogue of orchestral music from 1880 to the present, appropriate for performance by youth or amateur orchestras. The works of ten young composers from ten European countries were given public performance in 1953.

A recent initiative of the Council had to do with the production and international distribution of LP recordings, on the basis of a presubscription scheme which would guarantee an adequate return. Three kinds of records were to be produced: (1) a world collection of recorded folk music classified by themes of common human experience, such as songs of love and marriage, work songs, and funeral chants; (2) an international anthology of contemporary recorded music by composers in some thirty countries whose works have not yet been listed in record catalogues; and (3) contemporary musical experiments in developing new musical "language" or in using such new technical resources as electronic sound.[16]

The Council's emphasis on recordings and concerts, necessarily on a limited scale and apparently designed for an élite group, and the neglect of exchange of information and other clearing-house activities, has been criticized in several countries including the United States. It has been argued that instead of small projects with little international influence, the Council should distribute lists of contemporary composers and information on how and where material could be secured by a performing organization. This, it is held, would encourage the presentation of thousands of contemporary compositions for which material is already available.[17] Along this line the Council arranged for the 1956-57 season an exchange of radio programs featuring the work of contemporary composers of nine countries, including Canada, Brazil, and Japan outside of Europe.[18] In cooperation with the Austrian government and the organizers of the Salzburg Festival, the Council sponsored at Salzburg a conference on "Opera in Radio, Television and Film" which met in the late summer of 1956.[19]

Theater

The International Theater Institute was established in 1948 with J. B. Priestley as its first president. It now has national centers in more than thirty countries. The Institute advises Unesco on its program in the theatrical field, and consults with writers, directors, actors, and dancers. Part of the Institute's assistance in international exchange of information is a monthly bulletin in English and French, *World Premiers*, which provides a summary of plot, and press comment on new productions in the participating countries. The Institute also publishes three times a year an illustrated review, *World Theater*. To stimulate further the international exchange of experience, the Institute grants five traveling fellowships annually to younger artists for study of the theater in one or more foreign countries.[20]

Philosophy and the Humanities

Another area where Unesco has aided the exchange and enlargement of knowledge is philosophy and the humanities. The Preparatory Commission drew up a detailed list of activities in this field similar to those outlined for other subject areas. But as early as the 1946 session of the General Conference, groups working in this area proposed that projects be designed, not with an eye to what Unesco could do for philosophy and the humanities, but to what they could contribute to Unesco's broad objectives. It was therefore recommended that the diversified scheme of activities listed by the Preparatory Commission should be reduced to two continuing projects, one in philosophy and the other in the humanities.[21]

With regard to philosophy, knowledge might be advanced through analysis of fundamental philosophical questions involved in international cooperation. The first chosen was the concept of "human rights." An inquiry was proposed into the historical development and philosophical bases of human rights. Subsequently the concepts of democracy, liberty, and law were examined. Work on human rights and democracy centered in the Unesco secretariat. When a question was raised as to the wisdom of Unesco's undertaking research of this kind on its own, responsibility was shifted from the secretariat to private international organizations. The inquiry on liberty was undertaken by the International Federation of Philosophic Societies, and that on law by the International Council on Philosophy and Humanistic Studies. These studies and the volumes resulting from them are discussed more fully in Chapter XI. More recently the project has been broadened to include the preparation of a *Dictionary of Fundamental Terms of Philosophy and Political Thought,* whose purpose is to reveal the relationship among the basic ideas in different traditions of thought.

The project chosen in the humanities was a comparative examination of different cultures as they came in contact with one another in the modern world. What light may this cast on basic problems of international understanding? The Unesco secretariat undertook an inquiry which led to a symposium in 1951 at New Delhi, whose discussions and findings were published in *Humanism and Education in East and West,* and a second which culminated in a volume on *Interrelations of Cultures.* These studies provided background for a major project on mutual appreciation of Eastern and Western cultural values, approved at the 1956 General Conference at New Delhi. They, as well as the major project, are discussed in detail in Chapter XI.

Unesco helped to establish in 1949 the International Council for Philosophy and Humanistic Studies (CIPHS), set up on the general pattern of the International Council of Scientific Unions. The new Council and its member associations seek to develop contact, exchange of information, and collaboration among philosophers, philologists, classicists, historians, anthropologists, and other scholars in humanistic fields throughout the world. These organizations employ substantially the same methods as their counterparts in the natural and social sciences—international congresses, symposia and other meetings, and scholarly publications. Thirteen private international organizations, many of them federations of national or specialist groups, are represented in the Council.[22]

Unesco's annual subsidies to the Council have increased from about $60,000 in 1950 to $100,000 for 1956. Its quarterly review, *Diogenes,* is the first journal on a world scale which seeks to translate and interpret for the educated public the knowledge of scholars and research workers. It is issued in six editions—Arabic, English, French, German, Italian, and Spanish.[23]

The Council has made a special effort to undertake projects related to Unesco objectives, and not solely to scholarly goals. It has, for example, cooperated in the History of the Scientific and Cultural Development of Mankind, the translation of great works of world literature, and expansion of the teaching of the humanities, all to be discussed elsewhere in this volume. It has made a study of the philosophical bases of Nazism and the translation of this doctrine from intellectual theory into practical politics. This project was first proposed by an American labor leader in the hope that lessons drawn from this experience might help mankind to avoid similar follies in the future.[24]

The Council and its member organizations have also fostered encyclopedias and dictionaries of technical terms, to promote clarity of international discussion. Among these has been a *Dictionary of Terminology of International Law.* They have promoted international bibliographies, which make available to scholars throughout the world comprehensive lists of significant works in such fields as philosophy, linguistics, ethnology, history of art, history of religion, and comparative literature. A series of reproductions of ancient vases in the custody of the leading museums of the world, the *Corpus Vasorum Antiquorum,* makes available a valuable but fragile source for the family, religious, and military life of ancient peoples. A similar corpus of medieval stained glass is in process of development. Since much valuable glass has been destroyed, this enterprise is one of preservation as well as of study.

Another project is exploring the origins and growth of representative assemblies, the ancestors of modern democratic forms, which first appeared in medieval Europe and have since been extended throughout the world. Studies of African and Asian civilizations, especially of the languages and of the moral and religious ideas of these peoples, provide materials essential for an understanding of the dynamic currents of intellectual and social change occurring in these continents. An *International Directory of Musical Sources* from the earliest times is designed to cast light on developments antedating modern music.[25]

Mass Communication

Throughout the first part of the twentieth century there has been a growing interest in the direct influence of public opinion upon domestic and foreign policy. The extension of public education and the growth of radio, press, and motion pictures made these media important instruments of education and propaganda in influencing public opinion. During World War II authoritarian as well as democratic countries relied so extensively on the mass media of public persuasion that delegates to the San Francisco and London Conferences looked almost automatically to these media as aids in building the peace.

In some circles mass media were accepted as a major instrument to develop public opinion for peace. It was not enough, it was argued, to wait for the slow processes of education to build "the defenses of peace" in the minds of children. Adults must be stirred, for they would influence immediate decisions on public policy. Mass communication, it was urged, must be rapidly mobilized, particularly through a world-wide radio network. This might provide a new dimension in the quest for international understanding and cooperation.

The United States took the lead in urging inclusion of mass media in Unesco. Its delegation at the 1945 London Conference secured the inclusion in Article I of the Unesco Constitution of provisions stressing the organization's responsibility to "collaborate in the work of advancing the mutual knowledge and understanding of peoples, through all means of mass communication." In addition, it introduced at the London Conference a special resolution on "Media of Mass Communication and Their Place in Unesco," which referred to "the paramount importance of the media of mass communication . . . in advancing the purpose of the United Nations to maintain international peace and security by the spread of knowledge and mutual understanding."[26] At the First Session of the General Conference in 1946 the United States pressed for a world network of radio stations.

Mass communications, as a subject of Unesco concern, have not lived up to early hopes. This was due in part to the fear in many smaller countries that the nations most expert in using these powerful media—especially the United States—would employ them for "cultural imperialism," and that the smaller nations would be drowned out, their peoples overwhelmed and their cultures destroyed by a flood of alien propaganda. Another reason was lack of acceptable and imaginative projects.

There was, moreover, increasing recognition of the limitations of mass media for real communication between peoples. The Expert Committee on Education for International Understanding and Co-operation set up by the Director General in 1953 noted in its report that ideas related to international understanding and cooperation are well suited to radio, press, film, and television. It noted however, that the term "mass media of communication" is rather unfortunate, "since it conjures up the vision of someone in authority projecting an image or message to a great passive general public—mass man." While distorted views spread by some mass media programs may damage friendly relations between peoples, the Committee held that this monolithic notion of mass media is "a misleading and perhaps dangerous misconception. On the one hand it fails to take into account that each film, radio or television program selects or is selected by its own public—a sizeable group perhaps but rarely more than a minority. The recipients of the image or message have the power of choice; they respond or reject. Accordingly if the media are to be effective they must first be planned for a specific public and they must be utilized with effective methods and techniques usually involving further study and discussion. A great deal has already been learned about the most productive ways of using films and radio programmes but further research is needed. Television, which in many countries is becoming such an important feature in millions of middle and lower income homes, presents some unusual opportunities but much more needs to be learned."[27]

As regards the advancement of knowledge, Unesco's activities in mass communication have had two objects: to stimulate the flow of information, and to strengthen facilities for international communication through press, radio, film, and television. As a modest contribution to the first objective, Unesco issued the *Unesco World Review* and *Unesco Features*. The first was a weekly radio script in mimeographed form which carried material on educational, scientific, and cultural developments throughout the world. Stations in some countries used the script as basic documentation, and material was extracted from it for news bulletins, science programs, or women's programs. In other countries it was used in full. The Spanish edition was used in almost every Latin American country, either by national networks or by numerous individual stations.

Similarly, for the press, a fortnightly mimeographed bulletin,

Unesco Features, supplied educational, scientific, and cultural information, largely but not exclusively to the less economically developed countries.[28] In September 1955 *Unesco Features* and *Unesco World Review* merged under the title of the first publication. Published in English, French, Spanish, and Arabic versions, it goes to some 4,000 press and 1,000 radio outlets. Editions in Dutch, German, and Norwegian are published by national organizations in those countries.

Mention should also be made of the monthly *Courier,* Unesco's general periodical published in English, French, and Spanish. It originated as a house organ reporting the organization's activities, and it was often criticized for lack of appeal to the general reader. Neither its purpose nor its function was clearly defined. Repeated demands were made at the General Conference for its improvement. The 1952 General Conference decided that its primary audience should be the school teacher. Its editorial policy was gradually revised. Although the *Courier* has never achieved mass circulation, it has become a distinctive publication, presenting from a world viewpoint and in attractive format materials and news designed to promote international understanding. These materials are thus available for use by teachers and others in member states. Particularly successful have been special issues on human rights, Buddhist art and culture, the American Negro, and atomic energy. By December 1956 the paid circulation of the *Courier* had reached 71,000. The Unesco National Commissions in Denmark and Japan have published shortened editions in the languages of those countries. Starting in 1957 a Russian language edition of 20,000 copies was to be published in Moscow. Although the *Courier* is highly rated by both teachers and others interested in education on world affairs, it has lacked the enterprising support with which alone it can secure substantial circulation.

Other activities in press, radio, and films have advanced knowledge of Unesco's program and of other international efforts to spread information. Unesco provides press releases, articles, and background materials. It maintains a photographic library from which photographs are loaned on request to individual newspapers. "World Without End," a one-hour motion picture produced in 1953 by Unesco in cooperation with other United Nations agencies, reported on the work of these agencies in the less economically developed countries. It was telecast in both Great Britain and the United States. Unesco has also produced a number of shorter films on such projects as the fundamental education centers at Patzcuaro and Sirs-el-Layyan, the Delhi Public Library, arid zones, and museums.

In radio, the Unesco secretariat during 1956 produced more than 6,000 recordings on various aspects of Unesco's work which were distributed to almost one hundred countries and territories. Thirty feature programs were recorded in English, French, German, and Spanish, highlighting Unesco activities especially in human rights and technical assistance. But more important than this direct production was the effort to stimulate national radio chains and individual stations to develop programs in line with Unesco's purposes and projects. Some countries sent their producers to Unesco House in Paris; others produced programs after consultation with the secretariat; others used scripts from Unesco which were translated and adapted to programs in their own languages. Assistance was given by the secretariat to the exchange of cultural programs. For example, Vietnam was helped to obtain material on Mozart, and Poland on Indian music.

With the spread of television—by 1956 some thirty countries were carrying on regular operations—a number of governments asked Unesco to promote an exchange of information on television methods and programs about people and customs of other lands. Representatives of twelve countries took part in the first international seminar on television, which was convened at London in 1954 by Unesco and the BBC. In 1955 and 1956 Unesco had two small groups of specialists examine the problems involved in improving cooperation between the television and film industries for exchange of educational, scientific, and cultural films and kinerecordings.

An experiment in the combined use of various media to develop public understanding of a significant problem has been made by Unesco and other United Nations agencies in what are called *reportages*. The first, in 1950, was on *Man Against the Desert* and related especially to Unesco's work in arid zones. In 1951-52 a similar project was carried out on the subject *Man Against Disease*. Ritchie Calder, a British journalist, was joined by a Canadian radio reporter and a French photographer from the United Nations in a visit to India, Pakistan, Burma, Thailand, and Indonesia. The group reviewed progress in education, science, public health, agriculture, and national economy, and the cooperation extended by the United Nations and its specialized agencies. As a result, thirty articles appeared in English, French, Spanish, and other languages. A number of talks, three "features" and a television program were broadcast in Canada, the United States, and the United Kingdom. Broadcasting companies in twenty-four countries received on request recordings on the subject. In addition, photographs were supplied to newspapers and periodicals and used also for exhibitions and educational film-strips. Much of the material was made available to schools through filmstrips and pamphlets, and Calder on his return to England spoke to conferences of teachers and students.[29]

In addition to using mass media to spread information about its own activities and the character of its program, Unesco has aided individual countries to improve their technical equipment and personnel in press, radio, and film; and has helped to remove barriers to the free flow of information.

One of the organization's earliest activities was a survey of the needs of individual countries for technical equipment and personnel. This study was begun in the war-devastated countries as a part of the reconstruction effort, but later extended into a five-year undertaking which ultimately covered 152 countries and territories. The study examined the needs for raw materials, equipment, and trained personnel—such as raw film stock, pulp and paper; printing machinery and type; radio transmitting and receiving apparatus; film, cameras, and projectors. It explored the work of news agencies, and reviewed professional training, the status of press and radio correspondents, pertinent legislation, and government services and control. It brought together for the first time a world-wide review of technical facilities in the fields of press, film, and radio, and its results were published in five volumes.[30] These reports, revised and enlarged to cover 170 states and territories, were later brought together in a one-volume publication entitled *World Communications*.[31]

Among methods subsequently employed by Unesco to assist member states have been fellowships for study abroad and experts to advise on special problems. To cite only a few illustrations, fellowships were offered in 1956 to Haiti (for development of information services), to Spain (for radio and television), and to Yugoslavia (for news agencies). In the same year, specialists were sent to Libya to aid in the creation of a radio broadcasting system, to Costa Rica for establishment of a national television service, and to the University of

Strasbourg in France to help set up a regional center for training teachers of journalism.

This last enterprise resulted from the mounting interest in improving the education of journalists. This movement, which goes back to the early nineteenth century, had led to the establishment of many courses on journalism in educational institutions throughout the world.[32] One of the early proposals for giving an international character to this movement was considered at Unesco's 1947 General Conference. It called for establishment of an International Institute of Press and Information, which might serve as a research center on the technical needs of press, radio, and film, and as a place where journalists of various countries might come together for study and discussion. This idea encountered considerable opposition, especially from partisans of a free press who feared the effect of an international agency, supported and controlled by governments. As a result, the proposal was dropped; but a group of United States newspaper men took the lead in setting up an entirely private International Press Institute with headquarters at Zurich.

In recognition of the importance of journalists in improving the quality of information passing from one country to another, Unesco convened at Paris in April 1956 a meeting of sixty specialists from twenty-four countries to consider better professional training for journalists. This meeting drafted a series of recommendations on the selection and training of journalists, the role of universities in their education, and the cooperation of professional organizations. It urged creation of regional or international centers designed to raise the standards of training and the preparation of professors of journalism.[33]

Unesco's activities relating to mass communication have touched most of the media in some way but it has thus far failed to have a significant or even noticeable impact either in affecting the volume or scope of news that flows through the world or in the orientation of the media toward conscious efforts to increase objective understanding among the peoples of the United Nations. We shall discuss this question further in Chapter XII.

Libraries

Libraries perform an essential service in advancement and diffusion of knowledge. When they work together internationally, they help "to give the people of all countries access to the printed and published materials produced by any of them."

But a basic task of libraries is preservation of the knowledge acquired by mankind over the centuries, particularly "the world's inheritance of books."[34] Unesco has profited from earlier efforts in this field by the International Institute of Intellectual Cooperation and the Conference of Allied Ministers of Education meeting at London during World War II, as well as from the cooperation of numerous voluntary associations, particularly the International Federation of Library Associations, the International Federation for Documentation, the International Organization for Standardization, and the International Council on Archives.

Unesco's work has gone forward along three main lines: (1) promotion of libraries for the general public (which will be discussed in Chapter VII in relation to fundamental education); (2) encouragement of services to research and scholarship, particularly in bibliography; and (3) international exchange of material in library collections through gifts, loans, and microfilm. The basic plan for improvement of bibliography and documentation was laid down by a Unesco conference in 1950 and that for exchange of publications by a committee of specialists in 1948.

Bibliography, Documentation, and Abstracting[35]

Unesco's work in bibliography is directed primarily towards the scholar and scientist. It seeks to make known what has been published. Bibliography, it has been said, provides a guide for the intellectual explorer who sets forth to discover the treasures hidden in all languages and in all corners of the world. With the astounding increase in books and other publications during the last half century, bibliography has grown in importance. Its function is to "interpose a sort of filter between man and the torrent of books."[36] Unesco is concerned with listing and abstracting books, pamphlets, articles, pictures, films, and recordings, and also with problems of efficient and economical procedure.[37]

After a brief flirtation with the over-ambitious idea of establishing a union catalogue for all of Europe, Unesco has wisely sought to encourage national bibliographical centers in individual countries, of which some thirty-five now exist. A contract with the United States Library of Congress led to two publications surveying the situation in different countries and in certain subject fields, presenting basic problems and suggestions for their solution.[38] When these studies had been reviewed by member states, Unesco convened in 1950 an international conference on the improvement and coordination of bibliographical services. As the result of one of its recommendations, Unesco set up an International Advisory Committee on Bibliography, which has focused on the activities of national groups and coordinated national and specialized bibliographical activities in all fields and all countries. Under the auspices of this Committee there is now an annual report on world-wide progress in bibliography.[39]

Various Unesco publications have sought to improve bibliographical procedures, particularly by adoption of a uniform method of presenting references. A quarterly *Bibliographical Newsletter* circulates to the Advisory Committee and national groups. A series of practical handbooks on bibliographical services has been issued.[40] Unesco advises on a general international bibliographical program in natural science, social science, education, and cultural activities.[41]

Bibliographies, however useful, are inadequate for current material. Something more is needed: namely, short summaries of scientific and scholarly articles. Here the problem is often one of excessive wealth rather than poverty of material. Scholars face an increasingly complex problem because of the proliferation of research, not to mention the number of languages in which scientific papers appear. In the natural sciences more than a million articles (not including books and pamphlets) appear each year in 50,000 periodicals. An individual scientist cannot read all the journals which may bear on his research. He needs a short-cut to the articles that concern him. Consequently abstracting services have been developed.

One article bearing one single bit of knowledge may be of great practical importance. In the early months of 1949 an unknown disease practically brought to a halt France's largest automobile plant. The eyes of 500 workmen were swollen shut with a virulent infection. Scientists at the Pasteur Institute were consulted. In their files they found a small white card, an abstract of an article printed in the January 1943 issue of a medical journal published in the United States. During the war a similar infection had attacked workers in the Kaiser shipyards in California. Physicians at the Columbia Medical Center had produced a remedy. Thus the French scientists found information which stopped the epidemic.[42]

Unesco has helped to develop more effective and comprehensive abstracting. Although approximately 1,000 organizations were already producing abstracts, less than half of the million or so scientific articles published every year were being abstracted. Some sciences such as chemistry were better served than others, and the same was true of different geographic regions and different languages. There was some overlapping and duplication between abstracting journals. Unesco convoked a series of conferences of experts to examine the problem. As one result, the Abstracting Board of ICSU was created and has now taken leadership in the natural science field. Efforts have been launched to develop a cooperative plan to list periodicals in each field of science, together with information on where abstracts of their articles may be found.[43] The situation in physics has been cleared up by the ICSU Board through an exchange of proofs among editors of certain leading journals. A similar effort is under way in chemistry, with prospects that it will be broadened to include biological sciences, mathematics, and mechanics. In 1954 the Soviet Academy of Sciences offered to the Abstracting Board an exchange of scientific journals on physics, permitting a significant enlargement of its services.[44]

In the social sciences Unesco set up in 1950 an International Committee for Social Science Documentation to assist in collecting, classifying, and analyzing publications, articles and other materials. Each of the nongovernmental international organizations in the social sciences which Unesco helped to create has a committee which cooperates with this documentation group, with special attention to research in progress or completed. A series of specialized bibliographies in political science, economics, and sociology has been published.[45] Two quarterly reviews, *Current Sociology* and *International Political Science Abstracts*, keep bibliographical information up to date. Some publications are designed to encourage comparison of research methods in different countries. For example, the *International Register of Current Research in the Social Sciences* (1950-1952) contains references to several thousand projects under way in sixty-five countries and territories.[46] Finally, the quarterly *International Social Science Bulletin* carries, together with original articles, references to significant social science documents published by the United Nations and its specialized agencies, and information on international congresses and meetings.

Unesco has cooperated in setting up national or regional centers on scientific and technical documentation. These have had to do primarily with the natural sciences. With technical assistance funds, Unesco chose the staff and worked out methods of operation for such a center at Mexico City, established in 1951, to enable industry and research workers in Spanish speaking countries to keep abreast of the latest scientific information. A monthly bulletin was published listing the titles of more than 2,000 publications from almost 60 countries. By the end of two years requests for abstracts, summaries, and bibliographies totaled more than 120,000. The center provided copies of entire articles either on paper or on microfilm. After five years it was turned over to local staff trained through study abroad on Unesco fellowships, and working closely with the Unesco specialists on their return. Similar centers have been set up in Egypt (to serve all the Arab States), and in India, Turkey, Uruguay, and Yugoslavia.

The *Unesco Bulletin for Libraries* has helped the whole program on libraries and bibliographies. It has facilitated distribution of publications throughout the world. Offers of publications for exchange or as gifts are announced here. Information on libraries and document services is circulated. Seven thousand copies of the *Bulletin* are published in English, Spanish, and bilingual English and French editions. This journal was one of the first publications that the USSR asked to have translated into Russian.

Some activities in the field have been financed both from Unesco's regular budget and from the United Nations Technical Assistance Program. In Turkey Unesco has helped set up a National Institute of Bibliography linked to the National Library. In 1955 a specialist went to Indonesia to advise on the improvement of public and university libraries and bibliography. His work was so successful that in response to the government's request, three library experts are now at work in the country. Brazil was aided by a consultant in planning a long-term program of national bibliography. Aid was given to universities in Syria, Iran, and Iraq in improving their libraries and bibliographical services. A national bibliography of Iran appeared for the first time in 1955. The national committee on bibliography in Cuba in 1955 organized a seminar of representatives of ten countries which planned joint publication of bibliographies. The resources of these countries were too weak to attempt such an activity individually. The first Central American bibliography was published two years later.

Exchange of Publications

The Unesco Constitution gave the new organization responsibility for encouraging cooperation among nations in exchange of publications and for "initiating methods of international co-operation calculated to give the peoples of all countries access to the printed and published materials produced by any of them."[47] At the start, Unesco's most urgent task was restoration of war-damaged libraries in the formerly occupied countries. The Preparatory Commission recognized that this responsibility was temporary and that the big job was to improve normal means of acquisition. The *Unesco Libraries Questionnaire* drew from thousands of libraries throughout the world information on their individual needs. Unesco accepted a limited initial responsibility for actual operation of services of exchange and gift. After 1948 it moved to transfer major responsibility to national institutions, notably national exchange centers, of which some thirty-five existed in 1956. Unesco's role came to be primarily that of an intermediary. A scheme was worked out whereby books were sent only where they were wanted. In most cases offerings for gift or exchange were made up of duplicate and surplus copies, of which any library normally has a considerable stock.

Unesco published in 1952 a *Handbook on the International Exchange of Publications* which contained lists of organizations and publications for exchange; lists of bibliographies of official publications and exchange centers; and information on the legal character and administrative procedures for exchange agreements.[48] A revised edition of the *Handbook* issued in 1956 listed 10,000 titles available for exchange by 114 countries and territories. It covered some 3,500 institutions publishing educational, scientific, or cultural material. A substantial increase of publications available for exchange as compared with 1952 was reported for the Chinese People's Republic, France, both West and East Germany, Japan, Poland, the Soviet Union, the United States, and Yugoslavia.[49] Unesco's book and gift coupons were also used in the exchange program.

Two other methods have been available for movement of library material across frontiers. One is international loans, worked out particularly for research workers by the International Federation of Library Associations. The other is photocopy or microfilm, increasingly important in recent years. Information on this process has been published from time to time in the *Bulletin for Libraries,* and the International Federation for Documentation has prepared a *Manual on Document Reproduction and Selection.*[50]

Requests from member states have led Unesco to consider a new international convention on exchange of publications. An earlier convention was signed at Brussels in 1886, but by 1956 it had won adherence by only eighteen nations. An inter-American convention was approved in 1936. These two multilateral agreements were supplemented by bilateral agreements, mostly concluded by the United States. These related primarily to official documents and other materials, including important scholarly and scientific reports, which are not printed primarily for sale, and seldom circulate abroad through commercial channels. While government documents are produced chiefly for the issuing government and its nationals, copies are usually available for international exchange or gift, and such exchanges can be of great value. Seventy per cent of the annual increase in the holdings of the Library of the Department of Agriculture at Washington comes from international exchanges. The 1956 General Conference at New Delhi authorized the Director General to draft a new international convention on exchange of publications for consideration at the 1958 General Conference.[51]

Unesco has worked diligently for conservation and expansion of the world's heritage of books, but it recognizes that there are many new fields which call for urgent attention. The multitude of new literates want simple illustrated books. Hundreds or even thousands of books for children are needed. Books for adults which can inform, teach, and entertain are in demand. Scholars and scientists are eager for easier and more extensive access to learned works in all countries. Multitudes of human beings still suffer from book scarcity, even from book famine.[52]

Museums

The advancement of knowledge requires the preservation not only of books and documents but also of works of art, scientific and technical discoveries, and monuments of history and science. The museum is the oldest institution for preserving cultural property. Its collections illustrate our heritage of creative achievement and of knowledge of man and his world. Museums have a broader function than is often recognized; there are today throughout the world museums of art, archaeology, ethnography and folklore, health, history, natural history, science, and technology, as well as zoological and botanical gardens, and planetariums.

Unesco has also stressed the services which the museum can render to contemporary life. The modern idea of a museum originated some twenty or more years ago in certain countries where education for everyone was recognized as basic to a democratic society. The United States took the lead in museums of every kind—history, science, and art—with educational purposes, from the primary level to the university and adult education. The United Kingdom, many members of the British Commonwealth, and the Scandinavian countries were not far behind. Unesco presented an opportunity to extend this broad concept of the museum to other parts of the world where its role was still limited to the passive if important functions of collection and conservation. Museums have been used extensively in many of Unesco's educational activities, from fundamental education to research on the most specialized levels.

Unesco found to its hand a ready-made organization, the International Council of Museums (ICOM), which was established in November 1946 before the First Session of the Unesco General Conference. Unesco has given the Council an annual subsidy of approximately $20,000 and has delegated to it important responsibilities. By 1956 the Council had national committees in forty-two countries.

While serving as an international center for exchange of information, the Council has also carried on many kinds of activities. It has provided services on such problems as the care and preservation of valuable paintings and the use of natural and artificial illumination and air-conditioning in museums. An ICOM group was consulted by Belgium on the treatment of Jan van Eyck's altar-piece in Ghent Cathedral, the *Adoration of the Lamb,* damaged when taken from Belgium during the war. A similar approach was made on treatment of the paintings of Leonardo da Vinci in the Louvre. Another committee explored ways in which museums of history and archaeology might contribute to international understanding. A manual was issued on children's museums. The results of various ICOM projects are published in *ICOM News,* which reaches approximately 1,000 museum leaders throughout the world.[53]

Unesco publishes quarterly a technical review, *Museum,* designed to help museum workers improve their methods and enlarge their contribution to scholarship, public education, and general culture. The review, whose circulation is still limited, is perhaps better appreciated in far corners of the world, where museums and outside contacts are few, than in countries with numerous museums and well developed museum associations. Unesco has published manuals on traveling exhibitions, and on the organization of smaller museums.

Unesco organized in 1955 a "Campaign for Museums," in which the governments and National Commissions of member countries, together with the International Council of Museums, were invited to celebrate an International Museums Week on the occasion of Unesco's tenth anniversary. Exhibitions demonstrating common elements in the life of different peoples were on view in various parts of the world. Unesco has sponsored two seminars or international workshops on the use of museums in education, the first at Brooklyn in 1952 and the second at Athens in 1954.[54] A similar seminar for the Latin American countries is planned for Rio de Janeiro in 1958.

Unesco in 1955 approved requests from member states for experts to help Burma and Peru in planning national museums; India, Ceylon, and Pakistan in establishing scientific museums; Indonesia in developing the educational activities of museums; and Belgium, Guatemala, and Singapore on other museum problems. Additional requests from a number of countries called for fellowships for the training of museum personnel.[55]

Monuments and Historic Sites

At the request of the Egyptian government Unesco agreed in 1955 to help set up a special research center to study the ancient art and civilization of that country. Neither in Egypt nor elsewhere was there any complete record of the monuments and other vestiges of ancient Egyptian culture. In connection with plans for the Aswan dam in upper Egypt, the Egyptian government recognized that the temple of Abou-Simbel near the Nile in North Sudan and other monuments in an area of 500 kilometers would be inundated if the dam were constructed, and Egypt appealed to Unesco for assistance. In addition to preserving records it was hoped that by aerial photographic surveys it might be possible to identify other sites in regions as yet incompletely explored where, before inundation occurred, excavations might be carried out.

Ancient monuments in other parts of Egypt were suffering severe deterioration. Wind and sand storms together with erosion had been taking their toll. This was especially true of mural paintings in tombs recently opened. If the remains of one of the oldest artistic civilizations of the world were to be preserved, prompt action was necessary to make records of the vanishing relics, including architectural plans, drawings, photographs, descriptions, and copies of texts. The research center was to publish brochures and catalogues on its findings.

From the start the center was a cooperative venture between Unesco and the Egyptian government. During the first two years Unesco provided foreign experts and equipment at a cost of $18,000 annually. The Egyptian government offered to contribute approximately $110,000 to establish the center and $135,000 for its annual support.[56] It was anticipated that other countries might ultimately follow the Egyptian example.

This development in Egypt highlights what not infrequently happens with a Unesco project. At the start its value may seem questionable, but a turn of events may bring out its importance. This illustrates the need for flexibility in the Unesco program. Unesco had initiated in 1949 a proposal for protection of historic monuments, an idea suggested by the damage and devastation wrought by World War II.[57] The Netherlands government had taken a leading part in this endeavor, and at its instigation Unesco gave attention to the protection of monuments and "all objects of cultural value, particularly those kept in museums, libraries and archives, against the probable consequence of armed conflict.[58] The Italian delegation proposed to the 1950 General Conference that Unesco prepare an international convention for protection of cultural treasures. After extended consideration by succeeding General Conferences and other bodies, the Intergovernmental Conference on the Protection of Cultural Property in the Event of Armed Conflict met at The Hague in April and May 1954, with the Netherlands government serving as host, and with fifty-six governments represented.[59]

The Conference adopted a Convention for the Protection of Cultural Property in the Event of Armed Conflict, together with an accompanying Protocol and Regulations. The Convention sought to afford the same protection to historical monuments, museums, libraries, works of art, scientific collections, and other cultural treasures, and their personnel, as is generally given in wartime to medical staffs, hospitals, and ambulances. It provided that the contracting parties would prepare in time of peace facilities for safeguarding cultural property and would refrain from exposing such property to destruction or damage in time of war, subject to waiver in cases of imperative military necessity. All theft and pillage were forbidden. Special protection was pledged for a limited number of refuges sheltering movable objects, and for centers containing monuments and other immovable cultural property. In the Protocol, the contracting powers agreed to prevent exportation of cultural property from any territory occupied during war.[60] The Convention came into force in August 1956, and by December had been ratified by eight states.[61]

A proposal in 1949 to provide international financial assistance for preserving and restoring cultural property—income to be derived from a special tourist tax—met with scant support. Instead a plan was approved in 1952 for Unesco to provide assistance on the technical level. Member states were to be helped in learning and applying scientific methods for preserving museum collections, monuments, and historic and archaeological sites.[62] The New Delhi General Conference approved a proposal to set up an international study center which is to collect and distribute information, encourage research, help train research workers and technicians, provide advisory services, and recommend action on general and specific problems. Though an independent body, it will be connected with a national research institution in Italy.[63] Under the plan, Unesco would subsidize the center for a limited period, after which it would become self-supporting, it was hoped, on the basis of contributions from individual governments and private institutions.

Unesco since 1951 has furnished technical missions to member states requesting assistance on problems relating to historic and cultural monuments.[64] The first mission went to Peru to advise on restoration of the historic city of Cuzco following a disastrous earthquake. Another mission in 1951 proposed measures for preserving the frescoes and building of the Church of St. Sophia at Ochrida in Yugoslavia. Here the mission incidentally served the cause of international cooperation, for the Yugoslav government requested two Italian experts, in spite of political tensions between Yugoslavia and Italy over Trieste. Subsequent missions have assisted other countries in the preservation of historic monuments: Lebanon at Tarabulus and the Baalbek Acropolis; Syria at Aleppo, Damascus, Palmyra and other points; Iraq at Hatra; Israel at Acre and other towns; India in recording the wall paintings of the Ajanta caves in both ordinary and color photographs; Indonesia in the preservation of Buddhist temples and especially of the shrines at Borobudur in Java which date back to the eighth and ninth centuries A.D.[65]

Unesco during 1955 received numerous requests in connection with the new program of participation in the activities of member states adopted at the 1954 General Conference. Funds were available for only half of these requests, but assistance was approved for projects in fourteen countries.[66]

As both cause and effect of Unesco's activities in this field, there has been a growing sense of responsibility by individual countries for protection of monuments and other cultural property, and a recognition that these resources are not only national treasures but part of the heritage of mankind. Because so many of the countries possessing such treasures lack funds for protection and maintenance, it is more and more realized that this task represents a responsibility in which trusteeship is international as well as national. Unesco may be forced to become a world agent for conservation of the world's cultural heritage.

A question of international importance has also been emerging in connection with archaeological excavations. National governments sometimes look askance at foreign scholars seeking to study their national treasures. Should scholars have unrestricted access to historic sites which may throw light on mankind's past? Some earlier work on the problem had been done by the League of Nations. After consideration by successive Unesco General Conferences, study by ICOM, and review by Unesco's advisory International Committee on Monuments, Artistic and Historical Sites and Archaeological Excavations, a committee of experts and technicians met at Palermo in May 1956 to work out a statement on International Principles Governing Archaeological Excavations, which was approved by the 1956 General Conference at New Delhi and transmitted to Unesco's member states.[67]

Removal of Barriers to Free Flow of Information

In all the fields mentioned above, Unesco has made a determined effort to encourage the free flow of information, as laid down in its Constitution. The United Nations General Assembly has termed freedom of information "the touchstone of all our freedoms." Unesco and the United Nations have worked out a practical division of effort in this field, the UN dealing with political difficulties, while Unesco focuses on economic, administrative, and technical obstacles.

Unesco has promoted a series of international agreements, the most important being the Universal Copyright Convention, adopted at Geneva in 1952 by the Intergovernmental Copyright Conference after five years of negotiation. Forty states signed the Convention, which became effective on September 16, 1955. By the end of 1957 twenty-two states had ratified it. This convention removed an obstacle to the free flow of ideas which had long been of serious concern to authors, composers, and publishers. Previous conventions had been ineffective because they were not world-wide. The forty countries participating in the Berne Convention of 1886 were mainly from Europe and Asia. In the Western Hemisphere a separate inter-American system developed. The new convention provided a minimum standard of protection without prejudicing existing international agreements.

The Geneva convention standardizes international copyright procedure for literary, scientific, and artistic works, including books and other writings, music, records, films, painting, and sculpture. These are protected for a minimum of twenty-five years, and each signatory nation assures to authors and artists of other ratifying nations the same treatment as that given its own nationals, without special registration. The Convention also provides for translation rights on a basis mutually satisfactory to author and publisher.[68] More recently Unesco, in cooperation with the Berne Copyright Union and the International Labor Organization, has interested itself in the so-called "neighboring" rights of copyright. The rights of authors, composers, and publishers are covered by the Geneva convention; "neighboring" rights include those of performing artists, manufacturers of recordings, and broadcasting organizations.[69] The New Delhi Conference authorized the Director General, in cooperation with ILO, to convene an intergovernmental conference for the preparation and adoption of an agreement on such rights.

The Unesco General Conference has approved two international agreements to reduce trade and tariff difficulties affecting materials used in education. The Agreement on Importation of Educational, Scientific, and Cultural Materials was approved in 1950. It eliminates duties on books, newspapers, magazines, educational films and recordings, works of art, certain kinds of scientific equipment, and articles for education of the blind. The Agreement came into force in 1952, and by December 1956 twenty-four countries were applying it and ten others had signed but not yet ratified.

Unesco has also developed an Agreement for Facilitating the International Circulation of Visual and Auditory Materials of an Educational, Scientific and Cultural Character. This Agreement is limited to films, filmstrips, microfilm, recordings, maps, charts and other auditory and visual materials. The Agreement calls for freedom from tariffs, quotas, licensing systems and other import regulations. Twelve countries have ratified this treaty, which came into force on August 12, 1954; ten others have signed but not yet ratified, among them the United States.

In tariff negotiations at the 1956 Geneva Conference of parties to the General Agreement on Tariffs and Trade (GATT), fourteen countries responded to a suggestion from the Director General of Unesco to reduce import duties on educational, scientific, and cultural materials. Tariff reductions on various scientific instruments were agreed to by Australia, Canada, France, Italy, Sweden, and the United States; on radio receivers or parts by the German Federal Republic, Norway, Sweden, and the United Kingdom; on television receivers by Japan; on sound recordings by Belgium, the German Federal Republic, Italy, Luxembourg, and the Netherlands; and on films by Chile and Sweden.[70]

Further to promote the free flow of information Unesco has worked for reduction of postal, freight, and telegraph rates. At the 1952 Congress of the Universal Postal Union, the UN agency that fixes international postal rates, Unesco proposed changes in international postal regulations, which were adopted. Some thirty nations have acted on these recommendations. As a result, it is easier and cheaper to send books, periodicals, newspapers, and other printed matter from one country to another. One measure approved was a revised international system through which a person can subscribe to a foreign newspaper or magazine, pay for the subscription in his own national currency at his local post office, and receive the publication at reduced mail rates. Unesco has recommended that its member states revise their postal regulations to remove obstacles to the flow of ideas.

While postal reductions apply to individual copies of a book, newspaper, or magazine sent from one country to another, freight rates affect bulk shipments sent to bookstores, newspaper dealers, and other agencies. In August 1953 Unesco requested the International Air Transport Association, representing ninety-five percent of the world's civil aviation traffic, to cut rates on certain types of air freight. As a result books were granted a discount up to one-third the normal cargo rate in Europe and up to one-half in other areas. Unesco planned next to seek similar reductions in ocean freight rates for educational and scientific materials.

Newspapers and news agencies have long been concerned about high telephone, telegraph, and radio rates, as well as by delays in transmission, that limit coverage of news, especially in less developed areas. Smaller newspapers cannot subscribe to news services, let alone maintain correspondents abroad, and even the major agencies and newspapers cannot give their readers sufficient information. With the backing of international associations of newspapermen, Unesco has acted as spokesman of the public interest in this matter. In 1949, at a meeting in Paris of the International Telegraph and Telephone Conference, the United Nations body which establishes international rates, Unesco submitted proposals to reduce press rates and expedite transmission of press messages.

It was evident that the complex question of the international press-rate structure needed further study. Unesco commissioned a British newspaper editor to investigate the matter, and in 1953 published his findings in a volume entitled *Transmitting World News*. The study recommended measures to facilitate transmission of press messages; Unesco communicated their substance to member states, with a proposal that they be considered for submission to the next session of the International Telegraph and Telephone Conference scheduled for 1958.

The Economic and Social Council also requested Unesco and the International Telecommunications Union[71] to examine the transmission of press messages. The resulting study, entitled *The Problems of*

Transmitting Press Messages, was sent by the Economic and Social Council in 1955 to telephone, telegraph, and radio services throughout the world. It recommended abolition of taxes on all communications, and lower rates on ordinary press telegrams, press telephone messages, and certain radio communications.[72]

Censorship is another great obstacle to news-gathering. The International Telecommunication Convention explicitly allows governments to stop messages. A number of governments have used this provision as justification for censorship of press dispatches.

In connection with a conference at Buenos Aires in 1953 of the International Telecommunications Union, Unesco recommended that its member states support a United States amendment to the Convention which proposed abolition of censorship. The amendment was not adopted, but the conference recommended to governments measures to facilitate the free transmission of news. The Director General of Unesco is to formulate proposals which would incorporate the substance of this recommendation in the Convention. These proposals could be taken into consideration by member states represented at the 1959 conference of the International Telecommunications Union.

Recognizing the importance of world public opinion in the effort to reduce obstacles to the free flow of information, Unesco publishes every year a study to acquaint the public with issues in this field. In addition to *Transmitting World News,* mentioned above, Unesco has issued *Trade Barriers to Knowledge,* a manual of tariffs and regulations affecting educational, scientific, and cultural materials. This survey, made with the assistance of *The Economist* of London and covering ninety-one states and territories, proved of value to publishing houses, film libraries, and organizations interested in importing or exporting such materials. A succeeding publication was *Books for All,* a study of international circulation of books and obstacles encountered.[73]

Unesco and the Advancement of Knowledge

What can one say in conclusion about Unesco's program for advancing knowledge as discussed in these two chapters?

Within each of the major fields of education, science, and culture, its projects have been of five distinct kinds: collection and dissemination of technical information (clearing-house activities); strengthening professional contact among scholars and specialists (nongovernmental organizations); mobilizing of special talents on particular problems (meetings, conferences, and seminars); publications for professional audiences; and, finally, the opening to a wider public of the attainments of scholarship, the arts, and philosophy.

The program has evolved gradually. Its principal weakness in early years lay in the absence of clear criteria for deciding what activities Unesco should engage in. At first, literally no proposal however narrow its focus, however small the number of persons to be benefited, could be ignored by the secretariat because criteria of selection were lacking. Valuable weeks and months of staff time were spent in correspondence, meetings, conferences, and even top level discussions on many proposals that should have had no claim on the organization's time. They came from governments, individuals, sometimes from within the secretariat, sometimes apparently from nowhere at all. Translating somebody's favorite book, getting some person or group to a conference, recognizing some one-man organization, publishing someone's pet research—scores of demands descended upon Unesco with a claim that each would "advance knowledge." Choices of projects were therefore not always wise. Many consumed considerable time and money to produce a meagre result. Conferences and seminars were frequently called without a clear purpose or adequate planning for follow-up. More publications were proposed than the organization could produce efficiently at reasonable cost, or distribute effectively on a world-wide basis.

Objective criteria were slow in adoption, as were also the means for evaluation, not only because they might block pet projects, but also because both member states and the secretariat wanted action and were impatient of any delay caused by study or planning. As the contrast between needs and resources compelled critical choices and as the program took on a more rational shape, selection and evaluation became more acceptable.

In the early years most initiative for program planning came from the secretariat in Paris, partly because of the urgency to get action under way quickly and partly because member states only gradually became clear themselves as to their own pressing needs. Only gradually also did professional groups become articulate as to their desires. The natural scientists alone seemed ready almost from Unesco's beginning to make clear-cut demands upon the organization to aid in the advancement of knowledge. The social scientists, by contrast, were limited in number and slower in stating their needs.

Unesco was most effective in helping advance knowledge where its own limited resources could be multiplied into greater efforts through the work of national and international nongovernmental organizations or through governments. In such cases it was able to complement activities of existing organizations (as in the case of the International Council of Scientific Unions); respond to clearly defined needs of special professional groups (teachers, or persons interested in exchanges of persons) or of particular countries. It was able to help both professional groups and individuals.

Its work was most difficult, conversely, where the area of concern had been largely unexplored by other agencies (e.g. in the arts), or where the subject (the social sciences, for example) was relatively underdeveloped in most countries of the world.

Its work was relatively unsuccessful where its task required contacts with people not easily reached through established professional channels (mass communication activities and general sales of publications).

Subventions to Nongovernmental Organizations

During Unesco's first decade one problem relating to the advancement of knowledge became a subject of much controversy. Unesco from the beginning has granted subventions to nongovernmental organizations (NGO's), which now amount to six percent of the annual budget.[74] This practice has raised certain questions of principle and policy.

Debate first centered upon grants to international nongovernmental organizations in natural science. Some scientists expected Unesco to give fairly substantial sums to the organizations included in the International Council of Scientific Unions, to permit them to expand their activities. Debate turned on the basic issue of Unesco's purpose and whether all of Unesco's projects should immediately contribute to international peace. One school argued that subventions merely helped scientific endeavor and did not advance the prospects for peace. Many scientists declared that support for science, which is international, contributed to international understanding, and that leading scientists might exert a salutary influence on foreign policies to further the cause of peace. As the issue over Unesco's purpose gradually became less prominent and general acceptance was found for the three goals of human welfare, international understanding, and advancement of knowledge, the debate about natural science subventions began to subside.

New problems arose, however, concerning financing of nongovernmental organizations in other fields. Many of these organizations had little financial support outside the Unesco grants, which raised the question whether they would become permanently dependent upon Unesco's assistance. The question of subventions was related to contracts, which were often awarded to international organizations to perform services for Unesco, and at the same time helped to keep the organizations going. In some countries, like the United States, where large private funds are available for nongovernmental professional activities, the government is disinclined to favor public financial aid through Unesco, even to international NGO's. But in many, if not most other countries there is no such opposition and public funds are seen as an appropriate source to help maintain NGO's of both a national and an international character. At the insistence of the General Conference, criteria have been developed for granting subventions,[75] and a system of review adopted whereby the Executive Board and the General Conference examine both subventions and contracts.

A continuing problem is what proportion of the annual budget should go into subventions and contracts. The decision must depend on the effectiveness of the NGO's as compared with other means of carrying out Unesco's program. It is likely, however, that subventions for advancement of knowledge will receive a diminishing percentage of the total budget as Unesco concentrates more on major projects and on aid to member states of the kind discussed in succeeding chapters.

Attitude of Governments and Specialists

Governments have signified their approval of most Unesco projects in more positive ways than merely by conference votes. Many have actively cooperated in Unesco's clearing house in education. Others have taken over and continued projects started by Unesco such as the national fundamental education training center in Liberia; the university science faculty at Baghdad, with a carefully planned curriculum and well-equipped laboratories; the Cologne Social Science Institute, which has considerable aid from the German government; a permanent observatory at Quetta in Pakistan for research on earthquakes, earth magnetism, and weather; two centers in Yugoslavia, one for making scientific and technical documents more widely available, the other to produce school furniture and equipment.[76]

Although member state support of projects is recorded in the General Conference and although many member states participate in Unesco projects such as the educational clearing house, the extent of active governmental support is still limited. There are great differences among nations as to the proper role of government in relation to the advancement of knowledge. There are also basic constitutional questions in federal governmental systems regarding the role of national governments in dealing with such matters through international relations. Projects to strengthen professional contacts through nongovernmental organizations attract the attention of specialists but have had less systematic support from governments. The distribution and sale of Unesco publications have not had major support from governments and the organization's work for the advancement of knowledge remains largely unknown except among small professional groups.

Certain Unesco projects for the advancement of knowledge have won support from other international agencies. The United Nations Economic and Social Council in 1950 called attention of governments to the "practical importance" of the Agreement on the Importation of Educational, Scientific, and Cultural Materials earlier mentioned. The Committee of Ministers of the Council of Europe in 1953 urged governments to "take the necessary steps to obtain its ratification with a minimum of delay."

The attitude of specialists has been shown in the vigor with which they have fought, in National Commission meetings and in the General Conference, for Unesco projects in their own fields. In this the educators and natural scientists have been most outspoken. More significant, perhaps, is support coming from organized bodies of professional opinion. For example, the Unesco Agreement on the Importation of Educational, Scientific, and Cultural Materials was backed in numerous countries by more than twenty private organizations, including the International Publishers Association, the International Federation of Newspaper Editors and Publishers, the

League of Red Cross Societies, and the International Council of Women. Many testimonials have endorsed specific Unesco projects. For instance, the Curator of the Perth Museum in Australia testified that the traveling exhibition of color reproductions "proved a great stimulus to the art-loving public and created considerable interest among those to whose notice it brought the work of some contemporary artists for the first time."[77] Unesco's *Bulletin for Libraries* was termed by the Chief Assistant Librarian of the United States Library of Congress "the ideal of what such a publication should be."[78]

However, not all specialists have approved everything Unesco has done in their field. The usefulness of the *Index Translationum* has been questioned in various quarters.[79] Many writers and artists regard Unesco's activities in the arts with indifference if not hostility. Sometimes what seems a successful activity to one specialist may appear to another to create new problems.

Over the decade the secretariat, Executive Board, General Conference, and member states became clearer as to the organization's real potential and as to the methods best suited to the advancement of knowledge through Unesco. Greater maturity at all levels, including the level of governments of member states, contributed to growing efficiency and increasing effectiveness.

CHAPTER VII

Education and Human Welfare: FUNDAMENTAL AND ADULT EDUCATION

We come now to the third major field assigned to Unesco by member states: promotion of human welfare by an attack on world-wide educational, scientific, and cultural problems. In this chapter we examine Unesco's work in fundamental and adult education. In the following chapter we shall review its work in primary, secondary, and higher education.

Fundamental Education

What is fundamental education?

The Marbial Valley in Haiti is situated a few miles inland from the small southern port of Jacmel. The 30,000 to 40,000 inhabitants live in scattered wooden huts; there are no villages. In 1947 the region was plagued by overpopulation, soil erosion, and declining agriculture, and in consequence by poverty, undernourishment, and illiteracy. An eleven-month drought threatened famine. A less promising site than this dying valley was difficult to imagine. It was to be the scene of one of Unesco's earliest efforts at fundamental education.

The Marbial Valley Project

The purpose of the Unesco project was to attack illiteracy, providing the people with elementary instruction and a few simple skills that would help them raise their standard of living. It was to be a joint undertaking by the Haitian government and Unesco. It would train teachers and field workers for other parts of the country, and eventually be taken over by the Haitian government. The project was marked by a series of ups and downs which illustrate most of the problems found in such enterprises, including the critical one of assigning responsibility among various United Nations agencies.

Only after Unesco had committed itself to this undertaking did it arrange for what ideally should have been a prior step—a survey of the area by a competent social scientist. The survey was started in April 1948 by an anthropologist of international experience, assisted by several Haitian social scientists. In the meantime, as a result apparently of the eagerness of the Haitian authorities and particularly of the Marbial peasants, some health and educational activities were begun as the first step in a program of self-help. The Unesco anthropologist reported that the road or track into Marbial from Jacmel was impassable much of the time, that safe drinking water and suitable housing for the staff were lacking, and that there was friction over the project between the Catholic majority and the Protestant minority. Nevertheless he recommended that the project go forward, and he was supported by a United Nations mission then making an economic study of the whole Republic. The first director was appointed in June 1949, but he soon ran into difficulties with Haitian officials which led to his resignation. At this stage the undertaking reached its lowest point. The Valley's inhabitants lost faith in the enterprise and it became a laughingstock in the eyes of government officials at Port-au-Prince.[1]

In January 1950 the project took a turn for the better with the arrival of a new director, an administrator of long experience in the British Colonial Service. He was able to remain only twelve months, but recruited a staff of competent and interested Haitians, and the World Health Organization provided a doctor and a nurse. (As a result of WHO cooperation the disease of yaws, which had formerly affected eighty per cent of the people, was eliminated.) Faith in the enterprise revived and a clinic and dispensary, a community center, an industrial crafts building, and a dormitory and mess hall for the staff were constructed. By 1952 the enterprise had begun to train workers to carry the rudiments of practical education to illiterate peasants in other parts of Haiti. The Unesco center was serving as a demonstration point, with a primary school providing two classrooms for 105 pupils, a clinic conducted by a physician and a dentist, a small stock-raising station for poultry and pigs, and nurseries for vegetables and small trees. A credit cooperative had attracted more than a hundred members. Eight hundred people were attending adult classes conducted in nineteen small open-air centers, with an average of forty adult pupils in each group.[2]

Of the three groups of student-teachers graduated by the summer of 1953, the first was at work in the Marbial Valley itself, the other two elsewhere in Haiti. Additional provinces had requested the Marbial project to train instructors. These teachers returned to their own villages to lead in carrying out local improvements. Prominent villagers were marshaled to undertake soil conservation, improvement of roads and water resources, and construction of local education centers, clinics, and markets.[3] By agreement with the Haitian government, Unesco terminated direct assistance to the Marbial project at the end of 1953, but continued to help it as an "associated project."[4] Work in the Valley was carried forward by the Haitian government, primarily through rural schools, with assistance from graduates of Unesco's regional fundamental education center at Patzcuaro in Mexico.

Unesco's experiment in the Marbial Valley suffered more than its quota of mistakes. Its preparatory stage took two years. Success was uneven. Methods of cultivation were improved, but the problem of poor soil remained far from solution. Yet the people of this "forgotten valley" were learning to help themselves and others. Unesco's decision to work in such an unpromising area seemed to have been justified by its results in the Valley and in Haiti as a whole.

The experiment was also of value to Unesco, which may have learned more from it than from other activities judged more successful. It learned that in such projects a thorough preliminary study of the area is necessary in order to understand the people's way of life and special problems. Unofficial support, such as that given in the later stage of the Marbial undertaking by Catholic priests and Protestant churches, is helpful. Official support, especially in economic development, is needed if the initial impetus is to be sustained. Coordination of educational effort with agricultural, health, and other technical services, including assignment of responsibilities among several interested United Nations agencies, is essential but not always easy. The people must recognize that the purpose of outside help is to stimulate them to help themselves. They must understand what is being attempted and why. It is important to develop a sense of community participation through constructive cooperation by the local inhabitants. Literacy campaigns require expert guidance, solution of tough linguistic problems, and provision of appropriate reading material.[5] This last point is of great importance. Ability to read is useless unless there is something to read.

War on Ignorance and Illiteracy

The Marbial project illustrates what Unesco means by "fundamental education." This term, if not created, has at least been made current by Unesco. Half the people of the world—more than 1,200,-000,000, it is estimated—do not know how to read and write. Dr. Torres Bodet called the line that separates those who can read from those who cannot the "most unjust of all frontiers." He added: "We have terrible memories of the concentration camps, but we sometimes forget that, without prisons or barbed wire, more than 1,200 million men and women live in the implacable, invisible, inner dungeon of ignorance."[6] Only one person in two throughout the world can read the statement in the Universal Declaration of Human Rights proclaiming that "Everyone has the right to education."[7] Nor is there any prospect of early improvement. In many countries the number of children is outrunning the capacity of the schools. In 1952 at least half of the approximately 550 million children of school age (5-14 years) in the world were not in school, and of the remainder over four-fifths had not gone beyond the primary level. Thus of every ten children, five had no chance to go to school, four would not go beyond the primary grades, and only one could enter high school or college.[8]

Illiteracy is unevenly distributed throughout the world. According to the latest statistics available (estimated in some cases), the countries of northern Europe, Hungary and Czechoslovakia in Eastern Europe, the United States and Canada, Australia and New Zealand have come close to wiping out illiteracy. In Russia and Poland the proportion of illiterates has been reduced to nineteen and twenty-five per cent respectively; in countries of southern and southeastern Europe, such as Italy, Spain, Rumania, and Yugoslavia, it is around twenty-five per cent. In Latin America the percentage ranges from fourteen for Argentina to around fifty for Brazil, Mexico, Peru, and

Venezuela, seventy-four for the Dominican Republic, eighty for Bolivia, and ninety for Haiti. In Asia, outside Japan (where illiteracy has been almost eliminated), the rate is high—in the forties for Ceylon, the Philippines, and Thailand; fifty-six per cent for China, eighty-one for India, and ninety-two for Indonesia. For Africa the rate for the Belgian Congo is estimated at sixty-three per cent, and for Egypt and most areas south of the Sahara it runs in the eighties and nineties.[9]

Illiteracy is not only an obstacle to economic progress but to progress in the war on ignorance, poverty, and disease. True, illiteracy is not synonymous with ignorance. Many illiterates have a great store of folk knowledge and wisdom. But illiteracy makes for ignorance of the discoveries of modern science on hygiene and health, agriculture, and nutrition; and for ignorance of other peoples who live beyond the horizon. Thus ignorance is usually linked with underproduction and undernourishment, bad sanitary conditions, and endemic disease. It is both a cause and a consequence of such conditions.

The tremendous magnitude of the task confronting Unesco in fundamental education was recognized from the start. Within half an hour of the signing of the Constitution at the 1945 London Conference, Sir Alfred Zimmern, speaking to the first meeting of the Preparatory Commission, stressed Unesco's responsibility to help countries where large masses of human beings live "in conditions not only of poverty but of ignorance, and of removable ignorance."[10]

Unesco's potentialities in the war on ignorance and illiteracy were shown by its magnetic effect in drawing together widely dispersed persons and groups interested in fundamental education. Such groups had had little chance to compare methods, and little help from outside their own countries. Through discussions at London and later at Unesco headquarters in Paris, efforts associated with such names as Margaret Read of London, James Y. P. Yen of China, Jaime Torres Bodet of Mexico, Frank C. Laubach and Henry W. Holmes of the United States, and experiments of nearly half a century in colonial territories of the United Kingdom and in the Philippine Islands, were all brought to bear upon Unesco's task. Much of this material was assembled and published by Unesco in a volume edited by Dr. Holmes and entitled *Fundamental Education: Common Ground for All Peoples.*[11]

Expert opinions and records of various experiments were marshaled to help work out a practical plan to meet appeals from such newly independent countries as India, Burma, Pakistan, and later Indonesia, as well as the vaguer desires being voiced in the Middle East and Latin America. Colonial powers also, especially Great Britain, were showing a new awareness of the rising aspirations of subject peoples. The British Colonial Office was providing new types of training for its field staff. Every colonial power faced a popular demand for self-government and higher standards of living.

Unesco's immediate task was to stimulate awareness of the problem, define terms, and identify the best methods of work. It organized meetings of specialists, educational missions, and, perhaps most important, exchange of information on current projects. Provision for "associated projects" seemed at one stage to be a particularly ingenious scheme. Through this clearing-house arrangement Unesco would be kept informed of experiments, successful or unsuccessful, in many parts of the world. Ideas on fundamental education could be tried out systematically and the results compared.

Some of Unesco's early activities did not distinguish sharply between "fundamental education" and other kinds of education. This was true of its educational missions and of some conferences and seminars. In the initial stage of the Unesco program several member states requested guidance in working out their educational problems, and Unesco responded by sending an international team of specialists.[12] Some of these requests involved both reform of existing schools and fundamental education campaigns for illiterates. The first Unesco mission was sent in 1949 to the Philippines, a country devastated by war and newly independent. The mission examined primary education, adult education, and teacher-training.

Partly as a result of a Unesco mission to Afghanistan in the same year, sixty rural primary schools were opened by the government of that country and a new institute for secondary school teachers was set up; the agricultural college was reorganized and the engineering college enlarged. An educational mission to Burma in 1951 was a factor leading to doubling the budget for education and launching plans for 1,000 new elementary schools, 200 junior high schools, and 40 senior high schools, together with a new normal school. A Unesco mission requested by Pakistan in 1951 outlined methods for a national fundamental education campaign, with particular attention to education of women, fostering local arts and crafts, and improvement of agriculture.[13]

Unesco conferences and international seminars for teachers helped to spur member states to attack their educational problems. Unesco from the start encouraged educational leaders to meet and work together. In 1947 the organization sponsored two regional study conferences on fundamental education, one at Nanking and the other at Mexico City, just prior to the Second Session of the General Conference. In 1948 Unesco cooperated with the Organization of American States in a regional seminar held in Venezuela to discuss literacy campaigns and rural education. A result of this meeting was another seminar held the following year at Quitandinha in Brazil, dealing with measures by the American Republics to promote literacy and adult education. In the same year, 1949, a seminar on rural adult education was held at Mysore in India with representatives of fifty-six countries and territories.

UN Technical Assistance Program

A new phase in Unesco's fundamental education program began in 1949 with the launching of the United Nations Expanded Program of Technical Assistance. This program brought to light the fundamental importance of basic education to economic development and to the whole effort to raise living standards and to bring new nations into the world society. As noted elsewhere, the United Nations program of technical assistance had a tremendous impact on the methods and pace of Unesco activities.

When planning for the United Nations technical assistance program got under way, it became clear that full success would be achieved only by closer coordination among the specialized agencies than had been evident in the Marbial project. It was equally clear that at least three of the specialized agencies—FAO, ILO, and WHO—as well as the economic and social activities of the United Nations itself, needed the fundamental education approach that had become central in Unesco's work with less economically developed countries. Implicit in the idea of fundamental education is its impact on poverty and disease as well as on ignorance.

Ability to read and write is a step toward a better life, including improved housing, health, handicrafts, better agriculture and nutrition, and greater individual and community capacity to develop roads and bridges, schools and clinics, cooperative markets and community centers. It seeks to stimulate consciousness of human dignity and develop a sense of the cultural and moral solidarity of mankind. Fundamental education aims at achievement *by* the people rather than simply *for* the people.[14]

This also was the aim of the United Nations technical assistance program. With its advent came an attempt to define the part of fundamental education in a wider enterprise, that of "community development," which required a coordinated effort by several United Nations agencies. The idea of a "total approach" to community problems had to develop slowly, through experience. By 1956 the agencies concerned were able to reach an agreement defining their respective parts in the common task. Under this agreement central coordination, at least in planning, is the responsibility of the United Nations itself; and Unesco's concern is education.

How could Unesco best play its own part in the "total approach"? The experiments of its early years had by 1950 identified three main lines of activity: determining what were the best methods and materials for fundamental education; assistance to member states in applying such methods; and training specialists and field workers in their use, together with preparation of materials.[15]

Finding the Best Methods and Media

Transferring new methods and skills in fundamental education to multitudes of people in widely separated parts of the world, speaking hundreds of languages and dialects, is an extremely complicated task. In its efforts to assist member states, Unesco has worked out a sequence of operations. First, exploratory studies, promoted by the secretariat in Paris, to find out what methods are used in fundamental education in various parts of the world; then, meetings of specialists to analyze these practices and define the problems; third, field experiments for testing through specific projects how best to apply these methods; and finally, publication of the findings.

The question of what language to use in teaching illustrates this sequence. Both children and adults are best taught in their mother tongue. But often in many underdeveloped areas a vernacular is spoken by a relatively small group and has never been written down.

In one African territory more than 500 languages exist, of which only four have been put into writing. In other cases the national government is trying to establish a national language which is not the mother tongue of a large part of the people. The problem may be complicated by social and political considerations as well as by the technical problems of developing an alphabet for an unwritten language, outlining its structure, and listing its vocabulary, in order eventually to produce primers, readers, and dictionaries.

As early as 1947 Unesco called together a group of linguists to examine the problem of language in bringing education to illiterate or semiliterate peoples. The question became important in the initial stage of the Marbial Valley project in Haiti. Member states were queried for information and meetings of experts studied the problem. Several field experiments were carried out. Reports on various approaches have appeared in Unesco's *Educational Studies and Documents,* and elsewhere.

When it is decided what language to use in a given area, the next question is what methods to employ in teaching reading and writing. There are, broadly, two different approaches to this problem: those that begin with learning the alphabet and those that begin with learning phrases. William Scott Gray, formerly of the University of Chicago, was enlisted in 1952 to examine this question, and in 1956 a report was published reviewing the origin and development throughout the world of various methods for teaching adults as well as children, noting their advantages and limitations, and attempting to appraise their effectiveness.[16]

Applying Methods and Media

Unesco's second task in fundamental education is assisting member states in the application of methods and media. Libraries and museums can be useful instruments. An examination of how the library can be used in fundamental education was published as part of the report of the Unesco Seminar on Public Libraries held at Malmö, Sweden, in 1950. The seminar stressed the need for public libraries in the less developed countries. This factor was emphasized in the location of subsequent seminars on public libraries at São Paulo, Brazil, in 1951 (held in cooperation with the Organization of American States); at Ibadan, Nigeria, in 1953; and at Delhi, India, in 1955, where principles worked out at Malmö were applied to various geographical regions.[17] At the Ibadan seminar, the West African Library Association was organized; later the government accepted almost all the seminar's recommendations, approved library legislation, and established a regional library board.[18] At the Delhi meeting participants organized a committee to establish an Asian Federation of Library Associations, which would serve as a clearing house for library problems in that area. This committee was to encourage the formation of library associations throughout Asia.

The Delhi Library, opened in 1951 under the auspices of Unesco and the Indian government, illustrates the contribution of public libraries to fundamental and other education. It was the first modern, free public library in India. It has developed an extension program by depositing small collections of books at centers where adult literacy classes are held, thus seeking to bridge the gap between the person who has just learned to read and write and the habitual user of books. A mobile van extends services to literacy campaigns throughout a wide area. The library has produced for new literates easy-to-read material in vernacular languages. Answers to a recent questionnaire by library users indicated that one-fourth of them had no opportunity to read before contact with the library and that nearly half had no books whatever at home. During its first four years the library loaned almost a million books to its 20,000 listed readers. In 1956 it had on its shelves 62,000 volumes in Hindi, Urdu, and English, and was serving 2,000 readers a day.[19] During the first five years Unesco contributed to this project slightly more than $60,000, while the central and municipal governments, which furnished the building and most of the staff, contributed at least four times as much. In 1956 the Indian authorities assumed full responsibility for direction and support of the library, which, however, is still linked with Unesco as an associated project.

The Saõ Paulo seminar led to the founding of a similar pilot library at Medellin, Colombia, sponsored by the government and Unesco.[20] A third project was planned for Eastern Nigeria in 1957.

Museums, like libraries, are an important aid to education. At Unesco's seminars on the educational role of museums, at Brooklyn in 1952 and Athens in 1954, attention was given to the needs of fundamental education. Simple fundamental education museums were established at Unesco's centers at Patzcuaro, Mexico, and Sirs-el-Layyan, Egypt, as experimental projects.[21]

Experiments have been carried on in the use of visual aids—films, filmstrips, and posters. A Unesco seminar in 1953 at Messina reviewed the problems involved.[22] Unesco has published pamphlets such as *Visual Aids in Fundamental Education, The Use of Mobile Cinema and Radio Vans in Fundamental Education,* and *Radiò in Fundamental Education in Under-developed Countries.*

Radio has also proved a useful ally in some situations. In Sutatenza, an isolated hamlet high in the Colombian Andes one hundred miles north of Bogota, a young parish priest, Father José Joaquín Salcedo, started a campaign against illiteracy with the first educational broadcasts heard in Colombia. Around this village small farmers scratched out a livelihood from precipitous mountain slopes. According to local legend, some farms were seeded by shotgun. Two-thirds of the peasants could not read or write. The tavern was the principal source of diversion and alcoholism was widespread.

Today, as the result of generous gifts from the peasants themselves, an annual grant of $800,000 from the government, and some technical aid from Unesco experts, Colombia's most powerful transmitter broadcasts six hours daily to an estimated audience of 200,000 people gathered at 6,000 radio schools. The movement is called *Acción Cultural Popular.* Radio schools have been set up in villages and tiny hamlets, equipped with specially designed receivers installed in the homes of leading peasants, some of whom have given up one of their two rooms for this purpose. Local helpers follow instructions from the invisible radio instructor and write the lessons on the blackboard. Receiving sets and batteries are sold to the radio schools at a cost price of $18 and with them goes free a stock of chalk, erasers, textbooks, and an alarm clock to warn when the lesson time has arrived.

Lessons, starting at six o'clock in the morning, include reading and writing, agriculture, hygiene, history, religious instruction or civics, and a daily newscast. These are rebroadcast in the afternoon. Evening programs consist of music, news, variety shows, religious talks, and dramatic performances. *Acción Cultural Popular* publishes simple teaching materials and a monthly bulletin for the radio schools.

Father Salcedo sought Unesco's assistance in testing the teaching materials and methods employed. Two members of a Unesco technical assistance mission, brothers of a Catholic teaching order, prepared a series of posters which, reduced to book size, were used in the radio schools as primers for a six-month course in reading and writing. One of the brothers described the task as devising "teaching aids for a school where the teacher is blind and deaf and the pupils are completely mute." The posters were tested by being used in a special class made up of six stubborn women who previously had refused to have anything to do with the educational campaign. Described as "the rear guard of the march toward literacy," they consented to attend class only if paid to do so.

Five hundred thousand literacy charts and textbooks for the radio schools were distributed during 1955. Another Unesco mission, consisting of a French specialist in printing textbooks and a Mexican expert in textbook illustration, has worked on a training course for local assistants. The course is planned to train each year approximately 400 students who will supervise the group-listening of adults and children in the villages. By the middle of 1956 it was estimated that 120,000 persons had learned to read and write through the broadcasts of Radio Sutatenza.[23]

Acción Cultural Popular is aware of the inevitable limitations of its approach and of the need of working with other agencies. Its programs on contour plowing and other agricultural activities are prepared by an official of Colombia's Farm Credit Fund. A broadcast on the use of insecticides is followed by classes using posters, and by distribution of pamphlets. The local helper in the radio school assists pupils who have developed an interest. At this stage rural agents of the Farm Credit Fund enter the picture to teach farmers how to use insecticides on their farms. Similar efforts have been made to improve rural housing.[24]

Preparing Workers and Materials

Unesco's third task was to aid in training workers and preparing materials. In cooperation with the Organization of American States, Unesco set up at Patzcuaro, Mexico, in 1951 its first international training and production center. The Organization of American States also established in Washington, D. C., the Latin American

Fundamental Education Press, to produce reading materials specially adapted for fundamental education. FAO, ILO, WHO, and the United Nations Technical Assistance Administration (UNTAA) agreed to help at Patzcuaro by supplying members of the teaching staff. Former President Lázaro Cárdenas contributed his mansion, together with adjacent buildings and sixteen acres of land. The Mexican government provided new construction and land to the value of $100,000. Latin American governments were invited to send teams of five mature persons with experience in fundamental education, agriculture, handicrafts, home economics, cooperatives, health, and recreation. The team idea was stressed because of the need for concerted action on various phases of rural development. The governments agreed to continue the students' salaries during their course of study and to pay their transportation to and from the international center.

The four functions of the Regional Fundamental Education Training Center for Latin America (CREFAL) are teacher training, production of educational materials, technical and experimental studies, and practical assistance to nearby Tarascan villages. Some sixty-five students are admitted each year. The nineteen-month course at CREFAL is divided into three periods. In the first, lasting six months, students attend classes covering both theoretical and practical aspects of fundamental education, and produce primers, posters, films, filmstrips, and plays for puppet theaters. During the second period, of ten months, students organized in international teams of five spend most of their time in field work in surrounding villages. Here methods and materials prepared at the Center are applied and tested. Each student must live for a month in the community where he is working. For the final period of three months students are back again at headquarters, reviewing in classes and seminars what they have learned and thinking ahead to applying it in their home countries.[25]

By a special resolution approved at the 1951 Session of the General Conference, the Patzcuaro center was made part of a proposed world-wide network of six fundamental education centers, which in the course of a twelve-year period would be set up in Latin America, Equatorial Africa, the Middle East, India, and the Far East (where two centers were planned). These would have as a goal the training of 5,000 fundamental education specialists.[26] This proposal required more funds than were available from Unesco's regular budget. When special gifts did not materialize, the enterprise was limited to what could be financed from the regular Unesco budget and funds assigned to Unesco under the United Nations technical assistance program. With establishment of a second center at Cairo it was recognized that outside Latin America and the Arab states, no other regions of the world enjoyed a common language and culture permitting an international center to serve a group of countries. Emphasis was therefore shifted to establishment of national centers.

The Patzcuaro center has attracted students from two countries outside Latin America—Pakistan and the United States. Pakistan, in connection with a project to set up regional training centers for rural leaders, sent ten educators, agricultural experts, and social workers to study at Patzcuaro in 1954-55. The students, in addition to what they learned at CREFAL, taught fishermen on Lake Patzcuaro how to make their nets last two or three times longer than before; and in one Tarascan village the Indians have given up their traditional beds of mats strewn on the floor to sleep on Pakistani *charpoys*—simple wooden beds with mattresses of woven strings.[27]

The United States arranged for five students in 1955 and another five in 1956 to attend the Patzcuaro center. On return they were to work in Puerto Rico, in the U. S. Indian Service, and as rural nurses, librarians, and social workers elsewhere in the United States.[28]

Unesco's second international center, the Arab States Fundamental Education Center (ASFEC), was set up in January 1953 at Sirs-el-Layyan, a good-sized rambling village in the Menufia district of the Nile Delta, about forty-five miles from Cairo. The people of this densely populated area, with approximately 290 persons to the square mile, eked out a meager existence from small plots, many of which were less than one and a quarter acres in size. They shared with their animals the small dark rooms of their houses. Nine out of ten persons were sick from intestinal parasites which swarm in the irrigation canals. Other diseases such as tuberculosis and trachoma were widespread. Sixty-five per cent of the children died during their first five years. More than four-fifths of the people were illiterate.

The students, mature persons whose average age was thirty and who had already acquired a stock of practical experience, came to the Center from nine countries—Egypt, Iraq, Jordan, Lebanon, Libya, Saudi Arabia, Syria, Yemen, and the Sudan—and from among the

Palestine refugees. The teaching staff, including representatives of four United Nations specialized agencies besides Unesco, was even more widely international.[29] The purpose of the center was similar to that of Patzcuaro—to train teachers and field workers and to develop materials simple in language but of interest to adults in meeting their own practical problems. Sixty students were admitted each year. Work in the surrounding villages gave an opportunity to test and apply what had been learned, and at the same time to better the life of the *fellahin*. For part of each week during the second year, students resided overnight in the villages.

Perhaps the most significant achievement in field work at Sirs-el-Layyan, made possible by the aid of the more intelligent peasants, religious leaders, and young people who were awake to the need of progress, was a cooperative spirit in communities which were formerly riven with factional and religious rivalry, and whose people were suspicious of all outsiders. At the village of Deberki, possessing the least fertile land of the region, the peasants formed a cooperative and purchased a tractor. At Fisha, where Muslims and Coptic Christians had long been at odds, a house-to-house disinfection campaign was carried out and a theater was built. The plays presented, written first by an Iraqi student at ASFEC and later by the villagers themselves, satirized their own faults and those of government officials.

More important than concrete improvements was the change in the spirit of the people. The great need was to free peasants from their submissive, fatalistic acceptance of poverty, misery, and suffering, and to develop self-respect and consciousness of individual capacity and dignity. The students at Sirs-el-Layyan came to define fundamental education as cooperation with the people to be educated. Such work is a truly revolutionary enterprise which may modify the whole mentality of a people.

When a kindergarten was established in a shady courtyard at Fisha, it was a local peasant who donated the courtyard; volunteers built the kitchen, the shower, and the playground. For the public library opened at Sirs-el-Layyan, the building and grounds were given by the miller, the bookshelves were built by the carpenter, and everyone, it would seem, supplied the books.

Nor were peasants the only ones who profited by the cooperative process. One Egyptian student testified: "I am an engineer and have long been in charge of a major State agricultural enterprise. In other words, I did not come to the centre to learn my business. But what I did learn there at first dumbfounded me. I did not know that one could 'fraternize' with the *fellahin;* I am ashamed to admit this now, but it is the truth. If the centre had taught me nothing else, it would have taught me a great deal; you may try to help people with the best will in the world, but if you treat them as inferiors you are wasting your time."[30]

In the workshops at Sirs-el-Layyan, at Patzcuaro, and at the Latin American Fundamental Education Press in Washington, much material was prepared for newly literate adults. Textbooks, pamphlets, posters, and wall newspapers were produced. At Patzcuaro a new process was worked out for reproducing simply and inexpensively posters and other graphic material. At Sirs-el-Layyan pamphlets and posters were issued on gardening, beekeeping, control of insect pests, hygiene, and nutrition. Filmstrips were prepared on farming, home improvement, and the use of audio-visual materials in teaching. It was recognized that much of this material would need to be adapted for use in particular countries. The government of Mexico, with Unesco's aid, set up an educational film institute for Latin America.

Appraisal of the Fundamental Education Centers

At first, many people regarded fundamental education as a self-sufficient program for rural development, mainly through education supplemented by technical services in such fields as agriculture and health. It was initiated before the United Nations Expanded Technical Assistance Program had been launched and before the UN and its specialized agencies had developed service activities in the economic and social field. With the spread of such activities in public health, agricultural extension, rural industries, social welfare, and community development, fundamental education has come to be regarded as one element—the educational arm—in the general United Nations program for social and economic development. To clarify the relation of fundamental education to, for example, community development, the UN Administrative Committee on Coordination (ACC) initiated in 1955 an examination of all the activities involved in the UN effort to improve rural welfare.[31]

The appraisal focused particularly on Unesco's two regional fundamental education centers and the relation of their activities to the needs of participating countries. Two missions representing the UN, FAO, ILO, WHO, and Unesco surveyed the centers at first hand and discussed their work in visits to several countries in both areas.[32] Subsequently the reports of the two missions were reviewed by an inter-agency working group meeting at Paris in March 1956, and in May by the ACC itself.

How effective have the two centers been? The use made by governments of the graduates represents one significant test. CREFAL at Patzcuaro produced during its first four years (1952-55) 227 graduates from 18 out of the 20 Latin American Republics (all except Argentina and the Dominican Republic). These graduates have been used in four ways: (1) to staff national fundamental training centers (for example, in Cuba, Honduras, and Venezuela); (2) to direct fundamental education projects in the field (in Costa Rica, Haiti, and several other countries); (3) to supervise rural education, including fundamental education for adults (in Bolivia, Guatemala, and Peru); and (4) in the capital to head sections on fundamental education in the Ministries of Education or Indian Affairs (Bolivia, Ecuador, and El Salvador). One of the early Mexican graduates was appointed as a specialist on women's education with the Unesco Technical Assistance Mission in Iraq. Ministers of Education have in general expressed satisfaction with the work of the centers and the usefulness of the graduates. Applications for training grants have been double the number available.[33]

The ACC appraisal mission for Latin America reported on results in only four countries visited—Bolivia, Ecuador, Mexico, and Nicaragua. Of sixty-eight graduates who returned to these republics, sixty-one were in work which made use of their training in fundamental education. Most of them had been placed in supervisory positions or in teacher-training institutions, except for those in Nicaragua, who were carrying forward a fundamental education project on the Rio Coco. Officials in three of the four countries testified to their satisfaction with the character of the CREFAL training and with the work of the graduates. In Bolivia, however, some proposals advanced by the graduates were termed unrealistic and over-ambitious.[34]

At Sirs-el-Layyan 152 students were trained in the first three courses (1952-56). Of the 69 graduates who had returned to the countries visited—Egypt, Iraq, Jordan, and Syria (no Libyan students had yet graduated)—51 were working in positions related to fundamental education. Thirteen were engaged in ordinary school teaching, and the remaining five were in activities unrelated to fundamental education. The proportion in fundamental education varied. It was highest in Egypt (86 per cent), lowest in Syria (22 per cent), and in Iraq and Jordan stood at 73 per cent. Only one-third of the graduates were engaged in field projects. In Iraq some dissatisfaction with ASFEC graduates was voiced, but officials were enthusiastic in Jordan and in the UN-Unesco educational program for Palestinian refugees.

The appraisal mission for the Arab states concluded that on the whole the results of the training program had not come up to expectations, but recognized that immediate evidence of the value of educational activities is not usually to be expected. The mission reported a belief that ASFEC could provide the trained personnel these countries needed and "a growing appreciation on the part of all governments of the need for trained workers for rural, and in certain cases, urban services." In countries served by the two centers, there was evidently no clear understanding of the type of students to be selected for this special training, the kind of work they should do on return, or the benefits their training should produce.[35]

At both centers the plan had been to train mature students with some educational standing, technical knowledge, and experience, who could on return home become organizers, instructors, and supervisors. At ASFEC students were described as a heterogeneous group, some university graduates and some with a secondary school education or less. At CREFAL the situation was not dissimilar. One solution proposed was to develop two different training courses: a long course (eighteen to twenty-one months) for organizers of fundamental education projects, principals of village institutes, and other positions at the supervisor or instructor level; and a shorter and more intensive course for persons at a higher professional and technical level, such as mature specialists in agriculture and public health.[36]

The basic problem with regard to training, particularly at CREFAL, has been described as a choice between preparing students to work with illiterate rural people, or developing technical specialists in agriculture, health, and home economics who can provide expert knowledge at the farm or village level. CREFAL has centered on the first. In the students' home countries, ministries of agriculture and health are most interested in acquiring technical specialists. Even ministries of education are reported as at a loss where to fit into their pattern the "fundamental educator." He is often used to train rural teachers to expand their activities beyond school walls by working with adults in various community projects.[37]

The idea that students should work in teams, while appealing in theory, did not work out in practice. The original idea had been that each government should choose its candidates for the centers in teams of five, who would be selected not only by the Ministry of Education, but also by such ministries as those of agriculture, health, labor, and social welfare. On return to their own countries they would continue to work as a team. At the centers the students were also to be trained in groups of five, each with experience in a specialized field. Here the groups would be made up of students from different countries, in order to develop an international point of view. But this plan ran into difficulty from the start because in most participating countries each ministry was developing its own field services, with little or no coordination with other government agencies. (Similar organizational problems are faced in countries like India which have national programs for community development.)

Actually, some sixty per cent of the students at ASFEC and almost all those at CREFAL were recruited by ministries responsible for education. Only a minority of the candidates had any experience or training in agriculture, health, or home economics. In Latin America only half of the participating governments were using graduates in fundamental education teams. In Arab countries no ASFEC graduates were employed as interdepartmental teams; they worked only for individual ministries. In some cases students trained as members of teams were unwilling or unable to work as individuals. Certain governments viewed the team approach as too costly and too difficult to organize.[38]

While Unesco's two regional fundamental education centers had not succeeded in developing interdepartmental teams or in training any significant number of specialists whose previous experience had been outside the field of education, the ACC at its meeting in May 1956 concluded that the centers should be continued, provided major adjustments were made by governments in their choice and use of students and by the centers in their training programs. It was hoped that the centers could become increasingly useful as inter-agency institutions in the United Nations work for rural development.

The ACC outlined the future functions of the centers as follows:

"(a) to provide regular courses in fundamental education of eighteen to twenty-one months for persons mostly selected by Ministries of Education;

"(b) to provide short specialized courses in different aspects of education for social and economic development for persons drawn from various Departments of Governments concerned (these courses should be jointly planned, where appropriate, with the agencies concerned);

"(c) experimental study of educational methods and communication techniques in relation to development programs;

"(d) the production of tested prototype educational materials (books, films, filmstrips, posters, etc.) for use in rural development." Closer contacts between the centers and the various ministries in the participating countries were also recommended, as well as the use in individual countries of inter-agency committees.[39]

National fundamental education teacher-training centers, as we have seen, were set up in Cuba, Honduras, and Venezuela by graduates of CREFAL. These national centers represented the first step toward the original purpose of Patzcuaro and Sirs-el-Layyan. These international centers were to train leaders who would return to their own countries and in turn train an increasing number of other leaders. In addition, national centers began to sprout in various countries not represented at either Patzcuaro or Sirs-el-Layyan. A field project started in 1951 at Klay in Liberia, some twenty miles north of Monrovia, developed into a national training center from which thirty teachers graduated in June 1955. Returning to their home villages, they would act both as teachers in rural primary schools and as fundamental education field workers, linking the improvement of community life with expansion of elementary schools.[40] Other national training centers were opened at Ubol in Thailand[41] and at Delhi.

At the first stage, Unesco's efforts to stimulate the production of reading materials were directed mainly toward literacy campaigns and fundamental education centers. With advances in the teaching of adult illiterates, and with the expansion of primary education, the demand increased for periodicals, books, and pamphlets in simple language to conserve and develop the reading and writing skills of the "new literates." At least some of this material needed to be exciting as well as informative. Without it there was danger that what had been gained would soon be lost. Accordingly, the 1954 General Conference at Montevideo authorized the Director General to assist member states in planning and producing reading materials for new literates. It was suggested that these materials be of varied character, including adaptations of literary classics, folktales, material on arts and crafts, as well as publications dealing with housing, agriculture, health, citizenship, and human rights. During the initial period attention would center on South and Southeast Asia, particularly Burma, Ceylon, India, and Pakistan, which had voiced active interest.

Unesco's task was not to write or translate materials, but to enlist the services of experts; to help train personnel by granting fellowships; to provide advice and information on the principal producing agencies in other parts of Asia, Africa, Latin America, and the Pacific; to encourage publishing agencies to conduct research and experiments; and to issue reports on such aspects of publication as writing and testing, editing and distribution.[42] Information was already available bearing on earlier experience in various parts of the world, including the Latin American Fundamental Education Press of the Organization of American States, and on experiments in India and Burma and in such parts of Africa as the Belgian Congo, East Africa, the Gold Coast, and Nigeria.[43]

While Unesco's efforts to stimulate fundamental education in member states involved occasional errors and fell short of expectations, the growth of the movement in 1946-56 has been striking. At the start Unesco's capital was a single book (*Fundamental Education: Common Ground for All Peoples*) and the interest of a small number of specialists and officials throughout the world. Many governments were skeptical, including the French. More recently the territories of French Africa have shown a marked increase in this type of activity, which is due in large part to Unesco's stimulus.[44] Similar developments are taking place in connection with many of the almost sixty national enterprises in twenty countries linked with Unesco as "associated projects."

Adult Education

Although "fundamental education" is hard to define, experience has shown that Unesco's work in this field, in cooperation with other UN agencies, has met a genuine need of member states. In a related field, "adult education," there has been a similar need for aid from Unesco, but even greater difficulty in defining precisely what kind of aid is required. The phrase has different meanings in different countries. In a country with a high degree of illiteracy "adult education" becomes synonymous with fundamental education. In some highly industrialized countries it has come to signify primarily workers' education, which in turn may mean technical training to improve working skills, or training in trade-union organization, or cultural development and appreciation of the arts, or some combination of these. In many countries adult education is viewed as a means of promoting international understanding.

However, adult education during the decade under review has been principally associated by Unesco with the world-wide spread of democracy. Efforts to insure strong democratic systems in the new states of Asia, aspirations for democracy in African territories, the desire to achieve it in fuller measure in many of the Latin American republics, the struggle to maintain and expand it in various countries of Europe, the hope to regain it among some Soviet satellites— all testify to the necessity of equipping the common man to play his part as a citizen. Thomas Jefferson declared in 1820, "I know no safe depository of the ultimate powers of society but the people themselves; and if we think them not enlightened enough to exercise their control with a wholesome discretion, the remedy is not to take it from them but to inform their discretion by education."[45]

Combined with this democratic foundation for interest in adult education have been the rapid advances in technology which have increased the need for technical training and also the money and leisure available to the average worker. In many countries both the demand and the opportunity for adult education have been enlarged, either because today's adult missed educational opportunities in his youth, or because the changes in modern society require supplementary education to enable the adult to meet his present responsibility.

Unesco early faced the problem of defining adult education. Should the definition be broad or narrow? Broadly, a large part of Unesco's program is concerned with the education of adults. But the definition used by Unesco for this sector of its work is much narrower. In Unesco terminology and practice, "adult education" excludes fundamental education and higher education, but includes both general or "liberal" education and technical education. It is directed toward the continuing education of those adults (largely in the developed countries) who are literate but whose schooling often has not gone beyond primary or a limited degree of secondary education. Unesco has worked in this field in close cooperation with the ILO, which deals with vocational and technical training.

The need for definition became apparent in the International Conference on Adult Education which met under Unesco sponsorship at Elsinore, Denmark, in June 1949. The discussions revealed that adult education varied so much from country to country that it was impossible to frame a definition satisfactory to all. The best the conference could do was to declare that "adult education has the task of satisfying the needs and aspirations of adults in all their diversity." Its aims were listed thus: to foster a common culture which would narrow the gap between the "masses" and the "classes"; to stimulate a spirit of democracy and tolerance; to give to youth, in the face of world disorganization, "hope and confidence in life"; to restore the feeling of "belonging" to people isolated in an age of specialization; and to cultivate a sense of membership in the world community.[46]

Thus, as one speaker at Elsinore stressed, adult education should help the individual to find his place in the life of the modern world. He needs to understand his role as a worker, as a citizen with responsibilities, and as a personality in relation to other personalities. The task of adult education is to "help every man to become himself" and to be more a brother to his fellows by being more himself.[47]

The Elsinore Conference agreed that the time was not ripe to set up an international organization for adult education. Instead Unesco was requested to serve as a link among national leaders and organizations and private international organizations, a function which it has continued to perform with the aid of a Consultative Committee. To help educators learn what was being done in countries other than their own, Unesco published a volume entitled *Adult Education, Current Trends and Practices,* and in 1952 an *International Directory of Adult Education,* the first such survey since 1929. A third volume, *Universities in Adult Education,* reported experience in Canada, England, and the United States. Unesco has also published a series of discussions jointly with national educational journals.[48] Its quarterly *Bulletin of Adult and Fundamental Education* has carried articles and information on current developments.

Following recommendations from the United States and other member states, favoring a larger place for labor in Unesco's plans and activities, and the development of closer relations between Unesco and international workers' organizations, Unesco decided, in order to make its responsibilities in adult education more manageable, to focus for a period primarily on workers' education. As a result various international workers' organizations were given representation on Unesco's Consultative Committee. During 1952 and 1953 seminars and summer schools were held at the International Center of Workers' Education at La Brevière, near Compiègne, France. Some of the meetings were organized by Unesco itself and others by international workers' organizations.

By the end of 1953 it had become clear that while the meetings at La Brevière were theoretically international in character, they had benefited primarily those whose need was least, the urban workers in Europe and North America; and even in this area, differences had arisen between the American idea of training leaders for the labor movement and the European idea of a broader cultural education for workers. Consequently it was decided to decentralize the project. Member states were assisted by Unesco in holding regional seminars on regional problems. These met in Austria, France, and Jamaica in 1952, in the Dominican Republic and Italy in 1953, in Belgium in 1954, in the Scandinavian countries and Italy in 1955, and in Belgium, Chile, Poland, the United Kingdom, and Yugoslavia in 1956.

A Unesco seminar on rural adult education was held in Denmark in 1954. Unesco helped four international workers' organizations to hold conferences from 1954 through 1956 in different parts of the world: the International Confederation of Free Trade Unions, successively at Calcutta and the Gold Coast in Africa; the International Federation of Christian Trade Unions, Chile and Togoland; the Federation of Workers' Educational Associations, in the Gold Coast and Austria; the International Cooperative Alliance, in Haiti and Austria.[49]

The original emphasis on exchange of information, study groups and conferences, and the La Brevière center on workers' education, has shifted to adult education in the less developed countries, improvement of methods, and a sharper focus on international understanding.[50]

Some Unesco National Commissions have cooperated in seminars and conferences held with Unesco's assistance. In the field of adult education in the arts, seminars were held in 1956 in Germany and Sweden, organized by the National Commissions concerned. Both dealt with methods used in industrial and agricultural areas to encourage adults in the practice and appreciation of pictorial art, music, and theater. In the same year Unesco sponsored short holiday painting courses for workers in Austria, Belgium, Italy, and the United Kingdom.

Individual countries have carried on significant experiments. In 1954 Unesco collaborated with the French Broadcasting and Television Service in telecasts on rural life addressed to "tele-clubs" in villages east of Paris. These clubs had developed as a result of the limited number of television sets in France. Villagers had raised funds among themselves to purchase sets, which were installed in the village school and used by adults and children. Thirteen telecasts designed for adult education were given, dealing with modern methods of farming, credit cooperatives, community spirit, and other rural problems. This approach illustrates the similarity of adult education and fundamental education even in a country as developed as France. Each telecast was followed by a discussion in the local tele-club, often lasting far into the night. The response to these programs was so enthusiastic that a second series was given in 1955, showing how French country people had overcome specific difficulties.[51]

On request of the Italian government, Unesco sent Roger Louis, initiator of the French tele-clubs, to Rome to help educators and broadcasters develop tele-clubs in southern Italy. Unesco has helped Japan in an experiment on using television for adult education in rural areas. Following the visit to France of a Japanese educator on a Unesco fellowship, Japan began preparations during 1956 to telecast a series of programs for rural adult education which would be viewed and discussed by over sixty tele-clubs in areas covered by transmitters in Tokyo, Nagoya, and Osaka.[52]

In the United States the National Commission launched in 1954, as an experiment, a program of "citizen consultations" to examine in discussion groups such topics as the teaching of foreign languages, technical assistance for economic development, the American citizen as traveler and host, and moral and spiritual resources for international understanding. The recommendations of these groups, most of which were sponsored by a university or college, were forwarded to the National Commission to help it in formulating policy. During the first year twenty-eight colleges and universities in twenty-one states cooperated with the National Commission in such discussions.[53]

Unesco's activities in adult education have been more modest and have had less effect than those in fundamental education. They have been allotted fewer funds and a much smaller staff, and they have not been pushed with the same crusading zeal. Nor are results as immediately apparent. The situation may be likened to the education of a child, whose early progress in learning to read and write is obvious, but whose later advances in knowledge are more gradual, more complex, and less easy to see. Yet adult education cuts across most of Unesco's program areas, and experience accumulated in this field may make more effective almost every aspect of Unesco's work.

CHAPTER VIII

Education and Human Welfare: FORMAL EDUCATION

Extension of Free and Compulsory Education[1]

Fundamental and adult education may prove a losing enterprise unless schooling at the primary grades is rapidly expanded. The world's population is growing at the rate of one per cent annually, which means that 23 million prospective pupils are born every year.[2] As indicated in the preceding chapter, not more than half of the world's children of school age are now in school, and four-fifths of those in school do not go beyond the primary stage. Of these about half complete only the first two grades. One educator has estimated that children who have less than six years of primary education may forget how to read and write as they grow older.[3] Thus, the number of illiterates in the world is still on the increase, and fundamental and adult education will have to run fast even to maintain the present percentages of literacy.

During the nineteenth century primary education spread widely in Europe and North America, in response to national needs rather than, as earlier, to religious motivation. Industrialism with its reliance on science and technology required literate workers. Industrialism also, during the nineteenth century, increased ten-fold the national income of the economically advanced countries, thus providing the financial resources to expand primary education.[4] The spread of democracy, and the growing recognition that expenditures on education were a profitable investment in the development of national resources, stimulated the demand for wider schooling, which has expanded in the present century throughout Latin America, Asia, and Africa.[5] These factors stimulated development of compulsory education at public expense.

A whole complex of educational problems facing member states shaped their requests to Unesco. These problems included planning and financing the expansion of primary and secondary schools; improving the quality and quantity of teacher training; encouraging educational research; developing a well-rounded curriculum adjusted to both local and national needs; constructing school buildings; assuring equal access to education by girls and women; and, as will be seen in later chapters, encouraging understanding of international affairs and a broader world outlook.[6]

Approval by the United Nations General Assembly in 1948 of the Universal Declaration of Human Rights provided Unesco with a special incentive beyond the mandate in its constitution for activities in education. Article 26 declared: "1. Everyone has the right to education. Education shall be free, at least in the elementary and fundamental stages. Elementary education shall be compulsory. Technical and professional education shall be made generally available and higher education shall be equally accessible to all on the basis of merit."

The Size and Nature of the Task

The need throughout the world for free and compulsory education may be illustrated by a glance at the situation in certain important regions. In South and Southeast Asia[7] live approximately 600 million people, or about one-fourth of the world's population. Nine states in the region have achieved independence since World War II. According to current estimates, out of a total of 95 million children of school age, 55 million are not in school. Because the birth rate is high while the death rate, particularly among children, is declining, the proportion between the child population (six to twelve years of age) and the adult population is almost twice that of a country like England.[8] Thus in predominantly agricultural areas with per capita national incomes far lower than in Europe and North America, the burden of full compulsory education is double that of most European countries.

In Afghanistan ten per cent of the boys and one-third of one per cent of the girls of school age are in school. India, according to a 1948-49 survey, had schools for one-fourth of its children of school age. In Pakistan two-thirds of the children of school age had no opportunity for education. Although in Thailand almost all the children subject to compulsory education were in school, three-fifths of them in 1950 were in the first grade and only one-tenth had reached the fourth grade.[9] Throughout the area the demand for teachers exceeded the supply. Many teachers were untrained—more than one-fourth in Ceylon and Indonesia, more than one-third in India, about one-half in Pakistan, and four-fifths in Thailand. In most countries of the area, crowded classes and double sessions were common, equipment was scant and poor, school buildings were run down and sometimes entirely lacking, with classes meeting in the open air.[10]

But popular demand for education was growing rapidly, and among those in authority there was increasing recognition that education is basic to economic development. Governments were expanding educational facilities and some of them were stretching their resources to the limit. In 1952 Burma reported that sixteen per cent of its national budget was devoted to education. In the same year Afghanistan declared that it had increased by twenty per cent the budget for its Ministry of Education; two hundred new schools were opened in that year, as part of a campaign to establish 1,000 three-year schools. Article 45 of India's Constitution calls for free and compulsory education throughout the country by 1961. Indonesia has a ten-year plan to prepare for universal compulsory education for children and a parallel plan covering the same period for a fundamental education campaign to eliminate adult illiteracy. Its teacher-training program is expected to provide by 1961 enough teachers to make possible the introduction of compulsory primary education.[11]

Despite these efforts it was clear that the resources of these countries were not sufficient for the rapid progress their people were demanding. In India the estimated cost of universal primary education was greater than the present income of the central, state, and local governments combined. For the long pull the countries of South Asia must depend upon gradual economic growth to raise national income and make possible universal primary education.[12] But their own resources, technical and material, are at present inadequate.

The situation of the Arab states[13] is more favorable. The potential wealth of the region is greater than present economic conditions suggest. The economic problems of some countries stem not so much from absence of natural resources as from the difficulty of using them. In addition to vast reserves of oil, the Arab states possess other mineral riches, and the river valleys in Egypt, Iraq, and Syria are important sources of agricultural wealth. Yet much of the land is not cultivable. Libya and Saudi Arabia are almost entirely desert, and there are considerable desert areas in other countries. Industry is nowhere highly developed. While defective tax systems have kept government revenues low, the national income of all the countries except Libya, Jordan, and Yemen is probably adequate to carry out plans for educational expansion.[14]

The general educational position of the Arab states is midway between the high and low extremes.[15] Considerable advance has been made in recent years but much remains to be done. As regards compulsory education, the best conditions are found in Lebanon, Syria, and Jordan, where the schools provide for approximately three-fourths of the children of school age. Practically all boys are in school, but facilities for girls need improvement. Conceivably, effective compulsory education could be achieved in these three countries within five years. In Egypt the primary schools serve about half the children of school age. In Iraq the proportion is lower, roughly forty per cent. In the lowest group are Libya and Saudi Arabia, where modern education is only slowly taking hold. Within ten to twenty years, it is estimated, most of the Arab world could attain full compulsory education.[16]

This estimate is based on the significant progress already made. The number of government primary schools in these countries had increased from 750 in 1915 to over 10,000 in 1955. During the decade 1944-54 enrollment in primary schools had grown in Iraq from 90,000 to 258,000; in Jordan from 9,000 to 104,000; in Lebanon from 28,000 to 79,000; and in Syria from 77,000 to 245,000.[17] All the Arab states had statutory provisions for free education, at least at the elementary level; the majority had made primary education compulsory.[18]

Yet every Arab-speaking country still suffers from shortages in educational facilities, qualified teachers, school buildings and equipment. Curricula and textbooks are inadequate. The most serious lacks are in school buildings and teacher training. No country has yet achieved complete primary education, and the situation in secondary and higher education is even less promising. Educational advance has been made more difficult by the rapid increase of population and the influx of Palestinian refugees.[19]

In all the Latin American republics laws prescribing free and compulsory education have existed for thirty-five to nearly a hundred years, but in many cases these laws have not been fully enforced. The last thirty years have seen much progress; two republics have made primary education practically universal. Yet about half the children in the region are still without school facilities. The percentage varies from approximately twenty in some countries to almost seventy in others. Further, more than half the children who do go to school drop out within the first two years, and only about one-fifth complete the period of compulsory education.

The situation is particularly acute in rural areas, where four-fifths or more of the children have no schools. Here educational advance depends largely upon economic improvement and community development. The most feasible road to progress seems to be expansion of rural community schools where the teacher conducts classes for children and also helps adults in solving their practical problems.[20]

Recommendations and Regional Conferences

This brief sketch indicates the extent of the need and the complexity of the problem. We must remember that considerable assistance has been available from private sources as well as from bilateral programs such as that of the United States and from the Colombo Plan and other regional undertakings. But how have member states used Unesco to increase educational opportunities for the children of the world? In the first place, Unesco has helped to dramatize and spotlight the problem. Second, it has spread information on existing needs and practical ways to meet them. One country has been benefited by knowing what another country has done. Third, some tangible aid has been provided through Unesco. Progress along these three lines has been achieved through international meetings, publication of information, fellowships to teachers and educational officials for study abroad, and the loan of advisers and technical experts.

Unesco's effort to stimulate advance in free and compulsory education originated with the Fourteenth International Conference on Public Education sponsored by the International Bureau of Education and Unesco at Geneva in 1951. To provide this conference with factual material, Unesco sponsored studies on compulsory education in six countries, of which three had already achieved full compulsory education (Australia, England, and France), and three others were moving toward that goal (Ecuador, Iraq, and Thailand). Two more general publications were issued, one a comparative review by I. L. Kandel of the *Prolongation of Compulsory School-Age,* and the other *Child Labor and Compulsory Education* prepared by the International Labor Organization.[21]

The Geneva conference addressed to Ministers of Education a "recommendation" on compulsory education and its prolongation. It cited the Universal Declaration of Human Rights and particularly the language in the Draft Covenant on Human Rights under consideration by the United Nations, providing that any signatory state which had not achieved universal free and compulsory education should, within two years, work out a detailed plan to attain this goal within a reasonable period.[22]

It was recommended by the conference that the period of compulsory education, fixed in some countries at five, six, seven, or more years, should gradually be extended, as progress was made toward construction of schools. Increasing the number and improving the quality of teachers was also stressed. Since adequate financial support was essential to any forward movement, the recommendation recognized that account must be taken of a country's general economic position and its system of taxation, and emphasized that any plan for expansion of education should be coordinated with plans for economic and social development. It urged the International Bank for Reconstruction and Development to consider long-term loans to countries undertaking plans for expanded compulsory education, and requested Unesco, in consultation with other United Nations agencies, to formulate a program "to co-ordinate all sources of assistance now available, explore the possibility of loans, and raise funds from voluntary contributions."[23]

These proposals were translated into more specific terms through regional conferences on compulsory education held by Unesco at Bombay in 1952 for the countries of South Asia and the Pacific; at Cairo in 1954-55 for the Arab states;[24] and at Lima, Peru in 1956 for the republics of Latin America.[25] (Conferences may also be held in Africa and East Asia.)

Delegates at these conferences, a number of whom represented states that had just achieved independence, recognized that lifting the economic and social level of their people called for a bold forward step in the realm of education. They had to reconsider how schools could help to develop the human resources of their countries, retaining what was valuable in ancient tradition while introducing new knowledge that would be useful in attaining higher standards of living.

The value of the regional conferences was enhanced by published studies on the status of compulsory education in individual countries, reports from National Commissions, and a volume on economic conditions and compulsory education in Latin America. The Cairo conference provided the first opportunity in the history of the Arab states to consider their educational problems on a regional basis. As one of the Jordanian delegates remarked, "If there was nothing but that we all put our cards on the table and frankly discussed our problems and difficulties, that was enough."[26]

All these gatherings faced the basic question of how to finance more schools. At the Bombay conference delegates stressed the international character of the problem. They argued that if one-quarter of the world's population is left to struggle in the slough of poverty and misery, social and political unrest may develop into a threat to world peace. The need for compulsory education far exceeds the international help already available from the United Nations and its specialized agencies. Military aid has been given on a large scale; compulsory education, it was argued, requires action on a comparable scale. The Asian nations recognized that they must tap every possible domestic source, but they urged that the possibilities of outside aid be explored: grants from private foundations for pilot projects, research activities, and training programs; bilateral assistance from the United States and other countries; financial and technical assistance from regional enterprises like the Colombo Plan; grants or long-term low-interest loans from the International Bank for Reconstruction and Development, particularly for buildings and equipment.[27]

As a result of the Bombay meeting the Unesco draft program for 1955 and 1956, presented to the General Conference at Montevideo in 1954, included a proposal for "a movement through the machinery of the United Nations for the establishment of an International Educational Development Fund," later called the International Fund for Education, Science and Culture. Each dollar provided by the Fund would be matched with one or more dollars from receiving countries, and the money would be used for capital expenditures on school buildings and equipment and for teacher training.[28]

In 1951 the United Nations General Assembly had attacked a similar but broader problem. It requested the Economic and Social Council to prepare a plan for a Special United Nations Fund for Economic Development (SUNFED), which would provide grants and low-interest long-term loans to less developed countries. In the initial period of the technical assistance program, a good deal could be done with relatively small amounts of money. Visiting specialists could provide useful knowledge and advice; personnel could be trained through grants of fellowships; better methods of sanitation and farming could be taught.[29] But it was not long before the economically less developed countries reached a stage where larger amounts of capital were required, if progress was to continue. Only with such sums available over long periods of time could these countries build roads and other means of transportation, provide the power needed for industry and agriculture, and construct factories and schools. At the General Assembly meeting in December 1953, the SUNFED plan was compressed into a proposal, contingent on "sufficient progress" in internationally supervised world disarmament, to devote part of the savings thus achieved to assist less developed countries.[30] Discussion of the proposal continued from 1954 to 1956, but no action was taken. The governments best able to help were already contributing to the United Nations technical assistance activities, the Colombo Plan, and bilateral aid operations, as well as to the Arab refugees and Korean reconstruction.

The Unesco General Conference at New Delhi in 1956 recommended that the Director General prepare a plan for a Unesco fund separate from SUNFED, and request the International Bank for Reconstruction and Development to consider granting loans for the construction and equipment of schools, colleges, and universities of member states.[31] At this writing the prospect for international assistance through the Unesco fund remains as remote as that for SUNFED itself.

Following the Lima conference on compulsory education in 1956, a proposal was worked out for a long-term project to expand compulsory free primary education in Latin America, to run for six to eight years, with emphasis on training normal school teachers and educational specialists. This proposal was approved as a major project by the 1956 General Conference at New Delhi.

The project will go forward along five lines: (1) extension of primary education particularly in rural areas; (2) improvement of primary school teacher-training, both qualitative and quantitative, again with emphasis on rural school teachers; (3) preparation of normal school staff at the Inter-American Rural Normal School founded by the Organization of American States at Rubio, Venezuela; (4) university courses for curriculum experts, principals, and administrators; and (5) provision of fellowships.

Unesco and the OAS would jointly help individual republics to analyze their problems and outline a plan of action. Financial responsibility would fall principally on the countries themselves, if possible, with some aid from outside through bilateral or multilateral agreements. Individual governments would be mainly responsible for the three major aspects of the task: construction of school buildings, teacher training, and improvement of teachers' salaries.[32]

Finally, Unesco was able to provide some specialized aid to member states for the extension of free and compulsory education, but only on a limited scale. Following the Bombay conference, fellowships relating to compulsory education were awarded to senior educational officials in Cambodia, India, Indonesia, the Philippines, and Thailand. At the invitation of the Indonesian government a Unesco expert made a year's study resulting in recommendations on compulsory education, teacher training, curriculum improvement, and teaching methods. A specialist in Burma made suggestions on a new primary school program; another in Thailand on extension of the period of compulsory education from four to seven years.[33] The 1954 General Conference earmarked funds in the "participation program" to respond to requests for experts, equipment, and fellowships for training abroad. A New Zealand educational adviser was made available for a two-year term to the governments of Iraq, Jordan, and Lebanon. In Yemen, the country's first modern girls' school was to be established, staffed by women teachers from other Arab countries.[34] In all, some forty countries have been given assistance through specialists, fellowships, and equipment.

Access of Girls and Women to Education

A special problem in compulsory education has to do with women and girls. A leader of women in Pakistan has said, "Teach a man and you teach one person. Teach a woman and you teach a whole family."[35] The Universal Declaration of Human Rights proclaimed that women have the same right to education as men, but practice in many countries does not conform to this principle. Tradition and prejudice have made it difficult and at times impossible for girls to attend school or to have anything beyond the narrowest kind of education. The Arab states illustrate this problem.

Nearly all these countries have legislation prescribing equal educational opportunities for boys and girls, but not until recent decades have educational facilities for girls existed. In Iraq, between 1931 and 1954, the number of girls in primary schools increased from 7,000 to almost 63,000; in Lebanon from 27,000 to 63,000; in Syria from about 20,000 to 90,000; and in Egypt from 110,000 to almost 600,000. Yet the situation was still not satisfactory. Girls of school age enrolled in schools were markedly fewer than boys. At the time of the Cairo Conference neither Saudi Arabia nor Yemen provided any organized educational facilities for girls.[36]

In 1950 Unesco, at the request of the United Nations Commission on the Status of Women, prepared a report on the world-wide situation, based on the findings of a meeting of representatives of sixteen private women's organizations held at Unesco House in 1949.[37] The Fifteenth International Conference on Public Education at Geneva in 1952 gave major attention to the access of women to education. In preparation for that conference the International Bureau of Education carried out an inquiry in forty-seven countries, dealing with the social, economic, and educational factors which help or hinder the access of women to education. Unesco sponsored studies in Chile, India, and Yugoslavia. This 1952 Conference urged individual countries to examine the access of women to each level and type of education and how women could use the education they acquired.[38]

In a report to the Commission on the Status of Women in 1954, Unesco summarized its efforts to encourage member states to provide more opportunities for primary education and vocational and domestic training of girls and women.[39] In 1953 and 1954 three additional studies were made of educational opportunities for women in Japan, Mexico, and Pakistan.

The conference on compulsory education at Cairo in 1954-55 noted that "Islam urges the necessity of teaching both sexes and considers the search for learning a duty to be observed by every Muslim whether man or woman." It recommended that no distinction be made between boys and girls in providing educational opportunities, and urged all governments to establish the largest possible number of girls' schools and to awaken parents to the necessity of education for girls.[40]

Unesco has also given attention to the participation of women in political life. After a meeting of specialists in 1952, the International Political Science Association and the Social Sciences Institute of Unesco at Cologne undertook a review of the role of women in politics in France, the Federal Republic of Germany, Norway, and Yugoslavia.[41]

International Institute of Child Study at Bangkok

Efforts to extend and improve primary education have led many governments to introduce ideas and methods which have worked well in other countries. This borrowing is often done on a trial-and-error basis, overlooking the fact that a country's system of education must harmonize with its way of life, its traditions, values, and goals. Moreover, educational methods to be effective need to be adapted to the psychology of children, which may differ from country to country.

In recognition of this problem, Unesco secured the cooperation of Thailand to act as host and largely to finance an international institute for research and training on the psychology of education. Following preliminary explorations in Thailand by Professor William Line of Toronto University, and a year's study at Toronto by six Thai educators, the Institute began operation in August 1955. With fellowships for postgraduate training to educators and research workers—one each from Canada, Ceylon, India, Pakistan, and the Philippines—it lost no time in taking on an international character. The findings of the studies made at Bangkok will be compared with those of parallel research at the universities of the Saar and of Toronto in an effort to test whether universal factors can be identified with regard to child development and education. Later it is hoped to extend such collaboration to other research centers in Asia, the Middle East, and Europe.

Cooperating with the work at the Institute are two experimental schools at Bangkok, a teacher-training college at Prasanmitr, and Chulalongkorn University, together with teachers and school inspectors in all parts of the country. It is hoped that eventually the Institute will train each year some fifteen or twenty educators and psychologists from different countries who can help to adjust educational methods to national ways of life.[42]

Unesco has cooperated in other activities which apply the findings of social science and medicine to the problems of the classroom. In 1952 it helped organize a small conference in Europe on education and the mental health of children. It has cooperated with the United Nations, the World Health Organization, and qualified private organizations in studies and publications on mental hygiene in the nursery school, psychological services for schools, and similar topics. It has worked with advisory groups organized by WHO on physically handicapped and mentally subnormal children and with other groups on education of the deaf and training of teachers for handicapped children.[43] In 1956 Unesco provided several social scientists to the Brazilian Center for Educational Research, recently established to adjust the country's educational system to the needs and realities of Brazilian life. Among studies initiated or planned are a survey of the attitudes of parents and teachers toward schools, an analysis of national and racial stereotypes and of social and ethical values found in school textbooks, and an examination of the effect of social classes on educational goals.

Secondary and Higher Education

Unesco's activities in secondary and higher education have been more limited than in fundamental and primary education. Needs in these fields, however great, have been less urgently pressed. Fewer individuals are affected. There are four times as many children in primary schools as in higher institutions.[44]

As primary education expands and the school-leaving age is raised to twelve, or in some countries to fourteen or fifteen, a demand has been voiced for making some form of secondary education accessible to all children. Educators now prophesy that before long there will be as many pupils in secondary schools as in primary schools.[45] Traditionally many countries have had a dual system. Elementary schools were for all, but secondary schools only for a privileged few, who in many cases were going on to higher education. As educational opportunities have broadened, enrollment in secondary schools has risen. Economic development has created a need for workers with technical training, and hence for vocational schools. It has also been asserted that all secondary school pupils, if qualified, should have an opportunity for university education. The job of the secondary school, therefore, is no longer merely to prepare students for college. An "intermediate" school has been growing up which combines general and technical education. Secondary education has become more varied, ranging from the wholly academic to the wholly vocational, with all sorts of combinations in between.[46] Aid provided by Unesco with technical assistance funds has increasingly been applied to the improvement of secondary education, and especially to vocational training.

Unesco has used many methods to assist member states in advancing secondary education—missions of specialists, fellowships, cooperation with the International Bureau of Education in examining the training and status of secondary teachers, with the Organization of American States in a seminar on secondary education held in Chile in 1954, and with the ILO in projects on vocational and technical education.[47] It may be useful to examine here its work on the curriculum.

The Curriculum

Many of Unesco's undertakings have impinged on the curriculum in primary and secondary schools, teachers' colleges, and universities. It has been asked by member states to help improve teaching in numerous fields. In some subjects such as history, geography, and modern languages, and teaching about the United Nations and human rights, Unesco has focused principally on primary, secondary, and normal schools, though not excluding universities. These activities, together with the revision of textbooks, are reviewed in Chapter X, because of their relation to education for international understanding.

In respect to teaching natural sciences, as well as art and music, Unesco's emphasis has been on primary and secondary education, although it has contributed to natural science teaching at the higher level through visiting professors. In relation to the teaching of social sciences, philosophy, and the humanities, on the contrary, its work has been directed primarily toward higher education, with some attention to the secondary stage.

Natural Sciences

A survey of natural science teaching in secondary schools, made in connection with the Fifteenth International Conference on Public Education in 1952, revealed serious deficiencies in many countries. In no more than half of the countries covered was natural science compulsory for all students. The conference viewed science teaching as important not only to train scientists but also as part of general education. It recommended that the teaching of natural sciences in secondary schools should be as extensive as possible and should provide "a common core of knowledge for all pupils between eleven and fifteen years of age," as well as more intensive study for older pupils. It was agreed that science teaching should give the pupil fundamental facts about the world and man, provide some experience in scientific method, strengthen the capacity to observe, and foster love for nature and natural beauty.[48]

Member states have used Unesco in a number of ways. Under contract with Unesco the Oxford University Press has published since 1954 ten handbooks for elementary school teachers, including volumes on the teaching of mathematics, general science, physics, chemistry, biology, health sciences, and rural sciences. In the same year Unesco initiated a series of *Handbooks for Science Teaching in Tropical Countries,* of which four had been published by the end of 1956.[49] An earlier series of reports had appeared on the role of science in education. These included volumes on mathematical statistics, medical sciences, astronomy, chemistry, agricultural sciences, geology, geography, physics, and biology.[50]

A preliminary survey of science teaching in less developed countries was made in 1954, the findings to be used in briefing technical assistance specialists. A broader world survey of science teaching was planned as part of the review of the world-wide shortage in science personnel and teachers.[51] Representatives of fifteen countries of Asia and the South Pacific attended a study conference on science teaching at Bangkok in October 1956. The conference discussed how improved training of science teachers and better methods for teaching science in primary and secondary schools might lead to popular understanding and utilization of science.[52]

Unesco began in 1955 a *Science Teaching Newsletter* designed to promote common interests among associations of science teachers, encourage the exchange of ideas, and report new materials available. It was to be issued in mimeographed form at least three times a year.

In Chapter IV we discussed Unesco's efforts to help revive the teaching of science as part of postwar educational reconstruction. In 1948 Unesco sponsored publication of a small volume to help teachers and their classes make their own scientific apparatus and conduct experiments with makeshift equipment. The booklet was entitled *Suggestions for Science Teachers in Devastated Countries.* While highly useful in devastated areas, it achieved even greater success in countries where actual experiments had not previously been used in science teaching. It went through several editions and was translated into Arabic, Chinese, French, Spanish, and Thai. A revised and enlarged version was published by Unesco in 1956 under the title *Unesco Source Book for Science Teaching.*[53]

Unesco began in 1949 to publish a series of reference manuals to help science teachers in purchasing essential equipment. This series, *Inventories of Apparatus and Materials for Teaching Science,* comprised volumes for primary, secondary, and vocational schools; for universities; and for technical colleges in such fields as agricultural and veterinary sciences, physics and chemical engineering, electrical engineering and medical sciences (the last in cooperation with WHO). A collection of drawings and blueprints for the construction of scientific apparatus for low-cost laboratories has been published. These included equipment used in primary and secondary science teaching, and in training science teachers. With this "do-it-yourself" plan a laboratory can be produced at about one-third of its market price. This scheme is designed for countries with few specialized factories, where machine shops and vocational schools can manufacture ordinary laboratory equipment from local materials.[54]

In the production of scientific apparatus, particularly in the less developed countries, Unesco experts have tried to make a little go a long way. A Canadian science teacher sent to Indonesia on Unesco technical assistance funds found little or no apparatus for teaching science in the schools he visited. With the help of the government he opened a national center for science teaching at Bandung. His classes were made up of students from teacher-training schools and of secondary school teachers. With his students he assembled a simple kit of materials easily available—scissors, a hammer, saw and jackknife, tin snips, rubber tubing, nails, wire, string, some tin cans and burned-out light bulbs, a few test tubes, and glass tubing. He explained,

"With a pair of tin snips and a tin can you can soon make a tripod. Then, with an electric light bulb for a flask and an ink bottle transformed into an oil lamp, you can carry out a whole range of experiments—like expanding and contracting liquids and so on. With a cardboard box, you can soon have a simple camera." The Ministry of Education provided the equivalent of $100,000 for the purchase of the materials needed, and similar kits were sent out to all the elementary schools in the country.

A Unesco expert from Switzerland carried out a similar approach in the Philippines. His students were the science teachers of Manila. They began making simple equipment but ended up, such was their enthusiasm, constructing pressure gauges and even steam engines.[55] The Swiss expert had followed the example of an American teacher sent to Thailand who taught his students to build a "five-dollar laboratory" for elementary science teaching.

With Unesco assistance, science teaching during recent years has been given a place in the school curricula of Burma, Indonesia, Peru, and Thailand; and on the university level science faculties have been established in Iraq and Liberia. Missions of specialists have helped start new programs of scientific research in many lines. For example, Unesco scientists have initiated studies on earthquake problems in Turkey, papermaking in Brazil, and harbor construction in India.

Efforts to improve science teaching sometimes have important by-products. A Swiss specialist headed a Unesco team of scientists sent to Baghdad in 1951 to help establish courses in natural science and to start research at a university level. He was struck by the fact that Iraq, the world's largest producer of dates (whose sugar content is eighty-one per cent), was importing annually 80,000 tons of sugar. In years of large harvests many dates were left to rot since prices were so low that it was not profitable to move the fruit to market. During World War II this specialist, serving as chief of Zurich's Municipal Laboratory, had become familiar with Swiss research on the production of fruit sugar. Experiments in his laboratory in Iraq convinced him that dates could produce white sugar on an economic basis. But the refining equipment needed was in Switzerland. Accordingly, three tons of dates were shipped to Zurich and a short time later one ton of clear white sugar was returned. This was distributed in Baghdad to bakeries and manufacturers of candy and it met all tests. By 1955, in consequence, a factory was under construction in Iraq equipped to produce 9,000 tons of sugar a year, with a saving to Iraq annually of approximately 16 million dollars previously spent for imported sugar.[56]

In its educational work in the field of natural sciences, Unesco has kept in mind the layman and the general public, as well as the scholar and teacher. Traveling exhibitions have reached large masses of people. A quarterly review, *Impact*, discusses the material and cultural effect of scientific discoveries on modern society. Science clubs composed of young people or adults have been encouraged. The work of science writers and journalists has been stimulated. Unesco now administers the Kalinga Prize of £1,000 given by an Indian industrialist, Mr. B. Patnaik, and awarded annually to an author who has furthered the popularization of science.

Social Sciences

The social sciences during the past quarter century have undergone rapid development in a number of countries. Social scientists have contributed to the analysis of modern economic, social, and political problems, and in some cases to their solution. Social science teaching is essential not only to train competent economists, political scientists, sociologists, psychologists, and anthropologists, but also in the education of civil servants, administrators, jurists, journalists, and teachers. These sciences are also useful in giving the responsible citizen an understanding of his own and other societies. However, their development throughout the world has been highly uneven. In a few countries they occupy a leading place; in most others they are neglected.

Unesco began its examination of social science teaching as the result of a resolution approved at the 1950 General Conference at Florence.[57] Its procedure followed a planned sequence, as in its exploration of other new fields. First came an attempt to find out the facts about the status of social science teaching, with results made available in publications. Second, on the basis of this knowledge, general recommendations were drafted by a group of specialists. Third, a series of regional seminars reviewed and adapted the general recommendations to conditions in specific areas, and stimulated the countries in those areas to action. Finally, missions of specialists were provided to member states desiring to organize or reorganize their teaching of social science.

At the start Unesco requested private international organizations in the social sciences to scrutinize social science teaching in eight countries (Egypt, France, India, Mexico, Sweden, United Kingdom, United States, and Yugoslavia). Five booklets were published which provided a comparative review of the teaching of economics; political science; law; sociology, social psychology, and cultural anthropology; and international relations.[58] A second series of booklets described in greater detail the organization and aims of social science teaching in France, the United Kingdom, the United States, and India.

As a second step, these studies were examined by a score of specialists meeting at Paris in 1952. The principal questions before them were: (1) the status of the social sciences in universities; (2) the place of the social sciences in general education; (3) the training and recruitment of university teachers, and teaching methods. The specialists formulated a series of recommendations which were appraised at three regional round tables meeting in 1954, and a fourth held at Rio de Janeiro in 1956. One of these met at Delhi with representatives from South Asian states whose systems of higher education had been influenced by Great Britain and other English-speaking countries; a second at San José, Costa Rica for the Central American and Caribbean countries which had been influenced by Spain; and the third at Damascus for Middle Eastern countries whose universities had been patterned on French models. The fourth centered on the countries of South America.

These conferences all recommended that more attention and larger funds should be made available to promote the social sciences. Training for research, they said, was fundamental to good university teaching. Salaries should be increased to permit professors to devote full time to teaching and research. The round tables also gave attention to the problem of adequate textbooks, some favoring translation of existing texts and others urging the preparation of entirely new textbooks focused on local conditions and problems. These regional round tables were useful in furthering the 1952 recommendations and provided opportunity for an exchange of views on common problems and difficulties.

Finally, to reinforce these recommendations, Unesco offered to loan specialists to a limited number of member states to aid them in developing social science teaching. During 1954 and 1955, a large number of governments, twenty-seven in all, asked for such missions. In 1954 missions were sent to Costa Rica, Guatemala, Pakistan, and Greece.[59] In 1956 Unesco was scheduled to supply professors of economics to Afghanistan, Korea, Spain, Indonesia, and Nicaragua; sociologists to Costa Rica, Guatemala, Italy, and Syria; a teacher of psychology to Cairo University in Egypt; and specialists to assist in setting up social science institutes in Lebanon and Pakistan.

Unesco's survey of social science teaching carried out in 1951 and 1952 had indicated that better instruction in secondary schools was needed as a prelude to university courses. Unesco therefore undertook a comparative review in several countries of the situation in secondary schools. Further, as a background for the general public on how the social sciences can help to solve major social problems, Unesco initiated a series of books written for the layman, and particularly for secondary school teachers and leaders in adult education, which would outline leading theories, methods, and results in social science research. The first volume in this series, on economics, was written by Pierre Mendès-France and Gabriel Ardant.[60] Subsequent volumes were to treat social psychology and other subjects.

Because of the importance of statistics in the analysis of social problems and of the shortage of trained statisticians (especially in the less developed countries), Unesco has cooperated with the International Statistical Institute to improve the teaching of statistics. Assistance was given to the establishment of regional centers at Calcutta (1950) to serve the countries of South and East Asia, and at Beirut (1953) for the eastern Mediterranean and West Asia. Up to 1955 almost 200 students from some fifteen countries had received training at Calcutta; the Beirut center enrolled in its first year some thirty students from seven countries.[61]

Philosophy and Humanities

One of Unesco's earliest approaches to the educational curriculum was in the field of philosophy. Systematic philosophy had traditionally been taught in many countries at the university level, although the question had been raised of extending it to the secondary level. An exploration of the teaching of philosophy in different educational systems was carried out through questionnaires to member states, and the replies were analyzed by a committee of specialists in November 1951. This committee adopted a statement emphasizing the importance of philosophy teaching and urging that it be carried on in a spirit of free research and discussion. Subsequently the results of the inquiry were published in a volume containing suggestions on improvement of philosophy teaching, with particular attention to education for international understanding.[62]

It was not until 1954 that Unesco undertook an examination of the role of the humanities in education. It resulted from the discussion at New Delhi in 1951 on the cultural and philosophic relations between East and West (see Chapter XI). The teaching of the classics and humanities was studied on both secondary and college levels. The inquiry was addressed to National Commissions representing different cultures and to interested private international organizations. This inquiry was linked to the recommendations of a group of specialists in both Eastern and Western classical literature convened in 1955 by the International Council for Philosophy and Humanistic Studies. The latter group explored the possibilities of enlarging the teaching of the humanities in secondary schools and colleges in Eastern as well as Western school systems, so that any curriculum in East or West might include a balanced representation of the various classical heritages of world civilization. It was agreed that people in one culture should have a fairly broad knowledge of other major cultures. It was also emphasized that the teaching of humanities should not aim at an artificial synthesis or unification of cultures but rather at bettering their knowledge of each other.[63]

The Arts

Finally we turn to what Unesco has done about the arts in the educational curriculum. Following two meetings of specialists in 1948 and 1949, Unesco sponsored in 1951 at Bristol, England, an international seminar on the role of the arts in general education; assisted the International Theater Institute in holding two international conferences on theater and youth, one meeting at Paris in 1951, and the other at The Hague in 1953; organized, in cooperation with the International Music Council, a conference on music education at Brussels in 1953; and arranged for Tokyo in 1954 a regional seminar on arts and crafts in general education.

In these international meetings the role of the arts in general education was viewed as unique, since they stimulate not only the intellect but also the imagination and emotions. Through self-expression the individual develops toward self-realization and well-rounded maturity. In schools and colleges teaching of the arts has shifted from stereotyped practices—copying of models—to free expression by creative activity. Adult education has used the arts to release personality. Art education is needed not only for the future professional. It is useful for all children, as well as for adults.

At the Unesco seminar in 1951 it was agreed that no one "best" method of teaching art could be identified. The educational process was a creative experience in which the most important factor was the student. From this seminar emerged recommendations for exchange of teachers, students, and exhibits; publication of a symposium on *Education and Art,* presenting an international survey of art education; and organization of the International Society for Education through Art.[64]

The International Conference on the Role and Place of Music in the Education of Youth and Adults, which met under Unesco auspices at Brussels in 1953, focused on education whose purpose was to develop appreciation and critical judgment on the part of the listener. The training of professional musicians was considered at a conference held a little later in the same year at Bad Aussee and Salzburg in Austria, organized by the Musical Academies of Vienna and Salzburg, and sponsored by the International Music Council and Unesco.[65] Participating in the Brussels meeting were delegates from some thirty countries, plus two hundred individuals and approximately thirty music groups from Belgium, Canada, France, Germany, the United Kingdom, and the United States.[66]

The Brussels gathering requested Unesco to carry out an inquiry on music teaching throughout the world and recommended more exchange of information, persons, and teaching material. It also stressed the contribution of music education to international understanding. Among its results were the publication of *Music in Education* and the founding of the International Society for Music Education.[67]

A seminar on arts and crafts in general education and community development was held at Tokyo in 1954. This was a regional gathering for Southeast Asia and the South Pacific.[68] Its conclusions underlined the contribution of arts and crafts to the development of the individual personality and also to the cultural life of the community. Adults as well as children and adolescents should have opportunity for this kind of education. The seminar also gave attention to the training of professional artists and craftsmen and to the preparation of teachers in this field. It recommended international exchange of information on teaching methods and activities; establishment of national centers for display and sale of handicrafts; exchanges of teaching aids, of original craft work, and of teachers and practicing craftsmen; and publication of a handbook on education through crafts.[69]

From the above it is evident that Unesco activities on school and university curricula have proceeded not according to any preconceived plan, but on a piecemeal basis in response to the needs and requests of member states. Recognition has grown of the importance of seeing the curriculum as a whole in the light of the interests of the ordinary pupil. The extension of education at all levels has required radically new thinking. The curriculum must be related to the country's way of life, its political, economic, and social needs, and the psychological needs of its children. While it was clearly recognized that Unesco had no authority or desire to make even the smallest change in the course of study or the textbooks of a member state, it did have a responsibility to respond to requests for help and to bring together information on the experience of different countries.

In 1956 Unesco established an International Advisory Committee on the School Curriculum to advise the Director General and to assist member states in improving their curricula. The Committee was composed of ten members from Brazil, Burma, Costa Rica, Egypt, France, the German Federal Republic, Japan, the United Kingdom, the United States, and the USSR. An interdepartmental committee on curriculum was set up in the secretariat in 1955, and selected fourteen topics for study by specialists.[70]

Three regional seminars on the primary school curriculum were held in 1956: one at Geneva with participants from sixteen European countries; one near Lima, with participants from fifteen Latin American countries; and one at Karachi, with participants from five countries in South Asia. A publication on the primary school curriculum was planned for 1957, in preparation for study of that topic at the International Conference on Public Education in 1958.[71]

Braille for the Blind

One especially appealing Unesco project has dealt with helping develop a single universal Braille script, which promises great benefit to the seven million sightless persons in the world.

In April 1949 Dr. Humayan Kabir, then Joint Secretary of Education of the Government of India, wrote to the Director General seeking assistance in working out a universal script for the blind. The Indian government had evolved a system known as Uniform Indian Braille which covered the major scripts used in India including Sanskrit, Arabic, and Dravidian. On the basis of this system India was planning larger facilities for education of the blind. But it hesitated to proceed if there were a possibility of developing one uniform system of Braille for the whole world, which would serve for the Roman, Slavonic, Arabic, Indian, and Chinese scripts. It was known that in China, Persia, and the Arabic-speaking countries from five to eight Braille systems were competing with one another, and in other countries the promotion of rival systems further complicated the problem, with the result that the blind themselves were sometimes forgotten in the struggle.[72] During the 120 years since the publication of Louis Braille's system of six raised dots, the system had been modified and reconstructed until often the six dots no longer represented the same letters even in the same language.

Unesco secured the services as consultant of Sir Clutha Mackenzie of New Zealand, a leading authority on Braille who had lost his own sight during World War I. An International Braille Conference under Unesco auspices met at Paris in 1950; its members approved the creation of "a broadly uniform Braille system for all languages and scripts, which would be known as World Braille."[73]

The Unesco General Conference in 1950 took other steps, recommending a World Braille Chart, a reference book on Braille in various languages, and establishment of a World Braille Council. Other meetings worked on the adaptation of Braille to African tribal languages, the problems presented for Braille uniformity by the languages of the Middle East, India, and Southeast Asia, reduction of the differences among Braille methods used in Spanish and Portuguese, and music notation in Braille. By 1954 Unesco had substantially completed the task undertaken in 1949, to assist in developing Braille uniformity, and the World Council for the Welfare of the

Blind had assumed responsibility, aided in 1955-56 by a small grant from Unesco, for adapting Braille to further languages and acting as an international information center.[74]

Unesco and World Educational Needs

The last two chapters have reviewed the efforts made by member states through Unesco to forward human welfare by fostering the development of education. In actual practice these varied activities have not been carried on as a coordinated endeavor, but they have been grouped here for convenience because their purposes seemed closely interrelated.

Although Unesco makes a systematic effort to deal with educational problems of world-wide concern, it is important to recall that its projects are only a small segment of the total effort of governments and private agencies in this field. These national efforts, supplemented often by aid from foreign governments (through bilateral technical assistance from the United Kingdom and the United States, or through regional programs like those of the Colombo Plan and the Organization of American States), have a much more direct and immediate impact than those of Unesco.

Unesco's usefulness to member states comes from the kind of services and stimuli it is peculiarly well adapted to provide. It has furnished an important world forum for discussion. It has helped to develop a climate favorable to national and international action. Its most significant contribution to fundamental education and the elimination of illiteracy, for example, may have been its assistance in creating a world attitude that today prevents any government from remaining indifferent to widespread ignorance among its people. Unesco has helped link together widely separated endeavors, to develop awareness of the cost of ignorance and illiteracy, to spread information on educational needs of individual countries, and to draw together the experience of many nations.

Through Unesco the governments of member states have been able to give new emphasis to their belief that education is indispensable to a country's development; that it is vital for political democracy, for raising living standards, for adequate understanding of the discoveries of modern science, and for cultural as well as for economic growth.

Because Unesco is an agency of its member states, whose particular needs are different even if their general goals are the same, Unesco's projects have not provided a single comprehensive plan for raising educational levels. Its clearing-house facilities serve the whole world, but specific services vary for different states. Unesco's success depends upon its ability to remain sensitive to the diversity of needs while maintaining the unifying idea that the advancement of education is essential to human welfare.

In fundamental education, Unesco has found a major avenue of service to the peoples of the economically less developed countries. Francis O. Wilcox, Assistant Secretary of State (U.S.), has said that "Unesco's work in fundamental education alone . . . would more than justify its existence"[75] and this conviction has been echoed in many other countries by governments and educational specialists. It has been frequently stated by delegates to Unesco conferences. Tangible evidence of the value attached by governments to this kind of Unesco activity was provided when, after the establishment of the first international fundamental education training center in Mexico, nine countries asked to serve as hosts for additional centers: Bolivia, Brazil, Egypt, India, Iraq, Lebanon, the Philippines, Thailand, and Turkey.

Next to fundamental education, Unesco's projects relating to free and compulsory education at the primary level appear to have received the greatest attention from member states. In secondary and higher education, its focus has been largely upon the curriculum, though the finding and training of teachers has been increasingly prominent in its discussions.

The scope and progress of the Unesco program discussed in these two chapters have been due to the readiness of member states for this kind of international cooperation. The professional resources are available in many parts of the world. The needs are clear and the pressure for action is great. Through a good deal of experimentation and as the result of the interplay of many different interests and viewpoints, significant areas suitable for cooperation through Unesco have been identified. Continually apparent, however, as conditioning the effectiveness of Unesco's actions, has been the extent of readiness and the degree of willingness of member states themselves to provide the initiative and steady leadership in meeting their national responsibility to develop educational resources needed for the advancement of human welfare.

CHAPTER IX

Science and Human Welfare

The preceding two chapters have reviewed Unesco's efforts to combat ignorance by improving and extending educational facilities. Here we shall examine projects in which Unesco was asked to help member states apply the resources of natural and social science to some of the world's most urgent problems. These projects related to research facilities on nuclear energy; an international computation center; research on cell growth, on life in arid and humid zones, on oceanic resources, and on adjusting human life to the impact of modern industry and technology. Some projects were highly successful, some failed, and others are still developing.

Nuclear Energy[1]

The European Cultural Conference, meeting at Lausanne in 1949, recommended that international institutes be set up in specialized fields where the cost of research facilities would exceed the resources of any one country. It mentioned as one example an institute in nuclear physics. In the same year a small group of scientists, convened by the United Nations and Unesco, was asked to identify areas of scientific research where cooperative efforts might prove effective. A year later the Economic and Social Council approved a resolution[2] requesting Unesco to appraise in order of priority the outstanding problems of scientific research, to evaluate the ability of existing research centers to explore such problems, to analyze the need for regional international laboratories, and to examine the role of other specialized agencies and international organizations in aiding scientific research.

The next step took place at the session of the Unesco General

Conference at Florence in 1950. On the proposal of the United States delegation, voiced by Professor I. I. Rabi of Columbia University, a Nobel Prize winner, the General Conference authorized the Director General to assist the creation of regional research centers and laboratories in fields where the efforts of a single country would be inadequate. This resolution sought to establish the important principle that Unesco should help stimulate and plan such centers, but should not build or operate them. Informal discussions had led to agreement that the first center should bring together the countries of Western Europe for cooperative research on nuclear energy.[3]

Research on Structure of the Atom

The purpose of the center would be basic research on the structure of the atom, and particularly its nucleus. Such research was needed because the outstanding problem in physics had become the nature of matter—how the atom and especially its nucleus were held together. Around the turn of the century Roentgen, Becquerel, and the Curies had discovered the X-ray, radioactivity, and radium. In the nineteenth century no one had considered that the atom might have an internal structure; but later scientists began to delve into the interior of the atom and its nucleus to discover electrons and positrons, protons and neutrons, mesons and neutrinos. These new investigations, in contrast with the individual efforts of the forerunners, demanded teams of physicists, chemists, mathematicians, and engineers, as well as biologists and physicians. In comparison with the simple and inexpensive apparatus of the pioneers of research, the new studies demanded huge sums for equipment. A high-energy particle accelerator for exploring the interior of the atomic nucleus costs millions of dollars to build and thousands daily to operate. Few governments and far fewer universities could command such resources. Although the United States was rich enough to establish several research centers, many of the countries of Western Europe, where most of the pioneer work had been done, were unable either to provide the necessary equipment or to train their younger scientists for this new and all-important field of research. International cooperation had become a necessity.

Professor Rabi declared at Florence, "We scientists in the United States want to preserve the international fellowship of science, to keep the light of science burning brightly in Western Europe. Moreover, we want very much to help remove a sense of frustration which is growing among scientists of countries which do not have the material means which we have in the United States of America." Rabi urged that Unesco should serve as "the catalyst for the science of the world," emphasizing that Unesco should not run the research center itself, but that its help was needed in making plans and in translating them into reality.[4]

The United States resolution was approved by the Florence General Conference, despite some criticism that it was likely to advance the interests of natural scientists rather than to help mankind in any immediate way to achieve peace. Exploratory consultations were held with leading European scientists. Gifts from the governments of Belgium, France, and Italy made possible an office to continue inquiries, collect information, and maintain contact with interested national and international organizations. The preliminary plan for the European center was developed by the Unesco secretariat, with cooperation from outside scholars and specialists. It became evident that thorough studies on site, equipment, and costs would be essential before governments could commit themselves to this ambitious enterprise. Hence the Director General invited all of Unesco's European member states to a conference in December 1951, attended by delegates of twelve nations. An interim council of representatives of these nations was set up to study the problems involved in establishing an international laboratory and to draft a convention to that end.

Working with a budget of almost $500,000 supplied by interested states, and aided by the Unesco secretariat, the Council carried out its assignment in good time. It organized a scientific congress to survey the general situation in nuclear research and identify problems which might most usefully be attacked by an international organization. It selected Geneva as the site for the center and made plans for buildings and equipment. The Council was labelled CERN (from its French title, Conseil Européen pour la Recherche Nucléaire. Although the name was later changed to European Organization for Nuclear Research, its shorthand title continued to be CERN.). The Convention to establish the permanent organization was signed on July 1, 1953, and promptly ratified by all twelve governments.[5] The cornerstone of the main building was laid on June 10, 1956.

Specifications for the center's equipment were worked out by specialists chosen by the Director General. It will possess a 600 million electron-volt synchro-cyclotron and a 25 billion electron-volt proton-synchroton, which will have five times the power of the largest accelerator functioning in the United States in 1955 (the Berkeley Bevatron). It will take six to seven years to build and will generate particles whose speed will approach the velocity of light. But the research work of the center did not need to await completion of its equipment. It could call on accelerators already built or under construction in France, Great Britain, and Sweden and on resources for theoretical studies such as those of the Institute of Theoretical Physics at Copenhagen, headed by Niels Bohr.

One aspect of the work of CERN stressed by member countries is its training function for young scientists. It is considered essential that junior theoretical physicists be given advanced preparation in nuclear energy research if the impressive equipment at the new center is to be used most effectively.[6] CERN received in 1956 a grant of $400,000 from the Ford Foundation to cover the expenses of research at the center by scientists from countries not members of the organization.

Since the center had early been criticized as likely to forward destructive rather than constructive purposes, its supporters emphasized that its task would be research of a purely scientific and basic character on the structure of the atom and its nucleus. It will have nothing to do with atomic power and its military uses. It was planned to serve as "a common peaceful effort to master the secrets of nature in order to increase the resources of humanity." Its findings will be available to all mankind.[7]

The creation of CERN indicates how Unesco can make an effective contribution at only nominal cost. The idea for the center was crystallized and approved in a Unesco General Conference. The plan was developed, the international conference assembled, and the convention drawn up with the help of the Unesco secretariat. But the governments concerned determined what the agency's physical plant, equipment, and management should be. Unesco's budgetary contribution over three years was approximately $25,000. Three governments provided the half million dollars for the preliminary studies; the full membership later pledged 28 million dollars for construction, equipment, and operation during the first seven years.

Unesco's efforts touch upon many fields of knowledge and involve cooperation with many agencies, including those of the United Nations. It can draw on its established clearing-house activities and its contacts with scientists around the world. Its function is not to conduct research but to stimulate action by others on problems affecting human welfare.

"Atoms for Peace": Unesco's Role

In the meantime Unesco became involved in the efforts of the United Nations to focus world attention upon the peaceful uses of nuclear energy, in contrast to its destructive possibilities. How could atomic power be utilized in industry and transportation and in research for improvement of agriculture and health?

The background may be briefly summarized. On December 8, 1953, President Eisenhower, in his historic address to the General Assembly of the United Nations, brought forward his "atoms-for-peace" plan, calling for an international atomic energy agency under United Nations auspices, to which the governments principally concerned would "make joint contributions from their stockpiles of normal uranium and fissionable materials."

This dramatic initiative stirred hope and enthusiasm among the peoples of the world. But its realization had to await the willingness particularly of the USSR to contribute fissionable materials to the proposed agency. Negotiations on this point moved slowly. On December 4, 1954, the United Nations General Assembly unanimously adopted a resolution voicing the hope that "international cooperation in developing and expanding the peaceful uses of atomic energy will assist in lifting the burdens of hunger, poverty and disease" and proposing that "once the agency is established, it negotiate an appropriate form of agreement with the United Nations, similar to those of the Specialized Agencies." The resolution requested the Secretary General to convene a scientific and technical conference, which met at Geneva in August 1955, with 1,200 delegates in attendance and more than 1,000 papers submitted for consideration.[8]

On December 3, 1955, the General Assembly approved two resolutions which urged the prompt creation of the atomic energy agency, proposed a second international conference in 1957 or 1958 on the exchange of technical information concerning the peaceful uses of atomic energy, recommended that various interested agencies in the

UN family consult to assure coordination, and established a Scientific Committee of fifteen states to collect and publish information on the effects of atomic radiation.[9] Finally, a draft constitution for the atomic energy agency, prepared by representatives of twelve nations, was submitted to a special conference of eighty-two countries and unanimously approved on October 23, 1956. The constitution will come into effect when ratified by at least eighteen governments.

Various UN specialized agencies had given active attention to the uses of nuclear research in their own fields of activity. The Food and Agriculture Organization foresaw a wide variety of uses for radiation and radioactive isotopes in processing and conservation of foods, in breeding improved types of plants and animals, and in application of the tracer technique to research on crop production, animal husbandry, fisheries, and nutrition. Electric power from nuclear reactors would influence agricultural production and rural welfare. The World Health Organization was concerned with safeguarding the health of mankind against pollution of the air, earth, and sea by atomic waste and fall-out; and constructively, with employment of radioisotopes in medical diagnosis, treatment, and research.[10]

Unesco's concern with nuclear energy is both deeper and broader than that of the other specialized agencies. It is deeper in the sense that while FAO and WHO have to do with science mainly in its applied form, Unesco's responsibility is for pure or basic science. It is broader in that Unesco deals with education about science and with the effect of science on society. Unesco is particularly concerned with the educational, scientific, and cultural changes which nuclear energy and atomic power will bring throughout the world.[11]

At Unesco's General Conference in 1954 at Montevideo, a year after President Eisenhower's proposal to the United Nations, the governments represented instructed the Director General to cooperate with the United Nations, "with special reference to the urgent study of technical questions such as those involved in the effects of radioactivity on life in general, and to the dissemination of objective information concerning all aspects of the peaceful utilization of atomic energy; to study and, if necessary, to propose measures of an international scope to facilitate the use of radioisotopes in research and industry."[12]

Subsequent discussion made it clear that in carrying out the Montevideo decision, within the framework of UN coordination, Unesco could best proceed along four lines. These were (1) radioisotopes, (2) effects of radiation on life in general, (3) training of research personnel, and (4) diffusion of scientific knowledge in the field of atomic energy.

What has Unesco done with this four-fold assignment? At Montevideo the member states had requested Unesco to promote studies on the use of radioisotopes in scientific research and in industry. A meeting of specialists was organized in 1955.[13] Unesco was to help also in organizing training courses for research scientists and engineers working on radioisotopes. Toward this end an international conference bringing together more than 1,000 scientists was planned to meet in September 1957, to share knowledge on the latest developments in the use of radioisotopes as tools of research, as tracers, or as sources of radiation.

With regard to the biological effects of atomic radiation, Unesco turned to the International Council of Scientific Unions, which set up a special committee to define the problems to be studied. It was to report to Unesco at the end of 1956.[14]

The rapidity of scientific and technical progress in atomic energy had made training of necessary staff an urgent task. Without an adequate supply of qualified personnel any large-scale expansion in the peaceful use of atomic energy would be out of the question. The great majority of engineers, for example, were reported to lack knowledge and competence in this field. Unesco had submitted to the Geneva Conference a paper on training research personnel; even earlier it had organized, at the request of member states, several missions composed of specialists on nuclear physics and cosmic rays.

As the next step, Unesco was to organize, in cooperation with FAO and WHO, a conference to be held in 1958. This gathering would provide an opportunity for exchange of information on methods for training engineers, technicians, laboratory workers, and other specialists in all the sciences concerned with peaceful use of atomic energy. It would survey courses of study and teaching methods in various countries and recommend measures for more effective international cooperation. Unesco was to grant fellowships for special training abroad, and to encourage seminars and training courses for teachers of biology, chemistry, and mathematics.[15]

Finally, the fourth line of Unesco activity concerned the broadening of public knowledge about peaceful uses of atomic energy. It was

essential that both the benefits and the dangers of this new development be made clear to everyone. For this Unesco had various channels, ranging from contacts with learned societies in the natural
sciences, social sciences, and education, to activities in mass communication, including the Unesco *Chronicle* and *Impact* for serious
articles and the *Courier* for more popular articles,[16] the radio, films,
filmstrips, photographs, and exhibitions. The Director General was
also to assist member states by circulating information, by discussions
among specialists in cooperation with national commissions and with
national and international organizations, and by encouraging adult
education programs and youth organizations to give attention to this
topic.

Some of Unesco's supporters considered that it had been given too
limited an assignment in the field of atomic energy. They had hoped
that in this field the organization would play a leading role among
the United Nations agencies. However, political and scientific leaders
did not yet have enough confidence in the organization as a channel
for the exchange of scientific information and for stimulation of basic
research on a highly significant problem. The question raised in
1945 on the wisdom of including science in Unesco came to the fore
again with regard to peaceful uses of atomic energy. Unesco, in the
face of an opportunity for constructive and dramatic action, was assigned a secondary role.

International Computation Center

In contrast to CERN, Unesco's efforts to establish an International
Computation Center have been less successful. The small UN-Unesco
meeting of scientists in 1949, already mentioned, had given first priority to a computation center using the latest electronic equipment.

The need to share internationally the high cost of electronic com-
puting machines was an important factor behind the proposal for
such a center. An international convention to set up this center at
Rome was drafted under Unesco auspices in December 1951. It was
signed by eleven states, but only five of the necessary ten governments
(Belgium, Ceylon, Italy, Japan, and Mexico) had ratified the convention by 1956. The long delay in ratifying on the part of Italy, the host
country, was one element in holding up the approval of other countries. In addition, the rapid adoption in many nations of mechanical

and electronic computation processes led to the suggestion that the function of the center be re-examined. Some thought that the need for the machines to be set up at Rome had diminished; others contended that the value of the proposed institute as a center for international research and for training research workers had increased.

Unesco, in cooperation with the Preparatory Committee of the International Computation Center, sponsored a meeting of specialists at Rome in October 1956 to consider these questions. The participants recommended that the existing Preparatory Committee be enlarged and that, pending additional ratifications, it set up a provisional center with staff and suitable equipment, which would carry on activities desired by the signatory nations, including scientific symposia and training of specialists and research workers in computation.[17] But at this writing it remains to be seen what action will be taken on these recommendations.

Cell Biology

Another effort to involve Unesco in attacking a major problem of scientific research was in the field of cell biology. The UN-Unesco group of scientists meeting in 1949 had listed the chemistry of living matter (including cancer research) as one of the fields in which cooperative international research might be of value. For a time little progress was made on this proposal, partly because of the difficulty in defining Unesco's responsibility in science in relation to that of other United Nations agencies. In theory, Unesco was concerned with pure or basic science, while other agencies dealt with applied science. The World Health Organization, for example, was responsible for international activities in medicine. It was finally agreed that WHO, which was in touch with national and international medical organizations, should deal with cancer research. Unesco's responsibility lay rather in the area of basic scientific knowledge concerning cell growth, in the fields of biology, chemistry, and physics. This area, of course, was of fundamental importance in the fight against cancer.

The Unesco General Conference at Montevideo in 1954 authorized the Director General to encourage international research to improve basic knowledge on cell growth.[18] With Unesco's assistance, specialists met at Paris and at Brown University in the United States in 1955 and 1956 and recommended the creation by Unesco of an international commission on cell biology which would review research in progress and facilitate cooperation between existing international bodies through exchange of information, symposia, grants in aid for special tasks, and training of personnel. After further study and discussion, the commission will probably be set up in 1958. The specialists also recommended that Unesco encourage production of inbred strains of laboratory animals. As a result, an international committee for laboratory animals was created, and a world-wide survey of the problem was carried out.[19]

Living in Arid Zones

Quite a different type of world problem is that of human habitation in arid and in humid tropical zones. "The Unesco arid zone program has set in motion forces in the last four years which will undoubtedly have more beneficial effects on the arid regions of the world than any previous historical effort." Such was the judgment of a group of scientists and laymen interested in deserts who met at Cincinnati, Ohio, in November 1955.[20]

Between one-fourth and one-third of the land surface of the world is desert or semi-desert. These arid areas, which receive a restricted and erratic annual rainfall of less than fifteen inches on the average, stretch in an irregular arc from the Atlantic coast of North Africa through Egypt and the Middle East and on into Pakistan, Central Russia, and China. Another strip parallels the Pacific Ocean along many parts of the Western coast of North and South America. Approximately one-third of the territory of the continental United States is arid or semi-arid, as is one-half of Australia.[21]

The desert and semi-desert regions of the world cover almost three times as much land as the cultivated areas; and on some of their margins the deserts are on the march. In a few regions deserts are encroaching upon adjacent good lands at a steady pace, in part because of over-grazing and deforestation. These areas with too much sun and too little rain support only one-sixteenth of the world's population. It is estimated that if the present two-thirds of the world's people now on less than a subsistence diet are to have adequate nourishment, the food supply must be doubled during the next decade. More cultivable land is needed as well as greater and more stable production.[22]

The problem of making better use of the world's arid lands presents a multitude of scientific questions. Can better use be made of underground water and of dew? Can fresh water be distilled economically from salt water? Can rain be induced from reluctant clouds? Can plants be used to anchor the blowing sand dunes? Can man learn to take care of his soil? Can modern science hold back and reclaim the spreading deserts?[23]

Research into questions of this kind has been under way for some time, but the studies have been separate and independent efforts. Most of the research has been carried on in countries like the United States which were only partly arid and therefore had enough wealth from their richer areas to finance scientific study. Countries which were largely arid, like those of the Middle East, and which had greater need for research were too poor to support it on a large scale. An international approach would encourage pooling of effort.

When Unesco began its arid zone project, it centered attention on two international phases of the problem: to improve exchange of information and to stimulate research on desert problems. At the 1948 General Conference in Beirut, the Indian delegation proposed the establishment of an international institute of the arid zone.[24] After the proposal had been given critical examination by two groups of specialists and by the United Nations and FAO, a more modest approach was chosen. It was decided that an international research council meeting periodically would be better adapted to the situation than a permanent institute. An Advisory Committee on Arid Zone Research was appointed and held its first meeting at Algiers in 1951. Its members were drawn from different parts of the world and from different sciences.[25]

Stimulating Study of Desert Problems

The Advisory Committee does not carry on research. Each year a special topic is selected. The Committee requests scientists to summarize the research already done on the topic, appraise it critically, and point out gaps. These studies, after consideration by the Committee, are published by Unesco. Such analyses of major questions usually culminate in an annual symposium jointly organized by Unesco and a member state.[26]

Starting in 1951, the first topic selected for study was hydrology, with special attention to underground water. Scientists know less about underground water resources than about surface water. They are perfecting the means of determining safe yields of water and they are learning that many areas including deserts have beneath them great reservoirs of underground water. Extensive areas of water-bearing rock have been discovered under some parts of the Algerian Sahara, which when tapped can provide wells at artesian pressure. An international symposium held at Ankara in 1952 brought together findings which enabled research workers to recognize and measure these underground resources.

The second problem was that of plant ecology. The science of ecology deals with the relations of plant and animal groups to each other and to their environment, in this case the desert. A symposium on plant ecology was held at the University of Montpellier in France. In many countries lists of plants that flourish on arid lands have been drawn up. Plants that do well in one area can often be introduced into another. In Australia large expanses of almost useless semi-arid land have been transformed into grazing lands by the introduction of subterranean clover. Similarly the Australian eucalyptus tree has been introduced into Morocco and Israel. In 1956 the Committee recommended a critical review in cooperation with WHO of work on medicinal plants in arid regions. It has also been discovered that some plants are not hurt by concentration of salts in the soil. Date palms, asparagus, spinach, cabbage, and cotton will grow in salty ground.[27]

A third aspect of arid zone research undertaken in 1953 was the use of wind, solar, and other types of energy to pump water from the ground. The following year India was host to a symposium on this topic. Engineers have been at work on designs for windmills and sun motors to substitute for vegetable, animal, and other fuels and to pump water from the ground.[28] A fourth aspect taken up in 1954 was human and animal ecology. Grazing by goats, sheep, and cattle may be harmful to vegetation, and by wild animals even more so. Man's wasteful habits in the use of land have earlier been mentioned.

In the spring of 1955 Unesco's Advisory Committee met at Tucson, Arizona, and a few days later at Socorro, New Mexico, in connection with a large conference sponsored by the American Association for the Advancement of Science on "What is the Future of Our Arid Lands?" The conference was attended by scientists from twenty-eight countries and by farmers and businessmen from the arid regions in the American Southwest. An Australian participant emphasized that the greatest need today is "to make use of what knowledge we already have so as to help the little fellow—the man on the farm." A delegate from India pointed out that in many lands every drop of water must be budgeted, and suggested that the same water could be used in the cities and then after purification for irrigation in the rural areas.[29] One result of these meetings was a recommendation that greater efforts be made to apply available knowledge to the problems of arid lands, and that contacts between scientists and laymen be improved.

The most recent topic studied by the Advisory Committee has been the climate of arid zones. With the cooperation of the Food and Agriculture Organization and the World Meteorological Organization (WMO), and at the invitation of the Australian government, a symposium on this problem was held in October 1956 at Canberra. In opening the meeting Richard G. Casey, minister in charge of industrial scientific research, announced that Australian scientists experimenting with artificial rain-making were believed to be close to practical economic results. In the United States and Mexico a number of efforts have been made to induce rainfall by spraying clouds with crystals. Unesco with the aid of technical assistance funds has cooperated with Pakistan in experiments in atmospheric physics and rain-making, which were believed by some to have achieved promising results in parts of the semi-arid Punjab by blowing finely ground salt into the air. These procedures, however, are applicable only to certain situations and are by no means perfected or reliable.[30]

Besides the annual major topics, the Committee has encouraged the study of other matters, such as the preparation of maps showing arid and semi-arid areas which have similar climatic conditions, the evolution of arid areas in the past, the physiology of the camel, the purification and utilization of salt water, and the use of dew.[31]

One study, assisted by Unesco funds and of practical interest in arid areas, has been on the physiology of the camel, particularly its tolerance of heat and its capacity to conserve body moisture. This was carried on in 1953-54 at a French experiment station in the Algerian Sahara. In contrast to cattle, whose characteristics have been carefully examined, scant attention has been given to the camel. Yet in the desert the camel is the most useful domestic animal. Not only is it the main beast of burden, but its milk and meat are used as food, its wool is spun and woven for clothing and tents, and its skin is used as leather.

Tentative results of this study indicated that the camel can get along for considerable periods without drinking water because of several unusual traits. Although it cannot store water in its hump or one of its several stomachs, as was once believed, the camel guards every bit of water in its body tissues. It never pants, or breathes with its mouth open; and it perspires little, if at all, because of its capacity to adjust to changes in its body temperature. While man under desert heat cannot survive the loss of more than ten to twelve per cent of body water, the camel may survive a loss of as much as thirty per cent.[32]

Another question affecting arid zones has to do with the use of salt water and dew. Recently one of the world's great plants to distill fresh water from the sea opened at Kuwait in Arabia on the Persian Gulf, to be used by the petroleum industry. It will eventually produce five million gallons of pure water daily. This quantity would be enough, if used in agriculture, to furnish one inch of water for an expanse of 180 acres. The United States Department of the Interior has had for some years a Saline Water Conversion Program, with research projects which have helped to appraise the merits and costs of converting salt water to fresh. To date such production is too expensive for general use in irrigation. Unesco has undertaken to serve as a clearing house for research going on in the United States, Western Europe, and North Africa.

Dew or fog, it has been learned, can be absorbed by certain plants at night through their leaves and stored in the soil for later use. An Israeli scientist has been specializing for some years at the Dew Research Station at Karkur on the role of regular supplies of dew in plant nutrition. On recommendation of Unesco's Advisory Committee, he was awarded a grant of $1,000 to study this problem at the Earhart Plant Research Laboratory of the California Institute of Technology. As a result of this work it was possible to prove that a large number of plants absorb dew and transfer it to the soil through their roots. This phenomenon had never before been observed in such quantity, and the amount of water was measured for tomatoes, sugar beets, peas, squash, and mint.[33]

Cooperation with Other Agencies and with Member States

Unesco's activities have paralleled those carried on by other UN agencies, FAO, ILO, WHO, WMO, and by the International Union for the Conservation of Nature and Natural Resources. FAO, for example, has waged a far-ranging campaign against desert locusts which have attacked crops from the Nile Delta eastward to India. FAO has also called attention to the deterioration of irrigated land in arid countries due to waterlogging and increase of salt in the soil. Crop yields from irrigated lands in most arid zone countries are lessening and much land formerly productive has been taken out of cultivation.[34] WMO prepared a paper on "rain-making" with special reference to arid and semi-arid regions, and a report on the practicability of using wind energy to pump water for irrigation.[35]

Unesco's arid zone project is part of a broader undertaking on "the effective use and control of water resources" outlined by the United Nations Economic and Social Council in 1952. This scheme recognized that the problem of using water involves not only irrigation but also power development, flood control, navigation, and industrial and municipal use of water. It is related to improvement of agriculture, expansion of fisheries, development of industry, control of pollution, and watershed management. The Secretary General was asked by the 1952 ECOSOC resolution to promote international exchange of information and experience and to encourage and coordinate national and international activities concerning water resources. Two years later, in 1954, on the basis of a report from the Secretary General on "Development and Utilization of Water Resources," ECOSOC called attention to the heavy demands on the world's water supply made by growing population and rapid industrial and agricultural development, and urged studies of hydrological data, methods of watershed management, and the use of water for domestic, urban, agricultural, and industrial purposes.[36]

If Unesco's work on arid zones has on the one hand had numerous points of contact with other United Nations agencies, it is related on the other hand to activities in individual countries. Its staff has pro-

moted world-wide surveys of the work of national institutions engaged in arid zone research. The Advisory Committee recommended
issuance by Unesco of a handbook to assist member states in bringing together basic research data needed for the constructive development of an arid or semi-arid area. The Committee reviews projects
for basic research on arid zone problems submitted by national institutions and recommends modest financial assistance for some projects. It has helped member states in holding symposia and publishing
important studies. For example, Unesco cooperated in 1952 with the
National Institute of Sciences in India in a symposium on the semi-
arid tracts of peninsular India. In 1953 it aided the Fouad I Desert
Institute of Egypt in a symposium on desert research and development. It provided experts and equipment to assist Turkey in establishing an Institute of Hydrology, and Israel in surveying the feasi-
bility of using wind power for irrigation.[37] Unesco grants annually a
small number of fellowships to train advanced personnel on arid zone
problems. The procedure followed by the Advisory Committee as
outlined above has been remarkably economical, usually costing
Unesco less than $100,000 a year.

The importance of the arid zone problem and the value of Unesco's
work in this field were underlined by the decision of the 1956 General Conference at New Delhi to establish an arid zones major project.[38] This will involve an increase in financial support by Unesco
and in cooperative assistance from FAO, WHO, and WMO, but even
larger contributions from member states.[39] The international character of the activity is to continue under direction of the Advisory
Committee, but an effort will be made for approximately six years to
provide individual countries with enlarged facilities for training
research workers, organizing research teams equipped with apparatus
and documentation, planning research programs, and setting up
laboratories. Two research institutes in the Middle East and two in
South Asia (possibly in Egypt, Israel, India, and Pakistan) will be
strengthened to serve as organs for regional cooperation.

Research will continue to be focused annually on major topics.
For 1957 the choice will lie between the history of land use, particularly of agricultural practices in arid and semi-arid regions, and the
modification of soil structure resulting from different types of land
use such as grazing, dry-land farming, and irrigation. In 1958 study
will be directed either to the water requirements of plants and espe-

cially the efficiency of their transpiration or exhalation of water vapor, or to methods of discovering and measuring water reserves.

Three special projects will be undertaken. One will be the establishment of a clearing house on purification of salt water, a long-term endeavor. Development of an economical process for purifying saline water both from the sea and from underground sources would, it is recognized, represent the greatest single achievement in bettering living conditions in many arid lands. A second project would develop wider understanding and support among the public, and particularly new literates, on this topic. In addition, Unesco will undertake an educational program on watershed management as requested by ECOSOC, and cooperate in preparing a handbook on the subject. Finally, a special study will be made by social scientists on the best methods of settling nomadic and semi-nomadic groups in areas newly opened to cultivation and adjusting these groups to an agricultural way of life.[40]

The member states involved in this arid zone project will cooperate by establishing national and local committees, developing programs of arid zone research, providing fellowships to their nationals for work and study abroad, and carrying out educational activities, especially for new literates.

Living in Humid Tropical Zones

Unesco's success in stimulating scientific research and action to improve living conditions in the world's arid zones provoked the question whether similar methods could be applied to other regions where climatic conditions make it difficult for men to live—the tropical and rain-drenched areas bordering the Equator in Africa, Asia, and South America.

Fifteen million square miles or one-third of the world's usable land is warm and rainy. In these areas the average temperature of the coldest month does not go below 64 degrees Fahrenheit and the minimum annual rainfall is 27.5 inches. In the humid tropics of Africa, America, and New Guinea the population is sparse, not exceeding ten per square mile. But the hot, wet lands of Asia include areas with the densest population in the world, such as the Bengal delta, Cochin and Travancore in India, and the Red River delta in Tonkin, where the density is almost 4,000 per square mile. Despite the prodigal abundance of plant life, the standard of living is low because of the inadequate size of family farms, erosion caused by torrential rains, the rapidity of bacterial decay and the consequent lack of humus, and the prevalence of disease.[41]

One of Unesco's first projects to miscarry—the Hylean Amazon Institute—had been aimed at this problem. The Brazilian delegation proposed originally to the Preparatory Commission and later to Unesco's First General Conference the establishment of a center for scientific research in the Amazon Valley—an area which included territory belonging to Brazil, Bolivia, Colombia, Ecuador, Peru, and Venezuela, and also to British, Dutch, and French Guiana. This vast expanse of four and a quarter million square miles, almost a third of South America, had been called "Hylea" (meaning "great forest") by Von Humboldt and others. It extends from the Atlantic Ocean to the Andes and contains the largest drainage basin in the world as well as the most abundant forest reserves.

An international convention for the research center was drafted at Iquitos, Peru, in 1947 and signed by nine governments.[42] But in Brazil the project ran into political trouble. Among other counts, it was criticized as threatening Brazilian sovereignty in the Amazon area. The Brazilian Chamber of Deputies requested the views of the General Staff on the question. The latter reported to the Chamber on March 31, 1949, taking in general a favorable attitude on the proposal. It recommended that the convention require the Institute to secure the express approval of a signatory state before undertaking any activity in its territory. Brazil proposed a protocol to the convention containing this change and some others, and this document was signed by six of the nine original participating countries. Despite this modification of the agreement, the Brazilian Congress never ratified the convention; and since Brazil was the prime mover and largest participant in the undertaking, its failure to act killed the enterprise. Subsequently, the Brazilian government through its National Council for Scientific Research founded a national research institute in the Amazon region.[43]

Unesco's involvement in the Hylean Amazon project was unfortunate in various respects. The proposal stirred false hopes. Unesco did not have enough experience to manage such a scheme. The United Nations Expanded Technical Assistance Program was not yet in existence. The enterprise deflected Unesco's attention from more manageable projects.

Nearly five years later, when interest in the humid tropical zones had been revived by the evident usefulness of the work on arid zones, Unesco brought together information on the problem and on national efforts to attack it. At the Montevideo General Conference in 1954 a move to postpone action for one year was strongly opposed by the delegations of Ceylon, India, Liberia, Burma, and Brazil, who argued that the problem demanded immediate attention. Accordingly Unesco's member states were asked in 1955 to report on the scientific problems of their own humid tropical regions, on research so far undertaken, and on what future action they would recommend. In the same year the Congress of the World Meteorological Organization approved full collaboration with the Unesco project. Data received from these reports and from other scientific organizations were reviewed by a group of specialists meeting at Kandy in Ceylon in March 1956, immediately following a symposium on "Methods of Study of Tropical Vegetation." The group called for a more complete classification of tropical insects and tropical soils, and fellowships for research workers on the scientific problems of the humid tropics.

At the end of 1956 Unesco set up an International Advisory Committee for Humid Tropics Research, scheduled to hold its first meeting in Brazil in July 1957. A symposium on climate, vegetation, and land utilization in the humid tropics was proposed in connection with the Ninth Pacific Science Congress at Bangkok in November 1957.[44]

Marine Sciences

At the 1952 General Conference Japan took the lead in urging a cooperative effort for more effective use of food and other resources in the oceans of the world, particularly in the Indo-Pacific region. The Indo-Pacific Fisheries Council, affiliated with FAO, had already done some work on the problem.

While the oceans cover more than half the earth's surface, they provide less than one per cent of man's food. Fish are at present their most important product. Although some countries bordering the sea consume little fish, in others fishing techniques are so efficient as to threaten the extinction of certain species. The value of sea plants as food for domestic animals as well as for men has already been recognized. For the future, some students hold that the greatest promise for increase in food supply lies in plankton, the minute floating organisms of the sea, both animal and plant, which often cover large areas. Fat for production of margarine has already been extracted from plankton. In France seaweed has been used as food for horses as well as for making silage. Both plankton and seaweed can serve as sources for drugs, pharmaceuticals, and other biochemicals.

To realize the full potentialities of the sea as a source of food, research is needed on many questions: temperature variations, depths, and currents, as these and other factors determine plant and animal growth; the diseases and parasites of plant and animal life; the sea bottom and the character of its soils and sediments. Certain areas such as the Indian Ocean are said to be less known to scientists than the surface of the moon.[45] The goal of this research is to help man to farm the ocean as he has the land, and to replace destructive exploitation with carefully planned scientific cultivation of the sea's food resources.[46]

The development of marine resources was examined by a group of consultants at Manila in November 1953, during the Eighth Pacific Science Congress. Interest had developed also in Latin America, where a suggestion to establish a chain of marine biology laboratories had been made by experts at Montevideo in August 1952 at a meeting called by the Unesco Science Cooperation Office.[47]

Unesco's role in attacking this problem was discussed by its international advisory committee on natural sciences at its first meeting in April 1954. Members from Australia, the United Kingdom, and the United States advised against any over-ambitious scheme and favored strengthening existing bodies before creating a new international institute. The most urgent task, they argued, was to train specialists. Members from India and Japan, on the other hand, stressed the importance of prompt action to set up an international center with adequate equipment and financial resources. The FAO representative pointed out that the development of fisheries was a responsibility of that organization.[48]

The Unesco General Conference at Montevideo in 1954 approved the creation of an international advisory committee on marine sciences to recommend measures for "stimulation and better coordination of basic research in physical oceanography and marine biology. Among its tasks will be the coordination and mobilization of scientific knowledge and the initiation of scientific studies with a view to better utilization of marine resources."[49]

The Committee held an interim meeting at Tokyo in October 1955, in connection with a regional symposium on physical oceanography and a meeting of representatives of oceanographic institutions in the Indo-Pacific area. It noted that "the oceans are international and hence the marine sciences are a natural field for international collaboration. . . . No one country can find out all it needs to know about the sea, except through the cooperative activities of many other countries."[50] It agreed to concentrate on reinforcing existing institutions, through assistance in training staff, improving experimental methods, and developing better international collaboration. The Committee held its first formal meeting at Lima, Peru, in October 1956.[51] In collaboration with FAO a large symposium was planned for 1958 on the productivity of the sea.

The Social Impact of Technological Change

Modern industry and technology made their initial impact on Western Europe and North America during the first part of the nineteenth century. The turn of Latin America, Africa, and Asia came later, much of it in the present century. Travel was transformed by the railroad, steamship, and airplane; communication by the telegraph, telephone, radio, newspaper, moving picture, and most recently by television. The machine produced goods cheaply and abundantly, but at the same time it crushed out many handicrafts and village products. Giant corporations prospered at the expense of small industry. Labor organized in self-defense. Social and labor legislation sought to protect the worker from the worst abuses of the industrial system. Foreign capital transformed the non-industrial countries into producers of raw materials and markets for manufactured goods. This wave of economic and social change was largely unplanned and at first largely unregulated by public authority.

Today the industrial revolution has entered a new phase. In industrial countries efforts have been launched, and in non-industrial countries demands have been voiced, for regulation of technological change in order to achieve maximum progress at minimum human cost. Some efforts have been successful, others have not.[52]

Largely as a result of pressure from the new non-industrial states of Asia, together with United Nations efforts to assist economic development and industrialization, Unesco was asked in 1949 to call together a small group of specialists to identify problems resulting from technological change which could be attacked by the methods of the social sciences. The group found that three problems stood out: reform of general and technical education; the human factor in industry; and extension of modern technology to the "non-mechanized" peoples of the world.

Educational Needs

A changing society requires change in education. When a people who have lived primarily from farming acquire railroads and factories, individuals must learn new ways of working and living. Schools must not only teach new subjects but must prepare their pupils to live in a new and changing world, far different from the one their fathers knew.

To examine the relation of education and technical change, Unesco brought together in 1950 specialists from a dozen countries, whose conclusions were published in a report entitled *Education in a Technological Society*. The group agreed that changes were needed both in general or ordinary education and in technical education. General education, they suggested, should give the pupil more practical knowledge about the world he lives in. Technical education should teach him the skills needed in an industrial society. But technical education should give him something more than narrow vocational training. He should acquire some knowledge of economic and social questions and some appreciation of the arts. His curiosity and independence of thought should be stimulated so that he may view life as a process of learning, carried out through adult education and further technical training. Education in such a society must plan for the future, and the social sciences could provide knowledge essential for such planning.

The Human Factor in Industry

The second problem concerned the human factor in industry. The factory and the machine have raised man's standard of living, but at the same time have uprooted him from his ancestral community and drawn him to a city where, belonging to no group, he suffers from a pervasive sense of insecurity. Modern industry with its emphasis on the "production line," breaking down production into small routine tasks, has taken from the worker much of the satisfaction which the craftsman derived from a job well done. The resulting tensions have been reduced somewhat by the labor union, which restored for the worker the sense of belonging, and by application of scientific management, which has begun to give him a sense of participation in industry.

In an attack on this problem Unesco, with the assistance of the International Committee on Scientific Management, stimulated case studies of a dozen industrial enterprises in six countries which had succeeded in developing among factory workers some sense of cooperation and community in production. The findings of these studies were brought together in a volume on *The Community Factor in Modern Technology*. This publication, besides reviewing the disintegration of communities by modern technology, analyzed how industry can provide human satisfactions, and how the social sciences can point toward natural and companionable association in labor and can diffuse a spirit of social understanding and cooperation throughout communities and nations.

Orderly Social Change

We come now to the third problem. The extension of modern technology to "non-mechanized" peoples has been a major shock to the social systems of many countries. A rapid shift from a primitive or semi-primitive society to an industrial society is likely to upset customs and cultural traditions. Modern techniques call not only for new skills, but for new attitudes and values. The way of life of a people is "a living unity." A change in one element may make changes in others inevitable.

How could these countries achieve orderly social change and develop the forms of social life required by economic progress without disrupting or destroying the old values which made for social harmony? As a first step in analyzing this problem, Unesco sponsored through the World Federation for Mental Health a study of the effects on a society of the deliberate introduction of new methods. This resulted in the publication of *Cultural Patterns and Technical*

Change, which examined several cultures in different parts of the world: Burma, exemplifying the Buddhist tradition of Asia; Greece, with its ancient pagan tradition and its two millennia of Christian culture; the Tiv people of Nigeria, whose culture is not far from primitive but is receptive to outside influence; and the Spanish-Americans of the United States, an agricultural Spanish-speaking minority embedded in an English-speaking industrial civilization. On the basis of these case studies, an approach was made to different aspects of technical change as they relate to mental health: agriculture, nutrition, maternal and child care, public health, industrialization, and fundamental education.

Studies on the three problems listed above indicated that a critical attitude was gaining ground concerning the place of industry in modern life. Modern technical assistance, both UN and bilateral, therefore involves serious efforts to protect human groups from the destructive phases of technology, and to identify methods which will foster the introduction of technical assistance and the use of the machine with due respect for lasting human values.[53]

Supplementing the three studies just mentioned, Unesco undertook an analysis of the social results of increased productivity, convening together with the United Nations in 1953 a group of social scientists, technical assistance experts, and administrators of both national and UN technical aid programs.[54] Unesco sponsored several regional surveys of the problem. In February 1956 a meeting of international organizations held at Rome discussed a possible survey by the International Social Science Council on psychological, sociological, and cultural factors affecting productivity. Pilot studies in Europe and in India, Japan, and Mexico were recommended, with the assistance of local institutions and groups.[55] A symposium at Athens in October 1952, organized by the Greek Society for International Studies, reviewed changes in social and legal systems in the Near and Middle East as a result of technological development.[56]

The International African Institute of London analyzed the consequences of industrialization in Africa. A team of three social scientists made a comprehensive study of Stanleyville, a city in the Belgian Congo. Their findings and those of other surveys were examined by a regional conference at Abidjan, Ivory Coast, in the autumn of 1954.[57] Unesco published in 1956 an 800-page volume entitled *Social Implications of Industrialization and Urbanization in Africa South of the Sahara.* A third project in South Asia brought together data on the impact of technology and also acquainted sociologists of the region with the most recent analytical methods. The Economics Department of Dacca University in Pakistan studied the effects of industrial development on several groups of workers, and the Asian Relations Organization made surveys of industrialization and rural emigration in Bangkok, Jakarta, and Bombay.[58]

The growing importance of the whole problem of the social effects of technical change led to a proposal for a permanent international research center. As a first step, the International Social Science Council set up at Paris in October 1953 an International Research Office on the Social Implications of Technological Change. This office serves as a clearing house for information, documentation, and research; organizes meetings among specialists in different countries; prepares research projects to be supported by outside financing; and has planned the establishment of a regional research center.[59] It was suggested that to reduce its task to manageable dimensions, the Office should concentrate on influences from outside rather than inside a society; rapid rather than gradual technological change; unsuccessful as well as successful examples; effects on social structure, the family and the person; and the relation of technological change to traditional values and attitudes.[60]

Next, the 1954 General Conference approved the establishment at Calcutta of a regional research center (its full title being Research Center on the Social Implications of Industrialization in Southern Asia). India offered $35,000 annually for the center, approximately one-fourth its total cost. Plans for the new institution were worked out by an advisory group of representatives of the countries of the area, which met at New Delhi in 1955. The center was to help participating countries develop their social science resources in men and in institutions. It would on request analyze the social effects of any new plan for economic development. It would conduct comparative studies in different countries and explore the problem of combining social and economic development. The center was to focus on industry rather than agriculture, with attention, however, to cottage industries and to the repercussions of factory industry on rural life. It was to cooperate closely with the universities of the region.

The Research Center began work in January 1956, guided by an advisory committee including representatives of the participating countries and of the United Nations, ILO, FAO, WHO, and Unesco. The plan called for a staff of leading social scientists, largely from countries of the area. In addition to its research responsibilities, the Center was to provide fellowships for ten younger specialists, enabling them to secure research experience. After an initial period of three years, the Center would become an international institution on the model of CERN or would be taken over by the Government of India. The initial subject chosen for research was the psychological, cultural, and social factors affecting productivity.[61]

The work of Unesco on the social impact of technological change illustrates several characteristic functions of the organization. It has helped a large number of countries undergoing major social change to secure world-wide attention to their problem. It has brought together professional, scientific, government, and United Nations personnel to consider ways of coping with this problem. It has helped to state the issues, identify specific questions requiring analysis, and locate expert knowledge in various countries around the world, but has not itself attempted to conduct research. In the International Research Office at Paris already mentioned, it has created a center for continuous attention to an outstanding world problem. Finally, Unesco has attempted to apply in its own activities and through its technical assistance missions the knowledge which it has helped discover and develop.

Unesco, Science, and Welfare

It was a request from the United Nations that initiated Unesco's efforts to put science at the service of man in dealing with major problems of human welfare. In October 1946 the Economic and Social Council approved a resolution aimed at identifying those areas of scientific research where international cooperation might prove useful. The stimulus had come from the French, who urged the creation of "United Nations research laboratories." Subsequently requests came from member states for cooperative international research in special fields: in arid zones from India; in nuclear research from the United States; and in marine sciences from Japan. It was largely the new nations of Asia, facing the consequences of United Nations technical assistance, that furnished the stimulus for study of the social effects of technological change.

A foundation for Unesco's endeavors to advance human welfare through science had been laid by the activities outlined in Chapter V to encourage international scientific cooperation through exchange of knowledge and closer relations with and among nongovernmental international organizations.

In the course of the international research projects mentioned above, Unesco's role has been somewhat clarified, both in relation to other United Nations specialized agencies and to nongovernmental organizations, national and international. With regard to the first, a sharper line has been drawn between Unesco's responsibility for encouraging research in pure or basic science, and the responsibility of other specialized agencies for stimulating research in the applied sciences, where the findings of basic science are put to work. For example, Unesco has worked closely with FAO in the projects on arid and humid areas, and on marine sciences. The studies carried out have been of benefit to FAO, particularly in its activities in agriculture and fisheries. Unesco's relation to WHO was more precisely defined during the discussion of research on cell biology and cancer, where Unesco was assigned responsibility for the first of these fields and WHO for the second. In nuclear research and atomic energy, Unesco is to work within the over-all program of the United Nations family, carrying out specific tasks primarily educational in character.

Progress has also been made—though much remains to be done—in clarifying Unesco's role in scientific research in relation to nongovernmental organizations, national and international. Unesco itself, it is generally agreed, should not engage in scientific research. However, on the advice of scientists meeting in international groups, Unesco has helped to identify problems of international concern, particularly where scientific research may develop knowledge whose application will improve living conditions. On a similar basis, gaps in existing research programs have been pointed out. Unesco can provide little material assistance for research, but it has provided channels through which research workers can cooperate more effectively.

Unesco's General Conference as well as its Executive Board has served as a forum in which important problems have been brought to world attention. These problems have been submitted to scrutiny by the secretariat and by small meetings of experts. Through consultation and discussion, agreement has been progressively worked out on the significance of the problem and the most effective way of attacking it. A choice has usually been made between two approaches. The first, setting up a new international center or institute, was adopted for the study of nuclear energy (CERN), for the proposed international computation agency, and the social impact of technological change (the regional research center in India). The second, creating an international advisory committee meeting periodically (often only once a year), has been employed for the study of living conditions in arid and humid zones and for research in marine sciences. These advisory committees have also proposed exploration of new problems. Finally, publications have served to bring to the attention of scientists the discussions carried on at the new institutes and in the periodical meetings and symposiums of the advisory committees.

The two approaches outlined above have proved—in certain cases at least—to be economical and effective. Their demands on Unesco's financial resources have been moderate and the results achieved have been out of proportion to the cost.

The projects reviewed in this chapter illustrate successful efforts like CERN, the analysis of the social impact of technological change, and the arid zone project, which set the pattern for later projects on humid tropical zones and the marine sciences. They include an outstanding failure—the Hylean Amazon undertaking—and some which represent only a start, though a fairly promising start, such as the international computation center, participation in the atoms for peace plan, and cell biology.

Success or failure has depended on many factors, including the nature of the subject, the attitude of member states, organizational relations among the United Nations and other agencies, and the ability of the Unesco secretariat to provide effective leadership.

CHAPTER X

"PEACE THROUGH UNDERSTANDING"

In the early days of Unesco it was assumed, as in the past, that education could build understanding and that understanding would contribute to peace. At the 1945 London Conference, Prime Minister Attlee put forward as the watchword of the new organization, "educate so that the minds of the people shall be attuned to peace." The better men understand each other, he argued, the less likely they are to take up arms against each other. Léon Blum expressed the hope of founding "a world in which peace shall become a permanent or rather a natural state of affairs—a world in which the *spirit of peace* shall become one of the guarantees, and perhaps the surest guarantee of Peace."[1]

Defining the Concept

Unesco started with only a vague and hopeful assumption as to the relation between education, understanding, and peace. The term "international understanding" was not defined in the Constitution; nor was its meaning clarified by the Preparatory Commission or early sessions of the General Conference. This vagueness did not reflect any lack of faith that understanding could further peace—quite the contrary. Succeeding sessions of the General Conference have called for international understanding.[2] But critical analysis of the relation between "understanding" and "peace" was slow to develop.

Around 1950 program planning in this area began to achieve some degree of clarity. This was due in part to pressure from member states, especially the United States, to make clear that promotion of international understanding did not mean support of world government.[3] It resulted also from progress in formulating a social science program, which involved consideration of how social science could contribute to international understanding. Early optimism and enthusiasm were tempered by a more realistic appraisal of actual world conditions. The personal and national insecurity inherent in a world of perfected atomic and biological instruments of destruction might argue forcefully for more effective world cooperation, but it also intensified attachment to familiar national institutions and symbols.

From the start Unesco leaders sought to make clear that international understanding did not mean undermining of national loyalty. The relation between patriotism and international understanding and cooperation was clearly stated as early as 1945 in London and as late as 1954 in Paris. Miss Ellen Wilkinson, British Minister of Education, declared at the London Conference: "We here could not be interested in international work if we were not firmly rooted in our national loyalties. You cannot build a bridge unless there is solid earth at each end of the bridge. Our international organization, intended to be a bridge between nations, must rest firmly on foundations dug deeply in the national life and tradition of the member states. International fellowship and national personality are not incompatible."[4]

An Expert Committee on Education for International Understanding and Cooperation appointed by the Director General recognized the relation between national and international loyalties. It stated that "it is possible and necessary to teach that loyal citizenship of one's own country is consistent with world-mindedness and that national interests are bound to suffer if international interests are ignored."[5]

The term "international understanding," however, was sufficiently broad and vague to include at least two different ideas. The earlier, and more prevalent, view was expressed by Lyman Bryson of Columbia University, who in the summer of 1947 prepared a memorandum on the subject at the request of the Director General. To him international understanding meant "a kind of knowledge, an attitude, that will lead the people of every nation to feel friendliness toward the people of other nations and to cooperate in international enterprises."[6] To others international understanding implies an objective attitude, a sober comprehension of the behavior of other peoples, whether friends or enemies.[7]

The first concept is that of *sympathetic* understanding, implying a friendly and favorable attitude conducive to mutual accord. While partisans of this view do not claim that sympathetic understanding automatically begets cooperative and peaceful relations, they believe that such relations are a natural consequence of sympathetic understanding. The second concept is that of objective *intellectual* understanding. An increase in this type of understanding may render the points of disagreement clearer, and perhaps in some cases fewer. It may make agreement less difficult but it does not necessarily lead to cooperation and concord.

The Unesco program has not distinguished clearly between these two concepts. In practice, it has acted along both lines. This is in large part due to lack of scientific knowledge as to what kind of understanding of other people and their ways promotes cooperative and peaceful relations and under what conditions.

In the absence of such scientific knowledge, Unesco has had to proceed on a trial and error basis, and has experimented with a variety of activities. Actually, it has often been assumed that all of Unesco's activities contribute, directly or indirectly, to international understanding and cooperation.

A multitude of Unesco activities directed primarily toward other goals may have as byproducts a substantial increase in mutual knowledge and appreciation. For example, Unesco facilitates free communication among peoples. Through its publications and clearing-house activities it fosters exchange of information across frontiers. It encourages personal contacts through exchange of persons and international meetings. It tries to better understanding through education, particularly fundamental education and extension of free primary education. It encourages cooperation among educators, scientists and other scholars, writers, and artists. It helps people from different countries to work together on common problems, for it believes that the experience of working together may beget international understanding.

A group of Unesco activities during the decade under review was aimed directly at increasing international understanding. These activities may be grouped as follows: (1) those which provide opportunity for direct contact with people of other lands, specifically exchange of persons (see below); (2) those which seek to promote understanding of other peoples through education (see below); (3) those which foster comprehension of the values underlying the diversity of national and regional cultures—in other words, the contribution of philosophy to the understanding of different ways of life (see Chapter XI); (4) those which encourage research on basic problems affecting international understanding (see Chapter XI); and (5) those which promote comprehension of the United Nations system (see Chapter XII).

Exchange of Persons

The exchange of persons, often through fellowships, has been part of many Unesco projects. In 1946-56 Unesco awarded more than 1,300 fellowships. Most were intended to advance particular projects, such as fundamental and primary education, workers' education, aid to creative artists, museum and library methods, and projects in the natural and social sciences. Some six hundred were offered between 1951 and June 1956 in connection with the United Nations technical assistance program. For other fellowships, financial support came from governments or other agencies, but the grants were administered and sometimes sponsored by Unesco. In most of these awards international understanding was a secondary object.[8]

More directly aimed at international understanding were certain exchange projects for manual and non-manual workers, youth organizations, and teachers. In 1952 Unesco launched a project to help workers from one country to use their holidays to visit their "opposite numbers" in other countries. Included in the enterprise have been printers and paper workers; textile, shoe, and clothing workers; bus drivers, railroad conductors, dock workers, and shipyard engineers; electrical and metal workers. The selection was made by such groups as the International Confederation of Free Trade Unions and the international federations of Christian Trade Unions, Workers' Educational Associations, and Workers' Travel Associations. In the receiving country visitors were guided and entertained by members of a corresponding trade union organization. Danish bus drivers visited Paris and sat beside French drivers as the latter followed their routes through the city. Austrian and Swedish firemen in reciprocal visits were given accommodation in brigade fire houses. Belgian metal workers visited Vienna; and Yugoslav cooperative employees visited Denmark. By 1956 more than 4,000 workers, representing more than 40 occupations, had participated in the exchanges. During the initial period the project was limited to European countries because of the cost of travel. But in 1954 a Unesco grant assisted a CIO group from the United States, whose members paid for their own

ocean transport, to travel in Europe. In 1955 experiments were made
in Latin America and Asia. The Unesco National Commissions in
Japan and India worked out an exchange of fifteen young workers
from each country. The Japanese group made a one-month visit to
India in late 1956.

Unesco's small investment in the enterprise, to cover costs of travel,
is more than matched by contributions from individual workers,
grants from trade unions, and in some cases aid from employers. Numerous factories have been opened to the visiting groups, providing
hospitality at the employees' restaurants.

Many of the visitors acquired some knowledge of the language and
life of the host country, some carrying on their studies for a year or
longer beforehand. Some were required to pass an examination on
language proficiency. Their travel schedules included visits to art
galleries, the theater and opera, places of historical interest, parlia-
ments, local festivals, and private homes. They carried back to
their native lands a picture of the cultural as well as the economic
life of their hosts. Often visitors of one year have been hosts the
next year.

Friendships thus formed have led to correspondence and invita-
tions for family visits. Articles and booklets on host countries have
been published, and radio broadcasts made. Not only the visitors but
their colleagues who stayed at home have become conscious of the
international community. They have gained perspective on their own
country and on possibilities of improvement there, and have learned
to appreciate the value of diversity in national customs.[9]

In the project for exchanges of young people, emphasis is on travel
grants to international youth and student organizations. Some twenty-
five international youth organizations have consultative relations
with Unesco. Nominations for travel grants are submitted to Unesco
by the organizations. The recipients, besides attending an international meeting of the organization, must study abroad for three to
six months. For example, four young people—an Australian, an East
Indian, an Indonesian, and a Thai—received grants to attend an International Red Cross conference in Turkey, followed by a study trip
to observe Red Cross activities in Greece, Yugoslavia, Switzerland,
France, and the United Kingdom. Young people from distant regions
were helped to attend an international course in Germany for leaders
of youth movements, a congress in India for Asian students on the

United Nations organization, a world conference in Holland for university students on problems related to the expansion of technical assistance, a conference on the problems of African youth, and an international seminar in Brazil on the present-day situation of young workers.[10]

Exchange of university professors is facilitated by the publication *Teaching Abroad*, which lists scholars willing to serve in a foreign post. Issues of this pamphlet carry information on approximately 1,300 candidates and are sent to almost as many universities and technical colleges. In October 1955 candidates listed were under consideration for 120 vacancies in the universities of twenty countries. Unesco has facilitated the exchange of a limited number of secondary school teachers among the Latin American countries and among the Arab states. A newer Unesco project sought to encourage understanding especially between parts of the world which previously had not been closely linked. Universities were to receive graduate students and younger teachers from foreign countries who would spend several months studying the language, literature, and culture of the host country; these universities, particularly those with a definite interest in area studies, were to send their own students and teachers abroad for similar studies. By June 1956 twelve such grants had been made and an additional twenty-four were in negotiation. A Cuban professor of geography was to study in France; a faculty member of the Oriental Institute at Beirut was to carry on social and cultural studies in Japan; a historian from Malta was to work in the United States.

International Seminars for Teachers

Although direct contacts with people of other countries can be extremely valuable in developing international understanding, the opportunities for such exchanges are necessarily limited. A much larger number of persons can be reached through educational programs and institutions within member states. Among Unesco's activities to aid school children and youth to obtain better knowledge of the people of other countries are international "seminars" for teachers. The governments of member states have asked Unesco to bring together primary and secondary school teachers in working groups or study conferences. These groups, ranging in size from thirty to seventy members, meet for four, five, or six weeks. Member states choose their participants in the seminars and pay their traveling expenses, while Unesco pays for organizing and operating the seminar, including members' board and lodging.

In the early seminars Unesco was more interested in giving teachers and educational leaders an opportunity to meet and work together than with improving educational systems. On returning home, it was hoped, the participants would share their findings through lectures and articles with national leaders and organizations.

The first seminar, necessarily experimental, met in 1947 at Sèvres near Paris, to discuss education for international understanding.[11] Others have focused on the teaching of specific subjects and the contribution of such subjects to international understanding. A seminar on the teaching of geography was held in 1950 near Montreal, Canada. It examined how geography may provide information on other lands and peoples and reveal the common needs of all peoples for food, shelter, security, and social life. In 1951 a seminar on the teaching of history as a means of developing international understanding met in France, again at Sèvres. The relative merits of national and world history were reviewed. It was recognized that national history is the core of a history curriculum. But national history may view the nation as a part of mankind, noting the contributions made by other countries and the interdependence of peoples. A third seminar, on the teaching of modern languages, was held in Ceylon in 1953.[12] Other seminars on teaching about the United Nations and about human rights will be discussed in Chapter XII.

Although Unesco has given special attention through seminars to the teaching of geography, history, and modern languages because these studies affect attitudes toward other countries and can give a sense of unity with other times, places, and people, it was recognized that all subjects in the curriculum may contribute to the spirit of international understanding.[13]

A special comment may be appropriate on the seminar method. The selection and preparation of the participants by member states is of great importance, and in this respect the Unesco seminars have often been weak. In Unesco's early days the time for planning was too short; participants were too hastily selected and arrived without adequate information and study of the materials. Since 1949, as a partial remedy, seminars have been planned two years in advance.[14]

Experience has shown what is the most useful function of the seminars. A committee of specialists remarked in 1954 that the chief value of seminars lies in the actions of participants after they return home. "An international seminar is essentially a method of higher education and is not a good method of conducting research, of advising Unesco on its programme, or of producing publications that represent a real advance in human knowledge. The writing of reports by participants should not be a major purpose of the discussions."[15]

The effect of Unesco seminars may be gauged by the follow-up that has taken place in member states. Here only scattered information is available. After the 1947 seminar on education for international understanding, a Brazilian member, who was in charge of radio in the Ministry of Education, conducted broadcasts on the work of the seminar and wrote articles for newspapers. Two representatives from Australia devoted six weeks after their return to a trip designed to report on the seminar to leading educational groups. A participant from Sweden took part in the work of a committee on curriculum reform of the elementary schools in that country. Through the cooperation of French members of the seminar, the *Radiodiffusion française* broadcast an hour's program every week during 1947-48 on "Children of Other Lands," with scripts prepared and sometimes recorded by school children of other countries. Other radio programs were exchanged among various countries. Material was published in national journals; seminar members reported to professional meetings of educators and gave talks to civic groups.[16]

Following the 1951 seminar on the teaching of history, the Unesco National Commission in France appointed a committee to review ways to improve the teaching of history in line with the seminar's suggestions. The committee published two pamphlets, the first of which pointed out how the teacher can encourage international understanding by linking national with world history, by noting the interaction of peoples and civilizations, by interpreting facts objectively, and by viewing history as the evolution of human societies. This pamphlet included a study of French and British history textbooks used in secondary schools and covering the period of the Napoleonic wars, 1800-15. The second pamphlet made recommendations on the methods and content of history teaching and discussed the relation of history teaching to international understanding.[17]

A regional seminar organized in the summer of 1952 by the Swedish

National Commission, and attended by history teachers from the three Scandinavian countries, studied the findings both of the 1951 Sèvres seminar on the teaching of history and of the 1950 Brussels seminar on history textbooks (to be discussed later).[18]

In the United Kingdom the Standing Committee on Methods and Materials of the National Commission, which had nominated British participants in the Unesco seminars, published in 1952 a pamphlet on *Teaching for International Understanding*. It stressed teaching *for* international understanding rather than *of* international understanding. Four principles underlay the study: (1) that international understanding is man's most vital need today, and that civilized society will be destroyed unless it progresses toward some international control; (2) that foundations for international understanding must be laid in the schools if such understanding is to be a living influence in adult life; (3) that international understanding must be based on good local citizenship; and (4) that international understanding must appear throughout the curriculum of the schools and not simply in special courses.[19]

Prior to the seminar on modern languages in 1953, several Unesco National Commissions appointed committees to help collect material. A subcommittee of the French National Commission, composed of a score of modern language teachers together with scholars in classical studies, philosophers, and psychologists, met fortnightly over an eight-month period and prepared a study which was available in printed form to members of the seminar.[20] Following the same seminar the United States National Commission initiated as part of its citizen consultation program a "Discussion Guide and Work Paper" on *The National Interest and Foreign Languages,* written by William R. Parker, a member of the Commission.

As a follow-up of this seminar Unesco itself issued two publications, one entitled *The Teaching of Modern Languages,* the other *A Bibliography on the Teaching of Modern Languages.*[21]

Especially interesting was the effect in member states of the 1950 geography seminar. A book on its findings was published in Japan; the Turkish member was requested by the Turkish National Commission for Unesco to organize in Ankara a national conference for teachers of geography; an Australian participant reported on the seminar in visits to individual schools.[22] Moreover, as a result of the seminar the International Geographical Union established a Commission on the Teaching of Geography, which in 1956 issued a preliminary report on geography teaching, and initiated a world-wide survey of the content of geography courses.

Whether these seminars, if compared with other forms of action by Unesco, have been sufficiently productive, and how well they have been administered, are questions on which conclusive evidence is not yet available.

Cooperative Revision of Textbooks

On December 1, 1955, William Benton, just returned from a month's visit to the Soviet Union, wrote to Luther H. Evans, Director General of Unesco, noting that the Soviet Union had recently become a member of Unesco and recalling Unesco's long concern with national textbooks which distort history and deal unjustly with other nations. Mr. Benton, formerly Assistant Secretary of State and later United States Senator, cited misstatements about World War II in a fourth grade history textbook used in the USSR, and asked where Unesco could find a project more suitable than a study of textbooks of the USSR and other countries, together with efforts to persuade nations to make their textbooks fair and objective.[23]

Dr. Evans pointed out in reply that beginning with the 1946 General Conference resolutions had repeatedly been approved inviting member states to examine their textbooks and to report on improvements. "Unesco's role then is," continued Dr. Evans, "to fan interest in the question of giving children in schools a fair and truthful picture of other countries, to bring those concerned with textbooks together when they are willing and to leave them to work out agreed solutions." He added, "It is not within our power, nor do I think it would be wise, for us to indulge in public denunciation of passages in textbooks that have given offense, even when a consensus among historians might support the criticisms made. Were we to seem to claim the right to demand changes in any nation's textbooks this would be resented (and not least in the United States)."[24]

Every country wishes to have its history presented adequately and accurately in the textbooks of other countries. But no country can determine what should appear in the textbooks of a foreign state. That question is decided by authors, publishers, and users of textbooks in each country. Here the role of Unesco, as indicated by Dr.

Evans, is not that of a critic, much less of a censor or judge. Unesco cannot and does not write or rewrite national textbooks. Unesco can do two things. It can urge the appropriate authorities in member states to look carefully at their own textbooks. More important, it can encourage qualified persons from different member states to consult on improvement of textbooks and of teaching aids such as films, still pictures, and recordings. Hence it should be emphasized that much of the work mentioned in the following pages, while stimulated perhaps by Unesco, has gone forward independent of direct Unesco sponsorship.

Unesco's efforts toward improvement of textbooks profited from two decades of earlier activity. At first the emphasis had been negative—on cutting out inaccurate or biased passages and eliminating chauvinistic books. In 1926 one teachers' organization in France, the Syndicat National des Instituteurs, boycotted twenty-six works considered unsatisfactory and secured changes in numerous objectionable statements. Gradually the emphasis shifted to the positive aim of developing in children good will toward other peoples. Several governments set up official bodies for textbook revision.[25] Among active private groups were trade unions, churches, peace societies, professional historians, and educators.

The Institute of Intellectual Cooperation prepared in 1935 a *Declaration Regarding the Teaching of History,* which pointed out the value of presenting the history of other nations and of facts concerning the interdependence of nations.[26] The Norden Association ("The North") in Denmark, Finland, Iceland, Norway, and Sweden sponsored numerous activities on a regional basis for improvement of history textbooks. Similarly the American republics approved two conventions on the teaching of history, at the Montevideo and Buenos Aires conferences of the OAS in 1933 and 1936.[27]

In the United States textbook studies were actively continued during and after World War II. Under the auspices of the American Council on Education, United States textbooks were scrutinized as to their treatment of Latin America, of Canada, of Asian countries, of the Soviet Union, and of minority groups in the United States. In addition a group of United States and Canadian educators sponsored by the American Council on Education conducted in 1945 a study of history textbooks in both countries.[28]

In the twenty years preceding the establishment of Unesco it had become clear that the aim of textbook revision should be not merely factual accuracy. Errors of both omission and commission should be noted. The task required a multiple approach, including careful research by scholars, broader use of such research by authors, more sensitive editing by publishers, new criteria for the selection of textbooks, the support of teachers and other groups, cooperation by governments in bilateral and regional agreements, and bilateral and regional efforts by private agencies. One method of tested utility was the choice of topics whose analysis would be significant for international understanding and cooperation.

The Unesco program from its inception in the Preparatory Commission gave attention to improvement of textbooks and teaching materials, as one means of bettering international understanding. Many earlier efforts had been unilateral, as with some of the studies carried out in the United States. Unesco encouraged member states to review their own textbooks.[29] It also cooperated with occupying authorities for improvement of textbooks in Germany and Japan.

A major step in Unesco's program on textbook revision was a seminar on "The Improvement of Textbooks, Particularly History Books," held at Brussels in 1950. The group was composed of primary and secondary school teachers, professors in teachers' colleges and universities, textbook editors, and government employees and advisers. Several of the teachers were authors of textbooks or members of textbook selection committees.

The participants came to a number of conclusions: the textbook should be "the teacher's servant, not his master"; there was too much nationalism in textbooks on all subjects; textbook revision should be done on a reciprocal basis and by professional groups rather than by government officials; along with national history, the general story of civilization should be taught; world history should cover not Europe alone but other regions; it should emphasize the great religions, stress social as well as political developments, and include the story of international cooperation and of the United Nations.[30]

The Unesco seminar at Brussels stimulated a large number of bilateral consultations between national groups of historians and history teachers. The personal association developed among the participants in the seminar often provided the basis for subsequent collaboration. Of the twenty-eight bilateral groups functioning in 1953, twenty-three included at least one participant in a Unesco seminar.[31]

The procedure usually adopted in bilateral consultations included exchange of manuscripts and textbooks, and their examination; discussion of reports; and finally a list of conclusions approved by both groups.

Both Germany and France played a leading role in the revision of history textbooks following World War II. In the winter of 1947-48 the German Teachers' Association appointed a committee of specialists to work on reform of history teaching. The committee was made up of university professors, teachers of history at all school levels, textbook authors, and radio specialists. The committee was concerned with redressing the harm done under the Hitler regime by twisting textbooks into propaganda vehicles.

A series of Franco-German conversations began in 1949 along the lines encouraged by Unesco. The conclusions issued in 1951 covered forty points relating to the presentation of controversial issues dating from the French Revolution to the advent of Hitler.[32] In the same year the project was broadened to include geography, civics, modern languages, literature, and natural science. The textbook, it was believed, should make clear to the pupil that other countries have interpreted events in a way different from his own. Not only were textbooks exchanged for review by two joint committees, but attention was given to their use in the classroom. For example, during a meeting in Paris in 1953, members of the German group attended classes in ten French primary and secondary schools for a period of thirty class hours. The findings of the committees were published in educational and professional journals. Publishing firms manifested their interest by requesting that additional textbooks be revised.[33]

After the Unesco seminar on modern languages in 1953, the French High Commissioner in Germany invited German modern language teachers to participate in a reciprocal examination of textbooks in the field, to the end of reaching agreement on revisions. French and German language teachers' associations, the *Association des Professeurs de Langues Vivantes* and the *Allgemeiner Deutscher Neuphilologenverband,* held two meetings, one in Germany and the other in France. As a result all textbooks employed in teaching French in the schools of the German Federal Republic were reviewed by French teachers, and vice versa. Criticisms by the German teachers were sent to French publishers, and French criticisms went to German publishers. The significance of this exchange becomes evident when it is recognized that the two national organizations include the majority of teachers in their respective countries and in both countries it is the teachers who have the right of decision on textbooks. Meetings of a similar type took place in 1954-55 between German and English teachers. As one result two English and six German history textbooks were revised.[34]

Another consultation starting in 1951 involved United States and German history teachers. This grew out of the Brussels seminar mentioned above, but was carried on independently of Unesco. The majority of the leading American textbook publishers, whose volumes were used in Canada, Australia, and New Zealand as well as the United States, expressed their willingness to give attention to German criticisms. At a German-American conference at Braunschweig, Germany, in 1952, the United States representatives suggested that German textbooks among other matters should give greater attention to the role in American culture of education, philosophy, and the arts; the American idea of democracy; the family and social life of the average American; and the varied racial and national origins of the American people. The Germans suggested more careful use of emotionally tinged expressions; recognition of the European framework in presenting the history of individual European nations; a clearer picture of the democratic tendencies evident at various stages of German history; and some account of the German resistance movement during the Hitler regime.[35] Other bilateral consultations have involved Germany and Japan, and the United States and the United Kingdom, the last emphasizing not so much misstatements and omissions as making textbooks instruments for international understanding.[36]

The 1952 General Conference of Unesco proposed a new regional approach, namely, a study of the treatment given to one region of the world in textbooks and teaching materials of another region, and vice versa, specifically the ex-colonial powers and their former colonies in Asia. In metropolitan countries students have often been offered an account of European expansion rather than history of Asia. The picture of Europe given to pupils in ex-colonies has overemphasized the role of the former colonial power. This proposal is more challenging than the traditional European and North American approach to textbook revision. It involves special difficulties and has special relevance to the new major project on Eastern-Western relations adopted by the New Delhi General Conference, discussed in Chapter XI.

The first step in carrying out the project related to the treatment of Asian countries in textbooks of the countries of Western European tradition. Unesco member states in the latter area were asked to examine their textbooks in literature and language as well as in geography and history, for the information presented on Asian peoples, its accuracy, its manner of presentation, and its educational value.[37] Approximately twenty nations agreed to do so. Educators from most of these countries came together in a meeting organized by Unesco in May 1956.

The participants called for more balanced presentation of the contribution of Asian peoples to world civilization; for a more vivid and realistic picture of Asian life and thought by attention to the family, food, transportation, education, architecture, and literature; and study of the fundamental issues domestic and foreign in Asian countries. The meeting recommended development by Unesco of a plan for exchange of textbooks, bilateral consultations between educators in the two regions, and regional meetings sponsored by National Commissions. The group also stressed the importance of teacher education, noting that the fullest advantage from improved teaching materials could be gained only if the teachers themselves had an adequate knowledge of Asian countries. A reciprocal meeting was planned for the next biennium to review how textbooks in Asian countries treat the countries of Western European tradition.[38]

The story sketched above reveals an impressive amount of activity in the long effort to improve school textbooks all over the world. Precise information on what has been achieved is largely lacking, including the many changes actually made in texts. No careful study of the results has been made. (Here is a task to be done which Unesco might well promote.) The testimony received from a number of leaders in several countries provides some indication of results and suggests that the endeavor has not been in vain.[39]

In the view of various leaders, changes in the language of textbooks have been less important than the opportunity for textbook writers from different countries to meet and learn each other's point of view. More significant than particular text changes has been the creation of human bonds across frontiers, which may insure that future editions will be influenced by a new spirit.

Others believe that substantial although not spectacular progress has been made in improving school texts. They note in particular that it is becoming increasingly common for textbook authors to submit their manuscripts for criticism to colleagues in other countries. An English author has reported that three of his own books have been altered as the result of criticism from Germany, Canada, Denmark, and Turkey. In Germany a pamphlet on the history of the Weimar Republic was sent for examination to French and American writers. Similarly a source study for use in officers' training centers of the new German army was submitted to French authorities for comment and criticism. The prefaces of this and other works have frequently carried a statement that such a review had been made. Improvement has extended also to the material in textbooks about international affairs and institutions. Much more is said today about the United Nations than was ever said about the League of Nations, and more exactly and objectively.

In some cases the danger lies not in deliberate misstatement, but rather in a bias which may be as unconscious as it is strong. What causes harm is not so much what is said as what is hinted or omitted. Textbooks may have a nationalistic slant, not because they speak ill of other peoples, but because they speak well only of their own nation and say little or nothing of the people of other countries. For example, European textbooks in their treatment of Asian peoples are reported as a rule to "say hardly anything at all worth saying" and to omit nearly everything essential.

Another danger in textbook revision may be dull and neutral history. D. W. Brogan has remarked, "The deodorized history of some propagandists has one weakness, it may have no faults but it has few merits. It is boring and the young cannot learn if they are bored." He adds: "How much more useful than rewriting the story of English rule in India in an apologetic fashion would it be for English school textbooks to ignore the short period of English rule and make India before the European invasions an historical theme of the first magnitude."[40]

Unesco has assisted member states to develop through their schools a more genuine and realistic understanding of other peoples. In revision of textbooks, Unesco's most important service has been to stimulate member states to undertake both bilateral and unilateral analysis of current textbooks. As yet, little has been accomplished in comparison with what needs to be done. Unesco's indirect approach, working through educators in member states, necessarily makes for slow progress.

Education in Ex-Enemy Countries: Unesco Institutes in Germany

Unesco faced at its founding a special problem, that of education in ex-enemy countries. The problem seemed most acute with regard to Germany. The horror of German Nazism permeated the sessions of the London Conference in 1945, and was viewed as the chief evil to be rooted out of men's minds. Bad as Italian fascism and Japanese militarism had been, German Nazism looked even blacker to the delegations most influential at London. During the war it had de-bauched the schools of the occupied countries. But what had it done to the minds of the German people themselves, where it had had its way for a dozen years?

Responsibility for the use of education to remake the mind and spirit of the German people lay with the four occupying powers. The question was early asked whether Unesco could aid in the intellectual reconstruction of Germany and its reintegration into the international community.

At the First Session of the General Conference in 1946, the Dutch delegation called attention to the German question and the need for Unesco assistance to overcome the cultural and spiritual isolation of the German people from the democratic world.[41] A subsequent proffer of cooperation by the Director General drew a favorable response from the commanders of the British, French, and United States zones. The negative attitude of the USSR caused delay and later barred any participation of East Germany. It was only in April 1948 that the Executive Board, after extensive discussion, approved the initiation, in cooperation with the three occupying authorities, of a modest program in West Germany, including exchange of persons and publications between Germany and other countries; study of German textbooks; and participation of German experts as observers in certain Unesco technical meetings. Unesco offices were set up in the three Western occupation zones. A somewhat similar program, in cooperation with the Supreme Commander for the Allied Powers, developed in Japan.[42]

During 1948 and 1949, against strong opposition from Czechoslovakia, Hungary, and Poland of the Soviet bloc, the scope of Unesco activities in West Germany was gradually expanded.[43] With the establishment of a Federal Government at Bonn in 1949, Germany entered a new phase of its postwar development, in which the re-education of the German people could no longer be emphasized. At the 1950 General Conference, representatives of both the United Kingdom and the United States urged that Unesco should not consider its program in Germany as dealing with a special case, but rather as a group of activities which might apply to any country. While Unesco could provide Germany with an opportunity for self-education, Germany had something to contribute to other countries.[44]

The German Federal Republic was admitted to Unesco in 1951, and in that year the General Conference voted to terminate Unesco's special program in Germany. It approved, however, continuance of Unesco's cooperation in three Institutes in Germany, on education, social science, and youth movements, which had been in process of establishment since 1950.[45] These Institutes were planned as separate bodies, located in different cities, but their work would be interrelated. An analysis by social scientists of the situation in Germany would provide guidance for the education and youth centers; experience in these two fields would be of value to social science studies of contemporary problems.

All three Institutes had the common object of supporting Unesco's efforts to further international understanding and cooperation. Each was also to promote international contacts and exchange of information and ideas in its own field. The Education Institute was to carry out research on the aims and methods of education, helping, it was hoped, to counteract the Nazis' exaggerated nationalism by stimulating revision of textbooks and the study of human rights in the school curriculum. The Institute for Social Sciences was to focus research on some of the unprecedented postwar economic, social, and political problems in Germany, including those affecting youth, and to apply modern research methods. The Youth Institute was to encourage in youth "the spirit of international co-operation and a sense of responsibility with regard to the international community," and to help young people to study youth in different countries and methods of cooperation with them.[46]

Thus the Institutes were a practical experiment in international cooperation. Their staffs as well as their governing boards would be drawn from different countries and would naturally represent different points of view. Financial support was also to be international.[47] The Social Science Institute began work at Cologne in July 1951, that for Youth at Gauting near Munich in January 1952, and that for Education at Hamburg in March 1952.

The Institutes in Germany were originally seen in some quarters as means of international assistance in the re-education especially of German youth. By the time they were in operation, this idea had been outmoded by changes in the world situation and in Germany itself. The Institutes then came to be viewed as a project to promote international understanding. In practice, however, they have been concerned with advancement of knowledge as well as of understanding.[48] The Institutes were plagued, one should add, by uncertainty about financial support.[49]

A survey of the three centers was made by a special committee of the Executive Board in 1952. Three years later a small group of specialists appointed by the Director General made a more thorough review and presented in their report a clear picture of what the Institutes had done and planned to do in the future.[50] These surveys showed that the Youth Institute had been the least successful of the three, lacking both a clearly defined object and effective leadership.

By contrast the Institute for the Social Sciences at Cologne has a purpose which is easily understood by scholars and governments. It has carried on a number of research projects, largely with sociological orientation. More recently it has sought to break ground in areas which were international either in the character of the problem or in the comparative research procedures required—helping to coordinate studies made by social science groups in different countries. One such undertaking related to labor mobility within and between countries belonging to the European Coal and Steel Community.[51]

It is important that its focus on international and comparative studies be continued. For the Institute has been materially hampered in attaining its objectives by inadequate contact with and support from scholars and other social science centers both inside and outside Germany. The Institute is apparently viewed in Europe as a competitor with other social science research agencies which have been developing since the end of World War II, rather than as a collaborator. Outside Europe it is virtually unknown.

Continuance of the Cologne center depends upon maintaining its international character. Though located in Germany, it is in no way a German institution. A resolution of the Consultative Assembly of the Council of Europe in January 1957 declared that "maintenance

of this international Institute is of indisputable importance for the
development of social sciences in the European countries" and that
"the Council of Europe might make use of this Institute's studies in
planning its own work."[52] Here, as in relation to the Coal and Steel
Community, the projected common European market, and similar
enterprises, the Institute for the Social Sciences may find a research
area for which it is peculiarly well suited.

The Education Institute at Hamburg has had the least troubled
and steadiest development. Its work fell into a well-defined professional area, and secured general support from the start because it
met a recognized need. It undertook studies and arranged conferences
on the education of adults and young children. Many of its conferences have been regional, drawing together educators from Britain,
France, Italy, Portugal, Scandinavia, Spain, and Switzerland, as well
as from Germany.

At the suggestion of Dr. Maria Montessori the Institute held an
international conference to discuss influences in early childhood making for a creative and cooperative personality. A later meeting organized jointly with the Unesco secretariat examined psychological
services in education. Conferences were held on more general topics
such as the education and training of primary school teachers, and
problems of educational reform common to a number of countries.
The Institute for Education joined with the Institute for Social
Sciences in a meeting to discuss young people in industry; and with
the French National Commission for Unesco in an international
gathering of young teachers at Sèvres near Paris to explore the teacher's role in developing understanding and cooperation between nations and groups. Reports on these meetings were published.[53]

While the three Unesco Institutes in Germany achieved varying
success, their record was such as to warrant recommendations for
their continuance from both the 1952 committee of the Executive
Board and the 1955 committee of specialists. The initial motive of
re-educating the German people early gave way to the broader aim
of joining the resources of education, the social sciences, and youth
movements to improve educational programs, solve social problems
of an international character, and forward international understanding. As an experiment in international cooperation, their story in
general is one of constructive collaboration in applying intellectual
resources drawn from many different countries and from very differ-

ent cultures. In spite of the multi-national membership of governing boards and staffs, the operation has proceeded with harmony. Both the investigating groups strongly urged maintenance of the international character of the Institutes—in their activities, in the choice of their participants, and in their staff and governing boards. While their "geographic area of action" must primarily be Europe, the investigating groups urged that wherever possible they secure the participation of representatives from more distant countries.

History of the Scientific and Cultural Development of Mankind

One of Unesco's most adventurous and extended undertakings, designed to provide a sounder basis for international understanding, has been the project for a world history of the scientific and cultural development of mankind. Such a work, it was hoped, would contribute to scholarship and undergird national programs to foster peace through education. Its purpose was to develop "a wider understanding of the scientific and cultural aspects of the history of mankind, of the mutual interdependence of peoples and cultures and of their contributions to the common heritage."[54] The proposal differed from preceding "world histories" in that it was not to be written by one author or group of self-selected authors, but by scholars working together with an international commission established for this purpose.

A novel element in the plan was a quarterly *Journal of World History,* which has been published since 1953 with Lucien Febvre as editor. The *Journal,* with articles in English, French, and Spanish, provides opportunity for interested persons to read materials destined for the history, so as to assure their critical examination by scholars before they are incorporated in the work.

The Unesco proposal for a History of the Scientific and Cultural Development of Mankind originated in a decision of the 1947 General Conference.[55] Only after consideration by succeeding conferences and by interested nongovernmental organizations and various experts did the General Conference in 1950 authorize a start on the project by appointing an International Commission "to undertake, on behalf of Unesco, full responsibility for the preparation and execution of the work."[56] Unesco thus delegated to the Commission re-

sponsibility for the project, although it would be financially supported by Unesco funds.

In accord with this decision, the Director General invited nine
scholars to serve as members of the Commission.[57] The Commission
was enlarged in 1953 by adding the editor of the *Journal* and the principal author-editors of the six volumes. In September 1952 the Commission addressed letters to the appropriate scholarly bodies in the
USSR, Czechoslovakia, Hungary, and Poland, inviting them to take
part in the work, but no replies were received. However, at the Montevideo conference in 1954 these countries expressed a desire to participate in the enterprise, and during 1955 and early 1956 members
from these states were added to the Commission. Representatives of
ICSU and CIPHS, and since 1953 of the International Social Science
Council, regularly sit with the Commission. The Commission was
constituted as an autonomous international association and operates
under a contract with Unesco.[58] The total cost of the enterprise over
a period of approximately eight years was estimated at $412,000.[59]

Provisions to ensure the balanced and representative character of
the history included, in addition to the *Journal,* the naming as corresponding members of some 130 scholars drawn from approximately
45 countries. In addition a smaller group of consultants was named—
specialists in many branches of history as well as in the sciences, arts,
and letters—to whom the Commission could refer questions calling
for special exposition or investigation.[60]

The Commission decided that the history would be written in six
volumes as follows: Volume I, prehistoric and archaic periods, up to
about 1200 B.C.; Volume II, from about 1200 B.C. to 400 A.D.; Volume III, from about 400 to 1300; Volume IV, from 1300 to 1775;
Volume V, from 1775 to the beginning of the twentieth century; Volume VI, from the beginning of the twentieth century to 1950. Each
volume would have one or more author-editors, aided by a group
of associates.[61] Professor Ralph E. Turner of Yale University will act
as general editor of the English edition, and editions will be issued in
French and possibly other languages.

The schedule called for completion of the manuscript of the six
volumes by January 1958. Comment and criticism would then be
secured from the members and corresponding members of the Commission and from scholars of special competence or of a special point
of view. These would be considered by the author-editors in revision

of their texts, and would be used by the general editor in preparing notes to accompany each volume, which would indicate differences in viewpoint concerning the facts of history, certain historical events and movements, and general interpretations. Through this process it was hoped to ensure that scholars of Asia and Latin America, as well as those of Europe and North America, would have a voice in the preparation of the work. Publication of the six volumes in English and French was planned for 1960 or 1961.[62]

Wider circulation of the history will be achieved by preparation of two abridged editions which will presumably be translated into various languages: one in two volumes and a shorter version in a single volume.

Critics have argued that the project would take too much time and too much money. Some believed it impractical because scholars prefer to work independently rather than in cooperation. Others said that Unesco, despite its delegation of the task to an autonomous commission, would itself be held responsible for errors and omissions; that the history could not be completely objective; that explicitly or implicitly it would represent one philosophy of history; and that it could achieve objectivity only at the cost of colorless neutrality.

Any appraisal of the History of the Scientific and Cultural Development of Mankind must await its publication. Only two remarks will be made here. First, a great effort has been made to assure that the history will be an objective and scholarly work. Witness the membership of the Commission itself and the corresponding members and consultants; the list of author-editors; and the *Journal of World History* as an international forum for preliminary presentation of material. Second, the project has survived to date the inherent perils of such an unprecedented and long-term enterprise, the difficulty in maintaining financial support from an international assembly, and the periodic criticisms at General Conference sessions.

Consensus to the fullest possible degree on the facts about historical relations of nations and peoples is an essential element in the promotion of either objective or sympathetic understanding among nations. To this task, admittedly difficult, the governments of member states have asked Unesco to bring the best available resources of world scholarship.

CHAPTER XI

INTERNATIONAL UNDERSTANDING: THE SEARCH FOR UNITY IN DIVERSITY

In the twentieth century ideological issues have become a prominent feature in international relations. The struggle between the Western powers and the Soviet bloc turns in part on differences in values. More positively, the growing contacts between the peoples of Asia and those of Europe and the Americas have led to the view that philosophic and spiritual ideas may provide a basis for analyzing differences and exploring the possibility of adjustment and understanding. Accurate knowledge of the facts of history may contribute to better comprehension of one people by another. But there is also need for comprehension of other peoples' basic ideas, what they believe is good in their way of life, the standards they use in morals and religion as well as in politics and economics. Upon this problem Unesco has focused many projects in philosophy and humanities.

Such standards and values are at the core of the problem of international understanding or misunderstanding. They differ from people to people and are often antagonistic, as current ideological conflicts demonstrate. Men are passionately attached to their own values. Sometimes differences can be adjusted through compromise. Jacques Maritain has pointed out that "systems antagonistic in theory 'may converge' in their practical conclusions."[1] Sometimes, differences can be reconciled through objective understanding. But in some cases, as in the current struggle between Communism and democracy, an objective understanding of what each side seeks may intensify the conflict.

Unesco was founded on recognition of the vast diversity of customs, traditions, and values which exist among nations. This diversity is a fact and an asset of world society. But Unesco was lured by its member states into the hazardous exploration of philosophic and religious belief, in an effort to discover points of agreement underlying human diversity. To what extent has mankind's common struggle to satisfy common needs created basic values which are universally appreciated? Is it possible beneath diversity to find some unity?

Archibald MacLeish urged in 1948 that "Unesco must restore the sense of a human community. It should start by stressing the universality of the question which all men in all countries face—the question of how any man can live in the modern world of vast machines and inhuman environments in which the individual seems powerless. Unesco must express the vast and tragic but common human experience of trying to answer this one question. It is the question and not the attempts to answer it that is important."[2]

Irrespective of the degree to which widespread sense of human community ever existed in the past, Unesco early recognized the crucial character of this problem in the present. As the first session of the General Conference declared, "The philosophic problem of Unesco is the problem of finding common grounds for understanding and agreement between diverse philosophies and religions. This is a new and important problem for philosophy directly related to the cause of peace."[3]

Fundamental Concepts: Human Rights, Democracy, Liberty, Law

Unesco's first effort in this field came in 1947, with an examination of the philosophic principles of human rights. This undertaking was designed to assist the Commission on Human Rights of the UN Economic and Social Council, which was just beginning to draft the Universal Declaration of Human Rights. Unesco's task was to examine the history of human rights and the principles underlying notable declarations of rights in the past. As regards history, it would seek to clarify the nature of human rights, and review the institutions by which they were established and safeguarded, their extension to larger numbers of people, and the growing variety of rights which men have sought. As regards principles, it would investigate whether those used to justify the classic declarations of rights in the eighteenth century, such as the equality of man and the law of nature, were still valid.

Replies to a widely circulated questionnaire were analyzed by philosophers and other scholars brought together by Unesco, and their findings were transmitted to the Commission on Human Rights, and also published in a volume entitled *Human Rights, Comments and Interpretations.*

The group agreed on the importance of the projected Universal Declaration of Human Rights. It declared: "an international declaration of human rights must be the expression of a faith to be maintained, no less than a programme of actions to be carried out. It is a foundation for convictions universally shared by men, however great the differences of their circumstances and their manner of formulating human rights: it is an essential element in the constitutional structure of the United Nations." The group agreed also that the foundations of human rights in the twentieth century must differ from those in the eighteenth, and that philosophic agreement on human rights did not depend on a single philosophic doctrine. In spite of widely different philosophical and political views, members of the group were able to agree on a definition of rights and of freedom, and to list a broad array of human rights regarded as universal.[4]

A committee of specialists from sixteen countries, called together at Paris in September 1947 to advise the Director General on the Unesco program in philosophy and the humanities, pointed out that the "ideological conflict" accompanying the cold war involved philosophic questions. It recommended that the inquiry into basic ideas, initiated by the examination of human rights, be continued by a scrutiny of other ideas such as democracy, freedom, and law. This recommendation was approved by the Second Session of the General Conference.

Exploration of the idea of democracy was undertaken to uncover "the traditions of thought and the basic assumptions of theory" which it involved.[5] To provide a basis of discussion a list was drawn up of fundamental texts, ancient and modern, in which the idea of democracy had been considered. This together with a questionnaire was addressed to some 500 scholars in philosophy, history, political science, law, sociology, economics, logic, and communications analysis. About one-fourth of those addressed replied, and their answers were studied by a small committee. Its report, published in *Democracy in a World of Tensions,* noted that despite much ambiguity in the idea of democracy and despite many differences of interpretation, "none of the replies to the questionnaire defend antidemocratic doc-

trines. The ambiguity is old, but the Committee points out that the
unanimity in favoring and professing democracy is new."[6] Inquiries
were later undertaken into the ideas of liberty and of law, in cooperation with the International Federation of Philosophic Societies and
the International Council for Philosophy and Humanistic Studies.[7]

It was originally hoped that the findings of the inquiries would be
transmitted to Unesco National Commissions, scholarly bodies, and
other organizations for study and review. These discussions, it was
expected, would then find their way into programs of education and
mass communication. In certain areas, at least, the plan worked out.
The *Human Rights* volume published in 1949 was widely and favor-
ably reviewed, and the English version went into a second edition. It
has been used at various universities. In one course at Yale College,
term papers written by the students were sent to a Paris *lycée* to be
reviewed by the students there, whose own essays were sent back to
the American class. Following use of the volume as a textbook at the
University of Chicago, two radio broadcasts presented by the University of Chicago Round Table over a nation-wide network discussed the book. A home study course on human rights was continued
by the University for several years. The Unesco secretariat transmitted 400 copies of the broadcasts to National Commissions in other
member states, resulting in extensive correspondence with, for example, a group of Japanese Unesco clubs and an official in India. The
Kansas and Missouri State Councils on Unesco used the volume as
a basis for annual programs. The volume on democracy was used in
courses at Washington University in St. Louis and at Mysore University in India.

The project has acquired enough life to go forward on its own, with
occasional help from Unesco or CIPHS. The International Institute
of Philosophy focused its 1955 meeting at Athens on two problems—
the use of philosophy in intercultural communication and the application of philosophic principles in treatment of practical problems.
At the invitation of the Polish government, the Institute was to hold
its 1957 meeting at Warsaw, to examine "Philosophy in Action." This
session would be the first international meeting of philosophers to be
held behind the Iron Curtain under conditions of free discussion.

The influence of the project is illustrated by the agreement of the
editors of the *Revue Internationale de Philosophie,* published at
Brussels, to devote the Autumn 1957 issue of the journal to justice (one
of the terms included in the *Dictionary of Fundamental Terms of*

Philosophy and Political Thought). Five articles in English, French, German, Italian, and Spanish will treat the ideas of justice in these linguistic traditions, together with a general article outlining the problems presented by divergencies in the basic concept. Collaborators in India and Japan will extend to Asia this presentation of the traditions of Europe and the Americas.

Comparative Study of Cultures

Unesco has also sought to throw light on the process of international understanding by a comparative study of cultures or national ways of life, and of peoples' ideas and judgments about their own culture and its relations with other cultures. Traditionally each people has assumed that its culture is the only "right" one, and has viewed alien values as quaint superstition. The notions, whether accurate or distorted, which men have of their own and of foreign ways of life affect profoundly the understanding between peoples.[8]

Unesco embarked on a study of this problem by resolutions approved at the 1947 and 1948 General Conferences.[9] Contributions were invited from scientists, historians, ethnologists, humanists, and philosophers; these were presented to a group of specialists meeting in Paris near the end of 1949, whose conclusions were published, together with a number of papers on the cultures of Asia, Africa, and Latin America, in *Interrelations of Cultures,* initiating a new series of Unesco publications under the title *Unity and Diversity of Cultures.*

This preliminary exploration led to a breakdown of the question into two parts: one, on peoples whose traditions might be profoundly modified by industrialization and modern technology, as well as by progress toward self-government; the other on cultural understanding among nations already adjusted to industrialization and political independence.

Many activities of Unesco and other United Nations agencies relate to the first problem, the impact of modern technology (outlined in Chapter IX). Among the Unesco projects are fundamental education, social tensions, improvement of living conditions, application of the principles of the Universal Declaration of Human Rights, and raising the general level of culture. Any tendency to ignore the intellectual, moral, and spiritual values of each culture may make technical assistance for economic development not only sterile, but possibly ridiculous or even dangerous in the eyes of the people who are to profit from it. Countries in this category must be helped to preserve their traditional culture, while at the same time incorporating new values of technology and industrialism, and to enter gradually into a world community of cooperative progress and mutual understanding which will facilitate the development of political and economic institutions essential for world peace.[10]

Orient and Occident

Continuing the examination of relations among the different cultures, Unesco organized at New Delhi in December 1951 a discussion on the cultural and philosophical relations between Orient and Occident, specifically on the theme "The Concept of Man and the Philosophy of Education in East and West." A dozen or more eminent philosophers and educators took part, from India, Ceylon, Japan, Egypt, and Turkey as well as from France, Germany, Italy, Switzerland, the United Kingdom, and the United States. Prime Minister Nehru and the Indian Minister of Education, Dr. Maulana Abul Kalam Azad, also participated.

The discussions led to agreement that "the conventional distinction between the active West and the contemplative East was fallacious" and has been overemphasized. Instead of two basically different ideas of man in East and West, the regions shared fundamentally similar religious and cultural ideas. Attitudes supposedly "typical" in both regions had been conditioned by geography and climate. The result of evolution, they could be modified by contacts between cultures, which should be encouraged. While in India ethics and philosophy were more clearly based on religion than in the West, this was not true of other Eastern countries such as China. Delegates from both East and West voiced some fear of religion as a divisive influence. The participants differed, but not on an East-West basis, concerning man's ability through technology to master nature. While science had given to multitudes greater health and happiness, there was danger that it might numb and enslave the soul of man. Education should recognize that the intellect was only one element in man's nature, and it was important to cultivate also the imagination and the spirit. Ideals of equality and the dignity of the individual must be stressed, and the right of all to participate in cultural life. A "new humanism" must safeguard against an exaggerated emphasis on technology in the West and an "other worldly" tendency in the East. Aggressive nationalism which taught the superiority of one race over another was condemned, but the value of patriotism and pride in one's own country and culture was recognized. Tolerance was good but it must not degenerate into apathy.

It had been hoped that the discussion would identify areas of practical activity where the thinking of East and West might converge, in line with the ideas presented by Jacques Maritain at the Second Session of the General Conference. The seminar recommended more conferences of philosophers, scientists, artists, and educators; wider knowledge in the West of the classic books of the East; mutual revision of history textbooks (initiated by Unesco in 1946; see Chapter X); new textbooks on religious leaders of the world; more attention in schools to the imagination and aesthetic capacities of children; linking the teaching of science to the teaching of philosophy; and continuation of Unesco's efforts for exchange of knowledge and advancement of education.[11]

In a manner somewhat similar to the New Delhi discussion, the cultural relations between Western Europe and the Americas were examined in 1954 at two conferences of philosophers, scientists and other scholars, and writers, held at Saõ Paulo and Geneva, the latter in cooperation with the *Rencontres Internationales*.[12]

Eastern-Western discussions were carried forward in a series of international round tables on Asian-American relations sponsored during April and May 1956 by the United States National Commission at the request of Unesco. Outstanding educational and cultural leaders from ten Asian countries[13] came to the United States to participate. In sessions of three to four days each, held in six American cities—San Francisco, Minneapolis, Ann Arbor, Louisville, Boston, and Washington—these representative Asians sat down with American social scientists, historians, philosophers, and other scholars, as well as businessmen, labor leaders, newspaper publishers and writers, and educational and religious leaders.

The exchange of views focused on the dynamic changes taking place in both Asia and the United States (under the topic "Human Values in Social Change in South and Southeast Asia and the United States: Implications for Asian-American Cooperation"). The talks ranged widely over the political, economic, and social, and also the educational, cultural, and religious elements in two different civilizations. They sought to identify sources of misunderstanding and to discover approaches to international cooperation between the United States and Asian peoples.

Human values in the two areas were compared and contrasted. The effects of industrialization on family and community, on art and religion were assessed. Race relations in the United States, a topic of special interest to Asian participants, were examined. In Detroit the Indian representative at his request met for an extended conversation with almost a score of Negro leaders, who, while stating frankly the discriminations suffered by their race, informed him that in that city their people were better treated economically than anywhere in the world. The United States' Asian policies were reviewed and criticized, and possibilities for future Asian-American cooperation were explored.

The talks revealed, as one Asian member remarked, "that Asians and Americans have the same cycle of life and the same values. The differences lie largely in emphasis. . . . Each region must do its best to understand the psychology of the other, and each region must choose its friends and its policies with care, lest it back the wrong horse. In achieving both aims, these meetings have been of inestimable help. They have changed a meeting of minds into a meeting of hearts."[14]

The Mutual Appreciation of Eastern and Western Cultural Values was approved as a major project by Unesco's 1956 General Conference at New Delhi. It is to continue for ten years. This proposal probably excited more interest at the New Delhi gathering than any other.

Asian countries, India in particular, had repeatedly urged that Unesco help present to countries of the Occident the cultures of the Orient—painting, music, literature, the theater and dance, and especially the spiritual values of religion, "the pivotal force in culture."[15] While appreciation of this kind must be reciprocal, Asian countries had stressed that the prevailing current of influence during recent centuries had been from West to East, particularly with regard to science and education. This trend not only made for an incomplete picture of the Orient in the eyes of the Occident, but also created an inaccurate impression of Occidental civilization among countries of the Orient.

This proposal as presented to the New Delhi Conference was less precisely outlined than the other two major projects approved, dealing with teacher training in Latin America and improvement of living conditions in the arid zones. It called for action along four lines and included, as will be noted, various undertakings already initiated. Among suggestions advanced was encouragement of cooperation between Eastern and Western specialists specifically in the preparation of works of reference. This item and certain others were referred to the International Council for Philosophy and Humanistic Studies. Discussions among philosophers and other scholars were to continue; social science studies on the reciprocal influence of Orient and Occident were to be promoted; fellowships and travel grants for exchange of specialists, teachers, eminent scientists, and university lecturers were to be increased.

Second, schools were to be encouraged to foster international understanding through more contacts among educational leaders, research workers, and administrators; improvement of curricula; revision of textbooks; and experimental activities in teacher-training institutions.[16] Third, wider and better exchange of information for the general public would be promoted through publications, radio, films, and television. Translation of literary classics and significant contemporary works would be expanded, as would traveling exhibitions of art in reproduction and the diffusion of musical compositions. Libraries and museums would be extended, and the assistance of youth and adult education organizations enlisted. Finally, Unesco would assist national organizations to provide the necessary coordination and liaison.[17]

The General Conference approved the project only in general terms[18] because it was unable to reach agreement as to what activities should be carried on and what methods might prove effective. In consequence it provided for an advisory committee of eighteen members which would assist the Director General in selecting activities which would be put in operation after approval by the Executive Board. The Conference voted $850,000 to carry the project during 1957 and 1958.

The Arts and International Understanding

The arts—music, literature, painting, and sculpture—can help greatly in developing international understanding. When not strictly local, they also may reflect a community of tradition among peoples of divergent customs. We have reviewed in Chapter VI Unesco activities in the arts, which in addition to advancing knowledge in many cases have fostered among different peoples better mutual appreciation of each other's artistic achievements. For this reason only one or two projects which bear particularly on the development of international understanding will be mentioned here.

The International Theater Week illustrates how the stage may contribute to international understanding. A number of national centers of the International Theater Institute, whose founding was sponsored by Unesco, have organized annually a program through which each country becomes acquainted with significant foreign plays, particularly those bearing on human rights and international understanding. Among the countries where such programs have been produced are India, Japan, Mexico, Netherlands, Norway, Switzerland, the United Kingdom, and Yugoslavia. This movement began in the United States, where the month of March each year is given to the program.[19] Theater groups across the country, amateur as well as professional, are invited to present a play or other performance bearing on race relations, international understanding, and peace. In 1956 more than 250 theater groups in the United States took part in this effort.

Some Unesco fellowships to painters may have advanced international understanding. In 1956 on the recommendation of the United States Committee affiliated with the International Association of Plastic Arts, an American artist, long interested in the relations between African Negro culture and American art, who was a faculty member at Texas Southern University, was granted a fellowship to study African life and art in Ghana. This study was in preparation for a mural showing the contributions of Negro culture to American life.[20]

Many of Unesco's mass communication activities (reviewed in Chapter VI) have contributed to international understanding as well as to communication of information and advancement of knowledge. They will therefore not be reexamined at this point.

Research on Causes of Social Tensions

The Unesco projects to encourage better understanding, discussed in this and the preceding chapter, have included direct face-to-face relations, improvement of educational programs, analysis of basic ideas and values which may be either barriers or bonds in a world community, together with the arts and means of mass communication. In the absence of knowledge derived from objective evaluation of the efficacy of these approaches, Unesco has proceeded on a common-sense, trial-and-error basis. But some fundamental questions have been asked which clearly called for research. What factors lead to suspicion, contempt, or hostility between one people and another? What factors foster understanding, peace, and security? Governments rightly wanted Unesco to promote research which might help point the direction for more effective efforts.

Sociologists, social psychologists, and social anthropologists had done considerable research on social behavior within nations. These studies had cast some light on domestic tensions, and had helped to improve relations between different races and occupational groups. Could lessons from the national level be applied at the international level?

Social scientists are not in full agreement on exactly what social tensions are.[21] They have been defined as latent conflicts or "states of strain," arising from fear, anxiety, and frustration, which threaten to lead to conflict.[22] The purpose of Unesco's efforts is not so much to reduce tensions as to develop ways in which tensions may be understood, endured if necessary, adjusted if possible, thus becoming constructive factors for improvement of human relations. Tensions are normal in human affairs; they may provide a useful dynamic. They become dangerous when they reach the point beyond which lies open conflict.

One classification lists tensions on three main levels: within the individual, within a group or nation, and between nations.[23] Unesco's interest has centered on the last level, international tensions. Studies of other kinds of tension are important to Unesco principally as they provide tools of analysis and as they contribute to understanding of international tensions.

In the project on social tensions, beginning in 1947,[24] Unesco was asked by member states to explore four different fields:

(1) The relation to international understanding of differences in what is called "national character" and of the ideas people have about such differences;

(2) The effect of modern technology and industry on relations between peoples, particularly as regards educational, scientific, and cultural activities;

(3) Movements of people, from rural areas to cities as well as from country to country, and the tensions such movements may cause;

(4) Race relations as making for prejudice and hostility, or tolerance and understanding.

Unesco has not attempted to conduct research. Its function has been to stimulate cooperative research of an international character, securing and circulating information, encouraging studies by scholarly bodies and individuals which may augment the working stock of methods and ideas, and helping member states at their request to solve their most pressing problems.

As an initial step in making available knowledge about tensions, Unesco encouraged the publication in 1950 of two exploratory studies[25] by American social scientists: one edited by Professor Hadley Cantril of Princeton University entitled *Tensions that Cause Wars,* a symposium by eight scholars of different nationality and field of interest on the influences which foster either international understanding or aggressive nationalism; the other written by Professor Otto Klineberg of Columbia University on *Tensions Affecting International Understanding* which summarized the results of studies of national character, of stereotyped attitudes and how they may be modified, and of influences making for aggression.[26] Dr. Klineberg concluded that the material he had reviewed added up to "impressive evidence of the possibility of applying scientific method to the study of international relations." He noted the complexity of the problem and the need for more research and for better scientific methods. He declared that attitudes can be changed, but more knowledge is needed on the conditions under which one method rather than another yields more useful results.[27]

Differences in National Character

To begin the study of differences in national character or culture as a possible source of tensions, Unesco asked the International Studies Conference to take responsibility for a series of studies, under the title "The Way of Life," of the social organization and basic values of fifteen nations—Australia, Austria, Egypt, France, Greece, Italy, Lebanon, Mexico, New Zealand, Norway, Pakistan, Poland, Switzerland, the Union of South Africa, and the United Kingdom.[28] Seven of these studies have been published.

Besides possible differences in national character, there are the ideas people hold about these differences, how one people thinks of itself and of other peoples.[29] Sometimes these fixed ideas or stereotypes correspond to the facts; sometimes they do not. They are often wrong and out-of-date. They may distort like a concave or convex mirror. Surveys of public opinion in nine countries were undertaken to identify these stereotypes and appraise their importance.[30] Another approach was directed to the possibility of changing, especially in children, ideas underlying prejudice against "foreigners" or "colored people." An experiment revealing how such attitudes may change was carried out in an English school where two Negro teachers from Africa taught for two weeks.[31]

Thus attention began to shift from concern with the origin of tensions to evaluation of social instruments and processes that either reduce or increase tensions. Other studies of the methods developed by education and the social sciences for changing mental attitudes included an examination in Paris at the Centre d'Etudes Sociologiques of the various elements in the social education of a child—the influence of the family, of other groups, and of social attitudes; a study in New Zealand of the relation between the manner in which information is presented and the attitudes toward international relations which result; and an experiment at London University, where teachers analyzed their own prejudices.[32]

Unesco has sought to stimulate demands for assistance of the social sciences on the part of governments, and it has encouraged social scientists to respond to these requests. Two governments have asked for Unesco's help in analyzing their domestic tensions.

India in 1949 was the first government to ask for such aid. Unesco appointed Professor Gardner Murphy, then of the College of the City of New York, to serve for a six-month period as technical adviser to the Indian government. The study centered on Hindu-Muslim relations but involved also language, caste, economic and regional antagonisms. The government urged Indian universities to participate in the program and eventually ten or more research teams of Indian scientists were organized. Studies were conducted at Bombay University of the attitudes of Hindu residents, Hindu refugees, and Muslims toward one another and toward government policies on communal matters; one at Delhi University, of characteristic differences among Hindus, Sikhs, and Muslims in handling aggressive impulses arising from frustration; one at the Muslim University of Aligarh, of methods of reducing Hindu-Muslim tensions by establishing common goals for both communities; one at the University of Lucknow, of inter-caste hostilities in the villages of the United Provinces and also of sources of insecurity among members of a minority community; at the University of Poona, of reduction of inter-caste tensions among secondary school students; at Madras University, of the part played by textbooks in the development of tensions; at the Presidency College in Madras of the sources and forms of language tensions with special attention to Telugu and Tamil; and at Ahmedabad, a large textile city on the west coast, of relations between factory workers and their supervisors.[33]

The whole research program was carried on under a coordinating committee attached to the Indian National Commission for Unesco. After the Unesco grant of $20,000 had been spent, the Government of India gave approximately the same amount to continue the research.

Similarly the Government of Israel in 1952 asked Unesco for a specialist to help formulate a plan of study comparable to that carried out in India. Professor Arvid Brodersen of the New School for Social Research was appointed. In cooperation with scholars from the Hebrew University and the Israeli Institute for Applied Social Science Research, a program of studies was carried out along four lines: adjustment of new immigrants, particularly from North Africa, the Middle East, and Asia, to employment in industry; relations between older settlers and new immigrants in regard to leadership and power; the situation of young people in a society divided between "old-timers and newcomers"; and dislike and attraction among groups of new immigrants.[34]

Studies in Germany and Japan have focused on tensions between generations, and in Japan the authorities have followed up the initial study by a general investigation of tensions on different social levels.[35]

Another sector of the tensions project, dealing with the impact of industrialization and of modern technology, has already been discussed in Chapter IX.[36]

Problems of Immigrants

In the third sector, the relation between population problems and international understanding, Unesco's activities have supplemented those of the Population Commission of the United Nations. Unesco's focus has been on educational and cultural factors which make it easier for immigrants to be incorporated into the community where they have settled. Studies have been made of assimilation of immigrants in Australia, Belgium, Brazil, France, and Israel. Countries of emigration were queried concerning measures taken to prepare emigrants for new conditions of life, and countries of immigration about what they were doing to facilitate the assimilation of immigrants.

Investigations were followed in 1952 by an offer on the part of Unesco to assist countries directly concerned with migration to ascertain and identify the social conditions which forward assimilation of immigrants, facilitate their entry into the economic and cultural life of the country, and improve understanding between peoples. A study in Brazil by Professor Arca Parró of Peru, formerly Chairman of the United Nations Population Commission, provided emigration and immigration officials, welfare services, and local administrative bodies with an objective account of measures for facilitating the assimilation of immigrants. Another group of studies, which served as working papers for a Unesco-sponsored conference at Havana in April 1956, reviewed the influence exerted by racial and cultural minority groups on the foreign policy of their country, and the contributions of immigrants to the economic and cultural life of their country of adoption.[37]

Race Relations

The fourth area of the tensions project centered on race relations. Unesco began its activities in this field in 1949, as the result of a request from the United Nations. The Sub-Commission on Discrimination and Protection of Minorities of the Economic and Social Council had approved resolutions suggesting that Unesco disseminate scientific information "designed to remove what is commonly known as race prejudice."[38] Unesco has issued a series of semipopular pamphlets on The Race Question in Modern Science, written by leading scholars; one, *The Race Concept—Results of an Inquiry,* included a statement by an international group of physical anthropologists and geneticists, declaring that science provides no proof that one race is inherently superior to another. Other pamphlets outlined succinctly the known facts about *Racial Myths, The Roots of Preju-*

dice, Race and Biology, Race and Culture, Race and History, Race and Society, The Significance of Racial Differences, and *Race Mixture.* These pamphlets in revised form were later published together in a volume under the general title of the series, *The Race Question in Modern Science.*[39]

Unesco has thus helped to make more widely known the findings of scientists that racial differences in behavior or mentality are not primarily rooted in biological inheritance, but are due to historical development at different rates under different conditions. Nor do mental characteristics necessarily correspond to physical differences.

A second series of publications on The Race Question and Modern Thought has included pamphlets on *The Catholic Church and the Race Question, Jewish Thought as a Factor in Civilization, The Ecumenical Movement and the Racial Problem,* and *Hinduism and Tolerance. Buddhism and the Race Question* is scheduled for publication in 1958.[40] Finally, Unesco has encouraged a study of constructive efforts to improve relations among racial groups in the United States, Brazil, Mexico, the French West Indies, Germany, and Yugoslavia.[41]

More recently Unesco was asked by its members to examine the question how education, particularly in primary and secondary schools, can help children develop racial tolerance rather than prejudice. Also studies were planned of members of supposedly "primitive" or "inferior" groups who are becoming intellectual leaders and capable technicians and administrators. The survey of these new "élites" covers communities in West Africa (Nigeria, Dahomey, and the Gold Coast), including the progress of educated African women and the role of Negro students in Paris as potential leaders.[42]

Unesco and Actual Threats to Peace

Has Unesco's tensions project had any effect on situations which threaten world peace? Following the aggression in Korea, the General Conference in 1951 authorized the Director General, when requested by the Economic and Social Council, to assist through studies or the advice of experts action taken by the United Nations "either to maintain peace in areas where conflicts are liable to arise, or, after the cessation of hostilities, to restore the normal life of national communities in areas where conflicts have taken place."[43] To date no such request has come from the Economic and Social Council. Social scientists have suggested that their studies might be more effective in helping to "restore the normal life of national communities" than to "maintain peace in areas where conflicts are liable to arise."[44]

The question has been asked why Unesco ignored the greatest contemporary tension of all, that between the Soviet Union and the Western powers. One reason was that the task was greater than Unesco's powers. Another was that during the earlier years, Unesco was not in a position to bring together social scientists in the Iron Curtain countries with those of the West.[45] The USSR remained outside Unesco throughout the latter's first eight years, its attitude reflecting indifference at times and hostility at others. Czechoslovakia, Hungary, and Poland attempted to withdraw from Unesco in 1951, but renewed their active relationship when the USSR joined the organization in April 1954.

A way was opened for organized contact between social scientists of the two great power blocs when the Montevideo General Conference in December 1954 approved a resolution which (among other matters) authorized the Director General to "undertake an objective study of the means of promoting peaceful cooperation" among nations, applying "the resources of social science to the study of the factors which hinder and which encourage international understanding."[46] The Indian delegation at Montevideo had introduced a resolution on "peaceful coexistence," aimed at Soviet-Western tension. After suggestions from several delegations which sought to relate the proposal more closely to Unesco's objectives, the language of the resolution was modified into that quoted above. The purpose of the resolution has been interpreted as an attempt to search out the barriers between scholars of countries with different economic systems (e.g., Communism and capitalism), to ascertain whether these scholars could achieve mutual understanding, and to explore whether positive cooperation or only coexistence was possible between the two groups of countries.

An initial difficulty was the absence of agreement on the meaning of either "peaceful cooperation" or "peaceful coexistence," a concept which had been revived by the Soviet Union. The content of these terms was discussed in September 1956 at a round table sponsored by the International Political Science Association. One position was voiced by Professor P. A. Reynolds of the United Kingdom. He attempted to draw a distinction between the two ideas. In his view peaceful *cooperation* was possible only between states sharing the same fundamental philosophy; peaceful *coexistence* applied to relations between states holding different systems of thought. The idea of peaceful coexistence, he contended, rests on the premise that antagonism is inevitable between states with different economic systems. He declared that Marxist thought for a time had held that enmity between capitalist and proletarian states could end only in armed conflict; peaceful coexistence applied merely to a period of temporary equilibrium between the two camps. More recently Marxist philosophy has stated that the final triumph of socialism may be achieved without war. But according to Professor Reynolds hostility between the two camps makes impossible any real friendship or cooperation.

Another view was presented by Professor Djordjevic of Yugoslavia, who remarked on the absence of any clear and generally accepted definition of coexistence. He recognized that the two blocs are now in a state of armed truce, but hoped that positive cooperation, directed toward social progress, might eventually develop.[47] However, to avoid controversy, the Unesco secretariat and a number of nongovernmental organizations have made no distinction between peaceful cooperation and peaceful coexistence.

The Director General, following the Montevideo General Conference, consulted nongovernmental international organizations in the social sciences on measures to carry out the resolution approved by that body. Meetings were called by organizations in economics, law, and political science to propose topics which might be studied. Additional suggestions were received covering other fields. The International Association of Legal Science noted such legal aspects of peaceful cooperation as collective security, self-determination, nonintervention, and the idea of sovereignty. The International Economic Association brought together a small group of specialists at Geneva in 1956, including participants from Poland and the USSR, to plan an international conference of economists to meet in 1957 under sponsorship of Unesco and the Association.

In the same month Unesco convened at Geneva a meeting of social scientists—economists, jurists, political scientists, and sociologists. The participants were chosen after consultation with the various international social science associations and with the National Commissions of Czechoslovakia, Hungary, Poland, and the USSR, as well as of France, Sweden, Switzerland, the United Kingdom, and the United

States. This group had before it, in addition to reports from the meetings mentioned above, questions on the historical aspects of peaceful cooperation, drafted by scholars in Czechoslovakia, France, India, the United Kingdom, the United States, and the USSR. The group focused on the contribution which various social sciences might make to the study of problems involved in peaceful cooperation, and on plans for future research.[48] It was decided to explore two general themes: "the theory and historical development of concepts of peaceful co-operation (coexistence)," and "economic relations between countries with different economic and social systems."[49] Parallel studies would be made by each of the individual disciplines on special questions. For example, a round-table conference of the International Sociological Association held at Amsterdam in August 1956 proposed a seminar to be held in 1957 or 1958 to discuss selected problems and research projects relating to peaceful cooperation.[50] Two conferences to be held in 1958 would discuss the results of the work on the two main themes and suggest future activities. These proposals were approved by the General Conference at New Delhi.

It is evident that considerable time must pass before the value of these studies can be appraised. Social scientists recognize the limitations of research in this field. Their analysis may clarify the problem of international tensions, and may ultimately be significant. But they are the first to emphasize that any project which presumes an early solution for the problems outlined above is destined to frustration and failure. Moreover, in approaching a question so closely related to national rivalries and power politics, the difficulty of maintaining scientific objectivity is as great as the need to do so. It is harder to find common ground between Soviet and Western scholars in the social sciences than in the natural sciences. The meeting of social scientists at Geneva in July 1956 had, it is true, produced important exchanges of ideas, and the agreements achieved had been unanimous. Yet a number of delegations at New Delhi remained skeptical about Unesco's capacity to undertake a frontal attack on the relations between the Communist world and the West.

CHAPTER XII

INTERNATIONAL UNDERSTANDING: SUPPORTING THE UNITED NATIONS

Aids to Teaching About the United Nations

Finally we turn to Unesco's efforts to further international understanding by promoting support of the United Nations and its specialized agencies. From the start the governments that created Unesco, in general the same as those that created the United Nations, recognized that the UN system was the essential framework within which to achieve international understanding and world peace. The Unesco Constitution had pledged the organization to advance "the objectives of international peace and of the common welfare of mankind for which the United Nations Organization was established, and which its Charter proclaims." Conversely, the UN General Assembly declared in 1946 that the United Nations could not achieve its objectives "unless the peoples of the world are fully informed of its aims and activities." A year later the General Assembly adopted a resolution in which all member governments were urged to "encourage the teaching of the United Nations Charter and the purposes and principles, the structure, background and activities of the United Nations in the schools and institutes of higher learning of their countries, with particular emphasis on such instruction in elementary and secondary schools." The resolution invited Unesco to assist in this endeavor.[1]

Among Unesco's first activities in this field was an international seminar on teaching about the United Nations and its specialized agencies, held for six weeks in the summer of 1948 at Adelphi College on Long Island, New York. Its purpose was to examine methods by which school children could learn about the United Nations, and to review the need for teaching materials.

Following the seminar, a Danish participant published a book especially for secondary schools, *The United Nations—Background, Origins and Experience,* and lectured extensively in Sweden and Denmark. A teacher from the Philippines used his experience at the seminar to develop a series of lectures at Quezón College and an eight-month radio series on the United Nations. Another participant, a Norwegian writer, published a story book for children from twelve to seventeen years of age called *Friends All Over the World.* One of the United States participants made many speeches and cooperated in the educational program of the Catholic Association for International Peace.[2]

As a direct follow-up to the seminar, Australia held a national seminar in June 1949, attended by fifty persons from schools, universities, and youth organizations. This meeting resulted in three pamphlets: *Teaching about the United Nations,* a practical guide for teachers; *The United Nations in Action,* a reference book for teachers; and *Towards World Understanding,* a handbook for youth leaders.[3] Undoubtedly there were other results from the seminar comparable to these just listed.

In addition to international seminars, of which the one at Adelphi is an example, Unesco assisted the World Federation of United Nations Associations to hold fourteen regional seminars on teaching about the United Nations: in 1949 at Paris and Havana; in 1950 at Rome, Teheran, and Paris; in 1951 at Beirut and New Delhi; in 1952 at San Salvador; in 1953 at Monrovia and Mogadiscio; in 1954 at Manila and Montevideo; in 1955 at Heidelberg; and in 1956 at Copenhagen.[4] Two regional conferences of Unesco National Commissions—one at Havana in 1950 for the Western Hemisphere and another at Bangkok in 1951 for South Asia and the South Pacific—discussed teaching about the United Nations and human rights.

In response to requests from educators and public officials for information about the United Nations, Unesco published a pamphlet, *Some Suggestions on Teaching about the United Nations and Its Specialized Agencies,* and a *Selected Bibliography on Education for International Understanding,* an annotated list of books and pamphlets in fifteen languages containing a section on teaching about the United Nations and the specialized agencies. A third pamphlet, *The*

United Nations and World Citizenship, was a report by an international group of six teachers who attended the seminar at Adelphi College.[5] The phrase "world citizenship" was later abandoned by Unesco as subject to possible misinterpretation. Dr. Torres Bodet stated in 1952: "It has never been the purpose of Unesco to turn citizens from their national loyalties. We are trying to do something quite different: to train citizens—since we are concerned with education—who will be faithful in their duty to their own country, and who, for that very reason, will also be loyal to the international obligations which their country has assumed."[6]

The task of assisting member states—on whom rests the primary responsibility for teaching about the United Nations—has been shared by the United Nations and Unesco. A 1950 resolution of the Economic and Social Council defined their respective roles. The United Nations was to: (1) prepare basic materials and encourage member states to adapt and publish them; (2) provide information about the United Nations to press, radio, and film services and to individuals; and (3) study ways to increase public recognition and understanding of the United Nations.[7]

Unesco was assigned four functions: (1) to produce teaching aids on the United Nations for use by teachers and adult education groups; (2) to evaluate, in cooperation with member states, methods for teaching about and promoting interest in the United Nations; (3) to grant fellowships permitting educators to study the problems of teaching about the United Nations, both in educational institutions and at headquarters of the United Nations and the specialized agencies; and (4) to encourage teaching about the Universal Declaration of Human Rights in schools and adult education programs and through the press, radio, and films.[8]

Materials and Methods

Teaching materials are of great importance because of the difficulty of presenting to school children the abstract principles and complex structure of the United Nations. Unesco's special effort related to the UN defense action in Korea is discussed later in this chapter. It has also worked through publications, some of which have already been mentioned; through educational campaigns on certain problems which face the peoples of the United Nations, such as a campaign on Food and People initiated in 1949, which involved a series of pamphlets; through special "reportages" such as that on "Man Against Disease" discussed in Chapter VI; and through exhibits such as "Education and Peace."

Little progress has been made in Unesco's second assignment, on methods. As one element in a larger program to encourage education about the United Nations and about human rights, member states were requested in 1953 to carry on a "minimum" experiment, conducted on similar lines in all institutions taking part. This project was called the "Associated Schools Projects in Education for International Understanding." Its purpose would be to secure data on the effectiveness of different teaching methods and materials in developing attitudes favorable to international understanding and cooperation. Three themes were proposed for the experiment: the rights of women, the study of other countries, and the Universal Declaration of Human Rights. As the result of later difficulties, less emphasis was placed on the experimental character of the undertaking. It was rather regarded as a cooperative enterprise in which an international group of schools worked together and reported to each other.

Almost one hundred secondary schools in thirty-two countries, including five in Germany, were by 1956 participating in the project. More than half the schools at the start chose the study of other countries, and slightly less than a third selected the Universal Declaration of Human Rights. Only a few took the rights of women. It was planned to make tests of knowledge and attitudes both before and after a period of instruction in the topic adopted. In the meantime, it is reported that already new materials have been included in school courses and new methods of teaching have been adopted. During 1957-58 the project was to be expanded by adding twenty-five teacher-training institutions to the enterprise.[9] This associated schools project is a promising type of activity for Unesco because member states feel their full responsibility and teachers in different countries have opportunity to learn about each other's work and to try new methods used successfully in other countries.

In its third assignment, on fellowships, starting in 1950 Unesco has made more than thirty grants to educators, permitting periods of study and observation at the headquarters of the United Nations and its specialized agencies and the opportunity to observe in schools methods of teaching about the United Nations.

Teaching About Human Rights

Unesco's fourth assignment under the ECOSOC resolution concerned human rights. With the signing of the United Nations Charter in 1945, human rights became a matter of major concern, not alone to national governments but also to international organizations representing nearly all countries. In Article 55 of the Charter the United Nations was called upon to promote "universal respect for, and observance of, human rights and fundamental freedoms." The Charter did not define the rights to be promoted. This was done in the Universal Declaration of Human Rights, drafted by a United Nations Commission headed by Mrs. Franklin D. Roosevelt. The Declaration was no more than a statement of principles. Later, two international covenants of Human Rights were drafted.

Following the adoption of the Universal Declaration of Human Rights on December 10, 1948, by the United Nations General Assembly, the Assembly recommended that governments of member states use every means available to publicize the text of the Declaration and to have it explained in schools and other educational institutions. Specialized agencies and private international organizations were invited to bring the Declaration to the attention of their members. In consequence the 1948 Unesco General Conference, meeting at that moment at Beirut, by acclamation instructed the Director General to circulate widely and to "encourage the incorporation of the Declaration as subject matter in the teaching about the United Nations which is given in schools."[10] Work was promptly begun on two guides which would help any teacher wanting to prepare materials on human rights for national use.[11]

At the time of the 1949 General Conference, Unesco with the help of the French government organized for display in Paris a descriptive and historical exhibition on the Universal Declaration which remained on view for three months. In connection with the exhibition, Unesco produced an eight-minute film, "Droits de l'Enfant, Droits de l'Homme" (Rights of the Child, Rights of Man), which was shown throughout the exhibition, and on December 10, Human Rights Day, was run in twenty-five of the leading motion picture theaters of Paris.[12] The exhibition was then sent to various countries of Western Europe. Subsequently the panels and other materials included in the exhibition were reproduced in a loose-leaf *Human Rights Album*, which was widely distributed to member states for possible use in schools, clubs, and other groups.

In 1950 a series of six filmstrips on the history of human rights was produced, including such topics as "Abolition of Slavery," "Emancipation of Women," "Right to Education," and "Freedom of Thought." Member states were invited to celebrate Human Rights Day on December 10 (as well as United Nations Day on October 24) by commemorative exercises in which such materials and others could be used.

In 1952 Unesco organized a "Seminar on Active Methods of Education for Living in a World Community" at Woudschoten near Zeist, Holland, with particular attention to teaching about human rights. As part of the preparation for this seminar, a pamphlet of suggestions for teachers was prepared. In addition, four international teachers' organizations prepared, at the request of Unesco, reports of methods currently in use in schools.[13] Participants in this seminar, including teachers, administrators, and textbook authors, worked out suggestions on teaching about human rights to three different age groups— children under twelve, children between twelve and fifteen, and youths between fifteen and eighteen.[14]

Among activities in member states to develop practical application of the principles of the Declaration, the National Commission of the Philippines brought out in 1956 an illustrated handbook, *Understanding and Observing Human Rights,* for students in the upper elementary grades and the high schools. Each article in the Declaration was accompanied by illustrations and a story dealing with a situation where, for example, the right to education or to freedom of thought and religion was involved.[15]

Of special interest to Unesco are those individual articles of the Declaration which concern education, science, and culture. Article 26 refers to the right to education, recommending that elementary education should be free and compulsory. It urges that education strengthen respect for human rights and fundamental freedoms, "promote understanding, tolerance, and friendship among all nations, racial or religious groups," and advance United Nations efforts for the maintenance of peace. Article 27 speaks of the right to participate freely in the cultural life of the community, "to enjoy the arts and to share in scientific advancement and its benefits." It also mentions the right of protection by copyright. Article 18 stresses the right to freedom of thought and Article 19 the right to freedom of opinion and expression and of freedom "to seek, receive and impart information and ideas."

It may be argued that the whole, or almost the whole, of Unesco's program seeks in one way or another to promote these specific rights. The right to education is forwarded by Unesco's activities in favor of free and compulsory education, fundamental education, and education for international understanding. The right to participate in cultural life and to enjoy the arts is forwarded by development of public libraries and of museums; assistance to private organizations in the theater, visual arts, music, and literature; program activities in the area of philosophy and humanities; circulation of exhibitions of color reproductions and of music catalogues; the book coupon scheme facilitating the international circulation of books. Further, Unesco has sought to improve the situation of the creative artist in society.

Opportunity to share in scientific advances is furthered by Unesco's distribution of information on methods, discoveries, and applications of science. The right to information and freedom of expression is advanced by Unesco's efforts to encourage mass communication, to remove obstacles to the free flow of information, to facilitate the international movement of persons, and to forward the training of journalists.[16] Unesco has done much in the field of human rights through its project concerning race relations, discussed in the preceding chapter.

It should be noted also that because of its special responsibilities Unesco was asked for and provided many comments, in the drafting stages of the Declaration and of the proposed Covenants, on articles relating to educational and cultural rights and on freedom of information.

Finally, Unesco provided special assistance in relation to proposals advanced by the United States in 1953, when it announced its unwillingness to sign the proposed Covenants. These proposals were designed to initiate immediately, without waiting for the Covenants to come into force, progressive implementation of human rights. They were based on the assumption that education of the general public, designed to make clear the importance of the individual citizen and to raise the economic and social level of the less economically developed peoples, might further human rights more effectively than conventions which might fail of ratification or, if ratified, of application.[17]

The United States proposals called for reports from national governments on what they had done to improve individual rights; advisory services to member states by the United Nations agencies, to aid in application of human rights; and detailed studies on a worldwide basis of specific aspects of human rights, to be initiated by the Commission on Human Rights. In response to requests from the Commission, Unesco submitted a series of observations, outlining the forms of assistance which it might provide, including experts, fellowships, and international seminars or work groups. The Economic and Social Council proposed in 1956 that the first subject for study should be the right of freedom from arbitrary arrest, detention, and exile.

The Korean Crisis

The sharpest test of what Unesco might do to support the United Nations, particularly in an emergency, came in 1950, when on June 25 the North Korean forces invaded and attacked the Republic of Korea. That same day the Security Council termed the armed attack "a breach of the peace." Four days later the Council approved a resolution calling on members of the United Nations to furnish assistance "to repel the armed attack."

The initial step to mobilize the resources of Unesco in this situation was taken in a resolution approved on July 22 by the Executive Committee of the United States National Commission for Unesco. This recommended "That the Executive Board of Unesco meet immediately and take appropriate and vigorous action with respect to the impact of the Korean situation on the peace of the world and in regard to other areas where acts of aggression may occur."[18] Luther H. Evans, then member from the United States on the Executive Board, was joined by nine other members in requesting Count Jacini of Italy, Chairman of the Board, to call a special meeting. The date was set for August 26.

Meanwhile, in other United Nations agencies, support was expressed for action by Unesco. Ambassador Austin, the United States representative on the Security Council, speaking on July 31 in support of the resolution on relief and rehabilitation in Korea, declared that "Unesco can reorganize disrupted educational facilities in the aggrieved country and utilize its experience in mass communications to tell the great story of today's international effort and to make clear the nature of the aggression in Korea." The Economic and Social Council, in session in Geneva, approved on August 14 a resolution inviting "governments members of the United Nations, the Secretary General and appropriate nongovernmental organizations . . . to assist in developing among the peoples of the world the fullest possible understanding of and support for the action of the United Nations in Korea," and requesting the Secretary General "to seek on behalf of the Council the co-operation of the Specialized Agencies as appropriate for this service."[19]

Further, the Department of Public Information of the United Nations welcomed the assistance of Unesco. Benjamin Cohen, Assistant Secretary General for Public Information, was sent to Paris for the meeting of the Executive Board, carrying a message from Secretary General Trygve Lie, who said that Unesco could be extremely useful in the Korean crisis, without in any way impairing its fundamental role in world affairs. He noted that a vast job needed to be done in educational circles, which Unesco could perform.[20]

At the meeting of the Board on August 26, Dr. Torres Bodet, the Director General, outlined four activities for Unesco:

(1) Assistance to refugees, particularly education for refugee children;

(2) Encouragement of teaching about the United Nations, with emphasis on its efforts in support of collective security and international law;

(3) An information program to develop understanding of United Nations action in Korea;

(4) Participation on the cessation of hostilities in the reconstruction of Korea.[21]

In the Executive Board, Dr. Evans stressed the challenge to the United Nations of the Korean crisis and said:

The duty of Unesco is plain. It must fulfill its obligation to the United Nations by explaining to the peoples of the world, with the help of teachers, scholars, writers and other leaders in the communication of knowledge and ideas, that the issue in Korea is clearly drawn between the defense of peace and permitting brute aggression to succeed. It must help create throughout the world an understanding of the vital role that the United Nations has assumed in Korea and the responsibilities it faces in other areas of possible aggression. Naturally, Unesco must also do its full part in rebuilding the shattered life of the Korean nation.

The United Nations has spoken for the conscience of mankind. Unesco can have no greater task than to uphold the United Nations as the defender of peace. Let us get on with that task!

This view did not go unchallenged. As indicated earlier, supporters of the organization have differed from the start on whether Unesco's contribution to peace and security should be direct or indirect, immediate or long-term.[22] In the debate on Korea, these issues were raised: (1) whether Unesco should embark on "political action"[23] and (2) what the scope of Unesco's responsibility to the United Nations should be. The word "political" when used in Unesco debates is almost always ambiguous. Some have termed Unesco a political organization, in the sense that it employs educational, scientific, and cultural activities to achieve a political end—the maintenance of peace—and in the sense that it is an intergovernmental institution. Others have pointed out that when means rather than ends are emphasized, Unesco is a technical and non-political agency.[24] Its methods are educational, not coercive. It is to promote the process of learning rather than to enact legislation.

Some feared that if Unesco were drawn into "political controversy," it would be abandoning the "universal" role which many of its supporters had hoped to see it play—that of an unbiased agency giving technical services to, and drawing support from, all countries including the USSR. Some Unesco leaders had hoped from the start that the organization might serve as a "bridge" between the non-Communist world and the Soviet bloc. (President Eisenhower and other participants in the "Summit Conference" of 1955 have increasingly recognized the uses of cultural cooperation in this respect.) It was feared also that involvement of Unesco in the Korean struggle might mean alignment of the organization with the United States and against the Soviet Union.

Those who viewed Unesco's purpose as linked to the political purpose of the United Nations in assuring world peace claimed that the values of a free society represented in Unesco's Constitution were threatened by a challenge to collective security. They argued that Unesco was under obligation to strengthen resistance to aggression in Korea and elsewhere.

The other group interpreted Unesco's purpose as clearly separate from the political objectives of the United Nations, and believed it fatal for Unesco to become involved in the cold war or the Korean struggle. The majority of member states holding this view inclined to a certain neutralism, contending that the issues of the Korean conflict were not directly related to the world of education, science, and culture. Some argued that Unesco should even stand aloof from the United Nations.[25]

The public in many countries did not at first fully realize that the war in Korea was a United Nations matter, much less how and why the United Nations was involved. It was believed in many countries that the Korean struggle concerned primarily the United States, while in the United States itself there were many who saw neither the principle involved nor the immediate threat to national security from Communist aggression.

It may be of interest to recall that at the outbreak of World War II the League of Nations' Institute of Intellectual Cooperation consulted members of the International Committee, its governing board, all National Committees which could be reached, and many other national or international cooperating groups concerning conditions under which it should continue its work, and how it could take an open stand against aggression.

Henri Bonnet, Director of the Institute, reported that hundreds of replies were received from almost every free country in the world. They agreed that the activities of the Intellectual Organization should continue.

These responses showed very clearly that the Organization could not continue by taking an attitude of indifference in the face of the war. In addition, the intention was revealed of concentrating on points which could be of immediate importance for the grouping of democratic forces. There was a strong emphasis . . . on the necessity of rallying leaders of the spiritual and intellectual activities for the defense of the principles of civilization, and of the moral rules which were threatened by the Nazi philosophy and which should be proclaimed as the ideal for which free nations were fighting. . . .

The International Intellectual Organization [M. Bonnet continued] was not neutral about the war in Europe. It was, at most, prevented by censorship from publishing some truthful statements about fascism because too many people, in the belligerent as well as in the neutral countries, maintained incredible illusions about Mussolini's policy. On the whole, it was free to launch intellectual action. There was a great desire in many of the non-belligerent but free countries, notably outside Europe, for a united front of the people who were defending values threatened with destruction.[26]

The Unesco Executive Board, after long debate, on August 28,

1950, unanimously condemned the aggression against the Republic of Korea, and adopted two resolutions.

The first pledged Unesco to "give all possible aid and assistance to the action undertaken by the United Nations in Korea"; instructed the Director General to assist in emergency relief and reconstruction, and "to develop, within the resources at his disposal, including the periodical publications of the Organization, the execution of the programme resolutions concerning teaching about the United Nations and the Specialized Agencies, putting particular emphasis on the necessity for collective security, based on respect for law, with the aid of concrete examples, and to this end utilize appropriate documentation provided by the Secretary General of the United Nations"; and appealed to governments, National Commissions, and private organizations to cooperate in this endeavor "with a view to reinforcing in the minds of men the intellectual and moral defenses of peace through law which the United Nations are responsible for developing and safeguarding."

The second resolution authorized the Director General:

(1) To despatch a mission to Korea, upon request of the United Nations Secretary General, to investigate the needs of the civilian population and determine how Unesco could assist in relief and reconstruction;

(2) To prepare in collaboration with the United Nations materials for schools, adult classes, and universities, and to distribute these to member states.[27]

The Executive Board allocated $100,000 as a special fund for educational, scientific, and cultural aid to Korean civilians.

In the world press, the action of the Executive Board was interpreted as a step away from Unesco's former "neutral" position of taking no open stand on political issues between East and West.

How were the above resolutions carried out by the Unesco secretariat? The media of mass communication were not effectively utilized. The periodical publications of Unesco gave scant attention to the Korean situation.[28] Moreover, what was published was detached and colorless and avoided any reference to "aggression." Some Unesco supporters in the United States held that Unesco had failed to meet a challenging opportunity and responsibility. In defense of the secretariat, it was pointed out that many of the member states were either opposed or lukewarm to a vigorous follow-up of the Executive Board resolutions. As of April 1951, of the twenty-three member states which had commented on the resolutions of the Executive Board, only six had clearly supported the resolutions. Of remaining replies, three were protests from the Soviet satellites, four were negative, eight were merely acknowledgments, and two indicated willingness to support the United Nations action but outside the Unesco program. No answers had been received from such important countries as France, India, the United Kingdom, and other members of the British Commonwealth.

For its part, the secretariat had worked out a plan for publication of educational material on the United Nations and collective security. The plan called for the following publications, each in English, French, and Spanish editions, to be translated where necessary and adapted by member states to meet their own circumstances: (1) a pamphlet designed principally for primary and secondary school teachers and adult education groups; (2) a booklet containing classroom suggestions for teaching about collective security; (3) a scholarly study on collective security, directed to college and university audiences; and (4) visual aid wall charts illustrating how the United Nations system works as regards both collective security and the activities of Unesco and the other specialized agencies. Contracts for writing these materials were made with outside authors. This fact and the need for careful consultation with the United Nations on the content of these publications delayed their appearance.

At the Sixth Session of the Unesco General Conference which opened at Paris on June 18, 1951, Trygve Lie was present and spoke of the "great decision" made by the United Nations almost a year earlier to meet aggression with collective force. He declared that "Unesco has a key position in the efforts which the United Nations organizations must now make to fulfill, in an unsettled world, the great purposes for which they were established. . . . Through the nature of its work, it has the possibility of influencing the minds of men and the ideas which motivate men's actions. It has a vital role to play in support of the total United Nations effort for peace—a role with many different aspects."[29]

Some of Unesco's publications on collective security appeared in the latter half of 1951, but others were not issued until the latter half of 1952, more than two years after the aggression in Korea.[30] By this time the world situation had changed and the peak of interest in United Nations action in Korea had passed. The United States National Commission published, in the summer of 1951, 10,000 copies of a *Discussion Guide—The United Nations and Collective Action against Aggression.* Most of these were sent to voluntary organizations which indicated that they would encourage discussion of the pamphlet, but subsequent reports from these organizations were not adequate to indicate how much use had been made of the material.[31] Even in the country which had originally proposed that Unesco play an active part in the Korean crisis, effective follow-up was delayed and public interest twelve months later had shifted to the presidential election.

In summary, then, the effort to use Unesco's resources to support the United Nations in an emergency was largely abortive.[32] The opportunity had been welcomed by those member states, particularly the United States, who favored close association of Unesco with the United Nations in the latter's struggle against armed aggression. It was hoped that Unesco could demonstrate its capacity to provide prompt and effective support. Experience revealed that not many states were prepared to encourage Unesco and that the organization was not equipped to provide effective leadership.

Understanding and Peace: Evaluating Unesco's Work

What findings emerge from the review in the last three chapters of Unesco's endeavors to develop international understanding and cooperation as a contribution to peace? What were the assumptions underlying its efforts and how valid were they? How effective were its projects in promoting greater international understanding?

Unesco's activities in this area were based on several assumptions. The first was that men's minds can be influenced by information, education, and personal contacts. Social science research supports this view, subject to certain qualifications. The assumption is based on the premise that man is a rational being, able to make choices between courses of action.

A second assumption has been that education, information, and personal contacts can contribute both to "cold" or objective and to "warm" or sympathetic understanding of other peoples, depending on which result is sought. It is widely agreed that education and its related activities can develop international understanding. Discussion of the relations between educational efforts and international understanding has progressed to the stage of analyzing under what conditions and by what methods the greatest contribution can be made.

Third, it has been assumed that the connection between international understanding and peace is indirect rather than direct. Unesco's function, then, is to promote a world community of understanding and cooperation, which helps indirectly to prevent armed conflict. Reinhold Niebuhr has remarked: "Unesco must, in short, find its justification in the contributions it makes to the integration of the emergent world community, rather than its supposed but usually illusory contributions to 'peace.' "[33] Mutual knowledge and understanding are essential conditions for a world community but they do not automatically promote such a community. World community is necessary for enduring peace but it is only one among many factors. A contrasting assumption, that Unesco can influence world opinion and immediately contribute to international understanding, remains unproved. Unesco's one effort to promote a specific educational campaign in support of the United Nations actions in Korea was clearly ineffective. But this may have been due to the lack of a clear collective will to carry out its resolutions as well as to Unesco's own competence.

One assumption enshrined in the Preamble to the Unesco Constitution was that ignorance contributes to international conflict. Its corollary, that knowledge makes for cooperation and harmony, has been challenged by scholars. Again to quote Niebuhr, in a statement which has been often cited or paraphrased by writers on Unesco, "Ignorance may aggravate fear. But it is not true that knowledge of each other's ways necessarily allays suspicion and mistrust. Some of the most terrible conflicts in history have occurred between neighbors who knew each other quite well, Germany and France for instance. . . . Actually the most tragic conflicts are between disputants who know very well what the other party intends, but are forced by either principle or interest to oppose it."[34]

In spite of some qualifications it has been accepted by governments in Unesco that education and understanding and peace are somehow linked. This view is founded on an optimistic attitude toward human nature. Men have the capacity, it is believed, for understanding of one another. Prejudice is due to ignorance, which can be overcome and which men of good will want to overcome by knowledge and reason. Those who take a pessimistic view, however, are skeptical about how much influence reason has in human affairs and they sometimes view prejudice as "having its roots in the propensity of men towards evil."[35]

So much for assumptions. What of Unesco's activities in developing international understanding and cooperation? We are in no position to measure their influence. Understanding is the result of many factors. It develops slowly, and it manifests itself only as a reaction to specific events such as economic or political crisis or war, or in response to leadership. By their very nature certain activities—such as contacts among scholars, discussions of philosophers, translations of the classics, and research into social tensions—can affect international undertanding only gradually, and to an indeterminate degree.

In seeking evidence on which to appraise Unesco's activities we turn to the testimony of witnesses, notably the special committee appointed by the Director General in 1953 to examine what Unesco had been doing to advance education for international understanding and cooperation. It was made up of fourteen persons from as many different countries, chosen as combining objectivity with some knowledge of the Unesco program.[36]

The committee's report stressed the urgency of educating men and women for international understanding and cooperation. It noted that mankind has the power to make his world "desolate or fruitful." With the increasing complexity of contemporary society and the accelerating rate of change from old ways to new, the individual is subject to new strains which have been added to longer standing tensions and fears.

The committee took a favorable view on substantially all activities reviewed in these chapters, ranging from revision of textbooks to round-table discussions on philosophy, from mass communication to dissemination of art and music. But it was urged that Unesco's whole program, not merely certain projects, should aim more systematically to foster understanding between peoples. In such activities as exchange of persons, traveling exhibitions in art and science, and the entire program of technical assistance, it recommended that whatever the immediate purpose, the principal secondary objective in every case should be international understanding.[37]

The reactions of member states cast light both on the value of individual projects and on Unesco's ability to enlist cooperation. While Unesco has been directed in all its activities by decisions of governments, a project must be judged by the degree to which member states have themselves put it into operation at home.

Here it may be well to make a distinction between the capacity of a project to enlist participants and to affect recipients. Certain Unesco undertakings, such as discussions among philosophers and scholars in the humanities, translation of the classics, research in social tensions, and writing the History of the Scientific and Cultural Development of Mankind, involve initially only a small number of participants. Ultimately they may develop better international understanding among numerous recipients, including students and members of the public. In some cases recipients may become participants. For example, Unesco's social tensions studies have stimulated requests from member states for help in analyzing their own internal tensions, thus expanding the number of scholars taking part in the research and also increasing the number of recipients of the knowledge and insight to be gained from these studies.

Other projects, such as international seminars for teachers, analysis of textbooks, and teaching about the United Nations and human rights, enlisted in the initial stage a larger group of participants. In the teachers' seminars, many member states cooperated in both preparation and follow-up. Even more noticeable has been the extent to which the people of member states have participated in bilateral and multilateral consultations on revision of textbooks and teaching aids, although precise information is not available on specific results. In teaching about the United Nations and human rights, member states have carried on a wide range of activities. All these projects have had an effect on the public, including teachers and pupils, though they are still inadequate to the needs of the situation.

Exchange of persons has enlisted world-wide participation. This is an enterprise in which almost every country is active in some way, either by providing opportunities for its own citizens to study abroad, or by offering facilities to students from other lands. By far the greater part of this activity, it should be emphasized, has gone on independently of Unesco, whose basic role has been that of an information and service center. Its publications and projects have stimulated member states and have contributed to the quality and scope of the enterprise. Exchange of persons across frontiers does not lead automatically to better understanding. Results depend to a large degree on the conditions under which exchanges are carried out. It is hoped that studies of these exchanges will clarify the various factors in a complex process.

With regard to the arts, activities in the theater have affected producers, players, and audiences. Traveling exhibitions of reproductions in color of the world's masterpieces of painting have served primarily recipients, some of whom, such as teachers, have become participants in the fostering of international understanding through this medium.

In mass communication, Unesco has had limited success in recruiting the cooperation of newspapers, radio stations, and film and television producers in member states; and until greater participation on the part of such agencies is achieved, the number of recipients who are helped to understand other peoples will not be large. Here results have been much less significant than was anticipated. The principal weakness has been in the attitude of member states and in the inherent nature of the media.

Special reference should be made here to the Unesco *Courier,* easily the most imaginative of Unesco's publications and designed to reach a large and varied audience. It provides reports on what Unesco is doing, but more importantly, it is a vehicle of communication among the people of member states, reporting on and comparing activities in different countries. Profusely illustrated, it brings in monthly issues insights into educational developments and techniques, human problems of social organization and habitation, religion, race, human rights, and into the work of the United Nations agencies from all corners of the world. As a teaching device, as a source of information, and as a potential influence for international understanding, it probably has no peer among international publications. Its circulation, however, is very small and cannot be made much greater without more active cooperation in member states, for it is handicapped by language barriers and by lack of access to channels of circulation.

Unesco has had least success where, as in the case of the Korean crisis, its supporters were divided, and where success depended upon an immediate effect on world opinion. It has been most clearly effective where, as in the associated schools projects on education for international understanding, it has found devices for involving member states directly.

Unesco's progress in this entire area has been modest at best. The enthusiasm of member states for positive efforts to promote international understanding—stated in the early days of Unesco and the United Nations and often reiterated subsequently—has not been matched by practical ideas, adequate funds, or, most evidently, by necessary government action in any member state.[38] On the other hand, the limited resources available to Unesco during its first decade have yielded returns whose usefulness is already apparent, and whose value could be translated into much greater gains in the future.

PART 3

PROGRAM-MAKERS,
NATIONAL POLICIES, AND
AN APPRAISAL

CHAPTER XIII

Who makes Unesco's program?

The discussion in the preceding chapters has made clear the decisive part that member states play in making Unesco's program and putting it into operation. The program has been shaped by representatives of these states in the General Conference, by the Executive Board, and by the Director General. What have been the respective roles of these three organs?

The Constitution Divides Responsibility

Under Unesco's Constitution, these three organs share responsibility for determining its program. The General Conference, composed of delegates from each member state, has final authority. The delegates are, in theory, if not always in practice, under direct government instructions and therefore voice the official views of member states. During the period under review (1946-56), the authority of the General Conference has remained unchanged and every Unesco project has been approved by at least a majority of the states represented.

The second organ of Unesco is the Executive Board. Under the Constitution, adopted in 1945, the Executive Board was empowered to draw up the program submitted to the General Conference. The Board was also responsible "for the execution of the programme adopted by the Conference." These arrangements gave the Board great influence, and confused its authority with that of the Director General. Because of mounting evidence that these provisions of the Constitution were unworkable, amendments were adopted in 1952. The Director General was assigned the task of drawing up the program to be transmitted through the Board to the General Conference. The Board's responsibility was restricted to making recommendations to the Conference about the Director General's proposals. For "execution of the programme" the Board's responsibility was reduced to "ensuring the effective and rational execution of the Programme by the Director General."[1] These changes in the powers of the Executive Board clarified authority for both the formulation and the execution of the program. They made consistent and workable the responsibility of the Director General to the General Conference.

The Director General, with the secretariat, constitutes the third organ in determining Unesco's program. He has authority to "formulate proposals for appropriate action by the Conference and the Board,"[2] and he prepares the budget to accompany the program proposals.

In summary, therefore, full authority over the content of Unesco's program rests with government delegates at the General Conference. According to present practice, the program and budget are drawn up by the Director General and his associates on the secretariat. They are presented by the Director General to the Executive Board for advice and comment only and are thereafter submitted to the General Conference. At this Conference, the Director General's proposals are reviewed and approved, modified, or rejected. Each member state has one vote.

The program as approved by the General Conference goes to the Director General to be put into operation with general guidance from the Executive Board. It consists of resolutions authorizing the Director General to carry out specified activities. Other resolutions are addressed to governments of member states to ensure complementary national action. The organization has no authority to function within any member state except with its consent.[3] The program document may also include policy resolutions bearing on Unesco's relations with other United Nations agencies or on broad international issues. At the next session of the General Conference, the Director General's report on the execution of the program is presented by the Chairman of the Board, with whatever comments the Board may have. This report forms the basis for debate at the Conference on the work of the organization.

This brief summary of the location of program authority has been primarily in constitutional terms. In practice, of course, other factors influence the system. It will therefore be useful to look a little more closely at the way the three organs of Unesco operate.

Member States and the General Conference

Unesco's member states are characterized by an extraordinary variety in political institutions, national wealth, social structure, school facilities. They differ in their progress in every field of Unesco concern. They differ also in the degree of citizen participation in public affairs, in the efficiency of government administration, and in experience in the conduct of foreign affairs.

These differences among member states are of more than theoretical interest, for they have a potent effect on program-making in Unesco. This has been noticeable as more states joined the organization, and the program had to respond to this broadening membership. The discussions at the London Conference in 1945 revolved largely around educational reconstruction in Europe, intellectual cooperation and advancement of knowledge on the scholarly level, "fundamental education," and international understanding in the light of Western European history. With the addition to Unesco of countries from the Eastern Mediterranean and South and Southeast Asia came demands for work in other fields. Unesco was pressed to help member states or groups of states to cope with such problems as illiteracy, expansion of primary schools, elementary scientific training, and technological development.

An attempt to sum up the differences among Unesco's member states was made by Dr. Tara Chand of India at the 1949 General Conference. He divided Unesco's supporting countries into two groups: those whose principal concern was with peace, and those who put welfare before all else. The "peace states" were mainly the great powers of the West whose national policies might run at cross purposes and lead to war. They had taken the lead in setting up the United Nations and its related agencies. They were not lacking in education, science, and culture as ordinarily conceived.

The welfare states, on the other hand, immediately and urgently needed freedom from hunger, ignorance, and disease. They were backward in modern education and science, but in the countries of the East concern for cultural and spiritual values was "perhaps more frequently found among the illiterates . . . than among the educated elsewhere." The welfare states, Dr. Tara Chand said, were too weak to embark on wars endangering world peace. They were too engrossed in the problem of existence to give attention to international understanding. Their very weakness made them a threat to world peace. Traditionally they had served as "pawns in the game of power politics" and their present involvement from Morocco to China in the world-wide struggle for power illustrated their capacity for good or evil.

In Tara Chand's view, the two groups of states had no choice but to cooperate in Unesco. Both needed to lift themselves through education above fear and pride to recognize that "humanity suffers because its sense of oneness is weak."[4]

The diversity among Unesco's member states was mirrored in the multiplicity of proposals presented to the General Conference. At the Third Session in 1948 more than sixty new proposals were introduced; at the Fourth Session the number exceeded thirty-five; at the Fifth Session in 1950, one hundred and eight new proposals were made by twenty-five delegations.[5] Since many of these reflected special interests, such as restoration of archaeological monuments, they were of little concern to some member states, and were actively opposed by others. Other proposals, such as the Indian suggestion in 1948 for attention to arid zones, overcame initial hostility and eventually achieved widespread support.

These new proposals, particularly in the early days of Unesco, did not necessarily reflect the most urgent needs of states recommending them. Each state has decided what it wanted from Unesco and worked for that at the General Conference. But many countries lack information on their own requirements, for example, data on the age distribution of the school-age population, the extent of illiteracy, and similar questions. Unesco has often been asked to help member states determine their needs and to develop standards against which existing conditions could be measured.

The opportunity of member states to voice their needs and views at the General Conference is also affected by other factors. Language has been a serious difficulty. Delegations whose native language is not English, French, or Spanish (or Russian since 1954) have had to understand and try to express themselves in a foreign tongue. Many delegations come with virtually no briefing from their governments. Even when a delegation is under instructions from its government, the instructions are not always followed. On the question of the million-dollar increase in the budget at New Delhi, one major delegation voted against its instructions. A prominent member of another delegation was reported to have taken the lead on this issue, without knowledge of his government. Such irresponsibility may well mean that governments will not carry out what their delegations have approved at the General Conference.

On these delegates of varying competence, with very different national backgrounds, rests the responsibility for a program that ranges over science, education, culture, and mass communication, and that is intended to serve mankind at nearly every level of development. There is probably no international legislative body with as complex a responsibility as that which faces each session of the General Conference. All the other specialized agencies and the United Nations itself have more clearly defined tasks. Nor is any national legislative assembly in the world so culturally and linguistically heterogeneous.

Leadership does not easily develop in such a body, and the need for it has become more urgent with the increase in Unesco's membership. A meeting of delegations from seventy or more countries is unwieldy. Conference officers are elected for a single term; it is extremely rare for a delegate to be re-elected to the same office even if he chances to reappear on a national delegation. Only a few delegates are returned by their governments to successive sessions of the General Conference.[6]

Regional blocs appear, such as those formed by the Arab and Latin American nations and the Soviet group. Such blocs usually operate in elections to Conference Commissions and to the Executive Board, on political questions, and sometimes on questions of program. In the Conference itself, the delegations of the larger nations exercise some leadership at times. But in the past such delegations—for example, those of France, Great Britain, and the United States—have often been divided among themselves on major issues. At New Delhi the British and French delegations were separated from the United States because of the attack on Egypt.

Only infrequently have governments tried to make the General Conference a more effective instrument for shaping policy. Two problems are involved. One, as the New Zealand delegation pointed out in a report on the Montevideo Conference, is that the General Conference has sought to "dictate the programme in every detail, and to trust neither the Director General nor the Executive Board to exercise real initiative."[7] Commissions of the Conference have attempted to subject proposed plans of work to a detailed scrutiny which they were not equipped to perform effectively. Broad objectives tend to be lost in preoccupation with minutiae; the interests of specialists with a particular end in view tend to dominate. The discussions as a rule have little effect on the content of the program as submitted by the Director General.

The other problem is the failure of the General Conference to perform the function for which it is uniquely equipped. It should be an occasion for a periodic survey in the light of Unesco's purposes, of the ideals and values prevailing in member states, in order that these may be better understood by peoples and governments. The General Conference should be a place to discuss the educational, scientific, and cultural problems facing member states. Such a review would lead to better appreciation of similarities and greater understanding of differences, and thus promote a more rational system of priorities within Unesco's program. The General Conference as a meeting of representatives of nearly every government in the world might thus assume an importance that would be reflected in the policy of states and in the quality of delegations.

The General Conference, then, has not provided much leadership in planning during the first decade. That function has been performed by two other organs: the Executive Board and the Director General, particularly between sessions of the General Conference.

The Executive Board and the Director General

Experience demonstrated that both formulation and execution of program must be performed in large part by the Director General. His is a full-time job. He is the chief administrative officer; he appoints the secretariat; he is in daily charge of the work of the organization; he has direct contact with member states.

Originally, as noted above, the Unesco Constitution divided executive responsibility between the Director General and the Executive Board, neither being responsible to the other, and both being responsible to the General Conference. The problem was complicated by the character of the Board, which was made up of individuals under no apparent control (after election in the General Conference) except their personal judgment.

Because of the careful counterbalancing of power, successful administration of the program has depended upon harmonious rapport

between the Director General and the Executive Board. When friction has existed, the Board and the Director General have tended to
negate each other and to endanger the organization's prestige and influence. Over the ten-year period this difficulty has been to some extent overcome, but full agreement on the roles of the two organs is
still lacking.

The theory behind the division of executive responsibility appears
to have been that a board composed of individuals would free the
organization from direct governmental and especially "political"
control. Unesco, it was thought, would not be concerned with political
issues. In addition, this arrangement would provide Unesco with
disinterested professional guidance from distinguished intellectuals.
It would ensure representation of the principal world cultures, which
would thus become committed to cooperation through participation
of outstanding leaders.[8]

Further, it was argued that the Executive Board would provide a
check against excessive concentration of authority in the Director
General, a point much in mind at the end of World War II, which
had been a struggle against dictatorship. The delegates at London
failed to distinguish between responsible power and arbitrary power.
Moreover, on administrative questions there was a difference in
viewpoint between Europeans and Americans. The result was that
authority was so circumscribed and divided between the Director
General and the Board that responsible use of power was jeopardized.
It was not until 1952 that the governments of member states through
constitutional amendment cut through this organizational problem
to establish the present division of responsibilities, described earlier
in this chapter.

How did the original system of checks and balances work out? Because of concern in certain member states about the administrative
and political inexperience of the first Director General, a number of
resolutions approved at the First Session of the General Conference
in 1946 required that action by the Director General on purely administrative matters, as well as program execution, receive prior approval by the Executive Board. The Board was invited to do what
good administrative practice would have discouraged, and the
practical scope of its authority was thus enlarged.

The unresolved issue of Unesco's purpose—perhaps more accurately
described as its multiple purpose—together with uncertainty as to

what the organization was capable of doing increased the difficulty of making clear-cut decisions on program, notably at the First Session. The General Conference received from the Preparatory Commission a set of program proposals which exceeded the funds they were prepared to vote. Delegates were unable to agree either to reduce the program or to organize it in a manageable way. The Conference took a simple way out. It set a low budget for the first year of operation, and passed on to the Director General and the Executive Board the task of reducing the whole program, including items added by the Conference, to fit the budget.

This procedure was largely repeated by the Second Session at Mexico City in 1947. Such a transfer of responsibility from the General Conference to the Executive Board and the Director General augmented their task without suggesting a practicable division of authority. Meetings of the Board became more frequent; the secretariat's time was increasingly committed to processing Executive Board papers before, during, and after Board meetings. The time available to the Director General for attention to program matters dwindled proportionately, as did his time to cultivate member states and prepare for the General Conference.

Some members of the Board were not averse to enlarging their individual and institutional roles vis-à-vis the Director General; and the first two Directors General—possibly for protective reasons—found fuzzy lines of responsibility convenient, and not infrequently sought to involve the Board in important decisions on administrative as well as program questions. The Board gave the Director General an opportunity to test the reaction of representatives of different nations and cultures to projects developed within the secretariat. Yet it was often unclear whether Board members were reflecting purely personal views or the views of their countrymen, since a number of them appeared to have become permanent residents of Paris. The Board did on a few occasions provide useful political advice and partly relieved the Director General of embarrassment that might have resulted from his taking personal responsibility on certain critical issues. Mostly, however, the Board left the Director General without this help.

In the role which the Board might most usefully have played under the constitutional arrangement before 1952—defending at the General Conference the program submitted by it and the

Director General—it was singularly ineffective. Members of the Board came to sessions of the General Conference as members of national delegations, losing their special "international" status and voting necessarily under government instructions. Their influence at the Conference was determined by the prestige of the country they represented rather than by their status as Board members. Although the program was presented to the General Conference by the Chairman of the Board, its defense and leadership in developing a Conference consensus fell mainly to the Director General and his staff. The task of the Director General has been made more difficult by the practice of holding Executive Board meetings during the Conference.

The confused relation during Unesco's first years between the Board and the Director General took its toll. Many false starts were made. The organization was loaded with responsibilities that exceeded its resources, the secretariat's time and strength, and the ability of member states to respond to projects approved by the General Conference. A continual strain existed between the Executive Board on the one hand and the Director General and secretariat on the other.

While it is not easy to appraise the responsibility of the Director General and the Executive Board for the program proposals submitted to the General Conference, it is evident that the initiative usually lay with the Director General and his staff. The Board rarely offered new projects, and prior to 1950 it contributed little to clarifying program structure.

From 1950 on, the Executive Board showed signs of functioning more effectively. But it was not until the winter of 1953-54, following the resignation of Dr. Torres Bodet, that the Board came seriously to grips with the issue of program reform. Meantime, the Constitution had been amended to give the Director General clearer authority to formulate and execute the program. At its Eighth Session at Montevideo, the General Conference received proposals which could be identified as coming from the Director General and which reflected the participation of the Board in its new advisory capacity. The General Conference could for the first time look to the Director General for leadership within all three organs of the organization. The 1956 Conference at New Delhi was presented with a program similarly prepared, and based on directives from the previous Conference at Montevideo.

Three Directors General

Three men have occupied the post of Director General during Unesco's first decade. Their intellectual strength and force of character have been important factors in the evolution of the institution of Director General in relation to member states, the General Conference, the Executive Board, and the secretariat, as well as in program-making.

One of Unesco's problems has been that the Director General was expected to be both an intellectual leader and a competent administrator—a combination which is all too rare. The efforts of each Director General were conditioned by the broader influences shaping the work of the organization. Unesco's growth was bound to be affected, regardless of who was Director General, by such factors as the initial postwar enthusiasm for cooperation toward international understanding; the insistent voices of new member states from the Eastern Mediterranean, Asia, and Latin America; the course of the cold war from 1947 on; and the general deterioration in international relations.

Julian Huxley (1946–1948)

The first Director General, Julian Huxley, had served as Executive Secretary of the Preparatory Commission from February 1946 to the first session of the General Conference which opened in November of that year. The grandson of Thomas H. Huxley, he had taught and written widely on the biological sciences and on general scientific questions. His books reflected the same catholicity of interests that appeared in his leadership of Unesco. As one of his co-workers has written, "There was no province of education, science or culture, in which he was not at home. Ideas excited him, and he communicated that excitement to his colleagues. Almost all ideas excited him with equal intensity; whatever idea was before him was for the moment of transcendent importance."[9]

His wide interests led to personal leadership on matters as varied as fundamental education (related to his long-standing concern with colonial problems), reproduction of works of art, research on resources and problems of the tropics, development of the social sciences, and a cultural and scientific history of mankind. In each field he showed enthusiasm and insight, and he was able to persuade both the secretariat and the Executive Board of the merits of many new program ideas.

Probably no one person more directly influenced the content and direction of Unesco's program than did Dr. Huxley in the preparatory stage and during his two years as Director General. Indeed, he was largely responsible for charting the broad course to which the organization became committed during its early years.

Huxley was skeptical of Unesco's ability to make a direct or immediate contribution to peace. In response to suggestions that projects should promote peace and security, he stressed the "impossibility of Unesco producing the rabbit of political peace out of a cultural and scientific hat."[10] Instead he believed that Unesco's contribution would be indirect, using education, science, and culture to build gradually the foundations of future peace.

Since in his view the most important part of Unesco's support would come from scholarly and professional groups, he argued that the program should include projects in which the largest possible number of such groups would have an interest. He believed that "the programme of Unesco should consist mainly of a rather large series of projects, none of them singly of outstanding importance for world peace, but collectively forming the necessary foundation for any future peaceful world." It was the function of Unesco to contribute to the weaving of a world-wide fabric of international understanding and cooperation. According to this view, "each project of Unesco constitutes only a single thread for such a fabric." Unesco could not work alone; "other organizations must be responsible for other threads and other portions."[11]

Further, Huxley hoped, at least initially, that Unesco, by a nonpolitical approach to technical issues in education, science, and culture, might be a bridge between the democracies of the West and the countries under Soviet influence.[12] To this end he proposed that Unesco's philosophy should be "world scientific humanism," in hopeful expectation, as outlined in Chapter III, that some such system might reconcile the West and the Soviet bloc.

Huxley's concept of a diffuse and far-ranging program was mirrored in his view of Unesco's internal organization. Even before his association with the Preparatory Commission, he had seen the staff of the new organization as a group of loosely federated divisions, including "a separate and relatively autonomous division devoted to the sciences and their application."[13] His conduct as Director General accorded with this concept. The secretariat consisted of relatively autonomous sections, and coordinated action by the entire staff became the exception rather than the rule. It should be added that Huxley made a point of being easily accessible to members of the secretariat, and as a result of their personal loyalty to him he was successful in drawing to the organization a large number of able persons from many lands.

Huxley emphasized the importance of vigorous and vigilant National Commissions or cooperating bodies in member states, made up of specialists and experts, who could see that the objectives of Unesco were in fact pursued by national governments. The more he traveled and became acquainted with member countries, the more he recognized that Unesco's own secretariat could do little more than assist and spark program developments in individual countries. He appealed repeatedly for action by member states and in his closing address at the Beirut General Conference in 1948 he said, "It has often—and rightly—been said that Unesco can only operate efficiently with the active co-operation of Member States, through their governments, their National Commissions, their specialists and experts in the fields of education, science and culture, and the general mass of their peoples."[14]

Jaime Torres Bodet (1948–1952)

Huxley had been appointed to serve for two years. Consequently it was necessary to elect the second Director General at the Beirut Conference in 1948. The choice fell on Dr. Jaime Torres Bodet, then Foreign Minister of Mexico. As Minister of Education, Torres Bodet had won wide recognition for a campaign against illiteracy. He was a poet, novelist, and critic who had served his country in a number of diplomatic posts abroad. He had shown interest in Unesco from the start and as head of the Mexican delegation at the London Conference in 1945 had emphasized "the intellectual and moral solidarity of mankind" as a basis of world peace. He had stressed the needs of countries like his own for expansion of education at the most elementary level. At the same time he was closely linked in sympathy with the intellectuals of Western Europe, as a result of his education and diplomatic experience. He spoke French as fluently as his native Spanish.

Perhaps the outstanding characteristic of Torres Bodet was the high degree to which he appealed to both the economically less developed and the more developed countries. With this he combined knowledge of diplomatic procedures and political skill that made him seem the kind of leader Unesco needed at a stage when projects were too abundant, when the rush of new members placed the organization under strain, and when the relations of Unesco to the broader peace efforts of the United Nations were in need of development.

Torres Bodet was more experienced than Huxley in diplomacy and negotiation. He, too, realized the importance of maintaining the support of member states, and was highly persuasive in the early years of his administration in winning their support. His influence as expressed both through his many public statements and through private conversations was an important political factor during debates in the General Conference on program and particularly on the budget. Not infrequently he was able to mobilize the support of the Latin American and Arab "blocs." So strong was his influence with these groups that at the 1949 session of the General Conference, the Director General was privately warned of the danger of a course which brought to his support the votes of a numerical majority composed principally of the smaller, less economically developed countries, but left in opposition to him the votes of a minority composed of the leading contributors to Unesco's budget. (Seven years later at New Delhi, this kind of grouping of states actually did increase the budget by one million dollars over the ceiling voted earlier. As a general rule, states making the largest contributions have exerted more influence on the Unesco budget and program than those making smaller contributions. The first group had as a rule carried farther the development of their own educational, scientific, and cultural resources. They had often been more active in applying the Unesco program among their own nationals. Their influence was exerted more often toward preventing than supporting a budget increase.)

Torres Bodet influenced the Unesco program in many ways. He had an abiding concern for the services which Unesco might perform for the peoples of less economically developed countries. A citizen of a less developed country which during three decades had sought constantly to better the welfare of its people, he seized quickly upon the early results achieved under Huxley's leadership in defining Unesco's responsibility in fundamental education. He set himself without delay to further the coordination of all Unesco's fundamental education activities with the programs in agriculture and health carried on by the Food and Agriculture Organization and the World Health Organization. New funds for fundamental education were made available through the UN Expanded Program of Technical Assistance starting in 1949.

Torres Bodet was intellectually and emotionally responsive to the human needs of the less economically developed peoples, but he was also responsive to the growing political pressure from the considerable number of less developed countries which were soon to attain a voting majority in the United Nations agencies. In his personality and in his career Torres Bodet symbolized the rightful ambitions of these peoples to be heard and to be served by Unesco. That he was so recognized by the less economically developed countries was manifest at every session of the General Conference. As he moved among delegates in the corridors or addressed plenary sessions or commission meetings, he could always count on understanding from representatives of these countries in his efforts to make Unesco serve a wider portion of mankind.

If any other subject produced a response in Torres Bodet comparable to that of aid to less favored lands, it was that of human rights. At the Beirut General Conference, where he was elected Director General, he grasped the initiative in demanding a central role for Unesco in promoting recognition of human rights throughout the world. This he did in responding officially to the message from Trygve Lie reporting adoption by the United Nations General Assembly of the Universal Declaration of Human Rights. From that time until his resignation in 1952, Torres Bodet missed no chance by speech, message, draft resolution, or letter to governments to urge more effective recognition of the basic human rights that must form the foundation for any civilized and peaceful world community. At Beirut, referring to Unesco's task to stimulate education in human rights, he spoke of Unesco as the world's "ever-wakeful conscience," while the United Nations was the "body politic of a new world."[15] Like Huxley, Torres Bodet was a vigorous and militant believer in democracy based upon social justice and freedom of expression.

Torres Bodet's preoccupation with increasing Unesco's assistance to the less economically developed peoples did not blind him to the role of the intellectual elite, especially in Western Europe. His immersion in French culture and knowledge of the dynamics of Western European democracy made him aware of the significance of this group to Unesco's task. He sought to bring intellectual leaders from all over the world into closer contact with each other, that all mankind might be served. Intellectual cooperation, in his view, should not be encouraged solely for the benefit of a select minority; it should serve to improve the conditions of the great masses of people. Torres Bodet was concerned that Unesco had not made contact with the masses in any effective way. Likening Unesco to a nerve center for world communication, he said, "We cannot conceive of a nerve centre except in terms of the living organism whose cohesion and action it ensures. Yet in our case it is often as though, by some strange physiological paradox, the nervous system were still in search of its physical organism."[16]

Perhaps the changing international climate due to the cold war and his own greater experience in world politics made Torres Bodet more acutely aware than was Julian Huxley of the need to relate Unesco's work more closely to that of the United Nations. As tension between the Soviet bloc and the majority of the United Nations grew, he became concerned over Unesco's role in advancing human rights and educational, scientific, and cultural activities in a world threatened by totalitarian control. He encouraged discussion on the central issue at meetings of the heads of the several United Nations agencies. He urged more attention in Unesco's program to efforts that would contribute to education for living in a world community and to greater support of United Nations efforts for peace.

Elected at a time when numerous member states were urging concentration of the program to aim more directly at world peace, Torres Bodet warned at Beirut in 1948 against diversion of Unesco's attention to too many projects and consequent dissipation of energies and resources. He continued: "Let us keep to essentials and, if need be, reduce the extent of our activities so as to be able to pursue them thoroughly and to a finish."[17] But member states were divided in their views as to how much Unesco could contribute directly to peace and security. Torres Bodet's attempt to reduce the number of program projects, and particularly to eliminate those not closely related to the central tasks of Unesco as he saw them, met opposition in the secretariat, the Executive Board, and among member states. He came to accept the necessity of a "balanced program," the result of give-and-take, debate and discussion in the General Conference, a program which, being a compromise among the demands of different kinds of member states, was deficient in unity and focus. In such a situation he believed that the only possibility of achieving greater emphasis on world peace, beyond integration of existing projects, was a larger budget, the additional funds to be allocated to projects directly related to Unesco's principal objectives. Torres Bodet called therefore for more men, more money, and more materials. He declared, "Without a concurrent and combined increase in all these means, what we call the concentration of our Programme could not but lead to sheer surrender. To concentrate is not to contract, even less is it to paralyse."[18]

At the 1950 session of the General Conference in Florence, conflicting pressures on the issue of a direct contribution by Unesco to immediate problems of peace, as well as on the Director General's request for a larger budget, led Dr. Torres Bodet to offer his resignation. International tensions extending from the cold war were rising. The Director General urged the Conference to consider what Unesco could do to strengthen peace. Resolutions introduced by several delegations called for action to this end through meetings of intellectual leaders to outline immediate steps to peace by outlawing atomic weapons.[19]

Since these resolutions were new and had not been adequately considered, they were opposed by several delegations, who argued that the existing program represented Unesco's most effective contribution to peace and that concentration of this program would be more useful than new and untried activities. At the same time certain delegations, some of whose governments were carrying heavy rearmament costs, had shown themselves unwilling to enlarge the Unesco budget. The Director General entered the discussion to declare that if governments genuinely regarded Unesco's existing program as a contribution to peace, they should evidence that attitude by expanding its budget to permit it to do more effective work. If they were not convinced that Unesco's program contributed to peace, he would not wish to continue as Director General. He thus appeared to offer his resignation.[20]

The Conference promptly gave the Director General unanimous

assurance of its confidence. His offer of resignation was withdrawn, on condition of more effective concentration of the program on problems of peace and of a substantial future increase in the budget as recognition of the importance of Unesco's task. The 1951 General Conference a year later adopted resolutions pledging Unesco to cooperate with the United Nations for peace. This session as well as the following one in 1952, while approving slight increases in the budget, substantially cut the totals requested by the Director General. Following such action in the latter session, Torres Bodet on November 22, 1952, once more presented his resignation, declaring that this time his action was irrevocable.[21]

The General Conference appointed John W. Taylor, the Deputy Director General, as Acting Director General. He successfully guided the organization until election of Luther H. Evans as the third Director General seven months later in July 1953. Evans was elected for the full constitutional term of six years. Because the General Conference is not scheduled to meet in 1959, he has requested the Executive Board to place on the agenda of the 1958 session of the Conference the election of a Director General, the term of the person elected to begin at the close of that session.

Luther H. Evans (1953–   )

Luther H. Evans, a political scientist and at the time of his election head of the United States Library of Congress, became Unesco's third Director General on July 1, 1953. He had participated as a member of the United States delegation in the 1945 London Conference and in all succeeding sessions of the General Conference save one. He had served as a member of the Executive Board since 1949. In addition, he had been a leading member of the United States National Commission, serving as a member of the Executive Committee and as Chairman of the Commission. He was thus intimately acquainted with Unesco from its earliest beginnings.

In his inaugural address Dr. Evans avowed his belief that the Unesco program must be planned in long-range terms. "Let us leave to other agencies and other men" he said, "primary responsibility for peace in this generation; we are working to lay the foundations of permanent peace in terms of many generations." He would follow a policy of close cooperation with the United Nations. He came to

serve Unesco "as a professional administrator," and as such he would
seek to enlist the participation of the staff on all levels in formulating
policy. He would try to learn the needs and wishes of all member
states, recognizing that Unesco was an instrument to serve the views
of its members.[22]

During the first year of Evans' term as Director General, the effort
to give a new shape to Unesco's program reached its peak, in antici-
pation of the Montevideo Conference at the close of 1954. He recognized the shortcomings of Unesco's program to that date, the dis-
tinctly minor role that Unesco was accorded in the foreign policy of
member states, as well as the urgent necessity of developing a program
more responsive to the desires of those states, and the importance of
defining more clearly the location of leadership in the organization.

Evans accepted and strongly supported the new orientation of the
program. Once the Montevideo Conference had approved the idea
of major projects, he took leadership in developing plans for the
arid zone undertaking, the Latin American rural education proposal,
and the Eastern-Western project. He also encouraged new ideas with
regard to what Unesco could do concerning the peaceful uses of
atomic energy. Far from seeking to stifle initiative in program thinking, he tried to establish conditions which would permit new ideas to
emerge from both the secretariat and the Executive Board. He endeavored in fact to stimulate fresh thinking on the entire program.

His two predecessors had requested from the General Conference
larger budgets than the Conference as a rule wished to approve. In
contrast, Evans' attitude toward expansion of the program has been
conservative, because he recognized that the major contributors were
also conservative. He himself initially proposed only two major
projects in the remodeled program, whereas the General Conference
in 1956 approved three. He asked an increase of one million dollars
in the budget at New Delhi, but the Conference voted to add two
millions.

While discussion of program reform went forward, Evans gave
priority to establishing first-hand contact with member states. Many
of these had not been visited by previous Directors General, and a
number of members had only recently entered the organization. The
new Director General wished to obtain a clear personal understanding of the needs and interests of member states and of their ideas of

what Unesco should do. In these visits he was markedly successful in establishing frank and friendly contacts.

During 1953-54 he visited thirty-four member states and during the succeeding two years an additional thirty-five countries, so that by the opening of the New Delhi Conference in November 1956, all but eight of the countries then members had had an opportunity to discuss the work of the organization with the Director General face-to-face. For the first time in Unesco's history the Director General was in direct contact with nearly all the member states, as well as with the Executive Board and the secretariat—a basic requirement for leadership. Evans also sought to improve cooperation with the other specialized agencies and with the United Nations itself.

His policy of building contacts with member states entailed prolonged absences from Paris at a time when the new Director General was unknown to many members of the secretariat, and when a host of pressing problems required attention—many of them dating from the resignation of Dr. Torres Bodet. His extended trips were, therefore, not without cost to his relations with the secretariat. They did, however, indicate a new kind of political sensitivity in the office of the Director General, deeply rooted in a democratic philosophy and an optimistic faith in Unesco and in the democratic process applied to international organization.

The third Director General knew, like his predecessors, that Unesco is nothing without the active participation of member states. As a political scientist he attempted to find the wellsprings of member states' interest and support, and to adjust the organization's program to what was politically possible. He did not presume to prescribe what member states should want and studiously avoided lecturing them on their shortcomings.

Evans was aware of the deficiencies in coordination that marked relations among the General Conference, the Executive Board, and the Director General. He expressed his belief that leadership for the organization must come from the Director General and the Executive Board jointly. He also made it clear, as had Torres Bodet before him, that the Director General must assume major responsibility for leadership.

Several extraordinary factors affected Evans' role as Director General, especially his influence on the program. Chosen by the Executive

Board at a time when it was deadlocked on four other candidates, he was a "dark horse" nomination. No major group of member states strongly supported his candidacy, and the French opposed his election. The United States, recognizing that four other specialized agencies were headed by Americans at that time, did not favor the choice of a United States citizen for the top position in Unesco; but once Evans was nominated it voted for him. Undoubtedly the lack of any enthusiastic bloc of nations or individuals as promoters of his election was one factor inducing him to embark immediately upon a tour of member states both to understand their needs and to win their support before the next regular session of the General Conference.

The United States was in the midst of a critical reappraisal of its place in world affairs, one aspect of which was a challenge to the authority of international organizations, including Unesco, with regard to the selection and retention of their staff. This problem affected Evans' early administration because in the Unesco secretariat were several United States citizens in whom the United States government had voiced its lack of confidence.

The loyalty issue concerning American citizens confronted Evans at the outset of his relations with the secretariat. The great suspicion with which United States policy on this matter was widely viewed was inevitably manifested among members of the Unesco staff. Evans handled this thorny question with courage and firmness, seeking to give due protection to the rights of members of the secretariat. The issue was later revived on many occasions by persons desiring to undermine his position in Unesco. This situation illustrated the difficult problems involved in maintaining the principle that the staff of an intergovernmental organization are international civil servants.

A third factor was the change in the tactics of Soviet foreign policy, heralded in the spring of 1954 by the deposit of the USSR's ratification of the Unesco Constitution. Both major protagonists in the cold war were now Unesco members. For a period after the 1945 London Conference, the Soviet Union had ignored Unesco. Then its attitude changed to open hostility. Soviet delegations in other United Nations bodies heaped scorn and abuse on Unesco. They termed it an instrument of United States policy. The fact that Evans was an American, and as a member of the Executive Board had led the fight for Unesco's alignment against aggression in Korea, created obvious problems when the USSR joined Unesco.

Meanwhile Unesco's Executive Board was transformed by a constitutional amendment approved at Montevideo into a body of government representatives. In preceding General Conferences there had been a bitter struggle over this proposal, which had been pressed by the United States and the United Kingdom. Evans himself, when he was a member of the Executive Board, had supported the change.

These four factors emphasized as never before the political setting of which Unesco is a part and hence the political character of the leadership required from the Director General.

The three Directors General have been entirely different personalities, and each has faced special problems arising at different stages of Unesco's history. Running through the administration of all three men has been the central issue of fashioning out of the Unesco idea a vigorous and effective instrument for world peace. The need for imaginative and courageous leadership within the organization has been constantly apparent, and it has been equally clear that this leadership had to come from the Director General. It had to be political leadership, to gear Unesco's work to the desires of member states and to mobilize the creative forces in the General Conference and the Executive Board to attain the goals set for Unesco in its Constitution.

By the end of 1956, Unesco had come a long way toward achieving the conditions for such leadership. Constitutional reform had clarified the relation between the Director General and the Executive Board; member states were beginning to provide guidance for the Board in its role of advising the Director General. There were signs that with the help of the Director General and the secretariat, the Board might come to play a creative role. The Board had become a body of instructed government representatives whose actions tended to be more consistent with the policies of member states. Closer contact had been achieved between the headquarters staff and member states. The secretariat had matured in judgment and efficiency and had become more sensitive to its task and to the needs of member states.

Many factors contributed to these developments. The program

had passed through its most trying period in the first five years. Member states had become more aware of Unesco's value and of their own needs. The two-year period between conferences had reduced the pressure of program preparation and permitted more attention to execution and to requests from member states. This change had also made easier a reduction in the number of meetings of the Executive Board, thus relieving the secretariat of the strain and interference with program work previously entailed by four meetings each year.

Hopeful as the situation now appears, it is clear that much thought and constructive action are still required to achieve effective cooperation among the General Conference, the Executive Board, and the Director General, in both formation and execution of the program, and to outline more clearly the responsibility of each organ. The important problems facing the organization are to define the role of the Executive Board and to improve the General Conference as an orderly and efficient instrument for expressing the will of member states.

Secretariat Staff

Although the Director General, as chief administrative officer, is the head of the secretariat, no discussion of program-making or of program execution would be complete without reference to the nature and functions of the Unesco staff. In contrast to the Director General, the Executive Board, and the General Conference, this staff is a continuing international civil service. It is responsible to the organization alone, although each member of course retains his own nationality. Members of the staff are appointed by the Director General with advice from the Board and from member states and are recruited on a world-wide basis. The staff resides in or near Paris, except those who work elsewhere in connection with various projects. There is also a small staff at the headquarters of the United Nations to conduct the all-important liaison necessary for coordination with the United Nations on program, administration, and finance. There are small secretariat staffs at the Science Cooperation Offices. Salaries and other terms of employment are related to those of the United Nations and of other specialized agencies, and many of the staff have permanent career contracts.

This staff serves the entire organization. Most of its work is done in the name of the Director General in the same sense in which, for example, all federal civil servants in the United States are but extensions of the President as chief executive. They carry on the communications regarding the organization's administration, finance, policy formulation, and program planning and execution. They do the day-to-day work of maintaining relations with governments, nongovernmental organizations, other United Nations agencies, and various groups and individuals interested in Unesco's work. It is the staff that drafts program proposals under supervision of the Director General, and provides the vast quantity of reports and documents requested by governments and the Executive Board. A single session of the General Conference calls for preparation and distribution before and during the sessions of an average of 10 to 12 million pages of documents. It is the staff that implements General Conference or Executive Board directives for meetings of experts or other specialist groups related to the program, of which there are approximately sixty per year. For each one the participants must be selected and invited, documentation prepared in several languages, and reports made on conclusions or recommendations and on plans for next steps. During the sessions of the Board and the General Conference, and for all other meetings, the staff provides all conference services, including interpretation, translation, minutes, and a great deal of drafting of resolutions or texts of agreements. Because of its wide international experience and outlook the staff plays a major part in most negotiations to reconcile divergent national points of view. Upon the staff falls responsibility for writing, drafting, editing, mimeographing, and publishing all official documents and the many special publications and periodicals to which reference has been made in this book.

In an agency with as broad a program as Unesco's the secretariat staff is made up not only of many nationalities but of a wide variety of specialists in professions touched by education, science, or culture. To organize such a group into an effectively operating instrument for the attainment of broad program objectives is a difficult task, which is only gradually being achieved.

The staff, which has grown from 400 to about 1,100 within the decade, has been very influential in program-making as well as in program execution. At best the General Conference is in session for four weeks every two years. The Executive Board, even with its committees, can have only a superficial knowledge of daily activities. The Director General, with his complex world-wide responsibilities, must delegate most of the actual administration of the organization. He cannot himself supervise individual staff work on correspondence, meetings, documents, or publications. He can meet frequently with only a portion of his staff.

During the early years, and first of all during the Preparatory Commission stage, the secretariat provided primary initiative in program planning and in development of working procedures for Unesco. Only gradually did member states gear themselves for responsible action in Unesco affairs, and even now it is the secretariat that provides coordination among the various member states. The secretariat has therefore been the principal element of continuity in Unesco's development—an element that has often been conservative and resistant to new ideas, but also has often provided leadership and imagination in proposing action that would lead to more rapid attainment of Unesco's objectives. Professional loyalties in the staff have undoubtedly contributed to the continued fragmentation of Unesco's program within the formal academic bounds of education, science, and culture. But staff members also provided much of the stimulus that led to the reformulation of the program in 1954. From within the staff came the initiative to seize upon the United Nations Technical Assistance Program as a means of increasing Unesco's total effectiveness. The staff has brought forth and developed many of the more novel ideas, such as the Coupon Scheme; negotiations through GATT for easing international trade in materials of education, science, and culture; publication of *Study Abroad;* and the Science Cooperation Offices. The staff has developed, jointly with staff of other United Nations agencies, the standards and procedures needed in the administration of Unesco as an international organization.

With its responsibility to the international organization clearly defined by the Constitution and with opportunities for professional careers in the service of Unesco, the staff is the most stable influence in the program-making process. It guides, in many respects, the use of the program-making power formally lodged with the General Conference, the Executive Board, and the Director General.

Special Interest Groups

Special interest groups in education, science, and culture might be considered a fourth factor in shaping the Unesco program, in addition to the General Conference, Executive Board, Director General, and the staff. Such groups saw Unesco as a means of promoting projects in which they had a long-standing interest. For the first time in modern history there was a full-fledged intergovernmental agency dedicated to the promotion of objectives which these groups had sought to attain on a national or at most on a nongovernmental international level. It has been noted that only in the natural sciences and to a lesser degree in education and in the humanities had there been much effective and systematic international cooperation prior to 1945. It was the need for better cooperation in these and other fields combined with the political objectives of the United Nations that had particularly stimulated the creation of Unesco.

As soon as the organization had been set up, individuals and groups throughout the world sought its assistance. Thus from the start Unesco inevitably became a means through which, and an objective upon which, various organized groups of educational, scientific, and cultural specialists sought to exert influence. Their efforts were directed to national governments, the General Conference when it was in session, the Executive Board, and the Director General and the secretariat. In some countries the National Commission, to be described in more detail in Chapter XIV, became an especially important means for exerting influence upon national policy in relation to Unesco.

These educational, scientific, and cultural interest groups tended to support the view that Unesco's best contribution to peace and security was through the long-term indirect approach of encouraging the development of education, science, and culture. Hence they were disposed to resist efforts to apply to Unesco program items the criterion of immediate contribution to peace and security. They also tended to emphasize the need for nongovernmental organizations and for contacts among educators, scientists, and cultural specialists, and to oppose governmental or intergovernmental sponsorship of such contacts.

In the second place, the separate interests of specialists within the broad field of education, science, and culture have contributed to splintering Unesco's program and discouraging concentration except as this could be achieved by the General Conference under leadership from the Director General. The specialists were unable to persuade their governments to provide a budget for Unesco that was commen-

surate with its program responsibilities. Between 1946 and 1956
Unesco's annual budget, which had started at 6½ million dollars,
did not even double, in spite of the great expansion of program responsibilities, an increase of member states from thirty to eighty, and
a vast increase in the population served by the organization, not to
mention rising prices.

The Cold War

A final factor affecting the evolution of the program was the cold
war which began almost immediately after Unesco was founded.
Unesco, like the United Nations, was set up on the assumption that
it would operate in a world of nations which shared certain broad
aims—especially peace—and in which understanding could grow as
the result of the free movement of people and ideas. It was assumed
that the military and political peace achieved by the defeat of the
Axis would be expanded into a lasting peace through the United Nations system, to which all the great powers were expected to give
loyal cooperation. But all too soon the dream of "one world" en-
visaged by hope and faith gave way to the seeming reality of a divided
world; and Unesco, despite its goal of universality, was in a position
up to 1954 to function in only one part of that divided world. The cold
war had ranged on one side of the struggle a majority of Unesco's
leading member states, and on the other the most powerful non-
member states.

Thus the absence of the USSR from Unesco in contrast to its active
participation in the United Nations meant that Unesco was substantially in a spectator position when it came to the most acute and
dangerous tensions of the time. It was largely on the sidelines of the
central struggle upon which government energies were focused during the 1946-56 decade.

It was not surprising then that member states tended to look upon
the program of Unesco as of secondary importance. Problems of
program concentration and of adequate financial support did not
receive the attention they might have won, had governments not
been preoccupied with the critical problem of strengthening the free
world against the possibility of open aggression. This tendency was
reinforced by the fact that Unesco's member states themselves were
in many respects divided in their appraisal of the significance of the

cold war and in the policies they adopted toward it. In consequence they found it difficult to agree on how Unesco's program should be related to the current efforts of the United Nations to promote peace and security. Discussion on how Unesco could contribute to peace and security quickly took on a pro and con character in the cold war atmosphere. The issues of that struggle and how they should be met came to dominate debates on the character of program projects and the relative amount of financial support to be given them.

Thus, although Unesco had a task far beyond its powers in the part of the divided world open to it, it was relegated by the cold war to a sideline position in relation to the central struggle of the period; the financial support accorded it was probably less than it otherwise would have been; and its efforts to clarify and concentrate its program suffered from difficulty and delay. The period of Soviet participation in Unesco has been much too short to indicate changes which this new influence may bring about.

CHAPTER XIV

Unesco and member states

"Without the collaboration of member states, Unesco can do nothing and can be nothing. Without the collaboration of the peoples who compose the member nations, the undertakings of Unesco—undertakings which touch most nearly the lives of people everywhere—can have no reality and no true meaning."[1] These were the words of the Program Commission at Unesco's First General Conference in 1946. The idea they expressed has been stated and restated on many occasions during the last ten years. It is inherent in the Constitution and it has been fundamental to Unesco's philosophy. This chapter examines the place which Unesco holds in the policy and action of member governments and their peoples.

Only in the context of national policy toward Unesco can one understand the changing, growing, and experimental character of Unesco's program.

National Administrative Links with Unesco

Although Unesco's member states have all evidenced their support of the organization by ratifying the Constitution and by paying their annual contributions (the latter sometimes after considerable delay), few have thus far made adequate administrative arrangements for large-scale cooperation in Unesco's program. This lack can be illustrated in a number of ways.

Since membership in Unesco is a matter of foreign policy, the ministry of foreign affairs provides the principal link with the organization. In most countries, however, the ministry of education is chiefly responsible for activities related to the Unesco program, except in federal systems like those in Australia, Switzerland, or the United States, where the role of the national education office is limited.

Wherever the major responsibility on Unesco affairs is assigned, it is essential to have a staff that is adequate in competence, size, and influence to ensure that national action will conform to policy declarations. Such action involves analysis of program projects advanced by the Director General for consideration at the General Conference; careful development of additional program proposals that accord with national needs; integrating the government's Unesco policy with other aspects of its total foreign policy; developing the National Commission and other national activity necessary to carry out Unesco projects; assisting Unesco in locating qualified personnel for service on the Paris staff or in the field; briefing delegations to the General Conference and other meetings and, in pertinent cases, the representative on the Executive Board; and handling effectively the extensive communications that flow between Unesco and member states.

One observer reported in 1951 that some small nations had available "only one or two foreign office men to deal with the United Nations and all its Specialized Agencies. The documents flown from New York, Paris, Geneva, Washington, seem to each secretariat a mere trickle of minimum essential information. Yet they seem a flood to these harassed or indifferent officials. A visitor to their offices finds circular letters piled in dusty stacks."[2]

Partly because so many member nations have not been equipped to do their part in furthering Unesco's objectives, the Director General warned in 1951 that "All too often the Secretariat's work yields no practical results, because it is not followed up at the national level by the governmental action which it was intended to stimulate and facilitate."[3]

Even today most nations, great or small, have not provided adequate staff for full participation in Unesco activities. According to 1956 reports, Japan had the largest—a full-time staff of sixty-eight persons for its Unesco activities including the National Commission; the United States came next with twenty-two; India and the United Kingdom each had ten; Germany and Italy eight; Indonesia and the Philippines six; and Australia, Cambodia, and Iran five.[4] Whether these staffs actually devote all their time to Unesco affairs is not clear. Nor is it clear how much of the reported staff is junior or clerical. An inadequate staff may be due to lack of understanding of Unesco's role, to the nature and level of development of educational, scientific, and cultural organizations both private and governmental, or to the country's stage of political and administrative development. Frequently the nations that need Unesco most are the least well equipped for effective collaboration.

Even in countries like the United States, where there is a special Unesco unit in the Department of State, there has been little evidence of continuing interest in Unesco affairs on the part of high-ranking officials. Questions relating to Unesco do not seem to be matters of major concern in planning national foreign policy.

Another illustration of the lack of serious government concern has to do with the General Conference. It is composed exclusively of government delegates and the complexity of its task has been noted in the preceding chapter. So far, the Conference has not been a very effective device for discovering the common international will on Unesco matters. It is unwieldy in size and overburdened with details. The quality of national delegates has not usually been commensurate with the responsibilities of Unesco. Only rarely have delegations included persons of the rank of foreign minister or prime minister. Many delegations seem to be given inadequate instructions. They have often made proposals that clearly had not been studied by their governments. Many delegates have shown a stronger preference for the "fringe benefits" of Conference attendance than for the hard work that alone can make a conference successful. The lack of continuity in the membership of delegations has meant that a large proportion of the delegates has not been familiar either with the program or with Conference procedures.

Since 1954 members of the Executive Board have represented governments and hence have presumably reflected government instructions. Some Board members have been well prepared; they have been able, highly intelligent, industrious, and dedicated individuals. Others have tended to improvise, and have contributed little to the discussions. The variety in performance has largely been due to the same factors that have influenced the quality of representatives in the General Conference. Adequate briefing of delegates on the many matters that come before a Board meeting requires not only individual study and conscientious attention by the Board members, but also careful prior analysis of the agenda by government staff at home, in terms of national policy and of Unesco's purposes and functions. Many governments are not equipped to undertake this task. Others apparently have considered Unesco's work of minor importance to national policy, and have allowed their Board members complete freedom.

Some member nations have resident delegates at Unesco's Paris headquarters. Through them, national interests can be more effectively communicated to the Director General and Unesco projects can be more clearly interpreted to member states than if communication consists only of letters and cables. A capable and conscientious delegate, understanding his own country's educational, scientific, and cultural resources and needs, can significantly affect a member state's participation in the Unesco program. He can also help Unesco to understand better the needs of member states. Some delegates, however, have been little more than expatriates in Paris, and have exercised little influence toward increasing Unesco's impact.

Unesco is a new organization for which there is little precedent. During its first ten years member governments have made only a beginning, though a promising one, in linking their administrative procedures with those of Unesco. On the other hand, the Unesco secretariat has recognized more clearly the importance of knowing which governments are prepared to participate actively in carrying projects to completion. The extensive travels of the third Director General, Dr. Evans, who visited in person most member countries, helped the secretariat at Paris to respond more rapidly and efficiently to what national governments were willing and ready to do.

National Commissions

Unesco's National Commissions are a unique feature; no other United Nations agency has a comparable arrangement formally linking citizen groups to the work of the international organization.

The Unesco Constitution provides that each member state shall associate its principal educational, scientific, and cultural organizations with Unesco activities, preferably by setting up "National Commissions or national co-operating bodies." The exact character of these agencies was not prescribed in the Constitution, beyond the stipulation that they should be broadly representative of the government and of the nation's "principal bodies interested in educational, scientific and cultural matters." Each state was to "make such arrangements as suit its particular conditions."[5]

The National Commissions were fashioned somewhat in the image of the National Committees of the Intellectual Cooperation Organization of the League of Nations,[6] but were intended to be more broadly representative and more democratic. During World War II a number of unofficial groups in Great Britain and the United States had included in their proposals for an international education agency an emphasis on National Commissions in each member nation, to reinforce the activities of governments by the efforts of private groups.

It was hoped by some that Unesco might thus develop through citizen participation a firm democratic base. Others wanted merely to ensure that national policy on Unesco matters would have advice from leading professional groups and would not be guided by government bureaucrats alone.

Citizen groups to advise on government policy have been a device employed by democratic governments for many years. Special bodies, such as royal commissions in the United Kingdom, have frequently been asked to develop policy recommendations. In the United States advisory boards have been used by government agencies, both to formulate proposals and to provide public support on important problems—local, state, and federal. Precedents for the use of such bodies in foreign relations were furnished by the representative committees and conferences which advised on the development of the national program of cultural relations in the United States and by the invitation of the United States government to a small number of private organizations to send observers to aid its official delegation at the Pan American Conference in 1945 at Mexico City. This latter procedure was broadened in connection with the San Francisco Conference which drafted the Charter of the United Nations. More than forty voluntary agencies were invited to name consultants to the United States delegation. These organizations included agricultural, business, labor, women's, veterans', educational, civic, religious, and peace groups. Their representatives met frequently with members of the delegation. Some of their proposals eventually found a place in the Charter, such as provisions on human rights and inclusion of educational and cultural cooperation within the responsibility of the Economic and Social Council. Groups of this type also shaped the United States National Commission for Unesco when, in the course of hearings before committees of both the House and the Senate, the original proposal of the Department of State for a body of thirty members appointed by the Secretary of State was expanded into a plan for a body of one hundred members, sixty of whom were to be nominated by private organizations.[7]

The provisions for National Commissions in the Unesco Constitution were unique in several respects. First, the creation of National Commissions or Cooperating Bodies was to be a government obligation implicit in ratification of the Constitution. Second, the Constitution defined the functions of such bodies: to serve in both an advisory and a liaison capacity. Third, the functions so defined assumed a degree of participation by the National Commission in government action that went beyond the current practice of even the most democratic states. Fourth, these functions seemed to make National Commissions something more than agencies of government—perhaps actually the means of direct contact between Unesco and citizen groups interested in its work.

The idea for Unesco National Commissions emerged primarily from countries with experience in political democracy, which had numerous voluntary organizations in various fields. A large proportion of their citizens were accustomed to taking part in such private organizations, which often directly or indirectly participated in government affairs. In many other countries most of the people had previously had no opportunity for participation in public affairs, because of a feudal heritage, or a caste system, or foreign occupation, or general conditions of poverty, disease, and illiteracy.[8] In many countries no organized effort by citizens had been possible in any field (even social clubs) without government authorization of some kind. It is therefore not surprising that the influence of National Commissions varies widely among Unesco's member states and that in some the idea is viewed with suspicion. Although the number of National Commissions increased from six in 1946 to seventy-two in 1956, the majority of them exist largely on paper.

In democratic countries with responsible government agencies, establishment of a National Commission meant that this body would be officially related to the government's policy-making mechanism. This posed a question concerning the amount of influence in policy matters to be exercised by elected officials, on the one hand, and members of the National Commission on the other. The former, including members of the national legislative body, are chosen through democratic procedures to carry out the will of the people. The Unesco National Commission then would be an additional organ expressing the will of a portion of the people. If differences developed between the two groups, which should prevail? When some members of the National Commission were appointed as official government delegates to the Unesco General Conference, could they continue to represent the views of the Commission if these varied from government policy? In short, was the Unesco General Conference to become a parliament of specialists in education, science, and culture, speaking to each other directly as representatives of their National Commissions?

A similar issue was implied in President Eisenhower's proposal for developing closer people-to-people relations around the world, when he suggested keeping open channels of communication that might even "evade" the will of existing governments.[9] Something of this spirit has been evident at many Unesco conferences when professional specialists on various national delegations ignored government instructions and voted according to professional interest.

In democratic governments, where practice can be flexible, the potential conflicts arising from the existence of National Commissions have not caused much concern. In fact, the National Commission has been hailed as setting a new pattern with regard to foreign affairs. The first Chairman of the United States National Commission, Milton S. Eisenhower, described that body as "quasi-governmental. It is a body of private citizens, speaking their own minds, and yet giving advice—very effective advice—to the Department of State on one important phase of foreign policy. It is a unique arrangement —and a fascinating one to any student of social science. It avoids the mistake of divorcing the workers for peace altogether from governmental responsibility and effectiveness, and it at the same time leaves these workers free of the restrictions which must hamper them if they become official agents of the Department of State."[10]

In less democratic governments, including those of many economically less developed countries, the proposal for National Commissions has seemed to contain a threat to established authority, and this is undoubtedly one reason for the character of their development to date in such countries.

A report from one member, New Zealand, declared:

... it is obvious from experience that the more vigorous and influential the National Commission is in any particular country, the more telling the work of Unesco in that country. For it can work efficiently only by stimulating and coordinating the work of other bodies and individuals, quite apart from its task of stimulating governments. If it is merely a formal body, then its State's membership of Unesco will remain merely a formality; and Unesco, to use the words of the Director-General . . . will be in danger of becoming "a purely technical body in the narrowest sense, an official organization of national and international officials or a centre for specialized studies unconcerned with the social consequences of what it does."[11]

Who are members of the National Commissions, and how are they related to governments? The number of members varies from 7 to 330, with the average about 50. The Commissions may include representatives of various government agencies, universities and institutions of primary and secondary education, libraries, museums, academies, and learned societies, professional and occupational groups such as educators, scientists, artists, journalists, and specialists in radio, film, and television, labor and youth organizations, and sometimes regional groups.

A study of the structure and work of National Commissions was authorized by the Montevideo General Conference in 1954. Its findings, based on replies from more than two-thirds of the existing Commissions, were presented to the New Delhi Conference in 1956.[12] This study found that the proportion of government officials ranges from five to 100 per cent. In Western Europe and North America, members from outside the government are as a rule more numerous than in other areas. Less than half of the Commissions outside Europe include representatives of the press, radio, film, and television; and even fewer have representatives of labor and youth organizations.[13]

There is also wide variation among Unesco National Commissions in their relation with government. The essential questions are whether the Commission has an independent status in law, and whether its staff is autonomous or under control of a government agency. A few Commissions, such as that of Sweden, have no connection with the government, in law or in fact, and the majority of their members are usually drawn from outside the government. The secretariat in these cases is autonomous and has an independent budget. Other Commissions are independent in law, but their staffs actually are closely in touch with government circles. Some Commissions are essentially government bodies, attached to the ministry of education or of foreign affairs, with the government appointing all their members. The secretariat is paid by a government ministry and is often completely under the ministry's control.

Most Commissions, however, are of a mixed or intermediate character, with their members representing both the government and the private educational, scientific, and cultural life of the country. Such is the case in the United States, where the Commission was set up by Act of Congress, rather than by executive action, and where the staff, located in the Department of State and paid by it, has a double function: to serve as the secretariat for the National Commission and also as the focus within the government for Unesco matters.

The Unesco Constitution proposes that National Commissions should furnish advice "to their respective delegations to the General Conference and to their Governments in matters relating to the Organization" and also that they serve "as agencies of liaison in all matters of interest" to Unesco.[14] In practice the Commissions have provided three services: advice, liaison (including information), and assistance in carrying out the Unesco program in member states. But they have functioned in very different ways, depending upon the traditions and practices of their countries.

The "Democratic" Type

In the United States the National Commission has probably developed further than in any other member state. Upon ratification of the Unesco Constitution, the Congress created the National Commission with one hundred members. It includes sixty persons nominated by national voluntary organizations, fifteen members "at large," and twenty-five officials from federal, state, and local governments, the latter two groups chosen by the Secretary of State. Among the sixty organizations represented are highly specialized intellectual groups, as well as more popularly based national associations in agriculture, business, labor, and religion. The Commission convenes every two years a large national conference attended by a thousand or more representatives of voluntary organizations, to discuss major issues involved in United States participation in Unesco. Thus the National Commission in the United States is a broadly democratic body.

The Commission has given advice to the United States government on Unesco's policy, personnel, and program. It has been informally consulted about membership of delegations to the General Conference, appointment of American citizens for Unesco tasks, and at times about candidates for the office of Director General. Its most important advice has related to the Unesco program. Its views have been faithfully and consistently transmitted by the Department of State as part of the official instructions to United States delegations at the General Conference. The Department of State has not always, however, accepted the National Commission's advice on such matters as the Unesco budget and major political questions.

The U. S. National Commission, like others, has been consulted by the Unesco secretariat on many matters. These include preparation and execution of the program and choice of consultants, recipients of fellowships and scholarships, and members of the Paris staff.

The liaison and information role of the U. S. National Commission is closely linked to its advisory function. A National Commission has been defined as "essentially a system of relations." It has been likened to a turntable for directing questions and information to the appropriate place. The U. S. Commission through its secretariat maintains close relations with the Office of Education, the Library of Congress, and other interested federal agencies, as well as with national organizations of educators, scholars, and specialists in the natural and social sciences and in the arts and philosophy. The National Commission has made some efforts to maintain relations with the press, radio, film, and television, and to reach the public by promoting circulation of Unesco publications, by its own publications on Unesco activities, and by a wide variety of meetings, conferences, and exhibitions.

The most important task of the United States National Commission has to do with carrying out the Unesco program. Although many individuals become involved in Unesco's program independently of the National Commission, nearly all the organized participation is arranged through the Commission.

Activities of the Commission and its member organizations have included fund raising and other assistance to educational reconstruction abroad, including distribution and sale of Unesco coupons; stimulating programs of education for international understanding, revision of textbooks, and education about the United Nations and human rights; cooperation in International Theater Month, which was first launched in the United States; and encouragement of participation by scholars in philosophic inquiries and in research on social tensions and on problems of arid zones. Many national and regional conferences have been held in the United States to follow up the work of Unesco international seminars. For example, in 1952 regional conferences on improvement of teaching and teaching materials relating to international understanding were held at the University of Denver, the University of Florida, George Peabody College for Teachers at Nashville, Iowa State University, and Syracuse University.

Recent activities have featured a program of "citizen consultation" started in 1954 and continuing in 1957, and have emphasized understanding between Orient and Occident.[15] A series of roundtable discussions on Asian-American relations were held in the United States in 1956, with the participation of ten educational and cultural leaders from Asia; and in November 1957 the Sixth National Conference sponsored by the U. S. Commission at San Francisco was to have better Asian-American relations as its major theme.

The continuing element in the United States National Commission is the Unesco Relations Staff within the Department of State. Its Director is the Executive Secretary of the National Commission and the staff is responsible for all the services required by such a large body. This staff, at one time composed of more than forty persons, was reduced in 1953 to about half that number. The appropriation for staff salaries and activities and for travel expenses of members attending meetings of the Commission and its committees was $240,000 for the 1955-56 fiscal year. The staff arranges meetings, develops working papers on all important items of business, and prepares reports and publications. It transmits the Commission's advice to the Secretary of State. It serves also as a link between the Commission and the Unesco secretariat at Paris. To this staff come all Unesco documents for consideration by the United States government; the secretariat considers in what ways the National Commission should be involved, and at times develops proposals for activities by voluntary organizations. Finally, the Unesco Relations Staff has initial responsibility, in cooperation with other offices of the Department of State, for outlining American policy at sessions of the General Conference and for arranging the briefing of delegations. It performs a similar function for the United States member of the Executive Board.

Many of the apprehensions expressed at the time the National Commission was set up in the United States have proved unfounded. It has not, as some of its first members feared, been wholly ignored or used merely as a rubber stamp by the Department of State. Nor, despite the forebodings of some government officials, has the Commission behaved irresponsibly. It has accepted its duties seriously and has acted with restraint, at times even with diffidence.

The National Commission began its life with optimism and enthusiasm, and with the active participation of outstanding leaders in the fields of Unesco's responsibility, as well as of influential civic groups. At the end of the first decade, however, it adopted a recommendation which showed that its members were not satisfied with its role. The recommendation called for a study and an objective evaluation of the Commission's structure and organization, its work during the first ten years, and its relations "to the Government, to Unesco, to voluntary organizations in the United States, and to the American people."[16]

This recommendation reflected the fact that Unesco affairs were still not receiving high level attention within the United States government. The role of the United States in Unesco seemed to have no clear place in the broader frame of American foreign policy. At the same time the Commission had been able to hold the enthusiasm and interest of only a few of the persons of stature and leadership who were among its original members. Some of its critics charged that it had degenerated "into a collection of trade association secretaries." Nor had it been able to develop widespread support at "the grass roots," as had been attempted in the early days by such activities as those in Kansas under the leadership of Milton S. Eisenhower, then President of Kansas State College.[17] In a few professional areas such as the natural and social sciences, there had been some organized support for Unesco program activities, but these cases had been exceptional. Leading educational groups, which at the start had given Unesco strong backing, lost their enthusiasm, in part because of jurisdictional differences among themselves. An impressive number of American citizens were involved in undertakings related to Unesco. Nonetheless, the groups represented on the National Commission showed little vigor in developing among the mass of their supporters knowledge about Unesco or positive participation in activities in line with Unesco objectives. This is a failure which brings into question the ability of the Commission to perform one of the two major functions for which it was created.

In short, the United States National Commission finds itself limited to the role of adviser on program policy and observer of program activities. Its staff, originally planned to serve a clientele as wide as the range of Unesco's program, has been reduced by official action, as have its budgetary resources. It is time for a reappraisal of the role of the National Commission and of the part Unesco should play in United States foreign policy.

The "Aristocratic" Type

In contrast to the widely representative character of the United States National Commission, involving broad citizen groups as well as specialists, is a second type found for example in many countries of Western Europe. Here the Commission is made up primarily of members of the intellectual aristocracy—scholars, writers, and other intellectuals. In some cases, as in Great Britain, the National Commission is a loose federation of so-called "cooperating bodies" or working groups in such fields as education, natural sciences, social sciences, arts and letters, philosophy and humanities, libraries and museums. Representatives of these groups come together perhaps once a year. Their most important assignment is to scrutinize and comment on the program to come before the General Conference.

Seminars on various phases of Unesco activity have been sponsored by the National Commissions in Europe. For example, the Commissions of Denmark, Norway, and Sweden organized in 1955 a seminar on education for international understanding, held at the Unesco Institute for Education at Hamburg. A number of Commissions in Europe have cooperated in the showing of Unesco traveling exhibitions in both art and science.

Local activities have been encouraged by some of these National Commissions. France has promoted Unesco Clubs in various provincial cities. The Swedish National Commission helped the town of Vasteras organize in 1954 a "Unesco Week," which focused on the needs of the economically less developed countries and the kind of international aid that would be helpful to them. Ways through which the townspeople could help Unesco efforts in fostering literacy, human rights, and international understanding were presented through films, exhibitions, lectures in the schools, and evening meetings for adults. During the week, taxis in Vasteras flew Unesco flags and Unesco posters decorated the town's narrow streets.[18]

The "Bureaucratic" Type

A third type of National Commission is found in countries where the national government is in process of rapid evolution, or where democratic institutions have not become securely established. In many states in Latin America, the Middle East, and Asia, the Commissions are in effect government agencies. But they perform a useful function, for they bring about inter-agency attention to the Unesco program as a whole. No other agency has the necessary breadth of view. The foreign office is concerned primarily with formal international relations. The ministry of education is preoccupied with technical aspects of education. The National Commission is an instrument for fusing the concerns of various government agencies into a unified conception of the national interest as affected by Unesco activities. This is of special importance in the development of technical assistance projects under UNETAP.

Mention should be made of efforts to link National Commissions and the interests they represent on both a regional and a world-wide basis. Some fifteen Commissions in Europe maintain regular working relations with other Commissions, mostly in neighboring countries. This practice is growing in Asia. The United States National Commission has regularly invited Commissions in all parts of the world to send observers to its meetings, and a number have responded. Following two regional conferences of National Commissions organized by Unesco—one in 1950 at Havana for those of the Western Hemisphere, and one in 1951 at Bangkok for those in South Asia and the South Pacific—individual National Commissions took the initiative in promoting such meetings. Early in 1956 the Japanese National Commission was host to a regional conference of Asian Commissions. In addition to conferences, liaison among National Commissions is maintained by exchange of publications, visits of secretaries, and meetings on problems of common concern (for example, the revision of textbooks discussed in Chapter X).

On the international level, meetings of representatives of National Commissions were held in connection with several sessions of the General Conference. The representatives were usually members of official delegations, and the meetings served principally for an informal exchange of ideas on what was going on in each country. More important, Unesco has brought to Paris, usually for three-week periods, the executive officers of National Commissions, who could thus become acquainted with members of the secretariat, learn more of Unesco's work as a whole, and discuss the needs of their countries and the future program. Representatives of almost sixty Commissions had been accorded this privilege by the end of 1955. Such visits have brought the Paris secretariat closer to what was happening in member states. They have also provided an opportunity for the visitors, while en route, to establish contacts with other Commissions. The General Conference has likewise approved funds to permit members of the Unesco headquarters staff to visit National Commissions, to assist their development and operations, and to discuss plans for carrying out certain projects.

Improving the National Commissions

The study of National Commissions recommended by the General Conference at Montevideo in 1954, although covering only two-thirds of the total number, provided the first general picture of the work of these bodies. It cast some light on a problem which from the start has called for careful study, namely, the need to identify the factors in national tradition and social structure which favor the successful development of National Commissions.

Four main points emerged from this review. First, no Commission has a budget large enough to handle all the work in member states called for by General Conference resolutions. Second, all Commissions recognize that they are reaching the general public inadequately at best. Third, their relations with the Unesco secretariat at Paris need to be improved through opportunity for more effective consultation and guidance on program matters. Finally, they need closer relations with other National Commissions. In short, the National Commissions require a more representative membership, larger staff and budget, a clearer relation to the national government, and more sharply defined methods of work.[19]

The National Commission represents an essentially new idea for all member states—an idea related to a new agency of international cooperation. It is still far from clear what the role of these bodies may become in the future development of Unesco.

In its ideal form and in its most democratic setting, the National Commission is essential for stimulating widespread support of national activities to carry out Unesco aims. It must have strong roots in local communities which cannot be developed by a government staff alone; it requires the active efforts of voluntary agencies. Finally, the National Commission must be closely geared into high government policy and requires continued government support. It has become clear that the National Commission in its relation with Unesco is not something distinct from government. Unesco cannot use it to bypass governments and speak directly to the peoples. In fact, the National Commission in countries lacking a democratic tradition has served primarily as a device to bring together separate government interests concerned with Unesco matters.

In all three types mentioned above—democratic, aristocratic, and bureaucratic—the Commissions have been most useful in formulating the Unesco program. It would appear on the whole that their advisory function concerning the program as well as other matters has gained in importance. It is in efforts to carry out the program that their effectiveness has varied most widely.

Policies of Individual States toward Unesco

A detailed analysis of the policies of individual nations toward Unesco would go beyond the scope of this volume. A brief review of the interest shown by leading member states or groups of states, however, may help in understanding Unesco's record during its first decade. Without access to national archives, such a review will necessarily be sketchy and somewhat impressionistic.

France

The French sent probably the most distinguished delegation to the London Conference in 1945, and in several succeeding General Conferences their delegations were of a high order, often headed by leading statesmen. At London, France was primarily concerned that Paris should be the seat of Unesco. The International Institute of Intellectual Cooperation had previously been situated at Paris. France had long laid heavy stress in its foreign relations upon cultural affairs and the promotion of the French language and cultural influence. It was not surprising that France should view Unesco as an important element in its postwar foreign policy.

France has shown awareness of the value of being associated with organized international activities in Unesco's field of operations. Its primary focus has been upon projects that appealed to the intellectual élite and to specialized academic and artistic groups. It has strongly backed financial support from Unesco for private organizations in scholarly fields. Somewhat less interest has been shown in fundamental education, technical assistance, mass communication, and activities seeking to make immediate contributions to peace. This has not meant that France did not support such projects. For French representatives in Unesco have, as is the case in other countries, included many different interests and a variety of specialists.

The nature of French social and political life, in which the intellectual élite occupies a prominent place, has largely set the tone for French policy on Unesco affairs. This has been noticeable particularly in the composition and activities of the French National Commission, which has tended to represent primarily the intellectual élite and appears to have relatively little participation by popular and civic groups. Even so, many French intellectuals have been indifferent if not hostile to Unesco undertakings. The most consistent interest and cooperation has probably come from primary and secondary school teachers, but support from the government has been disappointing. A special reason has no doubt been the chronically unstable character of postwar French governments.

United Kingdom and Commonwealth of Nations

The United Kingdom during World War II was host to the Conference of Allied Ministers of Education and later to the Unesco Preparatory Commission, and it took a leading part in launching Unesco initially; it showed great interest in intellectual cooperation, and it supported efforts to strengthen the international scientific unions and other scholarly bodies. However, interest in Unesco among university professors and other intellectual leaders has been uneven at best. This group on the whole had been cool toward active association with the Paris Institute linked with the League of Nations. Primary and secondary school teachers have shown a more cordial attitude toward Unesco.

The United Kingdom has displayed keen interest in the problems of the economically less developed countries and in Unesco undertakings to expand educational oportunities and help build foundations for political stability in the new states that were formerly colonies. The British Colonial Office had already pioneered along this line. It was the United Kingdom that introduced the idea of associate membership in Unesco for territories not yet independent.

British and Commonwealth policy has shown throughout most of the decade considerable skepticism as to the practicability of educational activities intended specifically to promote international understanding. The United Kingdom, like France, appeared to be aware that Unesco's cultural relations program was competitive as well as complementary to its own. Perhaps partly for this reason and certainly partly because of special financial and commercial difficulties during the postwar period, the United Kingdom has led most of the economy drives to limit Unesco's budget and, accordingly, its program.

All the Commonwealth countries have consistently supported efforts to concentrate Unesco's program and to increase its impact in member states. While in this and other matters the policies of the United Kingdom and other members of the Commonwealth have often been similar, there have been some contrasts. India will be separately discussed below. South Africa, after showing initial interest in the Unesco program, gradually reduced its cooperation, and at the end of 1956 withdrew from the organization, mainly because of differences concerning the country's racial policy. Australia and New Zealand have cooperated actively in various phases of the Unesco program. Both provided funds for fellowships to nations of the countries of South and Southeast Asia, and both have been active in promoting national seminars on Unesco undertakings. Canada, though facing federal educational problems due to culturally divided English and French-speaking elements in its population, has been active in efforts to strengthen Unesco. It has not been able to develop much systematic program support at home, except during the early years in the field of educational reconstruction.

United States

The United States[20] has repeatedly declared that support of the United Nations is one of the pillars of its foreign policy. It has also expressed support of Unesco and attested to its importance in the

United Nations system.[21] However, the United States government has not always seemed to understand what could be done by cooperative action through Unesco to achieve the goals of the United Nations and those of United States foreign policy.

From the start responsibility for policy supervision of Unesco matters has been divided in the Department of State. Program questions were the responsibility of an Assistant Secretary of State charged with the whole range of "public affairs," including sometimes aspects of overseas information programs, educational exchanges, and domestic information activities of the Department of State. Another Assistand Secretary of State, having general oversight of United Nations affairs, was responsible for constitutional, administrative, budgetary, and personnel questions relating to Unesco, as well as for the relations of that organization to other agencies of the United Nations. Although many of the Assistant Secretaries responsible for Unesco affairs have given support to the development of the National Commission and have attended Unesco Conferences, there appears to have been little appreciation, at the central point of foreign policy determination, of how important Unesco is in strengthening the values needed in a free and peaceful world community. No major effect has been discernible to involve Unesco in alleviating the tensions of the cold war, before or since the Geneva Summit Conference of 1955. Except at intermediate levels of the Department of State there has been only occasional evidence of a wish for vigorous efforts to involve the American people in Unesco's world program. Attacks upon Unesco and upon U.S. cooperation with it have largely remained unanswered in official quarters. Again there has been lacking an awareness of the positive value to U.S. world prestige that can come from supporting the intellectual and cultural values for which Unesco stands. The advantage of U. S. participation in Unesco's multilateral technical assistance in the fields of education, science, and culture has often been overlooked through preoccupation with more traditional, bilateral programs. Finally, no consistent effort seems to have been made to use the resources of the National Commission to help prepare the American people for their new international responsibilities.

By the end of the decade under review the chairman of the United States delegation to the General Conference at New Delhi in 1956 felt constrained to declare that "the U. S. has not provided the initiative and influence commensurate with the potential value Unesco holds for this country. . . . This may be attributable to our reluctance to assign to Unesco an adequate place in American policy and to accord to Unesco appropriate consideration as a means of achieving foreign policy objectives." He stated that he had recommended a fresh appraisal on a high level of United States relations with Unesco.[22]

Although support for Unesco and cooperation through it have played a minor part in total U. S. foreign policy, it should be pointed out that cooperation with Unesco has been more widely based among the American people than has cooperation with any other United Nations specialized agency. As noted in the discussion of Unesco's origin, many individuals and private groups had favored the creation of Unesco. The government, even before the Unesco Constitution was drafted in 1945, sought the advice of a broad array of private organizations and groups concerning what Unesco should be and what it should do. Many of these organizations were also represented at the San Francisco Conference.

During its early years the United States National Commission secured for Unesco wide and enthusiastic support in the United States. The Commission counted among its members distinguished specialists from the major fields of Unesco's interest. They were well-known persons who inspired confidence in the general public, and many were associated with important civic and professional groups. They gave freely of their time and advice to strengthen United States participation in Unesco. Most of the major civic, professional, and educational organizations at least formally supported the work of the National Commission. In many communities throughout the country Unesco groups, including State Councils, were formed to further the objectives for which Unesco stands. Thus there were signs of roots developing for the National Commission.

Subsequently a wave of opposition to Unesco swept certain parts of the country. This was motivated by a variety of factors largely unrelated to facts about Unesco or its work. It was part of a broader attack upon international cooperation emanating from a few individuals and "professional" patriotic organizations. As a consequence of the attacks upon Unesco, President Eisenhower in 1953 requested a committee of three United States Delegates[23] to the Special Session of the Unesco General Conference to appraise the organization and its work. The committee itemized six charges made against Unesco and on the basis of its inquiry explicitly refuted them. They concluded their report with the hope "that the facts herein will clear the way for renewed and constructive support in the United States for Unesco's aim and program."[24] Subsequent reports on investigations of Unesco came to similar conclusions, including those of a Special Committee of the American Legion, the Chamber of Commerce of the United States, and a Subcommittee of the House of Representatives Committee on Foreign Affairs.[25]

Within the limitations noted above, the focus of U. S. policy in Unesco has been fairly consistent. In the London discussions and subsequently the United States has stressed a wide, popular basis for the membership of National Commissions. It has shown special interest in mass communication as an avenue to the man in the street. It has urged concentration of the Unesco program upon activities designed (1) to meet more effectively the needs of the economically less developed countries, and (2) to develop international understanding as a contribution to world peace. The first has involved strong backing for fundamental education, extension of primary education, and technical assistance—all focused on the less developed countries. With regard to the second, the United States has repeatedly emphasized the importance of education for international understanding and the value of the social sciences in identifying the factors which strengthen or weaken the sense of world community. The United States has supported closer cooperation between Unesco and other United Nations agencies and made a special point of relating Unesco to the United Nations efforts for peace in Korea.

One unfortunate aspect of the United States' attitude toward Unesco has been an assumption that the function of the United States was primarily to give rather than to receive. Many Americans have viewed the U. S. as a patron in the Unesco enterprise rather than as a member of a mutually beneficial partnership. It has been suggested that American educators, for example, should define clearly what Unesco can do for them in the task of achieving national educational progress. The United States might well profit from the help of other countries in furthering understanding by the American people of their new world responsibilities. It might use such help in a more systematic attack upon problems of underdeveloped areas within the United States and in combating illiteracy. One educator has remarked, "We need to cultivate an indebtedness to Unesco for educational lessons the organization can teach us. We are troubled about the teaching of languages in this country. Can Unesco help us solve that problem? We are re-examining our system of higher education. Can Unesco convey to us the experience of other countries. . . . ?"[26]

Most of the weaknesses in U. S. policy noted here can be found in the policies of all member states, though the reasons may differ. Actually, the United States has been among Unesco's most faithful members. United States delegations to the General Conference have often brought an enthusiasm and optimism lacking in most other delegations. They have, as a whole, been well briefed and have been professionally highly competent. The action of the United States Congress in establishing the U. S. National Commission for Unesco, as well as the early record of the Commission and its executive staff in the Department of State, provided example and inspiration for action in many other countries. Many professional individuals and organizations have taken seriously the opportunity afforded by U. S. membership in Unesco to strengthen international cooperation in education, science, and culture. Many also have served on Unesco's committees and have contributed to its deliberations and publications. In addition, scores of Americans have participated as loyal international civil servants in the secretariat and on technical assistance missions for Unesco.

Even though the most violent attacks upon Unesco, outside the Soviet bloc, seem to have occurred in the United States, Unesco has probably had more widespread popular support in the U. S. than in any other country. Indeed, the fact that Unesco policy has been the subject of extensive public debate may be the best evidence of the seriousness of public interest in Unesco itself.

USSR

In the spring of 1954 the entry of the Soviet Union into Unesco presented a challenge to the liberal democratic principles upon which the Unesco Constitution had been founded. The Yugoslav observer at the 1946 General Conference had remarked on the ideological problem faced by a Communist state. He declared that his government could not agree with the "abstract principles" of the Constitution. The Yugoslav delegation at London in 1945 had signed the Constitution, he continued, on the assumption that these principles would not have "any decisive influence on the future activities of Unesco."[27] It seemed doubtful that the USSR, after joining Unesco in 1954, would long be satisfied with this pragmatic solution of the problem. The Soviet entry into Unesco may presage the joining of battle within the organization between the liberal democratic doctrines of the West and the authoritarian philosophy of Communism. With the USSR as a member, Unesco had possibly been shifted from the fringe to a central position in this struggle which had given rise to the "cold war." Unesco had now acquired a clearer meaning for statesmen as well as scholars. It could not be relegated to the sidelines because it dealt only with ideas. As the New Zealand delegation reported to its government after the Unesco Conference at Montevideo, "Just because it deals with ideas, and because it now has members holding conflicting ideas over which nations are willing to go to war, Unesco can be the most useful, as it could be the most dangerous, of all the Specialized Agencies. It can never again be ignored."[28]

The USSR had had no direct contact with Unesco until it ratified the Constitution. Its Eastern European allies—Czechoslovakia, Hungary, Poland—had early joined the organization. As Soviet control tightened, they became increasingly abusive of Western countries in Unesco conferences and ceased to participate in program activities and to contribute to the Unesco budget. Their attempted withdrawal in 1952-53 was accompanied by a particularly virulent anti-Western political attack. They returned to active membership in 1954, when the USSR joined the organization together with Byelorussia and the Ukraine. Two other countries of the Soviet bloc—Bulgaria and Rumania—have subsequently become members.

At the 1954 and 1956 sessions of the General Conference, at which the Soviet Union was represented, it brought forward the theme of "warmongering" against nations with a free press. Its delegation at New Delhi in 1956, together with those of other members of the Soviet bloc, led the attack upon Great Britain, France, and Israel for their action in Egypt. The debate, which was heated and prolonged, impeded consideration of important program items on the Conference agenda. It may be assumed that whenever the cold war is injected into Unesco discussions at the General Conference or the Executive Board, the issue will be debated in more effective terms than was possible when the Soviet bloc was represented only by some of its lesser members.

Besides urging the strengthening of National Commissions and closer bilateral and regional relations among the Commissions, the Soviet Union and its allies have displayed active interest in various phases of the Unesco program. The first participation of the USSR in program activities was at the 1954 conference on protection of historic monuments, where it espoused with considerable vigor the cause of those seeking to spare valuable historic monuments from destruction in time of war. It has given special attention to the social sciences and to mass communication. It has sought to shift the social sciences from a focus on international understanding to one on "peaceful coexistence" of states having different economic and social systems. With Soviet backing, the Polish delegation introduced at the New Delhi General Conference a resolution inviting member states to develop peaceful coexistence. A resolution of similar tenor was presented subsequently by Czechoslovakia to the United Nations General Assembly.[29]

In the field of human rights, the Soviet Union has stressed a narrow emphasis on racial discrimination, rather than a broader one including other kinds of discrimination. In mass communication, the USSR emphasis has been on peaceful coexistence in a world of tensions caused by fear of atomic destruction. It has called for international cooperation in developing the peaceful uses of atomic energy. It has taken a major interest in Unesco's activities under the United Nations Expanded Technical Assistance Program, offering funds as well as technical experts. It backed the major project for mutual appreciation of Oriental and Occidental cultural values. It has requested Unesco to issue a volume on Russian icons as part of its art series.

The significance of the USSR's participation in Unesco is still a matter of debate and speculation. At least three schools of thought may be identified. One is moderately hopeful that contacts with the Soviet Union will be fruitful, insofar as they do not directly involve major political issues. Faith is expressed that more active exchanges of persons, ideas, and educational, scientific, and cultural materials may help to build a foundation for peaceful relations between the peoples on both sides of the Iron Curtain.

A second group doubts whether the Soviet entry into Unesco was anything more than a tactical move to use Unesco as another instrument for spreading the influence of aggressive and revolutionary Communism, especially among countries of neutralist persuasion. They hold that the basic and long-term purpose of the USSR is, through cultural exchanges and technical assistance, to align the economically less developed countries and certain elements in the more industrialized countries more closely in support of the aims of Soviet foreign policy.

A third view, to which the authors incline, is that, whatever the intentions of the Soviet government, its policy of permitting wider and more active contacts between its people and those of other nations may lead to a demand for an even greater degree of freedom, which the Soviet regime may not be able to curb or control. In this view, educational and cultural exchanges may act as a yeast whose ferment will overflow the limits supposed to contain its expansion. The more Soviet citizens take part in international exchange and cooperation on the so-called "technical" level, the greater the possibility of securing acceptance of the principles upon which Unesco's Constitution is founded.

Cooperation of the Soviet countries within Unesco is already a matter of great importance to the furtherance of Unesco's technical objectives. It is likely to become a major issue in the broader area of peace as well.

India

The singular character of the new nationalism in India and other countries of South and Southeast Asia has given Unesco special standing in that area. This nationalism combines a struggle for complete national independence in the political field with an effort to strengthen and expand cultural bonds with the rest of the world. Cultural ties are especially valued as bringing peoples together in understanding and friendship. Unesco has appeared to many Asians primarily as an agency for cultural exchange and hence a people's organization, while the United Nations is regarded as an intergovernmental organization. Unesco therefore has in some areas a wider popular appeal than the United Nations.

The governments of India and neighboring countries were no slow to recognize that education and science were essential to any improvement in the economic and social welfare of their peoples. From the start of Unesco, India has been the leading spokesman of these new states in requesting aid from the organization.

At the 1945 London Conference, the Indian representative stressed the needs of the economically less developed countries as more basic in the long run than those of the war-devastated areas. India has called on Unesco to give greater attention to the countries of Asia and Africa, particularly as regards fundamental education and technical assistance for scientific as well as for educational development. It took the initiative in calling for a study of the world's arid zones. At the same time it saw clearly that economic and social progress would bring new problems and perils to its national life. It sought Unesco's aid in carrying out an analysis by social scientists of tensions within India, and welcomed the establishment at Calcutta of a regional research institute to study the social changes brought by modern industry and technology. Recognizing the importance of public libraries in popular education, India secured help from Unesco in setting up as a pilot project at Delhi the country's first modern public library.

India was also a leader in urging that Unesco promote wider understanding and appreciation in the West of the traditional cultures of Asia, through symposia on philosophic questions, translation of literary classics, reproduction of paintings, and activities in theater and music. It strongly supported mutual appreciation of Oriental and Occidental cultural values as a major Unesco project. It stressed the contribution of Gandhi's philosophy to international understanding and peace. It has emphasized textbook revision as an aid to international understanding, and urged the preparation of such scholarly works as an Asian Encyclopedia covering the Hindu, Buddhist, and Confucian civilizations, a Sanskrit dictionary, and a study of manuscripts of Asian history.

India has on many occasions contended that Unesco should become more representative of all peoples of the world. It urged the entry of the Soviet Union and has favored that of the People's Republic of China. In Unesco, as elsewhere, India has tried to mediate between the Soviet Union and the Western powers. It has supported "peaceful coexistence," removal of racial discrimination, and peaceful uses of atomic energy. It has favored concentration of the program, a substantial increase in Unesco's budget, decentralizing program operations, and strengthening National Commissions, although its own National Commission has yet to acquire much influence.

Arab States

The governments of the Arab states have shown little concern for the content of the Unesco program, except as it might affect their own countries. Their policy has reflected their needs as economically less developed countries, and certain other special interests. They have welcomed the services provided by the Science Cooperation Office at Cairo and the fundamental education training center at Sirs-el-Layyan, as well as assistance in meeting the educational needs of the Palestine refugees. They have also sought to spread knowledge of Arab culture through Unesco aid for translation of Arabic classics into Western languages, and, less successfully than the Latin American bloc, they have pressed for special recognition in Unesco conferences of the Arabic language. Egypt and Lebanon have played a more active part in these endeavors than the other nations of the group.[30]

While the political policy of the Western powers, particularly toward Israel, has alienated the Arab states from the West, Unesco, largely through its conferences and meetings of specialists, has been an influence drawing the Arab peoples toward the West.

Latin American Republics

The Latin American countries, a number of which were among the earliest members of Unesco, have with few exceptions remained inactive. Part of this apathy toward Unesco may be due to their long and active association with the Organization of American States. They have traditionally been zealous in their devotion to international understanding and cooperation, but their devotion has more frequently been expressed in words than in actions. They have not displayed in Unesco a drive and enthusiasm for extension of education at all commensurate with that of the Asian countries. Many of these republics, however, have participated in regional educational seminars sponsored by Unesco. Colombia with some small assistance from Unesco has made a dramatic experiment with the use of radio in fundamental education, and has cooperated in the establishment, as a pilot project, of a public library at Medellín which has achieved success.

The Latin American states have been most active in support of Unesco projects which promised some direct advantage to their part of the world. They have sought aid under the United Nations Expanded Technical Assistance Program. They favored establishment of a Science Cooperation Office at Montevideo, and many of their scientists seem to have benefited thereby. They supported creation of a regional Unesco center at Havana, and have fought to continue it, despite questions as to its value and effectiveness.

They secured at New Delhi in 1956 a Unesco commitment to support a Latin American Center of Social Sciences in Chile and a regional research institute in Brazil on the social and cultural aspects of industrialization and technological change. Ten years earlier Brazil had sought Unesco's help for the Hylean Amazon project but then had doomed that ambitious proposal by its own hesitant support. Mexico, host to the 1947 General Conference, cooperated with Unesco and the Organization of American States in setting up the training center for fundamental education at Patzcuaro, but aside from that has shown little positive interest. Argentina has done little. Otherwise the voice of Latin America has been heard largely on such questions as making Spanish a third working language of the organization, and expanding the number of Latin American works to be translated into other languages.

Germany and Japan

Unesco was the first United Nations agency to include these ex-enemy countries. Both nations showed active interest in Unesco as soon as they were encouraged to do so by the occupying powers (the USSR, however, refused to permit any relations between Unesco and the Soviet zone in Germany). Germany and Japan saw in Unesco an opportunity to renew their contacts with both government and professional interests concerned with education, science, and culture, and to reassert their intellectual position in the world. Both joined the organization in 1951. They have sent able delegations to the General Conference, but have been content thus far to play a modest role. Germany has cooperated with the three Unesco Institutes established in that country and has maintained that they should be international rather than German in character.

In Japan the news of Unesco's establishment aroused great popular interest, even before the organization had any contact with that country. The nation's defeat in World War II had left the people confused and uncertain. They felt isolated from the rest of the world. Barred from the United Nations, they regarded Unesco as opening the door to their return to the international community. Their new constitution renounced war and Unesco offered a channel through which they could work for international peace. In addition, they viewed themselves as uniquely linked to both Orient and Occident.

Beginning in 1947 Unesco Associations sprang up spontaneously all over the country, their number ultimately exceeding one hundred. These associations sought to stimulate knowledge and support of Unesco through lectures, discussion groups, motion picture showings, and other activities. They worked also with Unesco Student Clubs which were formed at the high school as well as at the university level. A National Federation of Unesco Associations was organized in 1948. The following year almost 300 members of both houses of the Diet set up the Unesco League of National Diet Members. A Unesco section was established in the Ministry of Education, and in the same year, with the approval of SCAP (the Supreme Commander for the Allied Powers), Unesco itself opened an office in Japan.[31]

Following Japan's entry into Unesco, a National Commission was set up in 1952, with a full-time secretariat of approximately seventy persons, a considerable number of whom were engaged in translating Unesco documents and publications into Japanese. Japan has cooperated actively in revision of textbooks, in showing Unesco art and science exhibitions, and in education for international understanding. It has served as host to various Unesco international seminars and has held more than a score of national seminars on Unesco activities. It has provided technical assistance specialists to countries in Africa and Latin America as well as in Asia. Japan took the lead in proposing that Unesco embark on a project in the marine sciences.

Unesco in National Policies

During Unesco's first decade, no government gave the kind of support that might have been expected from the enthusiasm manifested at London in 1945. All subscribed to Unesco's principles by ratifying the Constitution and by appropriate declarations on official occasions. But few provided the necessary administrative and institutional support to translate these declarations into vigorous national programs of action, either government or private. National Commissions have received slight encouragement and have been of uneven utility, either as advisory bodies on national policies toward Unesco or as agencies for citizen participation in Unesco's work.

To date there has been little evidence, outside the economically less developed countries, that Unesco had been effectively related to national policy or to domestic activities in education, science, and culture. Some countries which had traditionally integrated cultural affairs into their foreign policy continued to do so in their participation in Unesco. The ex-enemy states clearly saw membership in Unesco as a means for regaining status in world affairs. For the economically underdeveloped countries Unesco offered assistance in problems critical to national economic and political development. In urging more Unesco activity along this line they could count on support from many other nations. Most countries have cooperated with such Unesco activities as clearing-house operations and exchange of persons, but few have made energetic efforts to work with Unesco. This is especially apparent in the reports of member states made at each session of the General Conference and in the desultory nature of the discussion which takes place on these reports.

Until the end of the decade there was little evidence that Unesco had been related to the broader political objectives of member states. The United States sought in 1950 to involve Unesco in the United Nations action in Korea, but not until 1956 did Unesco's relation to the political objectives of the United Nations again become a major issue at the General Conference. Then it was the Soviet bloc that sought Unesco's support in condemning British, French, and Israeli action in Egypt, while other delegations desired Unesco's condemnation of Soviet action in Hungary. On this as well as previous occasions it was evident that the Soviet Union and its allies had discerned the political implications of Unesco membership. Such an attitude was indicated by the withdrawal and later the renewal of cooperation on the part of Czechoslovakia, Hungary, and Poland. The USSR's entry into Unesco has stimulated greater political awareness by all member states of Unesco's place in international relations. It appears that with the Soviet Union as an active member, Unesco's efforts to contribute to peace and security through development of international understanding will become more controversial and more difficult; on the other hand, Russia's entry may give them new vigor.

Although by the end of the decade Unesco was generally recognized as an important arm of the United Nations for pursuing broad economic and social objectives, the larger countries have relied more upon bilateral and regional methods that are more directly amenable to control in the interest of national policy. The British Commonwealth countries are channeling a considerable portion of their aid through the Colombo Plan. The United States has put most of its contributions into bilateral undertakings.

The total picture of the policies of member states, however, is not all black. Unesco is inevitably a slow medium of communication and cooperation. Policy toward the organization is seen more clearly in the perspective of a decade. During the early years leadership had to come in the main from Western Europe, the British Commonwealth, and the United States. Traditionally these countries had not engaged in international cooperation in the educational and cultural field on any large scale, and when they did so the emphasis was on intellectual cooperation. The broader outlines provided by Unesco's Constitution had to be translated into a concrete program by the secretariat, guided by ideas emerging from international meetings and conferences. These proposals could not begin to engage effective national action until well along in the decade.

By that time the Arab, Asian, and Latin American states had gained a majority voice in the General Conference. Their persistent emphasis on meeting the needs of member states had led, through the United Nations technical assistance program as well as through Unesco's own program of aid to member states, to recognition that not only the economically less developed countries but the developed countries as well had needs to which Unesco should address itself.

Only by the end of the decade had virtually all member nations accepted the view that Unesco should give priority attention, through a few major projects, to great problems common to a number of countries. This approach was expected to achieve sharper concentration of the program, and may result in more effective support for Unesco activities from member states.

A principal reason for the lack of more positive support of Unesco by governments is that in the postwar world military and economic power has loomed large in international affairs. Educational, scientific, and cultural factors have been given relatively less attention by many countries. Groups directly concerned with the latter activities have not been able to exert much political influence, and national support for Unesco has had to rely largely upon enlightened leadership from within the government.

It remains to be seen whether support of Unesco by governments will increase. Certainly some of the factors responsible for assigning Unesco a marginal position in the foreign policy of member states— the diffuseness of the program, its alleged impracticality, and the absence of the Soviet Union—had lost much if not all of their importance by the end of the decade.

CHAPTER XV

Summary and Appraisal

The story of Unesco's first ten years has been told in considerable detail. We have described its origin and the expectations entertained by the governments that created it. We have outlined the scope of its program and the nature of its activities. We have examined some of the influences affecting its work, and surveyed the policies of member states toward Unesco. We have also noted that Unesco is not the only agency at work in the area of its concern.

Our review has shown that the purpose of Unesco, to contribute to peace and security, has been broadly interpreted to include the advancement of knowledge, the promotion of human welfare, and the development of international understanding.

In many respects it is too early for an appraisal of what Unesco has accomplished. Considerably more than a decade is required for the maturing of program ideas and program methods, and for projects to have a measurable impact. Nevertheless, it is useful to ask: In what areas has Unesco been most effective? How well has it served its members? What are its prospects for the future?

Where Has Unesco Been Most Effective?

Advancement of Knowledge

The experience of the first ten years indicates that Unesco has been a useful instrument toward conserving, increasing, and diffusing knowledge on an international scale. Communication among scholars, teachers, and specialists of many kinds in many countries has been eased and stimulated by the improvement of existing channels and opening of new ones. This has been done through fellowships and travel grants, encouragement of private international organizations in many fields, the science cooperation offices, meetings, seminars, symposia, and conferences. Communication by exchange of materials has been facilitated and speeded through clearing-house activities, through Unesco's own publications such as yearbooks, handbooks, and journals, through art reproductions and translations, and more widely through library services, bibliographies and scientific abstracts, radio, press, films, and television. The conservation of existing knowledge and of the cultural heritage of mankind has been promoted by aid to museums and libraries and by efforts for the protection of monuments and historic sites.

Through Unesco, existing barriers to the flow of information across frontiers have been substantially reduced by means of the Universal Copyright Convention, two international agreements to minimize tariff and other obstacles to trade in educational, scientific, and cultural materials, and reductions in postal, telegraph, and freight rates on news and printed matter. Some nations, however, including the United States, have failed to ratify or implement a number of these agreements.

Wider dissemination of the findings of research in both natural and social sciences has been achieved through international scientific meetings and publication of scientific papers and abstracts. Unesco has helped to identify areas which need investigation and to set up international institutions to do the necessary research. Thus Unesco has contributed to the increase as well as to the spread of knowledge.

Unesco has served as a bridge between the industrialized countries and those less highly developed, increasing opportunities for exchange of knowledge and furnishing means for better appreciation by each group of the other's point of view. Illustrations are the science cooperation offices and particularly the technical assistance projects.

Unesco has helped to formulate world standards for education, science, and cultural activities, which may assist member states to define their own most pressing needs and to take remedial action. It has helped its members to locate outside assistance and to apply it to the development of their own educational, scientific, and cultural resources. Such Unesco activities have obviously been more important to some nations than to others.

Unesco's record in the advancement of knowledge also reveals some major shortcomings. Certain early efforts, such as the proposal to establish a union library catalogue for all the countries of Europe, were too ambitious, not only in the light of Unesco's limited resources but also from the standpoint of effective use. Occasionally it has taken on projects which could be done better by private agencies. In the early years it was often forgotten that mankind's resources of education, science, and culture are located within member states and that Unesco must work through them. Sometimes, it has been charged, the exchange of information has been viewed as an end in itself.

Although an increasing number of persons are being involved in Unesco's work, the effect of some projects has been largely limited to the few specialists directly concerned. Many other specialists, whether in science, education, or the arts, have not been touched directly by Unesco's activities, though they are vaguely aware of its existence and may see some of its publications. The number who can participate in Unesco committees, seminars, and conferences is necessarily restricted. The responsibility for spreading their influence to a wider circle rests mainly with the member states, and has not always been fulfilled, owing to inadequate development of the National Commissions.

The publications of Unesco have been numerous and deal with a wide variety of important subjects. They have often suffered in style and quality from the complexities inherent in the production of printed matter by public authority and prepared by persons of many languages and great differences in cultural background. Yet many of its volumes and periodicals are outstanding in their contribution to the understanding of educational, cultural, and scientific problems in a world-wide setting. Disturbing is the fact that so much good material remains largely unread by the audience for which it was prepared. Governments have not thus far been able to conquer the challenging problem of distributing publications of an international organization.

Promotion of Human Welfare

Unesco has been used by member states to further the solution of certain major world problems affecting human welfare. The fundamental education project has helped to focus world attention on ignorance and illiteracy and has underlined the indispensable role of education in economic and social development. It has made possible a cooperative world-wide attack on educational problems facing many countries of Asia, the Middle East, Africa, and Latin America. Unesco's aid to member states through the United Nations Expanded Technical Assistance Program, particularly through training fellowships and expert advice, has marshaled help from many sources for many countries in achieving educational and scientific progress which otherwise would have been impossible. Unesco's work has influenced bilateral technical assistance programs such as that of the United States, other UN programs, and national projects for community development, as in India.

Unesco's project on the problems of living in arid zones has helped to clarify the issues, to stimulate interest, and to encourage cooperative research. The methods worked out in this undertaking are now being applied to analogous problems of the humid tropical zones and to more effective use of marine resources. Another important activity has been analysis of the impact of modern technology and industry upon traditionally agrarian societies, including the establishment of research centers in Paris and Calcutta.

Not all of Unesco's efforts to advance human welfare were immediately successful. There were two notable initial failures, the Marbial Valley and Hylean Amazon projects. The reasons for failure were clear: inadequate study and preparation by member states and by the Unesco secretariat, lack of experience, and inability to exploit fully the resources of national governments and other international agencies. The experience gained in the Marbial Valley project was of value in later fundamental education activities of Unesco and other agencies. What the Hylean Amazon project had taught was helpful in planning, nearly ten years later, the work on humid tropical zones.

Development of International Understanding

In its many efforts to foster international understanding (both "sympathetic" and "objective") Unesco seems to have had most success with projects that reached initially only small groups, but whose influence gradually spread to a much wider circle. Exchange of persons is a good example. Unesco's own efforts, through a modest program of fellowships and periodic inventories of exchange opportunities, have borne fruit by influencing the fellowship and foreign study programs now conducted by hundreds of educational institutions, which have enabled thousands of students and scholars to broaden their horizons.

Another example of working through small groups is the scientific and cultural history of mankind. Only a few persons will participate in this enterprise, but it is hoped that the finished work will influence all who read it and, eventually, the writers of future school textbooks. Ultimately it may contribute substantially to making whole peoples see world history from a universal viewpoint. Likewise the study of social tensions, with special attention to race and cultural differences, has been the work of individual scholars. Their initial audience has been small, but they have laid a basis for wider understanding among nations and peoples.

Still other projects have directly involved small groups of teachers and educational leaders. The international seminars for teachers were designed to improve understanding of other peoples through the teaching of history, geography, and modern languages. The efforts to encourage textbook revision have touched a somewhat wider group. Although the number of persons directly affected has not been large, the effect on generations of school children may be considerable. Similarly, efforts to encourage better educational programs on the United Nations and on human rights should have a constantly spreading influence.

While Unesco has had considerable success in promoting international understanding by working through special groups, it has developed no project of its own with a world-wide mass appeal, nor has it been able to stimulate action of this kind within member states. It has therefore had no extensive direct response from the public at large, though there is widespread latent interest in the Unesco idea and in developing international understanding.

A variety of special factors has contributed to Unesco's failure to reach a mass audience. Member states could not agree on what an international organization ought to do in this field. They have not encouraged efforts by Unesco to reach their citizens directly. Unesco's program in this respect has therefore depended for execution upon governments, private national groups, and individuals. These, however, have shown little interest or initiative. Even the more vigorous National Commissions have not developed positive programs to reach mass audiences. Nor have they found effective ways to help Unesco publications like the *Courier* reach the large public for which they are designed.

Unesco's attempts to persuade existing mass media to join the crusade for international understanding have not been successful. Leaders of the press, radio, and other media were reluctant to become involved in such an undertaking. Some feared they would have to accept external direction. Others held that news agencies should merely report the news and not try to influence opinion.

Unesco's failure to develop an effective project to promote people-to-people understanding through mass media illustrates especially well the paradox that nations desire the fruits of peaceful cooperation but are unwilling to pay the necessary price in adjustment of national attitudes.

In summary, Unesco has been most effective when it sought to strengthen and extend traditional methods of cooperation to advance knowledge. These efforts were easily understood and brought clear and immediate benefits to member states.

Unesco has also been successful in a newer field: marshaling the world's educational, scientific, and cultural resources for a cooperative solution of major problems affecting human welfare. As it appeared that Unesco could give concrete aid in solving their own national problems, member states have been increasingly willing to authorize and cooperate in Unesco action. There were difficulties, of course: determining priorities, finding the necessary resources, and above all, devising methods by which an international organization could help member states to do the job themselves, instead of trying to do it for them.

Unesco has been least successful in making direct and immediate contributions to international understanding.

Finally, it is well to remember always that many other governmental, nongovernmental, and individual efforts are being made and have been under way for decades—some for centuries—to advance education, science, culture, and international understanding and that Unesco's contribution can at most be complementary to the others. The causal relation between what it does and what is accomplished by mankind in this broad area of human endeavor must always remain unclear.

Unesco is also but one of the agencies of the United Nations created to promote jointly the maintenance of peace and the advancement of human welfare. Its success, especially because its scope is so broad, is in part dependent upon the success of the other agencies and its efforts must always be seen as complementary to theirs.

Unesco in the Perspective of History

In the longer perspective of history, Unesco's significance may well transcend the accomplishments or failures of its first decade. (1) It is a new kind of international effort to promote education, science, and culture. (2) It gives world-wide emphasis to the role of the individual in a democratic society and in the achievement of peace. (3) It promotes the assimilation of new states and former colonial areas into the fabric of modern international relations.[1]

A New Kind of World Influence

Unesco provides tangible evidence that people all over the world believe in the importance of education, science, and culture for the advancement of civilization. Both as a symbol and as an agency it thus has special significance at a moment in history when more materialistic factors are heavily emphasized in many kinds of societies. Unesco furnishes leadership and support for individuals, groups, and governments that wish to strengthen those intellectual values which they regard as basic to human progress.

Unesco's role in education, science, and culture is different from that of its member states, nor is it merely the sum of their national efforts. Unesco's secretariat, its General Conference, and its Executive Board view the problems confronting them in a global perspective.

The development of the secretariat has been a major contribution by Unesco to the growth of an international civil service within the framework of the UN system. Its responsibility is to the organization and to the collective will which it expresses. The secretariat of Unesco identifies and explores educational, scientific, or cultural problems from an international, not a national, standpoint. It secures the advice of individuals and organizations from all over the world. The groups which it brings together for this purpose tend, to a striking extent, to develop an international outlook in their analyses and recommendations. They show responsibility not to their nation or profession so much as to the world community. On the basis of their advice important proposals for action are often worked out by Unesco and by member states.

The General Conference, in turn, voices through its resolutions a common or collective will in which the sometimes conflicting views of member states are reconciled. The Executive Board expresses the collective will as formulated by the General Conference, although the individual opinions of Board members or of their countries are also heard. In short, the policies of Unesco are determined by representative international bodies and are designed to advance interests that are not merely national but world-wide.

Because it is international, Unesco has been able to do some things better than any individual government could do them. This is illustrated by India's request in 1949 for assistance in making a study of social tensions that threatened the internal unity of this newly independent nation. Such a request could hardly have been directed to any individual foreign government. The same point is illustrated in the educational missions, recruited by Unesco on an international basis, that have aided a number of countries to improve their educational systems. Unesco's world-wide orientation protected the recipient countries from the cultural and political bias inevitably found in any educational mission representing only one country.

Unesco's technical assistance program also owes much of its success to its international character. This program has been financed, like those of all UN agencies, from a common fund to which many countries have contributed. Technical assistance experts have been recruited on a world-wide basis and have functioned as international teams without national instructions. This has relieved the recipient nations from a sense of burdensome obligation toward any one country or countries. At the same time it has permitted many donor countries, which lacked sufficient financial resources to develop their own bilateral programs, to make highly useful contributions to Unesco's international efforts toward economic and social development.

Unesco's work, unlike that of individual states, provides continuity of international experience on a variety of problems in education, science, and culture. Sustained work on specific problems of a wide variety gives insight into the characteristics, interests, and needs of different nations and cultures. The project on arid zones pointed the way toward solutions for comparable problems in humid tropical zones, with which Unesco had grappled unsuccessfully ten years earlier. Fundamental education activities stimulated or aided by Unesco in one part of the world provided lessons which could be applied in other areas. Techniques such as cooperation with nongovernmental international organizations and the use of expert advisory groups, which had proved successful in natural sciences and the humanities, were utilized in the social sciences.

Unesco has also served as a sort of laboratory for experiments in social engineering in many fields. Notable in this connection were the various methods employed in the revision of textbooks, particularly bilateral consultations between national groups of teachers and historians, and, more recently, similar joint efforts by groups representing the cultural traditions of Western Europe and those of the new states of Asia. The more effective diffusion of knowledge about the artistic achievements of different cultures was studied by Unesco expert committees, and there emerged a plan for a catalogue of reproductions of paintings and for a series of albums on the art of such widely separated countries as Australia, Russia, Norway, India, and Mexico. Again, Unesco has fostered a project in which individual schools in twenty or more countries are testing methods for developing understanding of other peoples.

More effectively than any single state or private group, Unesco has been able to defend the interests of education, science, and culture before international bodies where policy decisions affecting these fields were under consideration. For example, at meetings of the United Nations Economic and Social Council and of the Technical Assistance Board, Unesco representatives have stressed repeatedly the idea that education is basic to all economic development. In successive conferences of parties to the General Agreement on Tariffs and Trade (GATT), Unesco has pressed for tariff reductions on educational, scientific, and cultural materials. In conferences on peaceful uses of atomic energy, Unesco was able to emphasize basic research needs and to indicate progress already under way. At the conference of foreign ministers following the Summit Conference of great powers in 1955, Unesco pointed out that its resources were available for any new program of cooperation between the Soviet and non-Soviet worlds.

Finally, Unesco can formulate, and win recognition of, internationally accepted standards of educational, scientific, and cultural achievement. Through its efforts governments can compare their own progress with that of other countries in expanding primary education and eliminating illiteracy. They become more conscious of the creative potential of their institutions for scientific research, and of the need to conserve archaeological treasures and to stimulate contemporary artistic expression. Discussions at the General Conference and other meetings have shown many delegates some of the things their countries need to do if they are to win respect and influence in world affairs.

Emphasis on the Individual

Unesco's emphasis upon individual initiative and democratic values may also prove to be significant in the perspective of world history. Its present significance is obvious in relation to the cold war and to colonies and newly independent states whose political institutions are still in the formative stage.

It has been said that the essence of Unesco's method lies "in associating in its work the people of the world. . . . In spite of the highly specialized character of the disciplines within its purview, Unesco's real objective is to have people work with people and for people." The same witness has testified, "The extent to which the National Commissions for Unesco are really at work is exactly the extent to which democracy prevails in the world today."[2]

In contrast with the political activities of the United Nations, which absorb the attention primarily of governments, Unesco projects are suitable for action by individuals. The scientist who exchanges information with colleagues in other countries; the educator preoccupied with problems of free and compulsory education, teacher training, or curriculum reform; the philosopher in search of a better understanding of the values men live by; the artist or musician who knows no political boundaries to the expression of his genius—all of these people can feel that because Unesco is concerned with their problems, they as individuals have a stake in its fortunes.

Unesco has also had an appeal for nonspecialists and for members of civic organizations. Many voluntary organizations in numerous countries have been associated with its work. Representatives of these groups have helped plan study programs, discussion groups, lecture series, exchanges of students, campaigns to raise funds for educational reconstruction abroad, community programs on international relations and the United Nations, and efforts through Unesco Gift Coupons to help schools and other institutions abroad.

The National Commission idea is implicitly democratic, for it contemplates greater participation by citizens in international affairs. The National Commission was intended to give citizens a direct voice in the formulation of national foreign policy for the promotion of peace through education, science, and culture and through international understanding. But it was also designed to bring citizens into close contact with citizens of other countries and with Unesco itself. Although the degree of actual citizen participation in Unesco activities has thus far been disappointing, the objective is clear: to permit the individual citizen, specialist or nonspecialist, freely to make himself part of an international effort to further world peace. Thus, in Unesco, he can supplement the official activities of his government.

In addition to encouraging citizen participation in its work, Unesco has emphasized democratic values by urging the expansion of educational opportunities for all and an active role by the individual in the advancement of knowledge. In its emphasis on human rights it has consistently upheld the dignity of man, and it has encouraged educational programs to prepare the citizen for his public responsibilities. It has emphasized the role of voluntary private organizations, both in the development of the educational, scientific, and cultural resources of mankind and in the promotion of closer relations among men and women of different nations and cultures.

Help to New States

Unesco has contributed much to one of the great tasks of our generation, that of assisting formerly dependent peoples to stand on their own feet, improve their conditions of life, and become full members of the international community. It has done this in several ways.

Unesco has helped the peoples of the economically less developed countries to realize their expectations of economic, social, and political improvement. The organization has come to symbolize for many of them the economic and social progress, political stability, and free way of life they seek to achieve. Fulfillment of their aspirations for self-development and for effective participation in world affairs depends in large measure upon raising their educational level. Helping them to do this is part of Unesco's job as defined in its Constitution. Its activities contribute directly to fulfilling the aspirations of these peoples on the basis of individual freedom, justice, and the rule of law.

Unesco has also assisted these peoples in their revolt against many conditions which have hitherto hindered their progress. In many nations of Asia, the eastern Mediterranean, and Latin America, as well as the emerging independent states of Africa, revolutionary pressures are mounting against traditional attitudes: resignation to poverty, distrust of modern science, fatalism, passive acceptance of caste systems and legal structures that restrict individual growth, or rigid and primitive social systems that impede social progress. These pressures rival in intensity those for independence. From Unesco these countries can learn of the experience of other peoples who have achieved progress by releasing human abilities through expansion of their educational, scientific, and cultural resources.

While accepting cultural diversity, Unesco stands unequivocally for human dignity, freedom of inquiry, and political and social democracy. Hence, if member states remain loyal to the principles of its Constitution, Unesco's influence may be of crucial importance in the world struggle between free and totalitarian states. Since so many countries of the free world are stigmatized by colonialism, it is especially important that an international agency free of such onus is at hand to help the newer states in developing their new institutions.

At the same time, Unesco has aided the peoples of the new states to take their rightful place in the family of nations. A nation's influence in international affairs is determined to a large extent by its economic, financial, and military strength. But there are other measures of greatness that can be applied to the advantage of nations which are as old in civilization as they are new in independence. These new nations, as their leaders at Unesco conferences have pointed out, insist upon being heard and upon being given the opportunity to make clear the basis for their claims to independence and equality. Their position must be understood by the currently dominant countries of Western tradition if the unity of the free world, within which the newer states will inevitably play a growing part, is to be maintained.

The United Nations provides a political forum for these countries.

Other UN agencies supply them with important services in health, social welfare, nutrition, and general economic improvement. But Unesco, besides its technical services in education, science, and culture, furnishes a forum for discussion of philosophies, values, and ways of life. Unesco provides opportunities for the new states to acquaint the Western world with evidence of the creative genius of their cultures. At the same time it enables them to experience at first hand and judge objectively the cultural values of the West.

What Are Unesco's Prospects for the Future?

Our appraisal of Unesco's record has shown that it has been able to perform many important tasks which its member governments wanted done. It has been an instrument and a symbol of international collaboration, adjustment, and understanding. It has contributed to the development of institutions needed in a world community.

Many of the weaknesses displayed within the organization in the early years have been overcome. Time and experience have brought greater maturity to the international staff and to the policy-making organs. Program objectives have been clarified and program activities much more effectively concentrated. Experience has also shown that Unesco's success depends upon its ability to stimulate action by governments, private organizations, and individuals, rather than upon building itself into a large international bureaucracy with extensive operational responsibilities.

The basic weakness that still conditions its prospects for the future lies in the policy and action of member states, for the area of Unesco's competence ends at their boundaries. Few members have yet taken adequate action to achieve at home the objectives to which they subscribe in Unesco's Constitution and to make possible the fullest execution of the Unesco program. Most member states have not given to Unesco affairs an appropriate place in their foreign policy.

Therefore, without more positive support from member states there is little prospect for strengthening the Unesco program or for increasing the effectiveness of its operations. Upon member states depends particularly the greater coordination of Unesco work with that of other United Nations agencies whose programs are made by the same states. They also must decide whether Unesco's role in helping tensions underlying the cold war shall be peripheral, as it has been to date, or part of a larger and more positive international effort to achieve peace and security.

Unesco as the world focus of men's aspirations in the vast realm of education, science, and culture must always fall short of the hopes placed in it, for those hopes are as limitless as the creative abilities of the human mind itself. But if Unesco is properly used as a means by which peoples, through their governments, can agree upon goals important to all and then devise practical ways of reaching these goals through joint effort, it is capable of almost unlimited achievement.

GUIDE TO SOURCES IN NOTES

Where no publisher is mentioned, the agency indicated is the publisher. E.g., Unesco, *Index Translationum*.

In recent years Unesco's documentation system has been standardized. All documents pertaining to the General Conference, for example, are classified by a symbol, indicating the number of the session (see Appendix F for a list of the sessions of the General Conference), the Commission or Committee if any, generally a chronological number, and the title. (E.g., Unesco, "Report of the Director General," Document 7C/3—"7C" indicating the Seventh Session of the General Conference and "3" being the chronological number. 7C/PRG/.. would indicate a document for the Program Commission for the Seventh Session.)

Documents issued in connection with sessions of the Executive Board are designated by a symbol indicating the number of the session and the chronological number of the document. (E.g., 44 EX/7 refers to a document issued for the Forty-fourth Session of the Executive Board.)

The Departments and Services of the Unesco Secretariat employ the following symbols to indicate documents pertaining to their operations as follows:

CUA	Cultural Activities
ED	Education
EXP	Exchange of Persons
MC	Mass Communication
NS	Natural Sciences
SS	Social Sciences
TA	Technical Assistance

The Secretariat issues periodically a subject list of publications and documents of the organization, which is designated by the symbol UNESCO/CPG/List/.., and a list of conferences and meetings held during the year, which is designated by the symbol UNESCO/CPG/...

Throughout the notes of this volume, documents of the categories described above are mentioned by title and symbol in the first citation, and subsequently within the same chapter by the symbol only.

Notes

INTRODUCTION

1. Hitler declared that the duty of Germans was "not to seek out objective truth, insofar as it may be favorable to others, but uninterruptedly to serve one's own truth." Quoted in I. L. Kandel, *Intellectual Cooperation: National and International* (New York: Teachers College, Columbia University, 1944), p. 15.

2. Unesco, Preparatory Commission, *Conference for the Establishment of the United Nations Educational, Scientific and Cultural Organization, London, 1945* (London, 1946), p. 27.

3. Two brief Extraordinary Sessions were held at Paris in September 1948 and July 1953.

CHAPTER I

1. Ten years later the Summit Conference met at Geneva in the shadow of an even greater fear of mutual destruction and again turned to cultural exchanges as a means for improving the world political climate.

2. Unesco, Preparatory Commission, *Conference for the Establishment of the United Nations Educational, Scientific and Cultural Organization, London, 1945* (London, 1946), p. 87, statement of Etienne Gilson. This source will hereafter be cited as *1945 London Conference.*

3. Ibid., pp. 54, 43, 85, 27, 22.

4. See Harold Stanley Thames, "An Analysis of Representative Ideological Criticism of the United Nations Educational, Scientific and Cultural Organization in the United States, 1946-1954" (unpublished Ph.D. dissertation, Duke University, 1955), pp. 273-74.

5. This reference to "the minds of men" was later incorporated in the opening sentence of the Unesco Constitution. Ascher reports that after Mr. Attlee's speech, which it was generally understood was drafted by Mr. Francis Williams, Mr. Mac-Leish asked Miss Ellen Wilkinson, the Chairman of the Conference and British Minister of Education, what Mr. Attlee's attitude would be to incorporating the phrase in the Preamble to the Constitution. She replied that the Prime Minister would be pleased. Accordingly, Mr. MacLeish, as chairman of the subcommittee to draft the Preamble and First Article of the Constitution, composed the sentence: "Since wars begin in the minds of men, it is in the minds of men that the defenses of peace must be constructed." This wording was accepted without change by the Conference. (Letter from Mr. MacLeish, January 11, 1950). Charles

S. Ascher, *Program-Making in Unesco, 1946-1951* (Chicago: Public Administration Clearing House, 1951), p. 15, footnote 1.

6. *1945 London Conference*, p. 52.

7. Ibid., pp. 27, 55, 60, 33. I. L. Kandel had written in 1944: "The meaning of the economic interdependence of the world has now been borne in on the consciousness even of the uneducated. The meaning of cultural interdependence still remains to be disseminated as the solid foundation of international cooperation." *Intellectual Cooperation: National and International* (New York: Teachers College, Columbia University, 1944), p. 54.

8. Jan Opocensky, "Unesco History," II (unpublished manuscript), p. 3.

9. *1945 London Conference*, p. 22.

10. Ibid., p. 38.

11. Ibid., p. 54.

12. Ibid., pp. 37, 30, 31.

13. Howard E. Wilson (ed.), "National Programs of International Cultural Relations," *International Conciliation*, No. 462 (June 1950), p. 304.

14. These organizations developed in response to "problems arising from new means of rapid world-communication, from growing economic interdependence, from the destructiveness of new methods of war, and from the growth of humanitarian and democratic sentiment—all fruits of the political and economic revolutions which began in the late eighteenth century." Quincy Wright, *A Study of War* (Chicago: University of Chicago Press, 1942), Vol. I, p. 365.

15. Waldo G. Leland, "The Background and Antecedents of Unesco," American Philosophical Society, *Proceedings*, Vol. XC, No. 4 (September 1946), pp. 295-99.

16. P. Rossello, *Forerunners of the International Bureau of Education* (London: Evans Brothers, 1944), pp. 9-71. This volume is an English edition, abridged and translated by Marie Butts, of P. Rossello, *Les Précurseurs du Bureau International d'Education* (Genève: Bureau International d'Education, 1943). For a brief reference to the activities during World War II of private educational groups in Great Britain and the United States, see p. 19 of this chapter.

17. See Chapter V, p. 92.

18. P. Rossello, *Forerunners of the International Bureau of Education*, pp. 35-43; and Lura G. Camery, "American Background of the United Nations Educational, Scientific and Cultural Organization" (unpublished Ph.D. dissertation, Stanford University, 1949), pp. 10-23.

19. Henri Bonnet, "Intellectual Cooperation in World Organization," in *World Organization* (Washington: American Council on Public Affairs, 1942), pp. 190-91. Monsieur Bonnet was Director of the Institute of Intellectual Cooperation 1931-40.

20. *L'Institut International de Coopération Intellectuelle, 1925-1946* (Paris, n.d.), pp. 10-15.

21. Ibid., p. 61. The French government granted to the Institute an annual subsidy of 2 million francs (approximately $100,000 at the 1925 rate of exchange). Additional donations were made by other governments and private institutions.

22. Ibid., pp. 43, 84 ff.

23. European intellectuals, it has been suggested, had become resentful that financial and commercial interests, for example, had found vehicles to influence international developments, but the intellectuals had not. The League's Organization thus served to meet this need.

24. The original resolution advanced by Léon Bourgeois of France provided for a committee to examine questions regarding intellectual cooperation and education. But it was approved only after deletion of the reference to education. Ibid., p. 14; Rossello, *Forerunners of the International Bureau of Education*, pp. 50-62.

25. Bonnet, op. cit., pp. 196, 206-07. *L'Institut International de Coopération Intellectuelle, 1925-1946* gives a comprehensive review of the activities of the Institute of Intellectual Cooperation. Its work is summarized in Gilbert Murray, "Intellectual Cooperation," *Annals of the American Academy of Political and Social Science*, Vol. 235 (September 1944), pp. 1-9.

26. The Chairman of the Committee on Intellectual Cooperation declared in his closing address at the first session (1922) that international agreement "could be more readily realized in high intellectual circles, and that it could then descend progressively among the nations." The *Minutes* of the Committee reported in 1926: "It was not the duty of the Committee . . . and the Institute, which was its working instrument, to obtain any concrete results, at least for the moment. . . . The Institute was essentially an intermediary organization whose duty it was to bring together the savants and artists of the whole world for two purposes:

"(1) To serve science and art, the savants and the artists;

"(2) By thus placing itself at the service of the intellectual élite of the world . . . the Committee would have helped another cause—that of peace and mutual understanding between peoples."

League of Nations, Committee on Intellectual Cooperation, *Minutes*, 1st Session, p. 38; 8th Session, p. 38. Quoted in Yen-Tsai Feng, "Analysis of the Impact of the Several Different Concepts of International Cooperation upon the Establishment and Development of the United Nations Educational, Scientific and Cultural Organization during its First Six Years" (unpublished Ph.D. dissertation, University of Denver, 1953).

27. Marie Butts, "The International Bureau of Education," *Annals of the American Academy of Political and Social Science*, Vol. 235 (September 1944), pp. 10-16. Howard E. Wilson has noted: "The separate histories of the Bureau of Education and the Committee and Institute of Intellectual Cooperation illustrate and to a degree accentuate the unfortunate rift between lower and higher education which has been characteristic of recent decades." Howard E. Wilson, "Education as an Implement of International Cooperation," *International Conciliation*, No. 415 (November 1945), p. 710.

28. The words "culture" and "cultural" present something of a semantic problem. There is the more limited meaning which refers to the works of creative genius in art, architecture, music, literature, and philosophy, or in the words of Matthew Arnold, "the acquainting ourselves with the best that has been known and said in the world." Second, there is the broader socio-anthropological concept which covers the whole pattern of life of a particular people.

29. For a study of such programs, see Ruth E. McMurray and Muna Lee, *The Cultural Approach, Another Way in International Relations* (Chapel Hill: University of North Carolina Press, 1947); and "National Programs of International Cultural Relations," *International Conciliation*, No. 462 (June 1950). See also Harold E. Snyder, *When Peoples Speak to Peoples, An Action Guide to International Cultural Relations for American Organizations, Institutions, and Individuals* (Washington: American Council on Education, 1953). A thoughtful review

of such developments in the United States is given in I. L. Kandel, *United States Activities in International Cultural Relations* (Washington: American Council on Education Studies, Vol. IX, September 1945).

30. McMurray and Lee, op. cit., pp. 15-16, 11.

31. Ibid., pp. 39-61.

32. Ibid., pp. 110-18.

33. Ibid., pp. 138-48.

34. U. S. Department of State, *The Program of the Department of State in Cultural Relations*, Extract from the "Department of State Appropriation Bill for 1941." Hearings before the Subcommittee of the Committee on Appropriations, House of Representatives, 76th Congress, Third Session, on the Department of State Appropriation Bill (Washington: Dept. of State Pub. No. 1441, 1940), p. 1.

At the beginning of the United States program of cultural relations, emphasis was placed on its divorcement from political policy. Ben M. Cherrington, Chief of the Division of Cultural Relations, stated, "in the first place I think it is clear that this new Division should not be considered as the peace department of the Department of State. . . . Because of the fact that this program obviously must stand on its own feet, it must be cultural exchange for its own sake and not serve some ulterior motive. It would seem to me very important to over-stress the divorcement of our activities from the diplomatic activities of the Department of State." Department of State, Division of Cultural Relations, *Minutes of General Advisory Committee,* Second Meeting, November 21, 1938, p. 16 (typescript). A good summary of the program in its initial stage is given in Haldore Hanson, *The Cultural Cooperation Program, 1938-1944* (Washington: Dept. of State Pub. No. 2137, 1944).

35. For an excellent preliminary analysis of this trend, see Unesco, "Report on Cultural Agreements," Document 8C/PRG/11.

36. MacLeish, in McMurray and Lee, op. cit., p. viii.

37. "Ironically enough, it was the aggressively minded dictators who first sensed the immense potentialities of this field of activity and learned to bend it to their purposes. To them it was not, of course, a means of enlisting the informed support of free men on the side of peaceful policies but rather an instrument for gaining political influence over other countries by subversion. . . ." Similarly, "the Kremlin turned its attention to the possibilities of expansion by means of indirect aggression short of full-scale war, a venture in which the whole variety of techniques of influencing men's minds would play a role of primary importance. . . . It is high time that the free nations of the world paid serious attention to this middle ground between the bargaining of diplomats and total war. It is here that the democracies can build the bulwarks against further gains of the Soviets by infiltration and indirect aggression. It is also here that they can discover the conditions under which the peaceful coexistence of free states may again become possible." Frederick S. Dunn, *War and the Minds of Men* (New York: Harper & Bros., 1950), pp. xi, xii, xiii.

38. *Allied Plan for Education,* The Story of the Conference of Allied Ministers of Education (London: H. M. Stationery Office, 1945), p. 2. See also Walter Kotschnig, "Toward an IOECD: Some Major Issues Involved," American Council on Education, *Educational Record* (July 1944), pp. 259-87. For a general review of the work of CAME, its commissions and committees, see C. Mildred Thompson,

"United Nations Plans for Post-War Education," *Foreign Policy Reports,* Vol. XX, No. 24 (March 1, 1945), pp. 310-19.

39. Ibid., p. 16. The policies and actions of the Axis powers relating to education in the occupied countries are outlined in Walter Kotschnig, *Slaves Need No Leaders* (New York: Oxford University Press, 1943), pp. 63-117.

40. *Education and the United Nations,* Report of a Joint Commission of the London International Assembly and the Council for Education in World Citizenship (U. S. ed., Washington: American Council on Public Affairs, 1943), pp. 3-10.

41. See Educational Policies Commission, *Education and the People's Peace* (Washington: National Education Association, May 1943); *Education for International Security,* Proposals of the International Educational Assembly (Harpers Ferry Meeting, September 1943); American Association for an International Office for Education, Inc., *Unesco and the Story of the American Association for an International Office for Education, Inc.* (New York: The Hecla Press, n.d.); and Commission to Study the Organization of Peace, especially *Third Report and Papers presented to the Commission* (New York, 8 West Fortieth Street: The Commission, 1943).

42. Jan Opocensky, "Annotated Unesco Constitution," I (unpublished manuscript), p. 2.

43. U. S. Department of State, *Postwar Foreign Policy Preparation, 1939-1945* (Washington: Dept. of State Pub. No. 3580, 1949), pp. 236-37.

44. U. S. Department of State, *Bulletin,* Vol. X, No. 249 (April 1, 1944), pp. 299-300.

45. On the return to the United States of the Fulbright Mission, Dr. Kefauver remained in London as a continuing United States representative, maintaining liaison with CAME until the London Conference in 1945.

46. For a summary of the provisions of this Tentative Draft Constitution, see C. Mildred Thompson, "United Nations Plans for Post-War Education."

47. UNRRA however could not use its funds for educational rehabilitation, either for replacement of school buildings or for provision of school supplies. It eventually was able to assist in appraising the extent of devastation and to help in procuring supplies and equipment and arranging for their shipment.

48. Opocensky, "Annotated Unesco Constitution," II, p. 23.

49. U. S. Department of State, *Report of the Delegation of the United States of America to the Inter-American Conference on Problems of War and Peace,* (Washington: Dept. of State Pub. No. 2497, 1946), p. 104.

50. United Nations Conference on International Organization, 1945, *Documents,* Vol. III (New York and London: United Nations Information Organization, published in cooperation with the Library of Congress, 1945), Dumbarton Oaks Proposals, Comments and Proposed Amendments, p. 25.

The other delegations were: Brazil, Cuba, Ecuador, Egypt, France, Haiti, Iran, Lebanon, Norway, Panama, Philippines, Uruguay, and Venezuela.

51. H. J. Res. 305 and S. J. Res. 135, see United States Congress, House of Representatives, *International Office of Education,* Hearings before the Committee on Foreign Affairs, 79th Congress, 1st session on H. Res. 215, May 10, 15 and 17, 1945 (Washington 1945); and also Camery, op. cit., pp. 334-44. Senator Taft declared, "I venture to suggest that no single element can increase the standard of living of a people as much as universal education. . . . Furthermore, an education

which includes complete knowledge of other peoples and their viewpoints is almost the only hope of peace, and any educational system which is not based on freedom of communications is hardly worth the name of education." United States, *Congressional Record,* Vol. 91 (1945), p. 4968.

52. For a review of the role of the consultants at San Francisco, see Camery, op. cit., pp. 281-87; and also Howard E. Wilson, "Education as an Implement of International Cooperation," *International Conciliation,* No. 415 (November 1945), pp. 712-14.

53. Articles 55, 56, 57, 63, and 76, 83, and 88, respectively.

54. United Nations Conference on International Organization, *Documents,* Vol. I, pp. 683-84.

CHAPTER II

1. From the British Commonwealth there were in addition to representatives of the United Kingdom, delegations from Australia, Canada, India, New Zealand, and the Union of South Africa; from Europe: delegations from Belgium, Czechoslovakia, Denmark, France, Greece, Luxembourg, Netherlands, Norway, Poland, and Yugoslavia; from the Middle East: Egypt, Iran, Iraq, Lebanon, Saudi Arabia, Syria, and Turkey; from East Asia: China and the Philippines; from Africa: Liberia; and from the Americas: Argentina, Bolivia, Brazil, Chile, Colombia, Cuba, the Dominican Republic, Ecuador, El Salvador, Guatemala, Haiti, Mexico, Nicaragua, Panama, Peru, the United States, and Uruguay. In addition Venezuela was represented by an observer.

2. For the text of the two documents, see *1945 London Conference,* pp. 1-9.

3. Article I, 3 of the Constitution as adopted declares: "With a view to preserving the independence, integrity and fruitful diversity of the cultures and educational systems of the States members of this Organisation, the Organisation is prohibited from intervening in matters which are essentially within their domestic jurisdiction."

4. A former deputy director general of the Food and Agriculture Organization has stated, "Without making invidious comparisons, it seems quite clear that Unesco has about as difficult an assignment as any of the United Nations Specialized Agencies. The organization has to deal with matters which are much less tangible than ships and airplanes and food and money, but which carry a powerful emotional charge. Inevitably progress has to be slow in getting nations to work together in matters of this kind." Noble Clark, "Education Must Come First," *Educational Record,* Vol. XXX (April, 1949), p. 180. Cited in Basil Karp, "The Development of the Philosophy of Unesco" (unpublished Ph.D. dissertation, University of Chicago, 1951), p. 183. Some comparisons on program-making in WHO and Unesco are presented in Charles S. Ascher, "Current Problems in the World Health Organization's Program," *International Organization,* Vol. VI (1952), pp. 27-50.

5. *1945 London Conference,* pp. 32, 40, 50.

6. Ibid., p. 99.

7. U. S. Department of State, *"The Defenses of Peace,"* Documents Relating to Unesco, Part I (Washington: Dept. of State Pub. No. 2457, 1946), p. 8,

8. *1945 London Conference,* p. 98.

9. Ibid., p. 91.

10. Jan Opocensky, "Annotated Unesco Constitution," II (unpublished manuscript), pp. 1-5.

11. *1945 London Conference*, p. 24. For a summary review of the campaign of the scientists, see Yen-Tsai Feng, "Analysis of the Impact of the Several Different Concepts of International Cooperation upon the Establishment and Development of the United Nations Educational, Scientific and Cultural Organization during its First Six Years," pp. 65-75.

12. *1945 London Conference*, p. 68.

13. Byron Dexter, "Unesco Faces Two Worlds," *Foreign Affairs*, Vol. 25, No. 3 (April, 1947), pp. 388-407.

14. An Indian scholar subsequently remarked, "we ought not to forget that the human mind is a complex almost unfathomable in its intricacies, made up of all kinds of harmonies and contradictions, subliminal drives, conscious and reasoned ideas and ideals, unsuspected capacities for sublime and heroic action—and also of their opposite." Unesco Document 4C/Proceedings, p. 141.

15. Cf. contrasting approaches in Julian Huxley, "Unesco: The First Phase, I—The Two Views," *The Manchester Guardian* (August 10, 1950); and Walter H. C. Laves, "Unesco and the Achievement of Peace," *Political Quarterly* (London), Vol. XXII (April, 1951), pp. 164 ff. At the request of Torres Bodet, Professor Quincy Wright of the University of Chicago prepared "A Juridical Analysis of the Scope and Method of Unesco" (unpublished), which found that Unesco had a single purpose, to contribute to peace and security, and that this criterion should be applied to each program proposal.

16. Unesco, *General Conference, First Session,* Document Unesco/C/30, pp. 21, 25.

17. Ibid., p. 219.

18. U. S. Department of State, *Report of the United States Delegation,* First Session of the General Conference of Unesco, Paris, November 19–December 10, 1946 (Washington: Dept. of State Pub. No. 2821, 1947), pp. 72-74.

19. For the complete text of the longer form, see U. S. Department of State, "The Defenses of Peace," Documents Relating to Unesco, Part II (Washington: Dept. of State Pub. No. 2475, 1946), pp. 57-58. See also pp. 17, 18. Feng, op. cit., presents an excellent analysis of the whole question of the purpose or purposes of Unesco.

20. The head of the Canadian delegation remarked at the 1947 General Conference, "the Constitution offers a vast expanse in which there is a great temptation to meander." Unesco "Proceedings," Document 2C/132, p. 70.

21. See U. S. National Commission for Unesco, *Summary Minutes of the Fifth Meeting,* Boston, Massachusetts, September 27-29, 1948 (Washington: Dept. of State [NC5/47, SM], 1948, mimeographed), pp. 25-33.

22. Unesco, Document 5C/Resolutions, pp. 61, 15.

23. Unesco, *Report to the United Nations, 1949-1950* (Pub. 714), p. 8.

24. The first Director General suggested as Unesco's basic aim "The Advance of World Civilization." Unesco, "Report of the Director General," Document 3C/3, p. 26.

25. Unesco, *Constitution*, IV, E. 13 and XI, 4; and *1945 London Conference*, pp. 6, 131.

26. Ibid., pp. 2-3, 7.

27. The issue of "citizen" and expert members also arose in ILO, WHO, and other international organizations.

28. Unesco, *Constitution,* V, A. 1 and V, B. 12; and *1945 London Conference,* pp. 128-30. The number of Board members was increased from eighteen to twenty in 1952, to twenty-two in 1954, and to twenty-four in 1956.

29. Unesco, Document 8/C Resolutions, pp. 12, 13.

30. Unesco *Constitution,* IV, A. 1 and VII, 1, 2; and *1945 London Conference,* pp. 75-76.

31. Frederick S. Dunn was later to refer to Unesco as "a young international agency that was largely ignored by the important policy makers of most countries and left to the unpolitical hands of educators, scientists and artists." Frederick S. Dunn, *War and the Minds of Men* (New York: Harper & Bros., 1950), p. xi.

32. Chapter I, p. 7.

33. *1945 London Conference,* p. 20. Dunn notes as reasons for this emphasis on the role of the "people" (1) a growing skepticism about the ability of traditional forms of defense to guarantee security in the atomic age; (2) increasing recognition of the expanding influence of the masses of men on the shaping of foreign policy; and (3) the development through the social sciences of knowledge and methods for modifying human behavior in desired directions. Dunn, op. cit., pp. 2-4. For a discussion of the contrast and also of the interdependence between the "minds-of-men" theory and the older, more traditional "sovereign states" view of international relations, see ibid., pp. 12-24.

34. Feng, op. cit., p. 150.

35. *1945 London Conference,* p. 37.

36. Unesco, Document 6C/Proceedings, p. 150. In 1954 an expert committee on education for international understanding recommended that Unesco use every possible means to make the media of mass communication more effective instruments of international understanding. But at the same time it stated, "Unesco can act most effectively through key individuals and groups, rather than directly through attempting to influence the mass of mankind. In Unesco's case the key individuals are largely those in positions of leadership and administrative responsibility in the educational, cultural and scientific world. . . ." Unesco, "Final Report of the Expert Committee on Education for International Understanding and Cooperation," Document Unesco/ED/142, 1955, pp. 4-5.

37. The agreement between the United Nations and Unesco, which had been negotiated by the Unesco Preparatory Commission, was approved by the First Session of the General Conference. It provided for reciprocal representation at meetings, the exchange of information and documents, and cooperation in the field of statistical, administrative, and technical services. Unesco was to be autonomous with regard to its budget, but the United Nations was to examine and propose recommendations concerning the budget. For the text of the agreement, see *Report of the United States Delegation,* First Session of the General Conference, pp. 148-57.

38. Unesco, *Constitution,* Article X.

39. Ibid., Articles XIII and XV, 3.

40. Byron Dexter, "Yardstick for Unesco," *Foreign Affairs,* Vol. 28, No. 1 (October 1949), pp. 56-67.

41. Unesco, Document 4C/Proceedings, p. 61.

42. Ibid., p. 71.

43. Unesco, Document 5C/Proceedings, p. 342.

44. For the texts, see *1945 London Conference,* pp. 89-98.

45. Applied science in fields such as agriculture and health is the province of other specialized agencies.

46. Clarence E. Beeby of the New Zealand delegation declared after the 1954 General Conference at Montevideo: "Whatever the future holds, it is certain that, from now on, Unesco will be of greater significance to politicians as well as to scholars. In the past there has been an unreality about some of its work . . . the time is past when Unesco can be lightly dismissed because it deals only with ideas. Just because it deals with ideas, and because it now has members holding conflicting ideas over which nations are willing to go to war, Unesco can be the most useful, as it could be the most dangerous, of all the Specialized Agencies. It can never again be ignored." New Zealand Department of External Affairs, *Report of the New Zealand Delegation to the Eighth Session of the General Conference,* Held at Montevideo, Uruguay, from 12 November to 11 December 1954 (Wellington, 1955), pp. 34-35.

CHAPTER III

1. Howard E. Wilson of the United States and Jean Thomas of France were appointed as Assistant Executive Secretaries of the Preparatory Commission. The original representative of the United States on the Commission was Grayson N. Kefauver. After his sudden and untimely death in January 1946, he was succeeded briefly by Donald Stone and then in March by Mrs. Esther C. Brunauer.

2. Unesco, Preparatory Commission, "Verbatim Record of the Seventh Meeting," July 9, 1946, Document Unesco Prep. Com./5th Session/P.V.7, p. 2.

3. Unesco, Preparatory Commission, "Report on the Program of the United Nations Educational, Scientific and Cultural Organization," Document Unesco/C/2, pp. 5-6. A review of the work of the Preparatory Commission is given in Howard E. Wilson, "The Development of Unesco," *International Conciliation,* No. 431 (May 1947), pp. 295-303.

4. Unesco, "General Conference, First Session," Document Unesco/C/30, p. 223. The Executive Board in April 1947 listed four major emphases or Unesco-wide projects: (1) reconstruction and rehabilitation; (2) fundamental education; (3) education for international understanding; and (4) the Hylean Amazon project, calling for a special institute to study the problems of the humid area of the Upper Amazon Valley. This action, however, was little more than symbolic since it was not implemented by organizational or budgetary changes. Charles S. Ascher, *Program-Making in Unesco; 1946-1951* (Chicago: Public Administration Clearing House, 1951), p. 20.

5. The Ninth Session of the General Conference at New Delhi in 1956 was to repeat substantially this procedure. After voting to add approximately $1,000,000 to the total of $21,600,000 requested by the Director General for 1957-58, it approved enough new projects to use up, not alone the additional million dollars, but $660,000 more. A committee appointed to eliminate the extra two-thirds of a

million failed to agree, and the Conference remanded the task which had proved impossible for it to the Director General and the Executive Board.

6. These headings were: raising the standards of education, science, and culture; the free flow of ideas; education for international understanding; and man and the modern world. Ascher, *Program-Making in Unesco*, p. 26.

7. See pp. 59, 60 of this chapter.

8. Julian Huxley, *Unesco: Its Purpose and Its Philosophy* (Washington: Public Affairs Press, 1947). For a detailed review of the debate on this question see Basil Karp, "The Development of the Philosophy of Unesco" (unpublished Ph. D. dissertation, University of Chicago, 1951), pp. 50-63.

9. Unesco, "General Conference, First Session," pp. 38-41. Ribnikar declared that the Yugoslav delegation at the London Conference had signed the Constitution feeling "that the more or less abstract principles of this Constitution, with which we cannot agree, will not have any decisive influence on the future activities of Unesco." He continued, " . . . the Yugoslav delegation signed this Constitution, firmly convinced that declarations of policy were of less importance than the opportunity offered for cultural co-operation between the United Nations."

But the Marxists were not alone in criticizing the Huxley approach. "Hindus, Thomists, and dialectical materialists, pragmatists, idealists and positivists, whether inspired by a like desire to avoid dogma and particularism or by their own aspirations to universality and their own convictions of adequacy and the truth, could see no peculiar advantage in Dr. Huxley's formulation of a philosophy for Unesco, nor any reason for omitting it from the list of philosophies to be excluded." Richard McKeon, "A Philosophy for Unesco," *Philosophy and Phenomenological Research*, Vol. III, No. 4 (June 1948), p. 576.

10. Unesco, "General Conference, First Session," p. 64.

11. Unesco, "Proceedings," Document 2C/132, pp. 30-33.

12. Jacques Havet, "Is There a Philosophy of Unesco?" in Lyman Bryson, Louis Finkelstein, and Robert MacIver (eds.), *Learning and World Peace*, Eighth Symposium, Conference on Science, Philosophy and Religion, September 1947 (New York: Harper & Bros., 1948), pp. 602, 603.

Richard McKeon of the University of Chicago contributed to the discussion by pointing out that Unesco is "an institution within which, in the first place, a frame of action is provided despite differences of philosophic basis; in the second place, cultural differences are not merely noted and tolerated, but recognized and appreciated as embodiments of values; and, in the third place, ideas are used to influence and modify attitudes and convictions by means of the reasons they embody rather than the force they adumbrate or conceal." McKeon, "A Philosophy for Unesco," pp. 573-86, particularly pp. 585-86.

13. See Introduction, pp. xviii-xix.

14. See Chapter XII, pp. 276-78.

15. Harold Stanley Thames, "An Analysis of Representative Ideological Criticism of the United Nations Educational, Scientific and Cultural Organization in the United States, 1946-1954" (unpublished Ph. D. dissertation, Duke University, 1955), pp. 282-83.

16. The relation between the Director General and the Executive Board is discussed more fully in Chapter XIII, pp. 285-86, 290-93.

17. Unesco, "Report of the Director General," Document 4C/3, p. 8.

18. Ascher, *Program-Making in Unesco*, p. 63.

19. United States, 81st Congress, 1st Session, *Senate Document No. 5.*

20. United Nations, Economic and Social Council, Resolution 222 (IX).

21. For an analysis of the program's activities and its possible future development, see United Nations, Economic and Social Council, Technical Assistance Committee, "The Expanded Program of Technical Assistance, A Forward Look," Report of the Technical Assistance Board, with comments thereon of the Administrative Committee on Coordination, Document E/2885, E/TAC/49, Corr. 1, May 11, 1956.

22. Unesco, "Report of the Director General," Document 6C/3, p. 106. Technical Assistance funds increased the 1950 Unesco budget by 12 percent; while the 1956 budget increased 44 percent by this means. For a summary review of the role of Unesco in the United Nations technical assistance program, see Malcolm S. Adiseshiah, "The Participation of Unesco in the Expanded Program of Technical Assistance," Unesco, *Chronicle*, No. 5 (November 1955), pp. 3-8. See also Appendix E.

23. Unesco, Document 4C/Resolutions, pp. 39-40.

24. Unesco, "The Program of Unesco Proposed by the Executive Board," Document 5C/5 (I), pp. 3-27.

25. For the text of the Decalogue, see Unesco, Document 5C/Resolutions, p. 16. The text of the United States resolution is contained in Document 5C/97.

26. U. S. Department of State, "Report of the United States Delegation to the Fifth Session of the General Conference" (Washington: Dept. of State Pub. No. 4050, 1951), pp. 87-88.

27. Ascher, *Program-Making in Unesco*, p. 64; and Unesco, "Resolutions and Recommendations of United Nations Organs Concerning Unesco," Document 7C/PRG/23, pp. 2, 3, 4, 5.

28. Unesco, "Draft Program for 1952 Proposed by the Executive Board," Document 6C/5 (I), pp. 8-13. This emphasis was stressed also in the program proposals for 1953-54. See Unesco, "Proposed Program and Budget Estimates for 1953 and 1954," Document 7C/5, p. 6.

29. Unesco, Document 7C/Resolutions, pp. 67-71; and "Summary Records," Document 37 EX/SR. 1-40, pp. 121 ff.

30. Unesco, "Summary Records," Document 36 EX/SR. 1-11, p. 3.

31. Indian National Commission for Cooperation with Unesco, *Proceedings of the First Conference* (Government of India, Ministry of Education, 1954), pp. 3-7.

32. Unesco, "Remodelling of the Future Program of Unesco, Report Presented by the Executive Board," Document 8C/PRG/13.

33. Unesco, Document 8C/Resolutions, p. 70. A detailed analysis of the character of major projects is given in René Maheu, "Major Projects," Unesco, *Chronicle*, No. 4 (October 1955), pp. 3-8. For further discussion of the relations between Unesco and national programs of cultural relations, see Chapter XIV of this volume.

34. Unesco, Document 8C/Resolutions, pp. 49-51 (Res. IV.3).

35. Unesco, "Report on the Status of Execution of the Program of Aid to Member States, 1 January 1955–15 September 1956," Document 9C/PRG/18.

36. Unesco, "Proposed Program and Budget for 1957-58," Document 9C/5, pp. vii-xii, 41-48, 67-75; Document 9C/5 Corr. 1, pp. 15-23, 31, 49-63; and 9C/Resolutions, pp. 14-15 (Res. IA), pp. 17-18 (Res. IIA), and pp. 27-28 (Res. IVA). The first source (pp. xvii-xviii) gives the text of the "Principles and Conditions for the Grant of Aid to Member States." The major project for teacher-training in Latin America is described in Chapter VIII, pp. 175-76; that for arid zones in Chapter IX, pp. 208-09; and that for mutual appreciation of Eastern and Western cultural values in Chapter XI, pp. 251-52.

37. Throughout the London Conference where the Unesco Constitution was drafted "hope was repeatedly expressed that the Soviet Union, which had contributed so much to winning the war, might find it possible to join Unesco." Speech of Congressman Chester E. Merrow of New Hampshire in the House of Representatives, November 26, 1945. *Congressional Record*, Vol. 91, Part 8, 79th Congress, 1st Session, p. 10998. The Conference in addition reserved a seat for the USSR on the Executive Committee of the Preparatory Commission. However, following the accession of the USSR in 1954, George N. Shuster, Chairman of the United States National Commission for Unesco, issued a statement recalling the indifference and hostility shown to Unesco since its founding by the Soviet Union, and the USSR violations of basic Unesco principles with regard to human rights and to the "perversion of education, science, and the arts for political purposes." He noted that Soviet membership in Unesco would provide "an unparalleled opportunity for a world audience to contrast Soviet promises and Soviet performance." U. S. National Commission for Unesco, "Statement of Dr. George N. Shuster," June 29, 1954, Document NC/ (54)7, p. 2 (mimeographed).

38. It cited the distribution in South Africa by a private organization, the South African Institute of Race Relations, of Unesco publications on racial questions. One such publication contained a chapter on the "South African Case" (Kenneth Little, *Race and Society*) and another made a passing reference to South Africa (Arnold Rose, *The Roots of Prejudice*, p. 11). The withdrawal took effect on December 31, 1956. In 1953 the South African Cabinet had decided to leave the Food and Agriculture Organization and the World Health Organization as well as Unesco, but the decision was later reversed. The Executive Board approved a resolution in November 1955 inviting the government of South Africa to reconsider its decision, but declaring that "in the matter of race problems, as in all other spheres, the planning and conduct of Unesco's activities, as decided upon by the General Conference, have never violated Article I, paragraph 3 of the Constitution, which prohibits the Organization from intervening in matters which are essentially within the domestic jurisdiction of the Member States." Unesco "Report of the Director General, 1955," p. 19.

39. Unesco, Document 6C/Resolutions, p. 83. Inclusion in the Constitution of provision to give voice to the people of "non-self-governing areas" was recommended prior to the 1945 London Conference by three American associations: The American Council on Education, the Liaison Committee, and the American Association for an International Office of Education. Professor Alain Locke of Howard University specifically proposed as one possibility the idea of adjunct or associate delegations. Lura G. Camery, "American Background of the United Nations Educational, Scientific and Cultural Organization" (unpublished Ph. D. dissertation, Stanford University, 1949), pp. 310-13.

40. These were (a) the Gold Coast; (b) Sierra Leone; (c) a Southeast Asia group: Sarawak, North Borneo, Brunei, Singapore, and the Federation of Malaya; and (d) a Caribbean group: Jamaica, Trinidad, Grenada, Dominica, and Barbados.

41. Ascher, *Program-Making in Unesco,* p. 13.

CHAPTER IV

1. A detailed listing of all Unesco's undertakings will be found in the program resolutions of the General Conference and in the annual reports of the Director General. See Unesco, Document 9C/Resolutions; and "Report of the Director General, 1955," for the most recent statements.

2. Chapter I, pp. 21-22, and II, p. 27.

3. Unesco, General Conference, First Session, *Report of the Reconstruction and Rehabilitation Commission* (Paris, 1947), pp. 3-7.

4. In addition it assumed administrative services during the same period costing more than $500,000. Unesco, *Report on the Effectiveness of the Reconstruction Program,* 1947-49, p. 45.

5. For a review of the activities of this organization, see Garnet T. Page, "Canadian Council for Reconstruction through Unesco," *External Affairs* (Ottawa, May 1953), pp. 154-60. As one result of this effort it was estimated that through the aid extended, 25,000 teachers and 800,000 pupils in European countries were put in touch with the Canadian people.

6. Unesco, *The Book of Needs of Fifteen War-Devastated Countries in Education, Science and Culture,* Vol. 1 (1947); and *The Book of Needs in Education, Science and Culture of Devastated Countries,* Vol. II (1949). The second volume gave special emphasis to the countries of Southeast Asia. In addition pamphlets were issued on *Children, War's Victims,* The Education of the Handicapped (1949); *Libraries in Need* (1949); *Science Museums in Need* (1949); *Science Laboratories in Need* (1949); *In Work Camps for Peace* (1949); *Organizing International Voluntary Work Camps* (1949); *Operation TICER* (1949); *School Bell in the Wilderness* (n. d.).

7. This figure represents only a very rough estimate. The total for 1946 was put at 62 million dollars; for 1947, 88 million; and for 1948, 64 million. Harold E. Snyder, *When Peoples Speak to Peoples* (Washington: American Council on Education, 1953), p. 55; and Unesco, *Report of the Reconstruction and Rehabilitation Commission,* pp. 18-21. The first source provides (pp. 32-57) a graphic picture of the needs for educational reconstruction and of the efforts coordinated by the Commission for International Educational Reconstruction (CIER).

8. The campaigns in the last three countries were carried out in cooperation with the United Nations Appeal for Children, Unesco receiving ten per cent of the total raised.

9. Unesco, *Study Abroad,* International Handbook, Fellowships, Scholarships, Educational Exchange, Vol. I (1948).

10. Letter of August 17, 1956 from E. N. Petersen to Walter H. C. Laves.

11. Unesco, "Proposed Program and Budget for 1957-58," Document 9C/5, p. 149 and Document 9C/Resolutions, p. 30 (Res. 5.33 and 5.34). See reports of the Director General to the General Conference for details about the Coupon Scheme.

12. Ibid., p. 27 [Res. 5.32 (D)]; and Unesco, *Gift Coupon News* (Paris, August 1955).

13. Unesco, "Resolutions," Document 3C/110, Vol. II, p. 17 (Res. 1.7); and p. 34 (Res. 8.3).

14. United Nations Relief and Works Agency, "Report of the Director," Fourteenth Session (15 July 1954), Document A/2978, June 30, 1955; Unesco, "Report by the Director General on the Activities of the Organization, 1 April–30 June 1956," Document 44 EX/20, pp. 19-20; and Unesco, "Proposed Program and Budget for 1957-58," pp. 33-35.

15. The first was dated December 1952 and the second February 1953.

CHAPTER V

1. *Unesco Features*, No. 180 (16 April 1956), pp. 3-5.

2. Unesco *Constitution*, Preamble and Article I.

3. United Nations, *Universal Declaration of Human Rights*, Article 19.

4. However the 1950 session of the General Conference adopted a "Statement of Methods" covering many of the procedures followed by the organization. Unesco, Document 5C/Resolutions, pp. 71-76.

5. See Chapter I, pp. 8-9 and Chapter II, p. 37.

6. The cooperation with Unesco of these organizations takes three forms: consultative arrangements, formal agreements, and informal relations. In June 1956 Unesco had consultative arrangements with 104 international nongovernmental organizations. These organizations have to do with matters in Unesco's field of interest. Under the consultative arrangements the organizations have opportunity to participate in conferences and meetings and in the preparation and execution of projects of interest to them. They also receive pertinent documents and information. In return they provide publicity to Unesco's program, do everything possible to promote support of that program, and provide Unesco with full information on their activities relating to the program.

Formal agreements have been concluded by Unesco with nine organizations whose cooperation is essential to the progress of Unesco projects. These are: Council of International Organizations of Medical Sciences, International Association of Universities, International Council of Museums, International Council for Philosophy and Humanistic Studies, International Council of Scientific Unions, International Council of Social Sciences, International Music Council, International Theater Institute, and World Federation of United Nations Associations.

Unesco has entered into informal relations with approximately 250 international nongovernmental organizations which, though not eligible for consultative status, possess some common interests with Unesco. Unesco, "Unesco's Cooperation with Nongovernmental Organizations" (26 June 1956, WX/066.72, mimeographed); "Quadrennial Review of the Directives Concerning Relations with International Nongovernmental Organizations," Document 8C/ADM/21; and Document 8C/Resolutions (Res. III.3.3), p. 24.

7. W. E. F. Ward, "Unesco's Education Programme," *Oversea Education* (London), Vol. XXVII, No. 1 (April 1955), p. 7. The Unesco Institute of Education at

Hamburg has carried out a useful clearing-house function. See Chapter X, p. 240.

8. Unesco, Document 9C/Resolutions, p. 11 (Res. 1.21).

9. A bibliography of educational periodicals published in 79 countries and territories, listing some 3,500 publications, was prepared by the Educational Press Association of America in cooperation with Unesco and published in *America's Education Press, Twenty-Sixth Yearbook* (Washington: Educational Press Association, 1957).

10. The only omissions are the People's Republic of Korea, Tibet, Oman, and Masoate. For a listing of other Unesco publications on education, see "Report of the Director General, 1954," pp. 54-55.

11. Unesco, "Education in Czechoslovakia, Poland and the U.S.S.R." *Education Abstracts,* Vol. VIII, No. 8 (October 1956).

12. International Association of Universities, "A Note on the Activities of the International Association of Universities" (prepared for its Second General Conference, Istanbul, September 1955).

13. The Association has also prepared *A Collection of Texts* of forty-five cultural agreements between two or more countries which have reference to "equivalences." Unesco, "Report of the Director General," Document 7C/3, pp. 135-36; International Association of Universities, *Administrative Reports, 1951, 1952, 1953, 1954* (Paris, n. d.), pp. 10, 20, 24 and 36; and M. G. de Miranda, "Les pratiques actuelles en matière d'équivalence: L'intervention universitaire," *Avenirs* (Paris), Supplément au No. 59, Janvier 1954, pp. 2-19. In the United States the Comparative Education Branch of the Division of International Education in the U. S. Office of Education assists universities and colleges in the evaluation of foreign student credentials.

14. Unesco, "Consideration of the List of International Nongovernmental Organizations approved by Unesco for Consultative Arrangements," Document 7C/ADM/34, Appendix 65, pp. 143-44.

15. World Confederation of Organizations of the Teaching Profession, *WCOTP Annual Report, 1956* (Washington), p. 15.

16. Ibid., p. 52.

17. In 1953, $6,000; 1954, $6,000; 1955, $4,000; 1956, $4,000, while the IAU received for the same years respectively $14,000, $9,000, $14,000, and $14,000.

18. *WCOTP Annual Report, 1955* (Washington), pp. 26-27.

19. *WCOTP Annual Report, 1955,* p. 37.

20. A meeting which took place in January 1957 laid the basis, it was believed, for more effective cooperation in the future.

21. Unesco, *Study Abroad,* International Handbook, Fellowships, Scholarships, Educational Exchange, VIII, 1956-57 (Paris, 1956). It was published in a trilingual edition of 5,000 copies. The volume contains a chapter on "Teaching Appointments Abroad" and a report on Unesco's fourth annual survey of students enrolled for higher studies at universities in countries other than their own, the estimated total coming to 126,000. The United States headed the list with almost 35,000 foreign students in its educational institutions; and also led in the number of fellowships and scholarships offered, more than 20,000.

22. For an account of Unesco's activities dealing with exchange of persons, see Unesco, *Other Men's Ways,* Unesco and Its Program, XIII (Paris, 1955). A thought-

ful analysis of the international exchange of persons from the standpoint of a cultural anthropologist is given in John F. Embree, "Exchange of Persons, Directed Cultural Change" (Paris: Unesco, 1954, mimeographed).

23. Unesco, *Science Liaison,* The Story of Unesco's Science Cooperation Offices (second edition, Paris, 1954), p. 9; and Unesco, "General Conference, First Session," Document Unesco/C/30, p. 233.

24. Unesco, Preparatory Commission, Natural Sciences Committee, "Science and Unesco," Document Unesco/Prep.Com./Nat.Sci.Com./12 (London: The Pilot Press, n.d.), pp. 2-11. For a comprehensive review of the evolution of Unesco's program activities relating to the natural sciences, see Marcel Florkin, "Ten Years of Science at Unesco," *Impact of Science on Society,* Vol. VII, No. 3 (September 1956), pp. 121-46.

25. Unesco, *Science Liaison,* p. 13.

26. Unesco, *Courier,* Vol. II, No. 8 (September 1949), p. 11.

27. Unesco, "Report of the Director General on the Activities of the Organization for January-February 1956," Document 43 EX/10, pp. 18-20.

28. "Report of the Official United States Delegation to the International Symposium on High Altitude Biology in Lima, Peru, November 23 to 30, 1949" (typescript). The delegation reported that a considerable amount of new scientific information was gained from the conference, and recommended that the United States participate fully in future conferences on high altitude biology.

It is of some interest to recall this event, since the discussion of this proposed symposium at Unesco's Mexico City General Conference in 1947 was carried in a widely syndicated critical news story in the United States under the heading, "Sex at High Altitudes." In a similar vein, a leading article in the *Saturday Evening Post* of October 2, 1948, under the heading, "Dr. Huxley's Wonderful Zoo," used the Mexico City discussions as ground for an attempt to ridicule Unesco.

29. Unesco, *1945 London Conference,* p. 69; and Charles S. Ascher, *Program-Making in Unesco, 1946-1951* (Chicago: Public Administration Clearing House, 1951), pp. 3-4. For a summary review of the history and development of ICSU (1919-50) and United States participation therein, see Esther C. Brunauer, "International Council of Scientific Unions," U. S. Department of State *Bulletin,* Vol. XIII, No. 324 (September 9, 1945), pp. 371-76; and National Academy of Sciences-National Research Council, *Information for Delegates to International Scientific Meetings,* A Brief Description of the International Council of Scientific Unions (ICSU), 1956.

30. It includes, in addition to national research organizations in thirty-five countries and four other countries that adhere directly, international unions in the fields of mathematics, astronomy, physics, chemistry, biochemistry, biology, crystallography, physiology, geodesy and geophysics, mechanics, scientific radio, geography, and history and philosophy of science. Unesco, "Consideration of the List of International Nongovernmental Organizations Approved by Unesco for Consultative Arrangements," Document 9C/ADM/15, Appendix 27. The six most recently established unions, those in mathematics, biochemistry, crystallography, physiology, mechanics, and history and philosophy of science, were set up with the help of Unesco.

31. 1947-49, $746,758; 1950, $177,874; 1951, $179,628; 1952, $188,403; 1953,

$191,948; 1954, $180,000; 1955, $180,000; 1956, $180,000; total $2,024,610. Unesco, "Quadrennial Review by the Executive Board of the Employment of Subventions Granted to International Nongovernmental Organizations," Document 8C/ADM/ 20, Appendix XIII, pp. 3-4; and "Approved Program and Budget for 1955-56" (limited distribution), p. 65.

32. Forerunners of this type of international scientific cooperation were the First and Second Polar Years celebrated respectively in 1882-83 and 1932-33.

33. For a general review of the project, see Wallace W. Atwood, Jr., "The International Geophysical Year: A Twentieth-Century Achievement in International Cooperation," U. S. Department of State *Bulletin,* Vol. XXXV, No. 910 (December 3, 1956), pp. 880-86.

34. Council for International Organizations of Medical Sciences, Third General Assembly, *Bulletin,* Vol. VI, No. 1-2-3-4 (January-December 1955), and *Rapport Annuel, 1955,* p. 2.

35. Unesco, *The Social Sciences,* Unesco and Its Program, XII (Paris, 1955), pp. 8, 9.

36. See Walter H. C. Laves, "The Social Sciences and Unesco," *International Social Science Bulletin,* Vol. II, No. 2 (Summer 1950), pp. 251-55.

37. The titles and number of countries represented in each of the above organizations (as of 1956) follow: International Economic Association (24); International Political Science Association (21); International Sociological Association (47); International Union of Scientific Psychology (21); and International Association of Legal Science (28). Unesco assisted in the establishment of all of these organizations except the International Union of Scientific Psychology. Unesco, *International Organizations in the Social Sciences,* Reports and Papers in the Social Sciences, No. 5, 1956.

Unesco's encouragement of international social science organizations has not been limited to those of its own creation. It has worked with the World Federation of Mental Health, the International Union of Scientific Psychology, the World Association for Public Opinion Research, the International Union for the Scientific Study of Population, the International Econometric Society, the International Institute of Administrative Sciences, the International Society of Criminology, and the International Statistical Institute.

38. Unesco, "Final Report, First Plenary General Assembly of the International Social Science Council," Document Unesco/SS/10, 1954, p. 10.

39. J. Meynaud, "International Cooperation in the Field of Social Science," Unesco, *International Organizations in the Social Sciences,* Reports and Papers in the Social Sciences, No. 5, 1956, pp. 12-15. The Unesco Institute for Social Sciences at Cologne has contributed to the advancement of knowledge. See Chapter X, pp. 238-40.

40. *International Social Science Bulletin,* published quarterly, Vol. VIII, 1956, Unesco, Paris.

41. For a review of the approaches which have attempted to develop scientific methods of evaluation, see Otto Klineberg, "The Problem of Evaluation," and M. Jahoda and E. Barnitz, "The Nature of Evaluation," *International Social Science Bulletin,* Vol. VII, No. 3 (1955), pp. 346-54. The stages in the process of evaluation have been listed as follows: "defining the *aims* of the programme;

selecting the *criteria* by which accomplishment is judged, and the methods of measuring them, deciding on the *logic* or design of evaluation; *collecting the data; analyzing the data*." Jahoda and Barnitz, "The Nature of Evaluation," p. 354.

42. Unesco, *International Social Science Bulletin*, Vol. VII, No. 3 (1955), pp. 345-442. Their authors and titles were as follows: Otto Klineberg, "The Problem of Evaluation;" M. Jahoda and E. Barnitz, "The Nature of Evaluation;" C. Selltiz and E. Barnitz, "The Evaluation of Inter-group Relations Programs;" Ernest Beaglehole, "Evaluation Techniques for Induced Technological Change;" M. Brewster Smith, "Evaluation of Exchange of Persons;" Louis Moss, "The Evaluation of Fundamental Education;" C. R. Wright, "Evaluating Mass Media Campaigns;" and K. M. Miller, "Evaluation in Adult Education."

43. Otto Klineberg, "The Problem of Evaluation," pp. 350-51.

44. Unesco, Frank M. Gardner, *The Delhi Public Library, An Evaluation Report* (Paris, 1957).

CHAPTER VI

1. Unesco, *The Artist in Modern Society* (n. d.), p. 123.

2. Dorothy G. Williams, "The Rural Museum of the Arab States Fundamental Education Centre," *Museum*, Vol. VII, No. 4 (1954), pp. 221-24.

3. Unesco, "General Conference, First Session," Document Unesco/C/30, pp. 221, 237.

4. Unesco, "Resolutions," Document 3C/110, Vol. II, pp. 26-27 (Res. 6.15).

5. Unesco, *The Artist in Modern Society*, p. 121.

6. Unesco, *Arts and Letters*, Unesco and Its Program, X, pp. 5-6; and *Catalogue of Color Reproductions of Painting from 1860 to 1955* (3rd ed., 1955); and *Catalogue of Color Reproductions Prior to 1860* (3rd ed., 1955). Charles Sterling, Curator of the Louvre Department of Paintings and Drawings, states in the introduction of this latter publication, "This catalogue is beginning to reflect the art of all countries and all periods. As has long been desired, entire schools of painting are now being included. . . . Little by little, the catalogue is achieving its aim of being a repertory of thousands of works which, by means of faithful reproductions, will become familiar to millions of human beings." (p. 10).

7. These volumes have been published by the New York Graphic Society by arrangement with Unesco. Unesco cooperates in this project by negotiating with the national government concerned for permission to make the necessary photographs, sometimes carries the cost of the photographer, and purchases approximately one hundred copies of each album for distribution to member states. The expense to Unesco per album averages $3,000 to $4,000. A review of *Iran: Persian Miniatures— Imperial Library* commented, "The sixth volume in the Unesco World Art Series is as well edited and prepared as its predecessors. Like its predecessors, too, it has the felicitous quality of finding interest and beauty in little-known fields of artistic endeavor." *The New Yorker*, December 15, 1956, p. 179.

8. International Association of Plastic Arts, *Information Bulletin*, No. 22 (Paris, January 1957), pp. 2, 6.

9. Unesco, "Report by the Director General, 1 January—30 June 1956," Docu-

ment 9C/3, p. 104. Fourteen fellowships for 1955-56 were assigned to writers, composers, and visual artists.

10. International Council for Philosophy and Humanistic Studies, *Bulletin, 1951-53* (Paris, n.d.), pp. 24-25.

11. Unesco, Document 9C/3, pp. 106-07; and Unesco *Chronicle*, Vol. II, No. 11 (November 1956), pp. 348-49.

12. Kushwant Singh, "The Translation of Masterpieces of Literature: An Anthology of Sikh Sacred Writings," Unesco *Chronicle*, No. 2 (August 1955), pp. 9-11.

13. Unesco, *Index Translationum*, 8 (1957).

14. Its nine member organizations are the International Society for Contemporary Music, the International Musicological Society, the International Folk Music Council, the International Federation of Musicians, the International Federation of Musical Youth, the International Federation of Popular Societies of Music, the International Committee for the Standardization of Instrumental Music, the International Association of Music Libraries, and the International Society for Music Education. The last two were formed with the assistance of the Council. In addition the Council's membership includes twenty-one National Music Committees. The National Music Council is the member organization in the United States. Unesco, "Quadrennial Review by the Executive Board of the Employment of Subventions Granted to International Nongovernmental Organizations," Document 8C/ADM/ 20, Annex XLI, p. 1.

15. United States National Commission for Unesco, *Newsletter*, Vol. III, No. 13 (August 10, 1956).

16. See Sir Stewart Wilson, "An International Recording Plan," *The Gramophone* (London), July 1955.

17. United States National Commission for Unesco, Third National Conference, January 27-31, 1952, Document III/GM.10/2, paper by Harold Spivacke.

18. Sir Compton Mackenzie, "Disks as a Tool of Unesco," *New York Times*, March 18, 1956, p. 1 M, Section 11; and *Unesco Features*, No. 185 (21 May 1956), p. 1.

19. *Unesco Features*, No. 187 (4 June 1956), p. 3.

20. In 1953 the fellowships were awarded to nationals of Australia, Cuba, Finland, Japan, and Sweden; in 1954, of Belgium, Italy, Spain, Turkey, and the United States; and in 1955, of Austria, Chile, France, Switzerland, and the United Kingdom. International Theater Institute, *Report of the Executive Secretary, 1953-1955* (Paris, n.d., ITI/6C/SGR, mimeographed), pp. 16-17; and Unesco, *Arts and Letters*, pp. 10-12.

21. Unesco, Preparatory Commission, *Report on the Program of the United Nations Educational, Scientific and Cultural Organization* (London: Frederick Printing Co., Ltd., 1946), pp. 111-20; and Unesco, "General Conference, First Session," p. 275.

22. The thirteen constituent organizations of the Council are the International Academic Union, the International Federation of Philosophic Societies, the Permanent International Committee of Linguists, the International Committee on Historical Sciences, the International Commission on Folk Arts and Folklore, the International Federation of Associations for Classical Studies, the International Union of Anthropological and Ethnological Sciences, the International Committee on the History of Art, the International Association for the Study of the History of

Religions, the International Federation of Societies for Modern Languages and Literatures, the International Musicological Society, the International Union of Orientalists, and the International Congress of Prehistoric and Protohistoric Sciences. Unesco, "Consideration of the List of International Nongovernmental Organizations Approved by Unesco for Consultative Arrangements," Document 9C/ADM/15, Appendix 25, pp. 1-3.

23. For an outline of the purpose and character of *Diogenes,* see Roger Caillois, "The Tasks and Ambitions of 'Diogenes,' " Unesco *Chronicle,* Vol. II, No. 1 (January 1956), pp. 3-8.

24. Weidenfeld and Nicolson, *The Third Reich* (London, 1954).

25. Unesco, Document 8C/ADM/20, Annex XXXV, pp. 11-40; and International Council for Philosophy and Humanistic Studies, *Bulletin, 1951-53,* pp. 8-13, 21-26; and *Bulletin, 1954-1955,* pp. 31-56. Among other publications bearing on parts of the world outside the area of Greco-Roman tradition have been the *Concordance and Indexes of Moslem Tradition,* the *Sanscrit Dictionary,* the *Sumerian Lexicography,* the *Corpus Inscriptionum Iranicarum,* and the *Compendium of Turkish Philology and Literature.* In 1953 publication in two languages was initiated of a series of great classical texts stressing the ideas of tolerance and liberty. The general title of the series is *Philosophy and World Community.*

26. U. S. Department of State, *The Defenses of Peace,* Documents Relating to Unesco, Part I (Washington: Dept. of State Pub. No. 2457, 1946), p. 26.

27. Unesco, "Final Report of the Expert Committee on Education for International Understanding and Cooperation," Document Unesco/ED/142 (1955), pp. 9-10.

28. Unesco, "Report by the Director General and the Executive Board," Document 8C/3, pp. 151-55; and "Report of the Director General, 1954," pp. 122-25.

29. Unesco, "Report of the Director General," Document 7C/3, pp. 233-34; and United Nations, *Teaching about the United Nations and the Specialized Agencies,* 1952, p. 56.

30. Unesco, *Press, Radio, Film, Report of the Commission on Technical Needs,* Vol. I, 1947; Vol. II, 1948; Vol. III, 1949; and *Press, Film, Radio, Reports on the Facilities of Mass Communication,* Vol. IV, 1950; Vol. V, 1951.

31. Unesco, *World Communications* (3rd ed., 1956).

32. Robert W. Desmond, "Professional Training of Journalists," *Education for Journalism,* 1953, Unesco, Reports and Papers on Mass Communication, No. 8 (January 1954).

33. Unesco, "International Expert Meeting on Training for Journalism," Report by the Director General, Document Unesco/MC/28 (1956).

34. Unesco, *Constitution,* Article I, 2 (c). For a statistical study of libraries throughout the world—national, university, special, school, and public—see Unesco, "International Statistics on Libraries and Book Production, Preliminary Report," Document Unesco/ST/R/15 (1956).

35. The terms bibliography and documentation are sometimes used synonymously. But more strictly speaking, documentation refers to the printed and unprinted material on a given subject. Bibliography is the orderly listing of such material. Bibliography is sometimes spoken of as a documentation service. Abstracts are short summaries of scholarly articles.

36. Unesco, "Notes sur l'avenir du Programme de la Division de Bibliothèques en Matières de Bibliographie," Document Unesco/LBA/Conf. 16/1. (1955, mimeographed), pp. 3, 7, 21. For a summary review of Unesco activities in bibliography and documentation 1946-56, see Julien Cain, "The Development of Bibliographical and Documentation Services over the Past Ten Years," Unesco *Bulletin for Libraries*, Vol. X, No. 11-12 (November–December 1956), pp. 262-70. This same issue provides (pp. 290-94) a list of Unesco's bibliographical and reference publications.

37. Unesco, "A Brief Outline of Unesco's Library and Bibliographical Programs, 1953-1954," Document Unesco/CUA/51 (1953), p. 3.

38. Unesco, Library of Congress, *Bibliographical Services, their present state and possibilities of improvement* (Washington, 1949); and Unesco, "National Development and International Planning of Bibliographical Services," Document Unesco/CUA/1 (1950).

39. This Committee met as a provisional body in 1951 and 1952, and for the first time as a standing committee in 1953. Its annual reports to date have been L. N. Macles, *Bibliographical Services throughout the World*, First and Second Annual Reports, 1951-1952, 1952-1953 (Paris: Unesco, 1955); and R. L. Collison, "Third Annual Report," 1953-1954, Document Unesco/CUA/72 (1955).

40. By 1956 the following had been published by Unesco: Knud Larsen, *National Bibliographical Services*, Their Creation and Operation; Henry Lemaitre, revised and enlarged by Anthony Thompson, *Vocabularium bibliothecarii; Guide des centres nationaux d'information bibliographique;* L. Brummel, *Union Catalogues*, Their Problems and Organization; and P. K. Garde, *Directory of Reference Works Published in Asia*. In preparation was a *Directory of Reference Books Published in Latin America*.

41. Unesco, in its endeavor to serve as a world center of information on educational, scientific, and cultural matters, has developed the following pattern of organization for coordinating abstracting and bibliographical services:

International Advisory Committee on Bibliography, 1951. This over-all Committee is advisory to the Director General and is based in the Libraries Divison of Unesco.

International Committee for Social Science Documentation, 1951.

International Advisory Committee for Documentation and Terminology in Pure and Applied Science, 1951.

Commission on Bibliography of the International Council for Philosophy and Humanistic Studies, 1949.

In addition Unesco has encouraged the formation and the continuing activity of international nongovernmental organizations, including the International Association of Archivists; the International Association of Music Libraries; the Science Abstracting Board of the International Council of Scientific Unions; and the Joint Committee of the International Federation of Library Associations, International Federation for Documentation, and the International Association of Archivists. For an outline of a proposed long-term program for improved bibliography and documentation, see Unesco *Bulletin for Libraries*, Vol. XI, No. 1 (January 1957), pp. 5-7.

42. Unesco, *Courier*, Vol. II, No. 8 (September 1949), p. 10.

43. Unesco, "Report of the Director General, 1954," p. 73; and Document

8C/ADM/20, Annex XIII, pp. 11, 14. See also *Courier*, Vol. II, No. 6 (July 1949), p. 9.

44. National Academy of Sciences–National Research Council, *Information for Delegates to International Scientific Meetings*, A Brief Description of the International Council of Scientific Unions (ICSU), 1956, pp. 5-7.

45. Unesco, *International Bibliography of Political Science*, Vol. I, 1954; Vol. II, 1955; Vol. III, 1956; *International Bibliography of Economics*, Vol. I, 1955; Vol. II, 1955; Vol. III, 1956; and *Current Sociology*, Vol. I, 1952; Vol. II, 1953; Vol. III, 1954-55; Vol. IV, 1956.

46. Unesco, *The Social Sciences*, Unesco and Its Program, XII, pp. 16-20. The United Kingdom has its own complete national directory. The material in the *Register* on the United States was supplemented by three booklets presenting trend reports on research, entitled *Economics in the United States of America, Political Science in the United States of America*, and *Sociology in the United States of America*. Some volumes of basic research information have also been published: *Selected Inventory of Periodical Publications and Documentation in the Social Sciences* (1951); *World List of Social Science Periodicals* (1953); and *International Repertory of Social Science Documentation Centers* (1952). For a comprehensive review of social science documentation published or stimulated by Unesco, see "The Improvement of Social Science Documentation," Unesco *Chronicle*, No. 5 (November 1955), pp. 29-34.

47. Unesco, *Constitution*, Article I, 2 (c). A review of Unesco's efforts to forward the international exchange of publications is given in Gisela von Busse, "Access to Books," Unesco *Bulletin for Libraries*, Vol. X, No. 11-12 (November–December 1956), pp. 273-78.

48. Unesco, Document Unesco/CUA/51, pp. 4-6.

49. Unesco, *Handbook on the International Exchange of Publications* (1956).

50. Unesco, *Access to Books* (1952), pp. 19-20.

51. Unesco, "Report of a Possible International Agreement Concerning the Exchange of Publications," Document 9C/PRG/5; and Document 9C/Resolutions, p. 23 (Res. 4.33).

52. Unesco, *Access to Books*, p. 20.

53. Unesco, Document 8C/ADM/20, Annex XXXVI, pp. 1-9; and Georges Fradier, "The Care of Old Paintings," Unesco *Courier*, Vol. No. 2 (February 1952).

54. One of the participants in this latter meeting, Dr. Helmut Wagner of the Bremen Uberseemuseum, said in speaking of modern trends in the museum field, "We want to exhibit everything in such a way that our visitors will be encouraged to see for themselves and think for themselves. We don't want to offer them 'preserved reality' but to make them eager for knowledge about real things, about life itself." United States National Commission, *Newsletter*, Vol. II, No. 13 (August 5, 1955), p. 2. In relation to the campaign for museums, the entire Unesco *Courier*, Vol. IX, No. 4 (October 1956, U. S. edition) was devoted to museum activities. Special issues were published of *Education Abstracts* (Vol. VIII, No. 2, 1956) on "Museums in Education"; and of *Educational Studies and Documents* (No. 17, 1957) on "Museum Techniques in Fundamental Education."

55. Unesco, "Report of the Director General, 1955," p. 112; and *Fundamental and Adult Education*, Vol. VIII, No. 2 (April 1956), pp. 85-86. This latter source

carried a series of articles on the educational work of museums in various parts of the world.

56. Respectively 40,000 and 50,000 Egyptian pounds, the amount in dollars calculated at the rate of one Egyptian pound to $2.70.

57. The geographical scale and the increased destructiveness of modern weapons evidenced in World War I as well as in its successor had vastly increased the danger of damage to the world's cultural treasures. During World War II some 5,000 churches and historic buildings, it has been estimated, were damaged or destroyed in Europe alone. As early as 1907 the Hague Conventions had tried to circumscribe this danger. Continuing study of the problem led in 1935 to an inter-American agreement, the Roerich Pact; and in 1938 to the presentation to the League of Nations of a draft convention prepared by the International Museums Office. During World War II the United States government set up a special commission for the protection of artistic and historic monuments in war areas. World War II also witnessed on an unprecedented scale the systematic pillage, particularly by Nazi Germany, of works of art and other cultural treasures from the occupied countries. See Unesco, Intergovernmental Conference on the Protection of Cultural Property in the Event of Armed Conflict, The Hague, 1954, "Historical Note," Document Unesco/CBC/7, pp. 1-5. For a summary review of Unesco activity on the over-all problem, see "Convention for the Protection of Cultural Property in the Event of Armed Conflict," Unesco *Chronicle*, Vol. II, No. 12 (December 1956), pp. 363-66.

58. Unesco, Document 4C/Resolutions, pp. 27-28 (Res. 6.42).

59. Unesco, Document Unesco/CBC/7, pp. 5-7. At this conference the USSR participated for the first time in an international gathering sponsored by Unesco.

60. For the text and an analysis of the Convention see Unesco, "Report on the Results of the Intergovernmental Conference on the Protection of Cultural Property in the Event of Armed Conflict," Document 8C/PRG/4 and Annex ("Final Act").

61. These were Bulgaria, Burma, Egypt, Hungary, Mexico, Poland, San Marino, and Yugoslavia. The Soviet Union ratified in January 1957. When San Marino deposited its ratification, it offered the mountainous slopes of its tiny territory, including a disused railway tunnel, as a sanctuary in any future war for the works of art of all countries. Its territory covers no more than thirty-two square miles, but for sixteen centuries this diminutive state has remained independent and neutral. See Jean Gachon, "San Marino and the Protection of Cultural Property," *Unesco Features*, No. 185 (21 May 1956), pp. 10-11.

62. Unesco, Document 7C/Resolutions, p. 27 (Res. 4.23).

63. For an outline of its proposed character and functions, see "International Center for the Study of the Preservation and Restoration of Cultural Property," Document 9C/PRG/10.

64. Such activity was authorized in Unesco, Document 6C/Resolutions, p. 25 (Res. 4.22).

65. Unesco has published monographs on the reports of certain of these missions. See Unesco, I, *Sites and Monuments: Problems of Today* (1953); II, *The Care of Paintings* (1952); III, *Cuzco: Reconstruction of the Town and Restoration of its Monuments* (1952); IV, *Saint-Sophia of Ochrida: Preservation and Restoration of the Building and its Frescoes* (1953); V, *Manual of Travelling Exhibitions* (1953);

VI, *Lebanon: Suggestions for the Plan of Tripoli and for the Surroundings of the Baalbek Acropolis* (1954); VII, *Syria: Problems of Preservation and Presentation of Sites and Monuments* (1954).

66. Unesco, "Report of the Director General, 1955," p. 106.

67. Unesco, "Draft Recommendations on International Principles Applicable to Archaeological Excavations," Document 9C/PRG/7.

68. For the text of the Convention and a detailed account of the Conference proceedings, see Unesco, *Records of the Intergovernmental Copyright Conference, Geneva, 18 August–6 September 1952* (1955). A summary review of Unesco activities to foster the free flow of information is given in Julian Behrstock, "The Free Flow of Information: Unesco's Program and Methods," Unesco *Chronicle*, Vol. II, No. 3 (March 1956), pp. 80-84.

69. Unesco, "Proposed Program and Budget for 1957-1958," Document 9C/5, p. 113; and "Report on the Participation of Unesco in the Preparation of a Draft International Agreement for the Protection of the Interests of Performers, Recorders and Broadcasters," Document 9C/PRG/6.

70. *Unesco Features*, No. 191 (2 July 1956), p. 1.

71. United Nations Economic and Social Council, Resolution 522 (XVII) G.

72. Unesco, *The Problems of Transmitting Press Messages* (1956).

73. Unesco, *Report of the Director General to the Economic and Social Council on the Activities of Unesco in 1954*, pp. 63-64; and "Report on the Activities of Unesco to Promote the Free Flow of Books," Document Unesco/MC/20 (1954); Francis Williams, *Transmitting World News* (Paris: Unesco, 1953); Unesco, *Trade Barriers to Knowledge* (1955); and R. E. Barker, *Books for All* (Paris: Unesco, 1956).

74. In 1947 Unesco granted subventions to NGO's totaling $291,000; in 1956 the total was $633,200, or approximately six per cent of the total expenditure for that year. Unesco, Document 9C/5, pp. 272-73, 276.

75. Unesco, Document 9C/Resolutions, pp. 74-79.

76. Unesco, "Progress Report on Unesco's Participation in the United Nations Expanded Program of Technical Assistance," Document 41EX/14 Add., pp. 7-15; *The Geophysical Observatory, Quetta* (Karachi, Pakistan: Ministry of Education, n.d.); and "Progress Report on Unesco's Participation in the United Nations Expanded Program of Technical Assistance (1 September–31 December 1955)," Document 43 EX/17, pp. 46-47. At Quetta, sixty miles south of the Khyber Pass, an earthquake in 1935 killed 30,000 persons, and in 1955 a village four miles north of the city was completely destroyed.

77. Unesco, *Arts and Letters*, pp. 5-6.

78. Letter of April 20, 1955 from Verner W. Clapp to Guy A. Lee, Unesco Relations Staff, U. S. Department of State.

79. However, when Unesco proposed in 1955 to discontinue it, so many vigorous protests arrived from libraries, publishers, and scholars that it was continued with only minor modifications.

CHAPTER VII

1. The report of the United Nations Mission is given in United Nations, *Mission to Haiti,* Report of the United Nations Mission of Technical Assistance to the

Republic of Haiti (1949). For the Marbial study see Unesco, Alfred Métraux (in collaboration with Mr. E. Berrouet and Dr. and Mrs. Jean Comhaire-Sylvain), "Making a Living in the Marbial Valley (Haiti)," *Occasional Papers in Education* (Unesco/ED/Occ/10, 7 December 1951). Its findings are summarized in Unesco, *The Haiti Pilot Project, Phase One, 1947-1949* (1951). This gives the text of the agreement between the Haitian government and Unesco. The history of the project up to 1950 is also given in Kendric Marshall, "The Fundamental Education Program of Unesco," *Harvard Educational Review*, Vol. XX, No. 3 (Summer 1950), pp. 139-48. For a vivid first-hand account of a visit to the Marbial Valley project, see Edmund Wilson, "Unesco at Marbial," *The Reporter*, Vol. 2, No. 11 (May 23, 1950), pp. 29-33.

2. Tibor Mende, "Things are Looking Up in the 'Forgotten Valley'," Unesco, *Courier*, Vol. V, No. 1 (January 1952), pp. 4-5.

3. *Unesco Features*, No. 100 (26 June 1953), pp. 6-8.

4. See p. 147.

5. Unesco, H. W. Howes, "Fundamental, Adult, Literacy and Community Education in the West Indies," *Educational Studies and Documents*, No. XV, pp. 41-42.

6. Unesco, *Learn and Live* (1951), p. 5.

7. Article 26.

8. Unesco, *World Survey of Education*, Handbook of Educational Organization and Statistics (1955), pp. 17, 19.

9. Ibid., pp. 13-16.

10. Unesco, Henry W. Holmes (ed.), *Fundamental Education: Common Ground for All Peoples*, Report of a Special Committee to the Preparatory Commission of the United Nations Educational, Scientific and Cultural Organization (New York: Macmillan, 1947), pp. 1-2.

11. See footnote 10.

12. For a general statement by Clarence E. Beeby on educational missions, see Unesco, *Courier*, Vol. II, No. 1 (February 1949), p. 11.

13. See Unesco, *Report of the Mission to Afghanistan* (1952); *Report of the Mission to Burma* (1952); *Report of the Mission to the Philippines* (1950); and *Report to the United Nations, 1951-1952*, pp. 20-21.

14. Unesco, "A Definition of Fundamental Education," Document Unesco/ED/94 (1951). See also Document Unesco/ED/94 (rev., 1952); "A note on the Relationship of Fundamental Education to Economic and Social Development," Document Unesco/ED/95 (1951); and Unesco, *Fundamental Education, Description and Program* (1949), pp. 7-48. The publication, *Fundamental Education: Common Ground for All Peoples* (see footnote 10), which was submitted to the First Session of Unesco's General Conference in 1946, as the report of the special committee of the Preparatory Commission, brought together the views and comments of a representative group of specialists. The volume contains (pp. 178-201) a thoughtful analysis by Margaret Read of assumptions underlying the concept of fundamental education.

15. Unesco, "Report of the Director General," Document 7C/3, p. 81.

16. William S. Gray, *The Teaching of Reading and Writing* (Chicago: Unesco/Scott Foresman, 1956). The content of the book is briefly summarized in *Unesco Features*, No. 190 (25 June 1956), pp. 8-9.

17. Unesco, *Public Library Manuals*, particularly the following numbers of

the series: "Libraries in Adult and Fundamental Education," "Development of Public Libraries in Latin America," "Development of Public Libraries in Africa," and "Public Libraries for Asia." A summary of Unesco activities relating to public libraries is given in Edward Sydney, "Public Library Development in the Post-War Years: the First Decade," *Unesco Bulletin for Libraries,* Vol. X, No. 11-12 (November–December 1956), pp. 255-61.

18. *Unesco Bulletin for Libraries,* Vol. X, No. 4 (April 1956), p. 94.

19. Unesco, Frank M. Gardner, "The Delhi Public Library Project," *Occasional Papers in Education* (Unesco/ED/Occ.16, 29 December 1952); and Unesco, *Public Library Manuals,* "The Delhi Public Library," An Evaluation Report by Frank M. Gardner (1956).

20. Unesco, "The Pilot Public Library, Medellín, Colombia," Document Unesco/CUA/69 (1955); and Unesco, Gobierno de Colombia, Biblioteca Pública Piloto de Medellín para Latinoamérica, *Primer Año de Labores, 1954-1955.*

21. The role of museums in education is reviewed in Unesco, "Museum Techniques in Fundamental Education," *Educational Studies and Documents,* No. 17; *Fundamental and Adult Education,* Vol. VIII, No. 2 (April 1956), pp. 56-66; and *Education Abstracts,* Vol. III, No. 2 (February 1956).

22. Unesco, "Report on the Seminar on Visual Aids in Fundamental Education, Messina, Italy, August 31–September 26, 1953," Document Unesco/MC/22; and "Report of the Director General," Document 7C/3, pp. 90-92.

23. *Unesco Features,* No. 192 (9 July 1956), p. 2.

24. Unesco, Daniel Behrman, *When the Mountains Move,* Technical Assistance and the Changing Face of Latin America (1954), pp. 31-42. See also *Unesco Features,* No. 132 (3 December 1954), pp. 16-19; and Unesco, *Fundamental and Adult Education,* Vol. VIII, No. 2 (April 1956), p. 88.

25. Unesco, "The Training of Fundamental Educators," *Education Abstracts,* Vol. VII, No. 8 (October 1955), pp. 7-8; and "Report of the Director General," Document 8C/3, p. 69.

26. Unesco, Document 6C/Resolution, pp. 33-35.

27. *Unesco World Review,* No. 327 (21 May 1955), p. 3.

28. U. S. National Commission, *Newsletter,* Vol. III, No. 8 (April 20, 1956), p. 3.

29. In 1954 it was composed of three Americans, a Dutchman, an Englishman, eight Egyptians, a Frenchman, a German, a Jordanian, a Palestinian, a Syrian, and a Yugoslav. The Director was an Egyptian educator. Unesco, *The Builders and the Books,* Technical Assistance Lends a Hand to the Progress of the Middle East (1955), p. 40.

30. Unesco, *Sirs-el-Layyan,* Life and Hope for the Arab World (1955), particularly p. 20. Much of the same material is given by Georges Fradier, "Sirs-el-Layyan," Unesco, *Courier,* Vol. VIII, No. 2 (July 1955, U. S. edition), pp. 5-10.

31. Unesco, "Report of the Ad Hoc Working Group on the Appraisal of Fundamental Education Centers," Document 44 EX/7, Annex I, pp. 1-2.

32. Bolivia, Ecuador, and Nicaragua in addition to Mexico in Latin America; and Iraq, Jordan, Libya, and Syria in addition to Egypt among the Arab States.

33. Unesco, "The Training of Fundamental Educators," pp. 8-9; and "Report of the Director General, 1955," p. 55.

34. Unesco, Document 44 EX/7, Annex I, p. 52.

35. Ibid., p. 19.

36. Ibid., p. 4. The two fundamental education centers at Patzcuaro and Sirs-el-Layyan are training leaders at an approximate rate of 125 a year, at a total estimated cost to Unesco and other participating agencies for 1957-58 (including also production of materials) of about $825,000 annually. On the basis of these figures the cost per student each year is $6,600. Unesco, "Proposed Program and Budget for 1957-58," Document 9C/5, p. 29.

37. American Universities Field Staff (New York). "United Nations Technical Assistance to Mexico, A Report from James G. Maddox," December 17, 1956 (Mexico, JGM-7-56), pp. 17-25.

38. Unesco, Document 44 EX/7, Annex I, pp. 2, 20.

39. United Nations, Administrative Committee on Co-ordination, "Nineteenth Report of the Committee to the Economic and Social Council," Document E/2884, May 16, 1956, paragraphs 23-28, cited in Unesco, Document 44 EX/7, pp. 6-7.

40. Unesco, *Fundamental and Adult Education*, Vol. VI, No. 4 (October 1954), pp. 191-92; and *Technical Assistance Bulletin*, Progress Report No. 25 (December 1, 1955), p. 5 (mimeographed).

41. *TUFEC, Provisional Program of Study*, Thailand-Unesco Fundamental Education Center, Ubol, Thailand, 1954 (Bangkok: Chatra Press, 1954).

42. Unesco, Document 8C/Resolutions, p. 35 (Res. IV.1.4.331); and "Report of the Director General, 1955," p. 54. For an analysis of the problems involved in this project, see Unesco, "Regional Meeting of Experts on the Production of Reading Material for New Literature, Pakistan, June 11-18, 1956, Final Report," Document Unesco/ED/146.

43. Unesco, "Literature Bureaus and Production Centers," *Educational Abstracts*, Vol. VI, No. 2 (February 1954), pp. 10-11. For an account of the Burma Translation Society, which began work in 1947 in a country where little or no printed material was available in Burmese for the general reader, the student, or the scholar, see Unesco, *Fundamental and Adult Education*, Vol. VIII, No. 2 (April 1956), pp. 79-81.

44. Unesco, "Experiments in Fundamental Education in French African Territories," *Educational Studies and Documents*, No. IX (January 1955).

45. Quoted in Unesco, *The Right to Education*, pp. 3-4.

46. Unesco, *Summary Report of the International Conference on Adult Education*, Elsinore, Denmark, June 19-25, 1949, p. 4. With regard to the feeling of "belonging" mentioned above, Dr. Torres Bodet, speaking at Elsinore, referred to man's sense of loneliness in modern society, and Sir John Maud emphasized "the sense of being powerless." Unesco, *Adult Education, Current Trends and Practices* (1949), pp. 12, 17.

47. Ibid., Jean Guehenno, "Adult Education and the Crisis of Civilization," p. 36.

48. Unesco, *International Directory of Adult Education* (1952); and Unesco, S. G. Raybould, E. A. Corbett, Baldwin M. Woods, Helen V. Hammarberg, *Universities in Adult Education* (2nd imp. 1953). For the discussion in national journals, see Canadian Association for Adult Education, *Food for Thought* (Toronto, 1955); National Institute of Adult Education, *Adult Education* (London, 1955); and Adult Education Association in the United States, *Adult Leadership* (Chicago, 1955).

49. A summary review of Unesco's adult education program (1946-50) is given in

Herbert C. Hunsaker, "Unesco's Work in Adult Education," *Harvard Educational Review*, Vol. XX, No. 3 (Summer 1950), pp. 169-75. See also Unesco, "International Center of Workers' Education, Meeting of Experts, 8-15 August 1953, Report of the Meeting and Recommendations to the Director General," Document Unesco/ED/135; "Consultative Committee on Adult Education, 12-14 August 1953, Report on the Meeting," Document Unesco/ED/134; "Summary Report on the International Seminar on Rural Adult Education, 14 August–4 September 1954," Document Unesco/ED/145; "Report on the Unesco La Brevière Seminar on Workers' Education, 1952," *Educational Studies and Documents*, No. 1 (June 1953); "Workers' Education for International Understanding," *Educational Studies and Documents*, No. VIII (July 1954); "Report of the Director General, 1955," p. 57; "Report of the Director General, 1 January–30 June 1956," Document 9C/3, p. 52; and U. S. National Commission for Unesco, Abbot Kaplan, "The Development of Mutual Understanding through Programs of Adult Education," Document National Conference 5/WG/5.

50. W. E. F. Ward, "Unesco at Montevideo," *Oversea Education*, Vol. XXVII, No. 1 (April 1955), p. 17.

51. Unesco, Roger Louis and Joseph Rovan, "Television and Tele-Clubs in Rural Communities, An Experiment in France," *Reports and Papers on Mass Communication*, No. 16 (July 1955); J. Dumazedier, *Television and Rural Adult Education* (1956); and Unesco, *Courier*, Vol. IX, No. 1 (July 1956, U. S. Edition), pp. 4-13.

52. *Unesco Features*, No. 192 (July 9, 1956), p. 1.

53. U. S. National Commission for Unesco, Document National Conference 5/WG/5, p. 7. The following pamphlets were prepared for these discussions: "The National Interest and Foreign Languages"; "The American Citizen's Stake in the Progress of Less Developed Areas of the World"; "The American as International Traveller and Host"; and "Our Moral and Spiritual Resources for International Cooperation."

CHAPTER VIII

1. This paradoxical title is not a contradiction in terms. "Free" means without cost rather than without control. "Compulsory" means obligatory by law.

2. Unesco, *The Right to Education*, Unesco and Its Program, VIII (1952), p. 7.

3. Unesco, G. E. R. Burroughs, "Evaluation of Fundamental Education Projects (A)," Document Unesco/SS/Eval/12 (1956, mimeographed), p. 3.

4. Unesco-IBE, XIVth International Conference on Public Education, "Proceedings and Recommendations," Pub. No. 135 (1951), p. 122.

5. Unesco, I. L. Kandel, *Raising the School-Leaving Age* (1951), pp. 11-17. A report of the Consultative Committee of the English Board of Education in 1926 declared: "There is no capital more productive than the energies of human beings. There is no investment more remunerative than expenditure devoted to developing them." The Committee on Education of the United States Chamber of Commerce stated in 1945: "The evidence is impressive that education is a causal factor as far as income is concerned. . . . The more the education increases, the

higher the income rises." See the Hadow Report on *Education of the Adolescent* (London, 1926), p. 145; and United States Chamber of Commerce, Committee on Education, *Education: An Investment in People* (1945), p. 16, both quoted in Kandel, pp. 23, 30.

6. See Chapters X, XI, and XII.

7. Afghanistan, Burma, Ceylon, India, Indonesia, Nepal, Pakistan, Philippines, Thailand, Cambodia, Laos, and Vietnam.

8. It is eight per cent in England and more than fifteen per cent in South Asia. Unesco, *Compulsory Education in South Asia and the Pacific* (1954), pp. 120, 14-15.

9. Ibid., pp. 26, 40, 80, 58, 60.

10. Ibid., pp. 95, 37, 43, 40, 51, 81, 94.

11. Ibid., pp. 94, 32, 82, 38, 44-45, 81.

12. Ibid., p. 79.

13. Egypt, Iraq, Jordan, Lebanon, Libya, Saudi Arabia, Syria, and Yemen.

14. Unesco, *Compulsory Education in the Arab States* (1956), pp. 72-73.

15. Unesco, "Report on the Conference on Free and Compulsory Education in the Arab Countries of the Middle East," Document Unesco/ED/144, p. 5.

16. Unesco, *Compulsory Education in the Arab States,* pp. 77-78.

17. Ibid., p. 29.

18. Ibid., pp. 32, 77.

19. Ibid., pp. 27, 77, 16.

20. Unesco, "Major Project on Extension of Primary Education in Latin America (Teacher-Training)," Document 44 EX/4 Add. II.

21. A year earlier an inter-American seminar on primary education had been held at Montevideo under the auspices of the Organization of American States, Unesco, and the government of Uruguay.

22. Unesco-IBE, Pub. No. 135, p. 129.

23. For the text of the recommendation see ibid., pp. 129-37.

24. Because of the unwillingness of the Arab States to join with Israel in an international gathering, this conference was not organized by Unesco but by Egypt. However, Unesco provided some technical services.

25. Unesco, "Report on the Regional Conference on Free and Compulsory Education in Latin America," Document Unesco/ED/148.

26. Unesco, Document Unesco/ED/144, p. 5; and *Compulsory Education in the Arab States,* p. 78.

27. Unesco, *Compulsory Education in South Asia and the Pacific* (1954), pp. 22, 23, 118-19.

28. Unesco, "Proposed Program and Budget for 1955-1956," Document 8C/5, p. 22.

29. United Nations, 520 A (VI), cited in Unesco, "Report on the Proposal to Establish an International Fund for Education, Science and Culture," Document 42 EX/23, p. 3.

30. Unesco, ibid., p. 3. President Eisenhower had recommended such a policy in a statement on April 16, 1953.

31. Unesco, Document 8C/Resolutions, p. 43 (Res. IV.1.7.5); "Report on the Establishment of an International Fund for Education, Science and Culture," Document 9C/PRG/20; and Document 9C/Resolutions, pp. 35-36 (Res. 7.61).

32. Unesco, "Proposed Program and Budget for 1957-1958," Document 9C/5 Corr. 1, pp. 15-23; and Document 9C/Resolutions, pp. 14-15.

33. Unesco, "Report of the Director General," Document 8C/3, pp. 74, 75; and "Report of the Director General, 1954," pp. 61-62.

34. Unesco, *Compulsory Education in the Arab States,* p. 80.

35. Unesco, *Courier,* Vol. VI, No. 1 (January 1953), p. 6.

36. Unesco, *Compulsory Education in the Arab States,* pp. 67-69.

37. Unesco, "Committee of Experts on Obstacles to Equality of Educational Opportunity for Women," Document Unesco/ED/Conf. 8/SR (mimeographed). Dr. Torres Bodet in an address to the Committee referred to the statement that "a child's education begins twenty years before he is born, with the education of his mother."

38. Unesco-IBE, XVth International Conference on Public Education, "Access of Women to Education," Pub. No. 141 (1952); and Unesco, *The Right to Education,* pp. 40-41.

39. United Nations, Economic and Social Council, Commission on the Status of Women, Eighth Session, "Access of Women to Education," Document E/CN.6/250 (1954).

40. Unesco, Document Unesco/ED/144, pp. 26-28.

41. Unesco, Maurice Duverger, *The Political Role of Women* (1955). For a general review of United Nations efforts in behalf of the political and educational rights of women, see Alva Myrdal, "Unesco and Women's Rights," Unesco, *Chronicle,* No. 6 (December 1955), pp. 3-8.

42. William D. Wall, "It's a Wise Teacher Who Knows His Pupils, Research and Psychology in Thailand," *Unesco Features,* No. 136 (11 February 1955), pp. 11-13; Unesco, "Report of the Director General, 1955," pp. 48-49; and W. D. Wall, "The International Institute of Child Study, Bangkok," Unesco, *Chronicle,* Vol. II, No. 6 (June 1956), pp. 171-77.

43. Unesco, "Proposed Program and Budget for 1955-1956," Document 8C/5, p. 23. See also, Unesco, *Education and Mental Health* (1955).

44. Of the countries which have eighty-five per cent or more of their children of school age enrolled in schools, the proportion of those in secondary school to the total covered in primary enrollment ranges from approximately twenty in Australia, Canada, and New Zealand to thirty-one for the United States and sixty-four for Japan; for those countries with fifty to eighty-four per cent of children enrolled, the proportion in secondary school is, for example, twenty-six in Greece and thirty-two in Puerto Rico; and for those countries with less than fifty per cent of their children enrolled, the proportion in secondary school ranges from five for Liberia, approximately fifteen for Egypt and Iraq, to twenty-five for Afghanistan. Unesco, *World Survey of Education* (1955), p. 23. A survey of educational progress in 1954-55 reported that enrollment of schools throughout the world increased eight per cent at the secondary level and five to six per cent at the primary level. Thus "secondary education continued to be the growing point in world educational development." Educational expenditures rose on the average eleven to twelve per cent. Teachers' salary scales improved in a third of the countries covered by the survey. Unesco-IBE, "International Yearbook of Education," Vol. XVII, 1955, Pub. No. 169, pp. 7-8.

45. Unesco-IBE, "XVIIIth International Conference on Public Education, 1955," Pub. No. 167, p. 126.

46. Unesco, Kandel, *Raising the School-Leaving Age,* pp. 19-21, 67-72; and "Report of the Director General," Document 7C/3, p. 112.

47. Unesco-IBE, XVIIth International Conference on Public Education, 1954, "Secondary Teacher Training," Pub. No. 154; "Secondary Teachers' Salaries," Pub. No. 157; and Unesco, "Report of the Director General, 1954," p. 62.

48. Unesco-IBE, XVth International Conference on Public Education, 1952, "Proceedings and Recommendations," Pub. No. 143, pp. 123, 125, 135.

49. Published by William Heinemann, London.

50. Unesco, "Report on the Study Conference on Science Teaching," (Bangkok, October 4-20, 1956), Document Unesco/NS/139.

51. For a review of science teaching in primary schools, see Unesco, *Education Abstracts,* Vol. VII, No. 7 (September 1955).

52. Unesco, "Report by the Director General, 1 July–10 October 1956," Document 45 EX/11, p. 15.

53. Unesco, J. P. Stephenson, *Suggestions for Science Teachers in Devastated Countries* (1948); and *Unesco Source Book for Science Teaching* (1956).

54. They were entitled *The Construction of Laboratory Apparatus—Workshop Designs with Specifications and Instructions* (Unesco: Paris, 1954). See also Unesco, "Report of the Director General," Document 7C/3, pp. 162-63.

55. *Unesco World Review,* No. 250 (28 November 1953), pp. 5-7; and Unesco, *Courier,* Vol. VI, No. 7 (July 1953), p. 15.

56. Unesco, *Courier,* Vol. VIII, No. 3 (August 1955, U. S. edition), pp. 9-11.

57. Earlier in 1949, it had surveyed the single field of political science, publishing a volume containing reports from some thirty countries, entitled *Contemporary Political Science,* A Survey of Methods, Research and Teaching (Paris: Unesco, 1950).

58. These studies were all published by Unesco in 1954 in the series *The University Teaching of Social Sciences.* A summary of the project is given in Unesco, "Development of Social Science Teaching, Progress Report and Analysis of Regional Round Tables," Document Unesco/SS/11 (1954). In 1955-56 similar surveys were made of the teaching of statistics, demography, public administration, and criminology.

59. Unesco, Document Unesco/SS/11, p. 2.

60. Unesco, *The Social Sciences,* Unesco and Its Program, XII, pp. 26-27; and Pierre Mendès-France and Gabriel Ardant, *Economics and Action* (New York: Columbia University Press, 1955).

61. Unesco, *The Social Sciences,* p. 26.

62. Unesco, "Report of the Director General," Document 7C/3, pp. 133-34; "Enquiry into the Teaching of Philosophy," Document Unesco/CUA/45 (1952); and *The Teaching of Philosophy* (1953).

63. Unesco, "The Place of Classical Studies and Humanities in Education," Document Unesco/PHS/ECH/1 (1955) (mimeographed); and Jean d'Ormesson, "The Diversity of Cultures and the World Community," Unesco, *Chronicle,* No. 3 (September 1955), pp. 9-15.

64. See Unesco, Edwin Ziegfeld (ed.), *Education and Art* (1953); and "The

Visual Arts in General Education, Report of the Bristol Seminar, 1951," Document Unesco/CUA/36. The teaching of art was also examined at the annual Unesco-IBE conference at Geneva in 1955. See Unesco-IBE, "XVIIIth International Conference on Public Education, 1955," Pub. No. 167, and "Teaching of Art in Primary and Secondary Schools," Pub. No. 165.

65. Unesco, "Report on the International Congress on the Professional Training of Musicians," Document Unesco/CUA/ME/4 (1953).

66. The United States was represented by groups from the Cleveland Heights School, Columbia University, Purdue University, Temple University, and the State Teachers College at Framingham, Massachusetts.

67. Unesco, *Music in Education* (1955), which contains the principal speeches and papers presented at the Conference; and "Report on the Role and Place of Music in the Education of Youth and Adults," Document Unesco/CUA/ME/3 (1953).

68. Delegates were present from Australia, Cambodia, China, India, Indonesia, Japan, Pakistan, the Philippines, and Thailand. Observers were also in attendance from France, United Kingdom, and United States.

69. Unesco, "The Arts and Crafts in General Education and Community Life," Document Unesco/CUA/66 (1955).

70. On the establishment of the Advisory Committee, see Unesco, "Proposed Program and Budget for 1955-1956," Document 8C/5, p. 25; "Draft Statutes of the International Advisory Committee on the School Curriculum," Document 42 EX/14; "Summary Records," Document 42 EX/SR. 1-27, pp. 247-51; "Resolutions and Decisions," Document 42 EX/Decisions, pp. 9-10; and Unesco, International Advisory Committee, Paris, September 1956, "Background Paper," Document Unesco/Int.Adv.Committee, School Curriculum, which had as attachments the text of the fourteen studies. For a summary review of recent Unesco activities concerning the curriculum, see "School Curriculum Reform," Unesco, *Chronicle*, Vol. II, No. 12 (December 1956), pp. 359-62.

Regarding the interdepartmental committee in the secretariat, see Unesco, "Report of the Director General, 1955," pp. 49, 60 (notes 20, 21).

71. Unesco, "Discussion Paper on the Program and Budget for 1957-58," Document 42 EX/8, p. 6.

72. Unesco, Sir Clutha Mackenzie, *World Braille Usage*, A Survey of Efforts towards Uniformity of Braille Notation (1954), pp. 9-10; and Unesco, *Courier*, Vol. V, No. 3 (March 1952), p. 11.

73. Ibid., p. 11.

74. Unesco, "Report of the Director General, 1954," p. 118.

75. In testimony before the House Subcommittee on International Organizations, June 25, 1956.

CHAPTER IX

1. "Nuclear energy" is a more accurate term than "atomic energy." The latter, however, is more generally used in public discussion. The two expressions will be used synonymously in this volume.

2. ECOSOC Resolution 318 (XI), 14 August 1950, is cited in Unesco, International Advisory Committee on Research in the Natural Sciences Program of Unesco, "Unesco's Methods of Action in the Field of International Scientific Research," Document Unesco/NS/114 (rev.) (1954), pp. 7-8.

3. Unesco, "Resolution on Unesco's Role in the Organization of International Research Centers," Document 5C/58; 5C/Proceedings, pp. 364-65; and 5C/Resolutions, p. 38 (Res. 2.21 and 2.211).

4. Quoted in speech by Luther H. Evans, "New Dimensions in International Cooperation: Unesco's Role," United States National Commission for Unesco, Fifth National Conference, Cincinnati, Ohio, November 3-5, 1955, Document National Conference 5/4, p. 4.

5. Belgium, Denmark, France, German Federal Republic, Greece, Italy, Netherlands, Norway, Sweden, Switzerland, United Kingdom, and Yugoslavia. Other states may be admitted by unanimous vote.

6. CERN, "First Report to Member States on the Organization and Financial Implications of Future European Cooperation in Nuclear Research," Document CERN/GEN/3 (1952), p. 10.

7. Unesco, *Courier*, Vol. VI, No. 12 (December 1953), p. 11; and Vol. VII, No. 10 (March 1955, U. S. edition), pp. 23-24. The first of these issues is devoted almost entirely and the second entirely to nuclear energy and atomic power.

8. United Nations General Assembly Resolution 810 (IX). For a summary review of the above developments, see Unesco, *Courier*, Vol. VII, No. 10 (March 1955, U. S. edition), pp. 5-9.

9. United Nations General Assembly Resolutions 334, 335, 912 and 913 (X), cited in Unesco, "Report of the Director General, 1955," pp. 31-32, 37. In order to coordinate the activities in the atomic field of the various agencies in the UN family, the UN Administrative Committee on Coordination (ACC), which brings together the heads of the specialized agencies under the chairmanship of the UN Secretary General, set up a special subcommittee. This subcommittee was linked to the Advisory Committee originally established in connection with the Geneva Conference through the Secretary General, who was the chairman of both groups. The responsibility of the Advisory Committee extended to all atomic energy matters except that of the effects of atomic radiation, which was the responsibility of the Scientific Committee established by the UN General Assembly at its tenth session in the fall of 1955.

10. Gerald Wendt, *Nuclear Energy and Its Uses in Peace,* Unesco and Its Program, XIV (1955), pp. 65-69.

11. Ibid., pp. 69-72.

12. Unesco, Document 8C/Resolutions, pp. 28-29 (Res. IV.1.2.22). For the resolution approved at the General Conference at New Delhi in 1956, see Document 9C/Resolutions, pp. 16-17 (Res. 2.32).

13. Unesco, "Final Report on the Meeting of Experts on Radio-Isotopes," Paris, June 23-24, 1955, Document Unesco/NS/131; and "Cooperation with the United Nations and the Specialized Agencies on Peaceful Uses of Atomic Energy," Document 43 EX/13, Add. 1.

"Isotope" comes from two Greek words meaning "same" and "place." The periodic table employed by chemists lists the chemical elements, giving usually one space to each element. But after the discovery of radium, it became clear that a number of elements existed in several varieties, the number of electrons being the same but with some difference in the structure and weight of the nucleus. These varieties in the same element were all listed in the "same place" in the periodic table and were called isotopes. Radioisotopes are "unstable and radioactive isotopes of the chemical elements." Wendt, *Nuclear Energy and Its Uses in Peace,* pp. 16, 75.

14. Unesco, "Unesco's Role in International Cooperation for the Utilization of Atomic Energy for Peaceful Purposes," Document 9C/PRG/1, p. 4.

15. Ibid., pp. 3, 4-6. For a review of what the proposed UN atomic energy agency and also the United States itself might do in the field of training and education, see the statement of Henry Cabot Lodge reported in Unesco, *Courier,* Vol. VII, No. 10 (March 1955, U. S. edition), pp. 16-18.

16. See footnote 7. In addition Unesco had published in 1955 a pamphlet for the general reader, *Nuclear Energy and Its Uses in Peace,* by Gerald Wendt.

17. Unesco, "Report on the Meeting of Experts on the Tasks, Organization and Equipment of the International Computation Center," Document Unesco/NS/138.

18. Unesco, Document 8C/Resolutions, p. 28 (Res. IV.1.2.221).

19. Unesco, "Proposed Program and Budget for 1957-1958," Document 9C/5 Corr. 1, pp. 27-28.

20. United States National Commission for Unesco, Fifth National Conference, Cincinnati, 1955, "Preliminary Report of the Work Group Sessions, Man Against the Desert," (typescript).

21. E. W. Golding, "Some Problems in Underdeveloped Areas," Unesco, *Impact,* Vol. VI, No. 2 (June 1955), p. 89. For a list of countries and territories having arid and semi-arid areas, see Unesco, "Report of the Second Session of the Advisory Committee on Arid Zone Research," 1951, Document Unesco/NS/88, pp. 26-28.

22. Unesco, *Courier,* Vol. V, No. 7 (July 1952), pp. 2-4.

23. *Unesco World Review,* No. 332 (25 June 1955), pp. 4-8.

24. Unesco, "Draft Resolution Presented by the Indian Delegation, International Institute of the Arid Zone (IIAZ)," Document 3C/20. In October 1947, the International Union of Theoretical and Applied Mechanics had called for the creation of such an institute. Other communications were received by Unesco from the International Union of Biological Sciences and the International Union of Geodesy and Geophysics.

25. Unesco, "Report on Activities of Unesco related to Arid Zone Research and Development," Document Unesco/NS/115 (1954). The Committee originally had seven members, which by 1956 had increased to ten. Representatives of the United Nations and the specialized agencies participate in its discussions. The basis for the Committee's work was broadened by the creation of a number of panels of honorary consultants, each member state being entitled to name up to three qualified experts. The members of these panels may be consulted from time to time by correspondence or appointed to sit on committees which may be convened by Unesco. As of 1954 panels had been set up for biology, climatology, energy sources and use, hydrology, animal ecology, and human ecology. Unesco, Arid Zone Program, "Activities Report for the Period 1 May–15 September 1954," Document Unesco/NS/120, p. 4.

26. By 1956 the following reports had been published by Unesco: *Reviews of Research on Arid Zone Hydrology; Proceedings of the Ankara Symposium on Arid Zone Hydrology; Directory of Institutions Engaged in Arid Zone Research; Reviews of Research on Problems of Utilization of Saline Water; Plant Ecology, Reviews of Research; Plant Ecology, Proceedings of the Montpellier Symposium; Wind and Solar Energy, Proceedings of the New Delhi Symposium;* and *Human and Animal Ecology, Reviews of Research.*

27. Unesco, *Courier*, Vol. V, No. 7 (July 1952), pp. 2-4; and *Unesco Features*, No. 99 (12 June 1953), pp. 11-13.

28. For efforts to harness wind and solar energy in arid areas, see articles by E. W. Golding, Gerald Wendt, and Daniel Behrman in Unesco, *Courier*, Vol. VIII, No. 6 (November 1955, U. S. edition), pp. 17-27.

29. *Unesco World Review*, No. 332 (25 June 1955), p. 6. For a brief summary of the recommendations approved at this symposium, see Gerald Wendt, "Science Attacks the Desert," *Unesco Features*, No. 145 (17 June 1955), pp. 18-23. A more detailed statement on the recommendations is given in United States National Commission for Unesco, "Man Against the Desert," Document 5/WG/10, pp. 10-15. The complete record of the proceedings and recommendations is presented in *The Future of Arid Lands* (Washington: American Association for the Advancement of Science, 1956).

30. For a review of experiments in rain-making in various countries and reference to a 1953 report on the question by the World Meteorological Organization, see Unesco, *Courier*, Vol. VIII, No. 6 (November 1955, U. S. edition), pp. 48-50, 52-55. This issue of the *Courier* is entirely devoted to the question of arid zones. On the 1956 meeting in Australia of the Advisory Committee, see Unesco, "Report of the Eleventh Session of the Advisory Committee on Arid Zone Research," Document Unesco/NS/140.

31. Unesco, Document Unesco/NS/115, p. 2.

32. Bodil and Knut Schmidt-Nielsen, "The Camel—Facts and Fables," Unesco, *Courier*, Vol. VIII, No. 6 (November 1955, U. S. edition), pp. 29-32, 63.

33. Unesco, "Report of the Seventh Session of the Advisory Committee on Arid Zone Research," 1954, Document Unesco/NS/117, Annex I; and Document Unesco/NS/120, p. 3.

34. Ibid.

35. WMO, Technical Note No. 1 (WMO-No. 24.T.P.7); and Technical Note No. 4, cited in Unesco, Arid Zone Program, "Activities Report for the Period 1 November 1953—15 April 1954," Document Unesco/NS/116, p. 2; and Document Unesco/NS/120, p. 4.

36. ECOSOC, Resolution E/2603 of June 2, 1952; and Resolution of August 2, 1954 [533 (XVIII)], cited in Unesco, Arid Zone Program, "Activities Report for the Period 25 March–5 September 1952," Document Unesco/NS/100, pp. 1-3; and Document Unesco/NS/120, p. 2.

37. Unesco, Documents Unesco/NS/100, pp. 3-5; "Report of the Fifth Session of the Advisory Committee on Arid Zone Research," 1953, Document Unesco/NS/109, p. 6; and Document Unesco/NS/115, p. 4.

38. Unesco, Document 9C/5, pp. 67-75; and 9C/Resolutions, pp. 17-18 (Res. 2.61).

39. The Advisory Committee had recommended in 1954 that attention be given to the possibility of securing from member states profiting from Unesco's arid zone activities direct financial contributions for research projects, thus freeing Unesco's resources for an attack on other problems. The Committee cited the wisdom of a policy which would permit countries benefiting from any particular activity of Unesco to contribute to that activity. Unesco, International Advisory Committee on Research in the Natural Sciences Program of Unesco, First Meeting, 12-15 April 1954, "Report of the Secretariat," Document Unesco/NS/118, pp. 4-5.

40. For a bibliography and a number of abstracts of articles on the education of the children of nomads and migrant workers, see Unesco, *Education Abstracts,* "The Education of Nomads and Migrants," Vol. VIII, No. 9 (November 1956). The nomad groups discussed include those in Iran, Jordan, the Hoggar area of French Sahara and other parts of Africa, and the Lapps of Finland, Norway, and Sweden. The migrant groups discussed were the families living on river and canal barges in Belgium, France, Germany, and the Netherlands, and migrant agricultural workers in the United States.

41. Gerald Wendt, "Unesco Begins Research Study on Humid Tropics," *Unesco Features,* No. 192 (9 July 1956), p. 7.

42. Bolivia, Brazil, Colombia, Ecuador, France, Holland, Italy, Peru, and Venezuela.

43. See Paulo E. de Berrêdo Carneiro, *O Instituto Internacional de Hiléia Amazônica* (Rio de Janeiro, 1951). The text of the statement by the General Staff is given in pp. 90-100, that of the additional protocol in pp. 53-63, and that of the convention as modified by the protocol in pp. 64-81.

44. Unesco, Humid Tropics Research Program, "Activities Report for the Period January 1955 to March 1956," Document Unesco/NS/136; "Report by the Secretariat on the Preparatory Meeting of Specialists in Humid Tropics Research, Kandy, Ceylon, March 1956," Document Unesco/NS/137, and Unesco, *Chronicle,* Vol. III, No. 3 (March 1957), p. 68.

45. Marcel Florkin, "Ten Years of Science at Unesco," Unesco, *Impact,* Vol. VII, No. 3 (September 1956), p. 135.

46. Unesco, *Courier,* Vol. VIII, No. 3 (August 1955, U. S. edition), pp. 23-26.

47. Unesco, Document Unesco/NS/114 (rev.), p. 6.

48. Unesco, Document Unesco/NS/118, p. 8.

49. Unesco, Document 8C/Resolutions, p. 28 (Res. IV.1.2.22).

50. Unesco, *Chronicle,* Vol. II, No. 7 (July 1956), p. 219.

51. Unesco, "Report of the First Session of the International Advisory Committee on Marine Sciences, Lima, Peru, 22-24 October 1956," Document Unesco/NS/141.

52. E. Beaglehole, "Evaluation Techniques for Induced Technological Change," Unesco, *International Social Science Bulletin,* Vol. VII, No. 3 (1955), p. 376.

53. See Unesco, "Unesco and the Social Consequences of Technical Change," *International Social Science Bulletin,* Vol. IV, No. 2 (Summer 1952), pp. 370-80; and Unesco, *The Social Sciences,* Unesco and Its Program, XII, pp. 41-46. The three studies mentioned above were all published in the Unesco series *Technology and Tensions:* A. Kahler, *Education in a Technological Society;* Jerome Scott

and R. Lynton, *The Community Factor in Modern Technology;* and Margaret Mead, *Cultural Patterns and Technical Change.* The third study was also published as a pocket book by the New American Library in 1955.

54. Unesco, *The Social Sciences,* p. 45. For the findings of this group see M. E. Opler, *Social Aspects of Technical Assistance in Operation,* (Paris: Unesco, 1954), with a preface by the Director of the Conference, Walter H. C. Laves.

55. Unesco, "Report of the Director General, January–February 1956," Document 43 EX/10, p. 25.

56. Unesco, *International Social Science Bulletin,* Vol. V, No. 4 (1953), pp. 766-86.

57. Unesco, "Conference of Social Scientists on the Social Impact of Industrialization and Urban Conditions in Africa," Abidjan, Ivory Coast, 29 September–7 October 1954, Document Unesco/SS/13. The content of the volume *Social Implications of Industrialization and Urbanization in Africa South of the Sahara* published by Unesco, Paris, 1956 is summarized in Unesco, *Chronicle,* Vol. II, Nos. 8-9 (August-September 1956), pp. 273-77.

58. Unesco, *The Social Sciences,* p. 46. A review of the problem of industrialization in Asia is given in Unesco, "Report by the Director General on the Joint UN/Unesco Seminar on Urbanization in the ECAFE Region, Bangkok, Thailand, 8-18 August, 1956," Document Unesco/SS/19.

59. Unesco, *International Social Science Bulletin,* Vol. VI, No. 1 (1954), "The International Research Office for the Study of the Social Implications of Technological Change," pp. 86-91. The Office issues a monthly mimeographed bulletin entitled *Information.*

60. Ibid., pp. 86-88.

61. Unesco, "Establishment of a Research Center for South Asia on the Social Implications of Industrialization," Document 42 EX/18; "Summary Records," Document 42 EX/SR. 1-27, pp. 84-92; Document 42 EX/Decisions, p. 12; and Unesco, *Chronicle,* Vol. II, Nos. 8-9 (August-September 1956), pp. 267-68.

CHAPTER X

1. Unesco, Preparatory Commission, "Conference for the Establishment of the United Nations Educational, Scientific and Cultural Organization," London, 1945 (London, 1946), pp. 22, 28.

2. For example, see: Unesco, "General Conference, First Session," Document Unesco/C/30, Resumé of Education Sub-Commission Report, pp. 223, 224; "Resolutions," Document 2C/132, Vol. II, pp. 20-21; "Resolutions," Document 3C/110, Vol. II, pp. 18, 19; Document 4C/Resolutions, pp. 15, 16; Document 5C/Resolutions, pp. 25, 35-36; Document 6C/Resolutions, pp. 19-20; Document 7C/Resolutions, pp. 19-20; Document 8C/Resolutions, p. 27; Document 9C/Resolutions, pp. 12, 13.

3. The appropriation bill for the Department of State covering the period July 1, 1952–June 30, 1953, included an amendment proposed by the late Senator McCarran, stipulating that no funds provided in the bill should be granted to any international organization engaged in the promotion or the furtherance of the

doctrine of one-world government or one-world citizenship. In connection with the circulation in the United States of such a charge against Unesco, a special committee of the American Legion concluded after a careful and comprehensive investigation that "Unesco is not, and does not support or tend to World Government." American Legion, *The United Nations Educational, Scientific and Cultural Organization (UNESCO)*, A Report by Special Committee on Covenant of Human Rights and United Nations to the National Executive Committee, the American Legion (Indianapolis, Indiana, May 5, 1955), p. 25. However, the national convention of the American Legion on October 12, 1955, adopted a resolution ignoring the findings of its special committee and attacking the alleged "educational materials of Unesco propounding world citizenship and adherence to a nebulous world government as a criteria of education of American citizens. . . ." *New York Times*, October 14, 1955, p. 2.

4. *1945 London Conference*, p. 24.

5. Unesco, "Final Report of the Expert Committee on Education for International Understanding and Cooperation," Document Unesco/ED/142, p. 4.

6. Unesco, Lyman Bryson, "Report on International Understanding" (Summer 1947, mimeographed), p. 1. The content of the memorandum is summarized in Unesco, "Report of the Director General," Document 2C/4, pp. 37-38.

7. One writer has argued, "International understanding, like any other kind, would seem to be a tool and technique which can be used in various ways, depending on one's purpose. If we increase our understanding of Russian national character, the nature of the Stalinist regime and the psychology of its leaders, we shall be better able to promote peace with the Kremlin or to wage war against it. The understanding in itself, however, like all knowledge, does not automatically lead to or preclude either of these courses." Morroe Berger, " 'Understanding National Character'—and War," *Commentary* (New York), Vol. XI (April 1951), p. 386. Otto Klineberg noted the two kinds of understanding in "The Unesco Project on International Tensions," Unesco, *International Social Science Bulletin*, Vol. I, No. 1-2 (1949), p. 12.

8. From 1950 to 1955 Unesco awarded thirty-one fellowships to encourage teaching about the United Nations in the schools of member states. Under these, teachers and other educational leaders visited the headquarters of the United Nations and some of the specialized agencies for a first-hand study of their work. Mention has already been made (Chapter V, pp. 93-94) of *Study Abroad* and other Unesco publications which provide information on the world-wide character of this development of face-to-face contacts.

9. Unesco, *Workers Abroad*, Vol. II (1953) and Vol. III (1957); "The Group Study Tour as an Instrument in Adult Education," Document Unesco/EXP/39 (1954); and *Other Men's Ways*, Unesco and Its Program, XIII (1955), pp. 15-16.

10. Unesco, *Other Men's Ways*, pp. 16-17; "Report of the Director General," Document 7C/3, pp. 238-39; and "Prospectus on Youth Travel Grants, 1957," Document Unesco/EXP/43.

11. Unesco, "Report of the Director General," Document 2C/4, pp. 38-40. During 1948 three other seminars were organized by Unesco: one at Podebrady, Czechoslovakia, to explore the psychological bases for the development of a world outlook among children; another at Ashridge College in England, to examine the professional, moral, and social training of teachers; and a third at Adelphi College in

New York, to consider teaching about the United Nations. This third seminar will be discussed in Chapter XII.

12. For the seminar on geography, see Unesco, *Geography Teaching for International Understanding* (n.d.); and *A Handbook of Suggestions on the Teaching of Geography* (1951). For the seminar on history, see C. P. Hill, *Suggestions on the Teaching of History* (Paris: Unesco, 1953). For the seminar on modern languages, see Unesco, "An Account of the International Seminar on the Contribution of the Teaching of Modern Languages towards Education for Living in a World Community," Document Unesco/ED/132 (1954).

13. Unesco, "A Comparative Study of Curricula in History, Geography and Social Studies," Document Unesco/ED/108 (1951), p. 1.

14. Karl W. Bigelow, "Unesco Seminars," *Harvard Educational Review*, Vol. XX, No. 3 (Summer 1950), pp. 158-68. (This special issue was devoted entirely to the educational program of Unesco, and carried articles among others on fundamental education, adult education, higher education, and education for international understanding.) In some cases only a minority of seminar participants, it was estimated, possessed the intellectual capacity for serious discussion, or the qualifications which would make them on return to their home country persons of significant influence.

15. Unesco, Document Unesco/ED/142, p. 6.

16. Unesco, *Courier*, Vol. I, No. 4 (May 1948), p. 4.

17. France, Commission nationale française pour l'Unesco, *L'Enseignement de l'histoire et la compréhension internationale* and *Recommendations pour l'enseignement de l'histoire* (Paris: Centre National de Documentation pédagogique, 1952).

18. Unesco, "Report of the Director General," Document 7C/3, p. 222.

19. C. F. Strong, *Teaching for International Understanding, An Examination of Methods and Materials*, A Statement Prepared for the U.K. National Commission for Unesco (London: H.M. Stationery Office, 1952).

20. France, *L'Enseignement des langues vivantes et la compréhension internationale*, Mémoires et Documents Scolaires, Nouvelle série, No. 2 (Paris: Service d'Edition et de Vente des Publications de l'Education Nationale, n.d.).

21. Unesco, *The Teaching of Modern Languages* (1955); and "A Bibliography on the Teaching of Modern Languages," *Educational Studies and Documents*, No. XIII (1955).

22. Frank E. Sorenson, "A Report from the Montreal Seminar," *Social Education*, Vol. XV, No. 4 (Washington: National Council for the Social Studies, April 1951), p. 190. This publication also contains (pp. 171-75) a general description and summary of Unesco's seminar program through 1950.

23. Letter of December 1, 1955, from William Benton to Luther H. Evans. The text of the Benton letter is summarized in the *New York Times*, December 4, 1955.

24. Letter of December 22, 1955, from Dr. Evans to Mr. Benton.

25. For reviews of the movement for revision of textbooks and teaching materials, see Merrill F. Hartshorn, "The Improvement of Instructional Materials," *Yearbook* (Washington: National Council for the Social Studies, 1954), pp. 441-73; and Unesco, *A Handbook for the Improvement of Textbooks and Teaching Materials* (1949), pp. 9-15.

26. For the text, see ibid., pp. 105-06.

27. Ibid., pp. 39-41, 100-02, 107-08, 110-11; and Unesco, Haakon Vigander, *Mutual Revision of History Textbooks in the Nordic Countries* (1950); and "Norwegian National Commission for Unesco, A Study of History and Geography School Textbooks," Document Unesco/ED/117 (1952).

28. Canada-United States Committee on Education, *A Study of National History Textbooks Used in the Schools of Canada and the United States* (Washington: American Council on Education, 1947).

29. By August 1953 nine member states had made such studies and reported on them to the Unesco secretariat. For examples, see Dorothy McClure, *The Treatment of International Agencies in School History Textbooks in the United States* (Washington: Unesco Relations Staff, Department of State, 1951); and Unesco, New Zealand National Commission for Unesco, "New Zealand School Textbooks and International Understanding," Document Unesco/ED/118 (1952). For the text of a model plan and a report on bilateral and multilateral textbook accords, see Unesco, *A Handbook for the Improvement of Textbooks and Teaching Materials,* pp. 69-90 and 100-19.

30. For a report on the seminar, see Unesco, *Better History Textbooks,* Unesco and Its Program, VI (n.d.). The reports of the five United States participants are given in *Social Education,* Vol. XV, No. 4 (April 1951), pp. 175-88.

31. Unesco, "Bilateral Consultations for the Improvement of History Textbooks," *Educational Studies and Documents,* No. IV (July 1953), p. 39. Reports have been published on the reciprocal evaluation of textbooks between France and Italy; Belgium and Norway; and between Germany on the one hand and respectively France, Italy, Japan, Norway, Turkey, United Kingdom, United States, and Yugoslavia. See also *Internationales Jahrbuch für Geschichtesunterricht,* Vols. I-III (Braunschweig: Albert Limbach Verlag, 1949-54).

32. Unesco, *Educational Studies and Documents,* No. IV, pp. 15-19. Tentative agreement on these points had been reached in earlier discussions in 1935 but the attitude of the Hitler regime and then World War II blocked final approval.

33. Ibid., pp. 19-22.

34. For a review of the movement for textbook revision in Germany, see Georg Eckert, "History Instruction and International Understanding: The Problem of International Textbook Improvement," *Yearbook* (Washington: National Council for the Social Studies, 1954), pp. 431-40.

35. Robert LaFollette, "History Textbooks and International Understanding," *Social Education* (Washington: National Council for the Social Studies) Vol. XVII, No. 5 (May 1953), pp. 201-06.

36. Unesco, *Educational Studies and Documents,* No. IV, pp. 36, 38. For a review of Unesco efforts toward revision of textbooks, see Herbert J. Abraham, "The Improvement of History Textbooks in the Interest of International Understanding," Unesco, *Chronicle,* Vol. II, No. 1 (January 1956), pp. 9-14.

37. Unesco, "Draft Plan for the Study of School Textbooks, Submitted to Member States and National Commissions under Resolution 1.331 of the 1953-1954 Program of Unesco," Document Unesco/ED/130.

38. The discussions of the May 1956 meeting are reported in Unesco, "The Treatment of Asia in Western Textbooks and Teaching Materials, Report of an International Committee of Educators," Document Unesco/ED/147. The conclu-

sions of the meeting are summarized by its chairman in Merrill F. Hartshorn, "Asia in Western Textbooks," *NEA Journal,* Vol. 46, No. 2 (February 1957). For an over-all report on the surveys made in individual countries, see Ronald Fenton, "Asian History through Western Glasses," Unesco, *Courier,* Vol. VIII, No. 12 (May 1956, U. S. edition), pp. 8-13.

39. Particularly E. Bruley of France, E. H. Dance of Great Britain, Georg Eckert of the German Federal Republic, and Haakon Vigander of Norway.

40. D. W. Brogan, "A Warning against Deodorized History," Unesco, *Courier,* Vol. VIII, No. 12 (May 1956, U. S. edition), p. 22.

41. Unesco, "General Conference, First Session," p. 32.

42. For Unesco activities in Japan 1948-50, see Unesco, "Report of the Director General," Document 3C/3, pp. 100-01; Document 4C/3, pp. 115-17; and Document 6C/3, pp. 156-61.

43. Unesco, "Resolutions," Document 3C/110, Vol. II, pp. 63-66; and Document 4C/Resolutions, pp. 75-79.

44. Unesco, Document 5C/Proceedings, pp. 470-71.

45. Unesco, Document 6C/Resolutions, p. 36 (Res. 9.51).

46. Unesco, "Unesco Institutes in Germany, Report by the Executive Board," Document 7C/PRG/2, pp. 4-5.

47. Each board would consist of fourteen members. Six would be Germans, seven non-Germans from different countries, and the remaining member a representative of the Unesco Director General. While the German state and municipal authorities would provide the necessary buildings and furniture, German federal sources would furnish twenty per cent of the budget, whose total was fixed at $679,000 for 1951-52, the remaining eighty per cent to come from other countries. Contributions equivalent to the following amounts had been offered: Government of Lebanon, $5,000; private donors in the Philippines, $1,025; Iran, $572; Government of France, $75,000; United States High Commission in Germany, $350,000; Federal Government of Switzerland, $10,000; and India, $210; for a total of $441,597. Unesco, "Report of the Director General," Document 6C/3, pp. 147-52; and Document 7C/3, pp. 226-29.

48. It has been noted in Chapter VI that the work of the Social Science Institute, but for its origin, would have been discussed there as part of Unesco's program for the advancement of knowledge.

49. The original grants from various countries could carry the Institutes for little more than two years (until March 1954), and it was known that the major part of these grants would not be renewed. To assure continuance of the centers, the 1952, 1954, and 1956 sessions of the General Conference successively approved contributions from the Unesco budget, the last one voting for the 1957-58 period $45,000 annually for the Institute of Education, $42,000 for the Social Science Institute, and $32,000 for the Youth Institute.

50. The members of this committee were Professor Ingemar Düring of Sweden, Dean C. J. Nuesse of the United States, and Professor Louis Verniers of Belgium. Its findings were supplemented by individual reports prepared by the three Institutes. Unesco, "Unesco Institutes in the German Federal Republic," Document 42 EX/11, Annex I, II/A, II/B, II/C.

51. The following publications have been issued by the Institute: (a) *Das Dorf*

im Spannungsfeld industrieller Entwicklung, by G. Wurzbacher and R. Pflaum, Ferdinand Enke Verlag, Stuttgart. No. 1 in the Institute Social Science Series. (b) *Soziale Verflechtungen in der Bundesrepublik,* by Erich Reigrotzki, J. C. B. Mohr (Paul Siebeck), Tübingen. No. 2 in the Institute Social Science Series. (c) *Recherches sur la Famille,* Volume I, J. C. B. Mohr (Paul Siebeck), Tübingen. No. 3 in the Institute Social Science Series. Articles in languages used by authors, English, French, or German, with abstracts in companion languages. (d) *Die politische Rolle der Frau in Deutschland,* by Gabriele Bremme, Vandenhoeck und Ruprecht, Göttingen. No. 4 in Institute Social Science Series. (e) *Bibliographie relative à la Mobilité interne et aux Migrations internationales des Travailleurs dans les Pays de l'Europe occidentale depuis la fin du XIXème Siècle,* a document of 350 pages printed by the European Coal and Steel Community, Luxembourg.

52. Consultative Assembly of the Council of Europe, Eighth Ordinary Session, Recommendation 129 (1957), Document 611.

53. Unesco, Document 42 EX/11, Annex I, pp. 7-11, and Annex II/A.

54. Unesco, "Resolutions," Document 2C/132, Vol. II, p. 27 (Res. 5.7). For a later and fuller statement of its purposes, see Unesco, "Annual Report from the Chairman of the International Commission for a History of the Scientific and Cultural Development of Mankind, Addressed to the Director General," Document 6C/PRG/12, pp. 11-12. Indian scholars looked to the history to "correct the myopia of Western savants, so many of whom, unable to see beyond Greece, have withheld from the East and especially from India the credit due for cultural priority." E. M. Hough, "Unesco and World Unity and Peace," *Transaction No. 13* (Basaganudi, Bangalore: Indian Institute of Culture, June 1952), p. 5.

55. Unesco, "Resolutions," Document 2C/132, p. 27. The Conference of Allied Ministers of Education had earlier discussed a volume on "the spiritual development of Europe as something to which each nation in the Continent has contributed its share." *Allied Plan for Education,* The Story of the Conference of Allied Ministers of Education (London: H.M. Stationery Office, 1945), pp. 26-27.

56. Unesco, Document 5C/Resolutions, p. 42 (Res. 4.123); and Document 6C/PRG/12, pp. 1-5.

57. Homi Bhabha (India), Carl J. Burckhardt (Switzerland), Paulo E. Carneiro (Brazil), Julian Huxley (United Kingdom), Charles Morazé (France), Mario Praz (Italy), Ralph E. Turner (United States), Silvio Zavala (Mexico), and Constantin K. Zurayk (Syria). Guy Métraux has served as Secretary General of the Commission.

58. For the text see Unesco, "Annual Report of the President of the International Commission for a Scientific and Cultural History of Mankind Addressed to the Director General," Document 7C/PRG/9, pp. 10-12. The Statutes of the Commission as drafted in 1952 and amended in 1954 are given in Unesco, "Annual Report of the President of the International Commission for a History . . . to the Director General," Document 8C/PRG/7, Annex I, pp. 12-15.

59. Unesco, "Annual Report of the President of the International Commission for a History of the Scientific and Cultural Development of Mankind," Document 9C/PRG/9 (rev.), p. 4.

60. Unesco, Document 9C/PRG/9 (rev.), pp. 9-13. Following criticism in the United States, largely from Catholic sources, that the history would have an anti-

religious bias, the President of the Commission, Professor Carneiro, issued a statement stressing the factual and objective character of the work, and declaring, "No Catholic, Protestant, Muslim, Jew, Hindu, Buddhist, or Confucian need fear to find in it interpretations of history which reveal any kind of bias on the part of the numerous collaborators invited to write the different chapters in this great treatise." Unesco, Document 7C/PRG/9, p. 22. Professor Carneiro also reported having been given a private audience with His Holiness Pope Pius XII, during which the project was discussed. Subsequently the Vatican had appointed two corresponding members to participate in the work of the Commission: Monsignor Blanchet, Rector of the Catholic Institute in Paris, and Father Antonio Messineo, editor of *Civiltà Cattolica,* in Rome. Ibid., p. 3.

61. For the original detailed outline of the contents of the work and its subsequent modification, see respectively Unesco, Documents 7C/PRG/9, pp. 13-21; and 8C/PRG/7, pp. 5-7. The following persons have served as author-editors: Vol. I: Jacquetta Hawkes (Mrs. J. B. Priestley) (United Kingdom), Part I; Sir Leonard Woolley (United Kingdom), Part II; Vol. II: Professor Luigi Pareti (Italy); associates: Professors Paolo Brezzi and Luciano Petech (Italy); Vol. III: Professor Gaston Wiet (France); co-author-editors: Dr. Vadime Elisséeff and Professor Philippe Wolff (France); Vol. IV: Professor Louis Gottschalk (USA); associates: Professors Loren C. MacKinney and Earl H. Pritchard (USA); Vol. V: Professor Charles Morazé (France); associates: Professor Georges Balandier (France), Dr. Jorge Basadre (Peru), Miss J. Cuisinier (France), Dr. Louis Dumont (France), Mr. A. Mazahéri (Iran), Dr. René Taton (France), Professor S. H. Brockunier (USA); Vol. VI: Professor Caroline Ware (USA); co-author-editors: Dr. K. M. Panikkar (India), Professor J. Romein (Netherlands). *Journal of World History,* Vol. III, No. 3 (1957).

62. Unesco, Document 9C/PRG/9 (rev.).

CHAPTER XI

1. Unesco, *Human Rights, Comments and Interpretations* (London and New York: Allan Wingate, 1949), p. 12.

2. U. S. National Commission for Unesco, "Summary Minutes of the Fifth Meeting," Boston, September 27-29, 1948, Document NC 5/47, SM/4-5, p. 25.

3. Unesco, "General Conference, First Session," Document Unesco/C/30, p. 222.

4. See *Human Rights, Comments and Interpretations,* pp. 258-72, particularly p. 258. This volume contains, in addition to the report of the committee entitled "The Grounds of an International Declaration of Human Rights," some thirty contributions to the Unesco symposium. For first-hand accounts by Richard McKeon of the development of Unesco activities in the field of philosophy and the humanities, see Lyman Bryson, Louis Finkelstein, Harold D. Lasswell, R. M. MacIver (eds.), *Foundations of World Organization: A Political and Cultural Appraisal,* Eleventh Symposium of the Conference on Science, Philosophy and Religion (New York: Harper & Bros., 1953); pp. 318-29; and Louis Finkelstein (ed.), *Thirteen Americans: Their Spiritual Autobiographies* (New York: Harper & Bros., 1953), pp. 107-110.

5. Richard McKeon (ed.), *Democracy in a World of Tensions* (Paris: Unesco, 1951), p. vii.

6. Ibid., p. viii. This volume includes in addition to the report of the committee a number of individual responses. It was published by Unesco in English and was translated at the initiative of Israel and Japan into the languages of those countries.

7. For the inquiry on liberty, see Fédération Internationale des Sociétés de Philosophie, *Enquête sur la Liberté* (Paris: Hermann & Cie., 1953); and H. J. Pos, "Unesco Report on the Investigation Concerning Freedom," *Journal of Philosophy*, Vol. XLIX, No. 2 (January–December 1952), pp. 29-45. Philosophic journals in six countries—Belgium, Denmark, France, Italy, Switzerland, and the United States—were asked to take up specific aspects of liberty. The examination of the concept of law "as a fundamental factor in human co-operation in international affairs and in the activities of the United Nations" has gone through several stages. See International Council for Philosophy and Humanistic Studies, *Bulletin, 1951-53* (Paris: Unesco, n.d.), pp. 25-26.

8. This problem comes close to the question of "stereotypes" studied in the social tensions project (see pp. 255-56 of this chapter). The two undertakings were complementary to each other. The project on "stereotypes" was concerned with the image formed by one people of another. The comparative study of cultures was concerned with the values expressed in the art, philosophy, religion, and history of one culture, and their relations with similar values in other cultures.

9. Unesco, "Resolutions," Document 2C/132, pp. 25-26; and "Resolutions," Document 3C/110, Vol. II, p. 25.

10. Unesco, *Interrelations of Cultures,* Their Contribution to International Understanding (1953), pp. 381-82. The conclusions of the committee of experts are given on pp. 379-82. See also *Foundations of World Organization*, pp. 327-29.

11. Unesco, *Humanism and Education in East and West* (1953), pp. 22-26. This source includes a report of the discussions and a series of essays written by the participants. See also Unesco, "Report of the Director General," Document 7C/3, pp. 218-19. One result of the New Delhi meeting was the decision of the Indian Philosophical Congress to discuss at its meeting at Colombo in December 1954 the question of "Human Relations and International Obligations in East and West." Unesco, "Report of the Director General," Document 8C/3, pp. 127-28; and "Report of the Director General, 1954," p. 102. For the report on the symposium at Colombo, of a series of round-table discussions in India which preceded it, and of a round table in the United States which followed it, see Richard McKeon, "Human Relations and International Obligations," *Journal of Philosophy*, Vol. LIII, No. 2 (1956), pp. 29-55. The papers prepared for the Colombo symposium were published in N. A. Nikam (ed.), *Human Relations and International Obligations* (Bangalore, India, 1956).

12. See Unesco, *The Old and the New World* (1956); and *Le Nouveau Monde et l'Europe* (Neuchâtel, Switzerland: Editions de la Baconnière, 1954). In 1936 the Commission on Intellectual Cooperation of the League of Nations had sponsored a scholarly conference at Buenos Aires on the relations between Europe and Latin America. Since 1950 Unesco has cooperated with *Rencontres Internationales* in annual conferences at Geneva. Its limited financial assistance has made possible a

wider geographic representation at the sessions. The 1955 meeting of *Rencontres Internationales,* which focused on the role in contemporary cultural life of the media of mass communication, is reviewed in Jacques Havet, "The Tenth of the Rencontres Internationales de Genève," *Unesco Chronicle,* No. 6 (December 1955), pp. 9-12.

13. Burma, Cambodia, Ceylon, India, Indonesia, Laos, Pakistan, Philippines, Thailand, and Vietnam.

14. Arthur Goodfriend, *Two Sides of One World* (Washington: Government Printing Office, 1957), p. 72; and Unesco, "Report of the Director General, 1 January-30 June 1956," Document 9C/3, pp. 100-03.

15. Chapter III, pp. 57-58; and Indian National Commission for Cooperation with Unesco, *Proceedings of the First Conference* (Government of India, Ministry of Education, 1954), p. 7.

16. The use of educational activities to promote international understanding is discussed also in Chapter X, pp. 226-43 and Chapter XII, pp. 263-70.

17. Unesco, "Proposed Program and Budget for 1957-1958," Document 9C/5, Corr. 1, pp. 49-63; and *Unesco Chronicle,* Vol. II, No. 11 (November 1956), pp. 330-31.

18. Unesco, Document 9C/Resolutions, pp. 27-28, (Res. 4.81).

19. Unesco, *Arts and Letters,* Unesco and Its Program, X, p. 11.

20. U. S. National Commission for Unesco, *Newsletter,* Vol. III, No. 21 (December 28, 1956), p. 3.

21. According to some social scientists, the concept of tensions is valid when applied to individual behavior, but it is little more than a metaphor when transferred to relations within or between social groups. When used in relation to the mental state of an individual, it signifies the strain resulting from the prospect of two discordant future events. If applied to group relations, it indicates the effort to achieve two divergent or inconsistent objectives. Historically speaking, however, the term was initially adopted by Unesco as a general heading for three problem areas involving, respectively, aggressive nationalism, shifts in population, and the impact of modern technology and industrialization. See articles by Jessie Bernard, T. H. Pear, and Raymond Aron, and an extensive bibliography prepared by the Centre d'Etudes Sociologiques of Paris, in International Sociological Association, *The Nature of Conflict,* Studies on the Sociological Aspects of International Tensions (Paris: Unesco, 1957); Lyman Bryson, Louis Finkelstein, R. M. MacIver (eds.), *Learning and World Peace* (New York and London: Harper & Bros., 1948), comment by Rudolf Allers, p. 2, footnote; and Quincy Wright, "The Importance of the Study of International Tensions," *International Social Science Bulletin,* Vol. II, No. 1 (Spring 1950), p. 90.

22. Otto Klineberg, "The Unesco Project on International Tensions," *International Social Science Bulletin,* Vol. I, No. 1-2 (1949), p. 12.

23. Loc. cit.

24. Unesco, "Resolutions," Document 2C/132, p. 25 (Res. 5.1). A summary review of the development of the tensions project is given in *The Nature of Conflict,* pp. 9-32.

25. Otto Klineberg, *Tensions Affecting International Understanding* (New York: Social Science Research Council, 1950); and Hadley Cantril, *Tensions that*

Cause Wars (Urbana: University of Illinois Press, 1950). Both Dr. Cantril and Dr. Klineberg served in the Unesco secretariat as directors of the Social Tensions Project. Dr. Klineberg was succeeded by Dr. Robert C. Angell of the University of Michigan, who served also as Acting Director of the Social Science Department.

26. This study was made possible by a grant from the Social Science Research Council of the United States.

27. Klineberg, *Tensions Affecting International Understanding*, pp. 213-14.

28. Five of "The Way of Life" studies have appeared in English, published by William Heinemann Ltd., London: that on Australia edited by George Caiger; on England by K. B. Smellie; on Norway by Frede Castberg; on Pakistan by Ishtaig Hussain Qureshi; on South Africa by G. H. Galpin. Three have appeared in French, published by Editions du Rocher, Monaco: on Canada by Miss True Davidson; on South Africa by G. H. Galpin; and on Switzerland by Denis de Rougemont. These and other studies resulting from the social tensions project are listed in "Improvement of Information about Foreign Countries," *Unesco Chronicle*, No. 6 (December 1955), pp. 34-38.

For a critical view of the concept of "national character" and of recent works on the psychological study of peoples, see Morroe Berger, " 'Understanding National Character'—and War," *Commentary*, April 1951, pp. 375-86. Berger points out (p. 384) several problems involved in the scientific study of national character, namely: "which features of national behavior are important in the study of character; the relative value of studies of individual behavior itself as against its manifestation in certain formal institutions like law, political organization, and so on; and the interpretation of some of these formal structures, especially law." He also questions the relation of national character to international understanding and that of international understanding to peace.

29. For example, in the United States the Italians are often pictured as emotional and musical; the Irish as pugnacious and witty; the Germans as industrious and stolid; the Negroes as lazy and amusing; the Jews as shrewd and mercenary. Americans are pictured in other countries as boastful and materialistic. See Otto Klineberg, "Pictures in Our Heads," Unesco, *Courier*, Vol. VIII, No. 4 (September 1955, U. S. edition), pp. 5-6.

30. William Buchanan and Hadley Cantril, *How Nations See Each Other* (Urbana: University of Illinois Press, 1953).

31. Unesco, H. E. O. James and L. Tenen, *The Teacher Was Black* (London: Heinemann, 1953). For a summary of this study and other articles on stereotypes, see *International Social Science Bulletin*, Vol. III, No. 3.

32. Unesco, *The Social Sciences*, Unesco and Its Program, XII, p. 31; and E. Beaglehole and J. R. McCreary, *The Modification of International Attitudes: A New Zealand Study*.

33. Unesco, Indian National Commission, "Project for Research on Social Tensions," Document Unesco/SS/4 (1951). For a summary report on the initiation of the project, see Gardner Murphy, *In the Minds of Men* (New York: Basic Books Inc., 1953), pp. 11-26.

34. See a series of articles by Arvid Broderson, Alfred Bonné, S. N. Eisenstadt, J. Ben-David, and Judith T. Shuval under the general title, "Cultural Assimilation

and Tensions in a Country of Large-scale Immigration: Israel," *International Social Science Bulletin,* Vol. VIII, No. 1 (1956), pp. 7-123.

35. For the German study, see Knut Pipping, Rudolf Abshagen, and Anne-Eva Brauneck, *Gespräche mit der Deutschen Jugend* (Helsingfors: Societas Scientiarum Fennica, 1954). For the Japanese study, see Jean Stoetzel, *Without the Chrysanthemum and the Sword* (New York: Columbia University Press–Unesco, 1955).

36. Chapter IX, pp. 213-18.

37. Unesco, "Report of the Director General," Document 7C/3, pp. 202-03, and Document 8C/3, pp. 111-12. Among recent publications by Unesco are *The Positive Contribution of Immigrants* (1955), dealing specially with developments in Argentina, Australia, Brazil, United Kingdom, and the United States; "Some Studies in Education of Immigrants for Citizenship," *Educational Studies and Documents,* No. XVI (1955), with particular reference to Australia, Brazil, Canada, and Israel; and H. B. M. Murphy and others, *Flight and Resettlement* (Paris: Unesco, 1955). On the Havana conference see W. D. Borrie, "The Cultural Integration of Immigrants," *Unesco Chronicle,* Vol. II, No. 10 (October 1956), pp. 289-93.

38. United Nations, Economic and Social Council, Resolution 116 B (VI).

39. *The Race Question in Modern Science,* A Symposium (New York: Unesco-William Morrow, 1956).

40. A contemporary bibliography on living religions, including studies made since 1950 (but not bearing particularly on race relations), was published in Unesco, "Sociology of Religions, A Trend Report and Bibliography," *Current Sociology,* Vol. V (1956).

41. Unesco, *The Social Sciences,* pp. 50-56. See also Unesco, "Report of the Director General," Document 7C/3, pp. 204-06. One study relating to the United States by Morroe Berger, *Racial Equality and the Law* (Paris: Unesco, 1954), reviews legislation against discrimination and efforts to make employment equally accessible to all.

42. Alfred Métraux, "The Problem of the New African Elites," *Unesco Chronicle,* No. 5 (November 1955), pp. 9-14; and United Nations, Economic and Social Council, "Conference of Nongovernmental Organizations Interested in the Eradication of Prejudice and Discrimination," Document E/NGO/Conf. 1/3. 25 February 1955, pp. 5-7.

43. Unesco, Document 6C/Resolutions, pp. 23-24 (Res. 3.26).

44. At the session of the General Conference in 1952, it was proposed to look at procedures of conciliation and arbitration which had proved useful in the solution of labor conflicts within nations, to ascertain whether they might be usefully applied to international tensions. Unesco, Document 7C/Resolutions, p. 23 (Res. 3.2111). The Indian government urged that procedures outlined in the teachings of Gandhi be considered in these investigations. Suggestions for future research, particularly with regard to the mediation of international conflict, are given by Robert C. Angell in a chapter on "Discovering Paths to Peace," in *The Nature of Conflict,* pp. 204-23.

45. Klineberg, "The Unesco Project on International Tensions," *International Social Science Bulletin,* Vol. I, No. 1-2 (1949), p. 20.

46. Unesco, Document 8C/Resolutions, p. 31. The resolution (IV.1.3.41) is en-

titled "Social Science and Problems of International Understanding and Tensions." The General Conference at New Delhi in 1956 authorized continuance of the study of "the means of promoting peaceful co-operation." Unesco, Document 9C/Resolutions, p. 20 (Res. 3.5).

47. Unesco, *International Social Science Bulletin*, Vol. VIII, No. 4 (1956), pp. 732-34. Earlier, in August 1955, at the Third Congress of the International Political Science Association held at Stockholm, a round-table discussion on peaceful coexistence had outlined six proposals in this area for study by political scientists. Ibid., Vol. VIII, No. 1 (1956), pp. 196-97.

48. Unesco, "Preliminary Meeting of Economists on Peaceful Cooperation," Document Unesco/SS/18; and "Meeting of Experts on the Contribution of the Social Sciences to Peaceful International Cooperation," Document Unesco/SS/20; and "Proposed Program and Budget for 1957-1958," Document 9C/5, pp. 88-90 and Document 9C/5, Corr. 1, pp. 35-36.

49. Unesco, Document Unesco/SS/20, p. 5.

50. International Sociological Association, Document ISA/Coop/1956 (mimeographed).

CHAPTER XII

1. In carrying out this recommendation Unesco has cooperated with the United Nations in issuing a series of reports, based on information provided by member states, which present the most comprehensive review of information available on teaching about the United Nations. See United Nations, *Teaching about the United Nations and the Specialized Agencies,* Report submitted to the Economic and Social Council by the Secretary General of the United Nations and the Director General of Unesco, covering the period 1950-52 (New York: United Nations, n.d.), p. 1. This source will hereafter be cited as *Teaching about the United Nations, 1952.* For a summary of the earlier experience of the League of Nations in teaching about international cooperation, see "Teaching about the United Nations and the Specialized Agencies, Report submitted by the Secretary General of the United Nations and the Director General of Unesco to the Economic and Social Council," Official Records, Fifth Year: Eleventh Session, Special Supplement No. 1, July 1950, New York, Document E/1667.

2. United Nations, Document E/1667, p. 27.

3. Ibid., pp. 8, 9, 46.

4. See for example, *Report of the Southeast Asia Teachers' Seminar on Teaching about the United Nations* (New Delhi: Indian Federation of United Nations Associations, n.d.).

5. These pamphlets were published in the series "Towards World Understanding" as follows: I. *Some Suggestions on Teaching about the United Nations and its Specialized Agencies,* 1949 (revised edition 1952); III. *Selected Bibliography on Education for International Understanding,* 1949; IV. *The United Nations and World Citizenship,* 1949. A supplementary bibliography listing mainly publications issued from 1950 to 1953 is found in Unesco, "Teaching about the United Nations, A Selected Bibliography," *Education Abstracts,* Vol. VI, No. 3 (March 1954).

6. Unesco, "Teaching about Human Rights, A Report on the Unesco Seminar on Active Methods of Education for Living in a World Community," Document Unesco/ED/124 (1953), p. 5.

7. Resolution 3.14 (XI). United Nations, *Teaching about the United Nations 1952*, p. 40.

8. Ibid., p. 52.

9. Unesco, "Education for International Understanding and Cooperation, Program of Coordinated Experimental Activities in Schools of Member States, Report on Activities in 1954," Document Unesco/ED/141; and "Interim Report, Activities in 1955 and 1956," Document Unesco/ED/149.

10. United Nations, Document E/1667, p. 11. The UN resolution was 217 D (III). The Constitution of Unesco provided (in Article I, 1.) that the organization should "further universal respect for . . . human rights and fundamental freedoms. . . ."

11. Unesco, "Report of the Director General," Document 4C/3, p. 35; and Document 5C/3, p. 37.

12. United Nations, Document E/1667, p. 13.

13. Unesco, Document Unesco/ED/124, pp. 2, 4. The four teachers' organizations were: The International Federation of Secondary Teachers; International Federation of Teachers' Associations; New Education Fellowship; and the World Organization of the Teaching Profession. The pamphlet on suggestions for teachers was subsequently published under the title, *The Universal Declaration of Human Rights, A Guide for Teachers* (Paris: Unesco, 1953).

14. Unesco, Document Unesco/ED/124, pp. 7-12.

15. *Unesco Features*, No. 178 (2 April 1956), p. 2.

16. Jacques Havet, "Unesco and Human Rights," *International Social Science Bulletin*, Vol. II, No. 4 (Winter 1950), pp. 550-51.

17. James Frederick Green, *The United Nations and Human Rights* (Washington: The Brookings Institution, 1956).

18. U. S. National Commission for Unesco, "Summary Minutes of the Fifteenth Meeting of the Executive Committee," Document XC(50)54, pp. 24-25.

19. United Nations, Economic and Social Council, 323 (XI). The title of the Resolution was "Assistance for the Civil Population of Korea."

20. Unesco, "Summary Records," Document 23 EX/SR.1, p. 4.

21. Ibid., pp. 5-6.

22. See Chapter II, pp. 29-33.

23. One scholar has written, "Intrusions of issues arising from political differences in the discussion of Unesco have been few, including little more than attack on 'war-mongering nations' at the Second Session of the General Conference in Mexico, a debate concerning the seating of Observers from International Jewish Organizations (who in turn had not accepted the invitation to send observers) at the Third Session in Beirut, a demonstration against a proposal to introduce Unesco's program into Germany at the Fourth Session in Paris, and the withdrawal of the representatives of Hungary and Czechoslovakia in protest against the seating of the delegation from Nationalist China at the Fifth Session in Florence." Richard McKeon, "Knowledge and World Organization," in Lyman Bryson, Louis Finkelstein, Harold D. Lasswell, R. M. MacIver (eds.), *Foundations of*

World Organization: A Political and Cultural Appraisal (New York: Harper & Bros., 1952), pp. 304-05.

24. The Director General declared at the Sixth Session of the General Conference, "Unesco is a technical institution, and as such not responsible for establishing political security. But it is responsible, at least in part, for establishing a more general form of security—pacification in its deepest sense, without which political security is no more than a truce between wars." Unesco, Document 6C/Proceedings, p. 62.

25. Roger Seydoux, the member of the Executive Board from France, had stated at an earlier session that "there was something to be said for standing aloof; if despite a world divided in two, Unesco has been able to carry out work of a purely technical nature, it was precisely because it had remained aloof from political and other considerations which practically paralyzed other international organizations." Unesco, "Summary Records," Document 20 EX/SR.2, p. 2. See also the statement of Monsieur Bidault, head of the French delegation at the Fourth Session of the General Conference, Chapter II, p. 41.

26. Henri Bonnet, "Intellectual Cooperation in World Organization," in *World Organization* (Washington: American Council on Public Affairs, 1941), pp. 208-09.

27. For the full text of the resolutions see Unesco, "Resolutions and Decisions," Document 23 EX/Decisions, pp. 2-5.

28. Considerable material appeared in the October 1950 issue of the *Courier*. Only one issue of *Unesco Features* for the press, that for November 15, 1950, gave any major attention to Korea and the resolutions of the Executive Board. The January 27, 1951 issue of the *World Review* for radio carried a feature article on the cultural heritage of Korea.

29. Unesco, Document 6C/Proceedings, p. 43.

30. Some wall charts and the pamphlets for teachers in French and English, the latter entitled *Collective Security*, by A. Appadorai, were published before the end of 1951 as was the booklet in French on classroom suggestions. But the corresponding booklet in English, *Some Suggestions on Teaching about Collective Security*, and the English edition of the scholarly study, *Collective Security, A Progress Report*, did not appear until late 1952. No French or Spanish edition of the study was published.

31. As to the Unesco publications, approximately 1,800 copies of the pamphlet for teachers by A. Appadorai were received in the United States and sent out mostly to the organizations which had received the *Discussion Guide* mentioned above. Some 2,000 copies of *Some Suggestions on Teaching about Collective Security* were received, of which 500 were used at the Fourth National Conference in 1953, and the others were distributed in general mailing. About 200 copies of the scholarly study, *Collective Security, A Progress Report*, by Andrew Martin, were received from Unesco and were sent out to a special list of interested individuals. Letters from Constance Roach, Unesco Relations Staff, of May 17, May 31, and June 29, 1955.

32. It may be noted, however, that Unesco was the only UN specialized agency which "aligned itself in any positive way in support of the collective measures" of

the United Nations. Leland M. Goodrich and Anne P. Simmons, *The United Nations and the Maintenance of International Peace and Security* (Washington: Brookings Institution, 1955), pp. 422-23.

33. Reinhold Niebuhr, "The Theory and Practice of Unesco," *International Organization*, Vol. IV (Boston: World Peace Foundation, 1950), p. 6.

Herbert W. Schneider has written, "A world community is an idea to which we have long paid theoretical tribute, but the practical cultivation of neighborly virtues on such a scale requires the invention of appropriate institutional machinery. A community cannot live without communication. . . . We must become reconciled to a revolution in social machinery analogous to the industrial revolution. For it is only through a continual increase in the variety and directness of personal contacts across cultural lines, only through an actual becoming acquainted on a world-wide scale, that world community can become a reality. And just because it is visionary and foolish to expect the whole world to become acquainted immediately, we must be on our guard against expecting too much from the so-called 'Great Community.' After all, it was world war that brought the world together in conflict; it would be a miracle if the contacts of fighting could be transformed into bonds of fraternity without the many means of communication and service by which local communities keep alive." Herbert W. Schneider, *Three Dimensions of Public Morality* (Bloomington, Indiana: Indiana University Press, 1956), pp. 148-49.

34. Reinhold Niebuhr, "The Theory and Practice of Unesco," p. 6. See also Hans J. Morgenthau, *Politics Among Nations,* The Struggle for Power and Peace (New York: Knopf, 1948), pp. 408-09.

35. Harold Stanley Thames, "An Analysis of Representative Ideological Criticism of the United Nations Educational, Scientific and Cultural Organization in the United States, 1946-1954" (unpublished Ph.D. dissertation, Duke University, 1955), p. 272.

36. For the list of members see Unesco, "Final Report of the Expert Committee on Education for International Understanding and Cooperation," Document Unesco/ED/142, p. 17. Joseph E. Johnson, President of the Carnegie Endowment for International Peace, was the member of the Committee from the United States.

37. Ibid., pp. 5-15.

38. President Eisenhower's press conference statement (as reported in *Time,* February 4, 1957, Vol. LXIX, No. 5, p. 9) gave emphasis to the need for government efforts:

"Look. Everything else fails, fades to unimportance beside this one: that we do make progress toward better world understanding—achieved, I would say, in several steps.

"First, a better understanding among the free nations of the world—that is, better and stronger confidence among them; the certainty that their economic and military strength is equal to the test.

"And after that, particularly better understanding with the Russians, the Russian government.

"And, finally, agreements in which we could all trust them."

CHAPTER XIII

1. Unesco, *Constitution*, Article V, B, 5 (a) and (b).

2. Ibid., Article VI, 3 (a).

3. Unesco's Constitution gave the organization no authority to police the educational systems of member countries, as had been proposed prior to the London Conference by certain private groups in Great Britain and the United States. Their purpose had been thus to scotch tendencies to use education to breed a war psychology.

4. Unesco, 4C/Proceedings, pp. 141-42.

5. Charles S. Ascher, *Program-Making in Unesco, 1946-1951* (Chicago: Public Administration Clearing House, 1951), pp. 53, 65, 78.

6. Of an estimated 1,200 persons who have attended nine Unesco General Conferences and the constituent assembly in London as delegates, alternates, or expert advisors, 261 have attended a total of 2 sessions, 25 have attended 5 sessions, 8 have attended 8, and only 1 has attended all sessions. (Figures compiled from Conference records in the secretariat.) Cf. Chapter XIV, p. 314.

7. New Zealand, Department of External Affairs, "Unesco, Report of the New Zealand Delegation to the Eighth Session of the General Conference" (Wellington: 1955, Pub. No. 153), p. 9.

8. The World Health Organization had from the start a Board of individuals, similar to that of Unesco. But WHO works in a single, identifiable field of responsibility, that of public health. The members of its Executive Board share common professional and technical interests, a situation far simpler than that of Unesco, with its varied array of differing fields of interests.

9. Ascher, *Program-Making in Unesco*, p. 9.

10. Julian Huxley, "Unesco, The First Phase," I—The Two Views, *Manchester Guardian*, August 10, 1950.

11. Ibid.

12. It is interesting to note the parallel between Huxley's belief in this possibility down to 1948 and the hopes stirred in Washington and other Western capitals by the Summit Conference at Geneva and the thaw in the cold war.

13. Julian Huxley, "Science and the United Nations," *Nature*, CLVI (November 10, 1945), p. 554, quoted in Basil Karp, "The Development of the Philosophy of Unesco" (unpublished Ph.D. dissertation, University of Chicago, 1951), p. 30.

14. Unesco, "Proceedings," Document 3C/110, Vol. I, p. 166.

15. Ibid., p. 168.

16. Unesco, Document 4C/Proceedings, p. 46.

17. Unesco, Document 3C/110, Vol. I, p. 170.

18. Unesco, Document 4C/Proceedings, p. 47.

19. The Czech delegation demanded prohibition of atomic weapons and support for the World Movement of the Defenders of Peace, a Communist-dominated organization. A Yugoslav proposal called for a conference of intellectual leaders to combat the existing war-psychosis and to discuss what Unesco might do for the immediate promotion of peace. A Belgian resolution urged appointment by the Director General of two commissions: one to report on new methods of warfare developed from recent discoveries in physics, chemistry, and bacteriology; and a

second, to report on the "economic, financial, social and moral repercussions of war." Unesco, mimeographed documents 5C/17, 19, 25, 67.

20. Unesco, Document 5C/Proceedings, p. 446. For analysis of the reasons for the resignation of Torres Bodet, see Alan Morehead, *The Scotsman* (Edinburgh, June 1950); and Julian Huxley, "Unesco: The First Phase," I—The Two Views, *Manchester Guardian,* August 10, 1950.

21. Unesco, Document 7C/Proceedings, pp. 206-07. Torres Bodet made it clear that he viewed the budget reduction as evidence of lack of confidence in his leadership.

22. Unesco, Document 2 XC/Resolutions and Proceedings (Second Extraordinary Session, Paris, 1953), pp. 104-07.

CHAPTER XIV

1. Unesco, "General Conference, First Session," Document Unesco/C/30, p. 223.

2. Charles S. Ascher, "Unesco Gathers Momentum," *Survey*, LXXXV (June 1949), p. 313. Unesco has stimulated a number of studies on the problems which participation in international organizations present to governments. See Walter R. Sharp, *National Administration and International Organization,* A Comparative Survey of Fourteen Countries (Brussels, 1951); Benjamin Akzin, *New States and International Organizations* (Paris: Unesco-International Political Science Association, 1955); and Roger Grégoire, *National Administration and International Organizations* (Brussels: International Institute of Administrative Sciences, n.d.).

3. Unesco, "Report of the Director General," Document 6C/3, p. 16.

4. Ceylon, Denmark, Liberia, Turkey, and Yugoslavia had four each; Belgium, Cuba, Ecuador, France, New Zealand, and Sweden had three; and Austria, Haiti, Israel, the Netherlands, Nicaragua, Norway, and Switzerland had two. In the remaining countries one official—sometimes only part-time—was assigned to Unesco matters.

5. Unesco, *Constitution,* VII, 1.

6. The National Committees were established in the first instance to serve not "an abstract idea but a concrete aim," that of providing information on the losses suffered during World War I by the universities and scientific institutions of the countries of Central Europe. When inquiries addressed to Ministries of Education yielded little response, Madame Curie suggested approaching unofficial bodies. *L'Institut International de Coopération Intellectuelle, 1925-1946* (Paris, n.d.), p. 538.

7. James Marshall, "Citizen Diplomacy," *American Political Science Review,* Vol. XLIII, No. 1 (February 1949), pp. 83-90.

8. Sally Liberman Smith, "Some Observations on the Role of Mental Health in the Middle East and Asia," *Bennington College Alumnae Quarterly,* Vol. VI, No. 2 (January 1955), pp. 8-9.

9. "White House Conference on a Program for People-to-People Partnership, Washington, D. C., September 11-12, 1956" (mimeographed), p. 1.

10. Quoted in Howard E. Wilson, *United States National Commission for Unesco* (New York: Macmillan, 1948), p. 35.

11. New Zealand, Department of External Affairs, "The United Nations Educational, Scientific and Cultural Organization, Report of the New Zealand Delegation to the Fifth Session of the General Conference" (Wellington, 1951, Pub. No. 93), p. 22.

12. Unesco, "Decentralization of Unesco's Activities, Structure and Methods of National Commissions," Document 9C/PRG/21. The succeeding account is largely based on this source and on Unesco, *Guide for National Commissions* (Paris, 1956). For a discussion of National Commissions in the Arab states, see Rajai Abou-Khadra, "Unesco and the Arab Community" (unpublished Ph.D. dissertation, Indiana University, 1957), pp. 247-67.

13. Unesco, Document 9C/PRG/21, p. 4.

14. Unesco, *Constitution*, VII, 2.

15. See Chapter VII, pp. 166-67, and Chapter XI, pp. 250-51.

16. United States National Commission for Unesco, *Minutes* (Fifteenth Meeting).

17. United States National Commission for Unesco, *The Kansas Story on Unesco* (Washington: Government Printing Office, 1949).

18. Unesco World Review, No. 264 (6 March 1954), p. 1.

19. Unesco, Document 9C/PRG/21, pp. 12-14.

20. For reasons which should be apparent the authors have considered it appropriate to discuss United States policy toward Unesco somewhat more fully than that of other countries.

21. "The people of the United States do gain or can gain many valuable benefits from their participation in Unesco. The advancement by Unesco of human welfare through education, science and culture promotes international understanding which contributes to peace." John Foster Dulles, Sept. 15, 1953, Department of State Publication 5209, *An Appraisal of the United Nations Educational, Scientific and Cultural Organization*, Washington, 1953.

22. U. S. National Commission for Unesco, "Statement by Stanley C. Allyn, Member of the U. S. National Commission for Unesco and President of the National Cash Register Company" (Washington: n.d., mimeographed), p. 3.

23. The members of the Committee were: Irving Salomon of California, Chairman; Mrs. Elizabeth Heffelfinger of Minnesota, and President John A. Perkins of the University of Delaware.

24. Secretary Dulles summarized the Committee's conclusions as follows:

"1. The top officers in the Secretariat, both Americans and non-Americans, who are responsible for administration and program execution, are doing so with fidelity to Unesco's aims and purposes.

2. The influences which predominate in the Organization derive from a full regard for the Human Rights and fundamental freedoms affirmed in the Charter of the United Nations.

3. Unesco does not advocate world government, or world citizenship in the political sense. The U. S. delegation found no official expression of the General Conference, the Executive Board, the Director General, or the Secretariat that gives the slightest support to this charge. They found no fear on this point among the representatives of other governments who, on the contrary, find it difficult to comprehend the American fear on this matter.

4. The delegation reported that Unesco does not attempt, directly or indirectly, to undermine national loyalties or to encourage the substitution of loyalty to and love for a supranational authority for loyalty to and love for one's own country, as has been alleged in some quarters.

5. The delegates reaffirmed that the official bodies and the personnel of Unesco observe the provision of the Unesco Constitution which prohibits Unesco from interfering in matters within the domestic jurisdiction of Member States. Unesco does not attempt to interfere in the American school system.

6. The delegation could find no evidence of atheism or anti-religious bias in any of Unesco's work. I am happy to report to you these observations of the delegation." John Foster Dulles, September 15, 1953, Department of State Publication 5209, *An Appraisal of the United Nations Educational, Scientific and Cultural Organization.*

25. *Report by a Special Committee on Covenant of Human Rights and United Nations to the National Executive Committee, American Legion.* Ray Murphy, Chairman. Indianapolis, Ind., 1955. The 1955 National Convention of the Legion, in spite of the Committee findings that the most common criticisms of Unesco and the National Commission had no basis in fact, adopted a resolution calling for the dissolution of the National Commission.

A Study of Unesco, by the Chamber of Commerce of the United States. See the text of the policy statement adopted by the Chamber's annual meeting, 1954, and report of its committee findings in Extension of Remarks of Hon. Chester E. Merrow in the House of Representatives, July 15, 1954.

Report of the Subcommittee on International Organizations and Movements of the House Committee on Foreign Affairs, July 1, 1957, Government Printing Office, Washington, D. C. The subcommittee, after considering the charges made by the American Legion, declared that the National Commission "has served the Nation well."

See also Extension of Remarks of Hon. A. S. J. Carnahan in the House of Representatives, April 1, 1952, *The Facts of Unesco Pamphlets,* and his Extension of Remarks of June 2, 1954, *American Legion Report on Unesco.*

26. United States National Commission for Unesco, Howard E. Wilson, "Unesco's Cooperation in Education for Human Progress and Mutual Understanding," Document National Conference 5/3, p. 6.

27. See Chapter III, note 9 (p. 368).

28. New Zealand, Department of External Affairs, "Unesco, Report of the New Zealand Delegation to the Eighth Session of the General Conference" (Wellington: 1955, Pub. No. 153), p. 35.

29. Unesco, "Contribution by Unesco to the Development of Peaceful Coexistence," Document 9C/DR/83 and Rev. 3; and United Nations, Document A/3544, pp. 11-12 (draft resolution A/C.3/L.598).

30. See Abou-Khadra, "Unesco and the Arab Community," pp. 190-246.

31. Japan, National Commission for Unesco, *Unesco Activities in Japan* (Tokyo: Kasai Publishing & Printing Co., 1953), pp. 2-4.

CHAPTER XV

1. Cf. Walter H. C. Laves, "Unesco in the United Nations System," in *United States Foreign Policy and the United Nations,* Norman Wait Harris Foundation Lectures, University of Chicago, 1956 (American Association for the United Nations, Chicago, 1957), pp. 16-30. For an earlier appraisal of Unesco's place in the United Nations by the same author see "Unesco: Progress and Prospects," *Virginia Quarterly Review,* Vol. 27 (1951), pp. 321-33.

2. René Maheu, in address to the Fifteenth Meeting of the United States National Commission for Unesco, New York, September 17, 1956.

APPENDIX A

CONSTITUTION *of the United Nations Educational, Scientific and Cultural Organization*[1]

The Governments of the States Parties to this Constitution on behalf of their peoples declare:

That since wars begin in the minds of men, it is in the minds of men that the defences of peace must be constructed;

That ignorance of each other's ways and lives has been a common cause, throughout the history of mankind, of that suspicion and mistrust between peoples of the world through which their differences have all too often broken into war;

That the great and terrible war which has now ended was a war made possible by the denial of the democratic principles of the dignity, equality and mutual respect of men, and by the propagation, in their place, through ignorance and prejudice, of the doctrine of the inequality of men and races;

That the wide diffusion of culture, and the education of humanity for justice and liberty and peace are indispensable to the dignity of man and constitute a sacred duty which all the nations must fulfill in a spirit of mutual assistance and concern;

That a peace based exclusively upon the political and economic arrangements of governments would not be a peace which could secure the unanimous, lasting and sincere support of the peoples of the world, and that the peace must therefore be founded, if it is not to fail, upon the intellectual and moral solidarity of mankind.

1. Adopted in London on November 16, 1945, and amended by the General Conference at its second, third, fourth, fifth, sixth, seventh, eighth, and ninth sessions. See ECO/Conf./29, pp. 93–7; 2C/132, Vol. II, p. 63; 3C/110, Vol. II, p. 113; 4C/Resolutions, pp. 8–9; 5C/Resolutions, pp. 9–10; 6C/Resolutions, pp. 83–5; 7C/Resolutions, pp. 103–5; 8C/Resolutions, pp. 12–13; 9C/Resolutions, p. 70.

For these reasons, the States Parties to this Constitution, believing in full and equal opportunities for education for all, in the unrestricted pursuit of objective truth, and in the free exchange of ideas and knowledge, are agreed and determined to develop and to increase the means of communication between their peoples and to employ these means for the purposes of mutual understanding and a truer and more perfect knowledge of each other's lives;

In consequence whereof they do hereby create the United Nations Educational, Scientific and Cultural Organization for the purpose of advancing, through the educational and scientific and cultural relations of the peoples of the world, the objectives of international peace and of the common welfare of mankind for which the United Nations Organization was established and which its Charter proclaims.

Article I. Purposes and Functions

1. The purpose of the Organization is to contribute to peace and security by promoting collaboration among the nations through education, science and culture in order to further universal respect for justice, for the rule of law and for the human rights and fundamental freedoms which are affirmed for the peoples of the world, without distinction of race, sex, language or religion, by the Charter of the United Nations.

2. To realize this purpose the Organization will:

    (a) Collaborate in the work of advancing the mutual knowledge and understanding of peoples, through all means of mass communication and to that end recommend such international agreements as may be necessary to promote the free flow of ideas by word and image;

    (b) Give fresh impulse to popular education and to the spread of culture;

    by collaborating with Members, at their request, in the development of educational activities;

    by instituting collaboration among the nations to advance the ideal of equality of educational opportunity without regard to race, sex or any distinctions, economic or social;

    by suggesting educational methods best suited to prepare the children of the world for the responsibilities of freedom;

    (c) Maintain, increase and diffuse knowledge;

    by assuring the conservation and protection of the world's inheritance of books, works of art and monuments of history and science, and recommending to the nations concerned the necessary international conventions;

    by encouraging cooperation among the nations in all branches of intellectual activity, including the international exchange of persons active in the fields of education, science and culture and the exchange of publications, objects of artistic and scientific interest and other materials of information;

by initiating methods of international cooperation calculated to give the people of all countries access to the printed and published materials produced by any of them.

3. With a view to preserving the independence, integrity and fruitful diversity of the cultures and educational systems of the States members of this Organization, the Organization is prohibited from intervening in matters which are essentially within their domestic jurisdiction.

Article II. Membership

1. Membership of the United Nations Organization shall carry with it the right to membership of the United Nations Educational, Scientific and Cultural Organization.

2. Subject to the conditions of the Agreement between this Organization and the United Nations Organization, approved pursuant to Article X of this Constitution, States not members of the United Nations Organization may be admitted to membership of the Organization, upon recommendation of the Executive Board, by a two-thirds majority vote of the General Conference.

3. Territories or groups of territories which are not responsible for the conduct of their international relations may be admitted as Associate Members by the General Conference by a two-thirds majority of Members present and voting, upon application made on behalf of such territory or group of territories by the Member or other authority having responsibility for their international relations. The nature and extent of the rights and obligations of Associate Members shall be determined by the General Conference.

4. Members of the Organization which are suspended from the exercise of the rights and privileges of membership of the United Nations Organization shall, upon the request of the latter, be suspended from the rights and privileges of this Organization.

5. Members of the Organization which are expelled from the United Nations Organization shall automatically cease to be members of this Organization.

6. Any Member State or Associate Member of the Organization may withdraw from the Organization by notice addressed to the Director-General. Such notice shall take effect on December 31, of the year following that during which the notice was given. No such withdrawal shall affect the financial obligations owed to the Organization on the date the withdrawal takes effect. Notice of withdrawal by an Associate Member shall be given on its behalf by the Member State or other authority having responsibility for its international relations.

Article III.   Organs

The Organization shall include a General Conference, an Executive Board and a Secretariat.

Article IV.   The General Conference

A. COMPOSITION

1. The General Conference shall consist of the representatives of the States members of the Organization. The Government of each Member State shall appoint not more than five delegates, who shall be selected after consultation with the National Commission, if established, or with educational, scientific and cultural bodies.

B. FUNCTIONS

2. The General Conference shall determine the policies and the main lines of work of the Organization. It shall take decisions on programmes submitted to it by the Executive Board.

3. The General Conference shall, when it deems desirable and in accordance with the regulations to be made by it, summon international conferences of States on education, the sciences and humanities or the dissemination of knowledge; non-governmental conferences on the same subjects may be summoned by the General Conference or by the Executive Board in accordance with such regulations.

4. The General Conference shall, in adopting proposals for submission to the Member States, distinguish between recommendations and international conventions submitted for their approval. In the former case a majority vote shall suffice; in the latter case a two-thirds majority shall be required. Each of the Member States shall submit recommendations or conventions to its competent authorities within a period of one year from the close of the session of the General Conference at which they were adopted.

5. Subject to the provisions of Article V, paragraph 5(c), the General Conference shall advise the United Nations Organization on the educational, scientific and cultural aspects of matters of concern to the latter; in accordance with the terms and procedure agreed upon between the appropriate authorities of the two Organizations.

6. The General Conference shall receive and consider the reports submitted periodically by Member States as provided by Article VIII.

7. The General Conference shall elect the members of the Executive Board and, on the recommendation of the Board, shall appoint the Director-General.

C. VOTING

8. (a) Each Member State shall have one vote in the General Conference. Decisions shall be made by a simple majority except in cases in

which a two-thirds majority is required by the provisions of this Constitution. A majority shall be a majority of the Members present and voting.

(b) A Member State shall have no vote in the General Conference if the total amount of contributions due from it exceeds the total amount of contributions payable by it for the current year and the immediately preceding calendar year.

(c) The General Conference may nevertheless permit such a Member State to vote, if it is satisfied that the failure to pay is due to conditions beyond the control of the Member Nation.

D. PROCEDURE

9. (a) The General Conference shall meet in ordinary session every two years. It may meet in extraordinary session if it decides to do so itself or if summoned by the Executive Board, or on the demand of at least one-third of the Member States.

(b) At each session the location of its next ordinary session shall be designated by the General Conference. The location of an extraordinary session shall be decided by the General Conference if the session is summoned by it, or otherwise by the Executive Board.

10. The General Conference shall adopt its own rules of procedure. It shall at each session elect a President and other officers.

11. The General Conference shall set up special and technical committees and such other subordinate bodies as may be necessary for its purposes.

12. The General Conference shall cause arrangements to be made for public access to meetings, subject to such regulations as it shall prescribe.

E. OBSERVERS

13. The General Conference, on the recommendation of the Executive Board and by a two-thirds majority may, subject to its rules of procedure, invite as observers at specified sessions of the Conference or of its Commissions representatives of international organizations, such as those referred to in Article XI, paragraph 4.

14. When consultative arrangements have been approved by the Executive Board for such international non-governmental or semi-governmental organizations in the manner provided in Article XI, paragraph 4, those organizations shall be invited to send observers to sessions of the General Conference and its Commissions.

Article V. Executive Board

A. COMPOSITION

1. The Executive Board shall be elected by the General Conference from among the delegates appointed by the Member States and shall consist of twenty-four members, each of whom shall represent the Government

of the State of which he is a national. The President of the General
Conference shall sit *ex officio* in an advisory capacity on the Executive
Board.

2. In electing the members of the Executive Board the General Conference
shall endeavor to include persons competent in the arts, the humanities,
the sciences, education and the diffusion of ideas, and qualified by their
experience and capacity to fulfill the administrative and executive
duties of the Board. It shall also have regard to the diversity of cultures
and a balanced geographical distribution. Not more than one national
of any Member State shall serve on the Board at any one time, the
President of the Conference excepted.

3. Members of the Board shall serve from the close of the session of the
General Conference which elected them until the close of the second
ordinary session of the General Conference following that election.
They shall be immediately eligible for a second term, but shall not serve
consecutively for more than two terms. Half of the members of the
Board shall be elected every two years.

4. In the event of the death or resignation of a member of the Executive
Board, his replacement for the remainder of his term shall be appointed
by the Executive Board on the nomination of the Government of the
State the former member represented. The Government making the
nomination and the Executive Board shall have regard to the factors set
forth in paragraph 2 of this Article.

B. FUNCTIONS

5. (*a*) The Executive Board shall prepare the agenda for the General
Conference. It shall examine the program of work for the Organization and corresponding budget estimates submitted to it by the
Director-General in accordance with paragraph 3 of Article VI and
shall submit them with such recommendations as it considers desirable to the General Conference.

(*b*) The Executive Board, acting under the authority of the General
Conference, shall be responsible for the execution of the program
adopted by the Conference. In accordance with the decisions of the
General Conference and having regard to circumstances arising between two ordinary sessions, the Executive Board shall take all
necessary measures to ensure the effective and rational execution
of the program by the Director-General.

(*c*) Between ordinary sessions of the General Conference, the Board
may discharge the functions of adviser to the United Nations, set
forth in Article IV, paragraph 5, whenever the problem upon which
advice is sought has already been dealt with in principle by the
Conference, or when the solution is implicit in decisions of the
Conference.

6. The Executive Board shall recommend to the General Conference the admission of new Members to the Organization.

7. Subject to decisions of the General Conference, the Executive Board shall adopt its own rules of procedure. It shall elect its officers from among its members.

8. The Executive Board shall meet in regular session at least twice a year and may meet in special session if convoked by the Chairman on his own initiative or upon the request of six members of the Board.

9. The Chairman of the Executive Board shall present, on behalf of the Board, to each ordinary session of the General Conference, with or without comments, the reports on the activities of the Organization which the Director-General is required to prepare in accordance with the provisions of Article VI.3 (b).

10. The Executive Board shall make all necessary arrangements to consult the representatives of international organizations or qualified persons concerned with questions within its competence.

11. Between sessions of the General Conference, the Executive Board may request advisory opinions from the International Court of Justice on legal questions arising within the field of the Organization's activities.

12. Although the members of the Executive Board are representative of their respective Governments they shall exercise the powers delegated to them by the General Conference on behalf of the Conference as a whole.

C. TRANSITIONAL PROVISIONS

13. At the Ninth Session of the General Conference thirteen members shall be elected to the Executive Board pursuant to the provisions of this Article. One of them shall retire at the close of the tenth session of the General Conference, the retiring member being chosen by the drawing of lots. Thereafter, twelve members shall be elected at each ordinary session of the General Conference.

Article VI.—Secretariat

1. The Secretariat shall consist of a Director-General and such staff as may be required.

2. The Director-General shall be nominated by the Executive Board and appointed by the General Conference for a period of six years, under such conditions as the Conference may approve, and shall be eligible for reappointment. He shall be the chief administrative officer of the Organization.

3. (a) The Director-General, or a deputy designated by him, shall participate without the right to vote, in all meetings of the General Conference, of the Executive Board, and of the Committees of the Organization. He shall formulate proposals for appropriate action

by the Conference and the Board, and shall prepare for submission to the Board a draft programme of work for the Organization with corresponding budget estimates.

(b) The Director-General shall prepare and communicate to Member States and to the Executive Board periodic reports on the activities of the Organization. The General Conference shall determine the periods to be covered by these reports.

4. The Director-General shall appoint the staff of the Secretariat in accordance with staff regulations to be approved by the General Conference. Subject to the paramount consideration of securing the highest standards of integrity, appointment to the staff shall be on as wide a geographical basis as possible.

5. The responsibilities of the Director-General and of the staff shall be exclusively international in character. In the discharge of their duties they shall not seek or receive instructions from any Government or from any authority external to the Organization. They shall refrain from any action which might prejudice their position as international officials. Each State member of the Organization undertakes to respect the international character of the responsibilities of the Director-General and the staff, and not to seek to influence them in the discharge of their duties.

6. Nothing in this Article shall preclude the Organization from entering into special arrangements within the United Nations Organization for common services and staff and for the interchange of personnel.

Article VII.　National Co-operating Bodies

1. Each Member State shall make such arrangements as suit its particular conditions for the purpose of associating its principal bodies interested in educational, scientific and cultural matters with the work of the Organization, preferably by the formation of a National Commission broadly representative of the Government and such bodies.

2. National Commissions or National Co-operating Bodies, where they exist, shall act in an advisory capacity to their respective delegations to the General Conference and to their Governments in matters relating to the Organization and shall function as agencies of liaison in all matters of interest to it.

3. The Organization may, on the request of a Member State, delegate, either temporarily or permanently, a member of its Secretariat to serve on the National Commission of that State, in order to assist in the development of its work.

Article VIII. Reports by Member States

Each Member State shall report periodically to the Organization, in a manner to be determined by the General Conference, on its laws, regulations and statistics relating to educational, scientific and cultural life and institutions, and on the action taken upon the recommendations and conventions referred to in Article IV, paragraph 4.

Article IX. Budget

1. The Budget shall be administered by the Organization.
2. The General Conference shall approve and give final effect to the budget and to the apportionment of financial responsibility among the States members of the Organization subject to such arrangement with the United Nations as may be provided in the agreement to be entered into pursuant to Article X.
3. The Director-General, with the approval of the Executive Board, may receive gifts, bequests, and subventions directly from Governments, public and private institutions, associations and private persons.

Article X. Relations with the United Nations Organization

This Organization shall be brought into relations with the United Nations Organization, as soon as practicable, as one of the Specialized Agencies referred to in Article 57 of the Charter of the United Nations. This relationship shall be effected through an agreement with the United Nations Organization under Article 63 of the Charter, which agreement shall be subject to the approval of the General Conference of this Organization. The agreement shall provide for effective cooperation between the two Organizations in the pursuit of their common purposes, and at the same time shall recognize the autonomy of this Organization, within the fields of its competence as defined in this Constitution. Such agreement may, among other matters, provide for the approval and financing of the budget of the Organization by the General Assembly of the United Nations.

Article XI. Relations with other Specialized International Organizations and Agencies

1. This Organization may co-operate with other specialized intergovernmental organizations and agencies whose interests and activities are related to its purpose. To this end the Director-General, acting under the general authority of the Executive Board, may establish effective working relationships with such organizations and agencies and establish such joint committees as may be necessary to assure effective co-operation. Any formal arrangements entered into with such organizations or agencies shall be subject to the approval of the Executive Board.

2. Whenever the General Conference of this Organization and the competent authorities of any other specialized intergovernmental organizations or agencies whose purposes and functions lie within the competence of this Organization, deem it desirable to effect a transfer of their resources and activities to this Organization, the Director-General, subject to the approval of the Conference, may enter into mutually acceptable arrangements for this purpose.

3. This Organization may make appropriate arrangements with other intergovernmental organizations for reciprocal representation at meetings.

4. The United Nations Educational, Scientific and Cultural Organization may make suitable arrangements for consultation and cooperation with non-governmental international organizations concerned with matters within its competence, and may invite them to undertake specific tasks. Such cooperation may also include appropriate participation by representatives of such organizations on advisory committees set up by the General Conference.

Article XII. *Legal Status of the Organization*

The provisions of Articles 104 and 105 of the Charter of the United Nations Organization concerning the legal status of that Organization, its privileges and immunities, shall apply in the same way to this Organization.

Article XIII. *Amendments*

1. Proposals for amendments to this Constitution shall become effective upon receiving the approval of the General Conference by a two-thirds majority; provided, however, that those amendments which involve fundamental alterations in the aims of the Organization or new obligations for the Member States shall require subsequent acceptance on the part of two-thirds of the Member States before they come into force. The draft texts of proposed amendments shall be communicated by the Director-General to the Member States at least six months in advance of their consideration by the General Conference.

2. The General Conference shall have power to adopt by a two-thirds majority rules of procedure for carrying out the provisions of this Article.

Article XIV. *Interpretation*

1. The English and French texts of this Constitution shall be regarded as equally authoritative.

2. Any question or dispute concerning the interpretation of this Constitution shall be referred for determination to the International Court of Justice or to an arbitral tribunal, as the General Conference may determine under its rules of procedure.

Article XV. Entry into Force

1. This Constitution shall be subject to acceptance. The instruments of acceptance shall be deposited with the Government of the United Kingdom.

2. This Constitution shall remain open for signature in the archives of the Government of the United Kingdom. Signature may take place either before or after the deposit of the instrument of acceptance. No acceptance shall be valid unless preceded or followed by signature.

3. This Constitution shall come into force when it has been accepted by twenty of its signatories. Subsequent acceptances shall take effect immediately.

4. The Government of the United Kingdom will inform all Members of the United Nations of the receipt of all instruments of acceptance and of the date on which the Constitution comes into force in accordance with the preceding paragraph.

In faith whereof, the undersigned, duly authorized to that effect, have signed this Constitution in the English and French languages, both texts being equally authentic.

Done in London the sixteenth day of November, one thousand nine hundred and forty-five, in a single copy, in the English and French languages, of which certified copies will be communicated by the Government of the United Kingdom to the Governments of all the Members of the United Nations.

APPENDIX B

PROVISIONS *of United Nations Charter Applicable to Unesco*

Article 1

The Purposes of the United Nations are:

1. To maintain international peace and security, and to that end: to take effective collective measures for the prevention and removal of threats to the peace, and for the suppression of acts of aggression or other breaches of the peace, and to bring about by peaceful means, and in conformity with the principles of justice and international law, adjustment or settlement of international disputes or situations which might lead to a breach of the peace;

2. To develop friendly relations among nations based on respect for the principle of equal rights and self-determination of peoples, and to take other appropriate measures to strengthen universal peace;

3. To achieve international cooperation in solving international problems of an economic, social, cultural, or humanitarian character, and in promoting and encouraging respect for human rights and for fundamental freedoms for all without distinction as to race, sex, language, or religion; and

4. To be a center for harmonizing the actions of nations in the attainment of these common ends.

Article 2

.   .   .   .

7. Nothing contained in the present Charter shall authorize the United Nations to intervene in matters which are essentially within the domestic jurisdiction of any state or shall require the Members to submit such matters to settlement under the present Charter; but this principle shall not prejudice the application of enforcement measures under Chapter VII.

Article 13

1. The General Assembly shall initiate studies and make recommendations for the purpose of:

a. promoting international cooperation in the political field and encouraging the progressive development of international law and its codification;

b. promoting international cooperation in the economic, social, cultural, educational, and health fields, and assisting in the realization of human rights and fundamental freedoms for all without distinction as to race, sex, language, or religion.

2. The further responsibilities, functions, and powers of the General Assembly with respect to matters mentioned in paragraph 1 (b) above are set forth in Chapters IX and X.

Article 17

1. The General Assembly shall consider and approve the budget of the Organization.

2. The expenses of the Organization shall be borne by the Members as apportioned by the General Assembly.

3. The General Assembly shall consider and approve any financial and budgetary arrangements with specialized agencies referred to in Article 57 and shall examine the administrative budgets of such specialized agencies with a view to making recommendations to the agencies concerned.

Article 48

1. The action required to carry out the decisions of the Security Council for the maintenance of international peace and security shall be taken by all the Members of the United Nations or by some of them, as the Security Council may determine.

2. Such decisions shall be carried out by the Members of the United Nations directly and through their action in the appropriate international agencies of which they are members.

Article 55

With a view to the creation of conditions of stability and well-being which are necessary for peaceful and friendly relations among nations based on respect for the principle of equal rights and self-determination of peoples, the United Nations shall promote:

a. higher standards of living, full employment, and conditions of economic and social progress and development;

b. solutions of international economic, social, health, and related problems; and international cultural and educational cooperation; and

c. universal respect for, and observance of, human rights and fundamental freedoms for all without distinction as to race, sex, language, or religion.

Article 56

All Members pledge themselves to take joint and separate action in cooperation with the Organization for the achievement of the purposes set forth in Article 55.

Article 57

1. The various specialized agencies, established by intergovernmental agreement and having wide international responsibilities, as defined in their basic instruments in economic, social, cultural, educational, health, and related fields, shall be brought into relationship with the United Nations in accordance with the provisions of Article 63.

2. Such agencies thus brought into relationship with the United Nations are hereinafter referred to as specialized agencies.

Article 58

The Organization shall make recommendations for the coordination of the policies and activities of the specialized agencies.

Article 62

1. The Economic and Social Council may make or initiate studies and reports with respect to international economic, social, cultural, educational, health, and related matters and may make recommendations with respect to any such matters to the General Assembly, to the Members of the United Nations, and to the specialized agencies concerned.

2. It may make recommendations for the purpose of promoting respect for, and observance of, human rights and fundamental freedoms for all.

3. It may prepare draft conventions for submission to the General Assembly, with respect to matters falling within its competence.

4. It may call, in accordance with the rules prescribed by the United Nations, international conferences on matters falling within its competence.

Article 63

1. The Economic and Social Council may enter into agreements with any of the agencies referred to in Article 57, defining the terms on which the

agency concerned shall be brought into relationship with the United Nations. Such agreements shall be subject to approval by the General Assembly.

2. It may coordinate the activities of the specialized agencies through consultation with and recommendations to such agencies and through recommendations to the General Assembly and to the Members of the United Nations.

Article 64

1. The Economic and Social Council may take appropriate steps to obtain regular reports from the specialized agencies. It may make arrangements with the Members of the United Nations and with the specialized agencies to obtain reports on the steps taken to give effect to its own recommendations and to recommendations on matters falling within its competence made by the General Assembly.

2. It may communicate its observations on these reports to the General Assembly.

Article 65

The Economic and Social Council may furnish information to the Security Council and shall assist the Security Council upon its request.

Article 66

1. The Economic and Social Council shall perform such functions as fall within its competence in connection with the carrying out of the recommendations of the General Assembly.

2. It may, with the approval of the General Assembly, perform services at the request of Members of the United Nations and at the request of specialized agencies.

3. It shall perform such other functions as are specified elsewhere in the present Charter or as may be assigned to it by the General Assembly.

Article 73

Members of the United Nations which have or assume responsibilities for the administration of territories whose peoples have not yet attained a full measure of self-government recognize the principle that the interests of the inhabitants of these territories are paramount, and accept as a sacred trust the obligation to promote to the utmost, within the system of international peace and security established by the present Charter, the well-being of the inhabitants of these territories, and, to this end:

   a. to ensure, with due respect for the culture of the peoples concerned, their political, economic, social, and educational advancement, their just treatment, and their protection against abuses;

. . . .

d. to promote constructive measures of development, to encourage research, and to cooperate with one another and, when and where appropriate, with specialized international bodies with a view to the practical achievement of the social, economic, and scientific purposes set forth in this article;

. . . .

Article 76

The basic objectives of the trusteeship system, in accordance with the Purposes of the United Nations laid down in Article 1 of the present Charter, shall be:

a. to further international peace and security;

b. to promote the political, economic, social, and educational advancement of the inhabitants of the trust territories, and their progressive development towards self-government or independence as may be appropriate to the particular circumstances of each territory and its peoples and the freely expressed wishes of the peoples concerned, and as may be provided by the terms of each trusteeship agreement;

c. to encourage respect for human rights and for fundamental freedoms for all without distinction as to race, sex, language, or religion, and to encourage recognition of the interdependence of the peoples of the world;

. . . .

Article 88

The Trusteeship Council shall formulate a questionnaire on the political, economic, social, and educational advancement of the inhabitants of each trust territory, and the administering authority for each trust territory within the competence of the General Assembly shall make an annual report to the General Assembly upon the basis of such questionnaire.

Article 91

The Trusteeship Council shall, when appropriate, avail itself of the assistance of the Economic and Social Council and of the specialized agencies in regard to matters with which they are respectively concerned.

Article 96

1. The General Assembly or the Security Council may request the Inter-

national Court of Justice to give an advisory opinion on any legal question.

2. Other organs of the United Nations and specialized agencies, which may at any time be so authorized by the General Assembly, may also request advisory opinions of the Court on legal questions arising within the scope of their activities.

Article 104

The Organization shall enjoy in the territory of each of its Members such legal capacity as may be necessary for the exercise of its functions and the fulfillment of its purposes.

Article 105

1. The Organization shall enjoy in the territory of each of its Members such privileges and immunities as are necessary for the fulfillment of its purposes.

2. Representatives of the Members of the United Nations and officials of the Organization shall similarly enjoy such privileges and immunities as are necessary for the independent exercise of their functions in connection with the Organization.

3. The General Assembly may make recommendations with a view to determining the details of the application of paragraphs 1 and 2 of this Article or may propose conventions to the Members of the United Nations for this purpose.

APPENDIX C

UNIVERSAL DECLARATION OF HUMAN RIGHTS

Adopted by the General Assembly of the United Nations on December 10, 1948

Preamble

Whereas recognition of the inherent dignity and of the equal and inalienable rights of all members of the human family is the foundation of freedom, justice and peace in the world,

Whereas disregard and contempt for human rights have resulted in barbarous acts which have outraged the conscience of mankind, and the advent of a world in which human beings shall enjoy freedom of speech and belief and freedom from fear and want has been proclaimed as the highest aspiration of the common people,

Whereas it is essential, if man is not to be compelled to have recourse, as a last resort, to rebellion against tyranny and oppression, that human rights should be protected by the rule of law,

Whereas it is essential to promote the development of friendly relations among nations,

Whereas the peoples of the United Nations have in the Charter reaffirmed their faith in fundamental human rights, in the dignity and worth of the human person and in the equal rights of men and women and have determined to promote social progress and better standards of life in larger freedom,

Whereas Member States have pledged themselves to achieve, in co-operation with the United Nations, the promotion of universal respect for and observance of human rights and fundamental freedoms,

Whereas a common understanding of these rights and freedoms is of the greatest importance for the full realisation of this pledge,

Now Therefore

THE GENERAL ASSEMBLY

proclaims

THIS UNIVERSAL DECLARATION OF HUMAN RIGHTS as a common standard of achievement for all peoples and all nations, to the end that every individual and every organ of society, keeping this Declaration constantly in mind, shall strive by teaching and education to promote respect for these rights and freedoms and by progressive measures, national and international, to secure their universal and effective recognition and observance, both among the peoples of Member States themselves and among the peoples of territories under their jurisdiction.

Article 1. All human beings are born free and equal in dignity and rights. They are endowed with reason and conscience and should act towards one another in a spirit of brotherhood.

Article 2. (1) Everyone is entitled to all the rights and freedoms set forth in this Declaration, without distinction of any kind, such as race, colour, sex, language, religion, political or other opinion, national or social origin, property, birth or other status.

(2) Furthermore, no distinction shall be made on the basis of the political, jurisdictional or international status of the country or territory to which a person belongs, whether this territory be an independent, Trust, Non-Self-Governing territory, or under any other limitation of sovereignty.

Article 3. Everyone has the right to life, liberty and the security of person.

Article 4. No one shall be held in slavery or servitude; slavery and the slave trade shall be prohibited in all their forms.

Article 5. No one shall be subjected to torture or to cruel, inhuman or degrading treatment or punishment.

Article 6. Everyone has the right to recognition everywhere as a person before the law.

Article 7. All are equal before the law and are entitled without any discrimination to equal protection of the law. All are entitled to equal protection against any discrimination in violation of this Declaration and against any incitement to such discrimination.

Article 8. Everyone has the right to an effective remedy by the competent national tribunals for acts violating the fundamental rights granted him by the constitution or by law.

Article 9. No one shall be subjected to arbitrary arrest, detention or exile.

Article 10. Everyone is entitled in full equality to a fair and public hearing by an independent and impartial tribunal, in the determination of his rights and obligations and of any criminal charge against him.

Article 11. (1) Everyone charged with a penal offence has the right to be presumed innocent until proved guilty according to law in a public trial at which he has had all the guarantees necessary for his defence.

(2) No one shall be held guilty of any penal offence on account of any act or omission which did not constitute a penal offence, under national or international law, at the time when it was committed. Nor shall a heavier penalty be imposed than the one that was applicable at the time the penal offence was committed.

Article 12. No one shall be subjected to arbitrary interference with his privacy, family, home or correspondence, nor to attacks upon his honour and reputation. Everyone has the right to the protection of the law against such interference or attacks.

Article 13. (1) Everyone has the right to freedom of movement and residence within the borders of each state.

(2) Everyone has the right to leave any country, including his own, and to return to his country.

Article 14. (1) Everyone has the right to seek and to enjoy in other countries asylum from persecution.

(2) This right may not be invoked in the case of prosecutions genuinely arising from non-political crimes or from acts contrary to the purposes and principles of the United Nations.

Article 15. (1) Everyone has the right to a nationality.

(2) No one shall be arbitrarily deprived of his nationality nor denied the right to change his nationality.

Article 16. (1) Men and women of full age, without any limitation due to race, nationality or religion, have the right to marry and to found a family. They are entitled to equal rights as to marriage, during marriage and at its dissolution.

(2) Marriage shall be entered into only with the free and full consent of the intending spouses.

(3) The family is the natural and fundamental group unit of society and is entitled to protection by society and the State.

Article 17. (1) Everyone has the right to own property alone as well as in association with others.

(2) No one shall be arbitrarily deprived of his property.

Article 18. Everyone has the right to freedom of thought, conscience and religion; this right includes freedom to change his religion or belief, and freedom, either alone or in community with others and in public or private, to manifest his religion or belief in teaching, practice, worship and observance.

Article 19. Everyone has the right to freedom of opinion and expression; this right includes freedom to hold opinions without interference and to seek, receive and impart information and ideas through any media and regardless of frontiers.

Article 20. (1) Everyone has the right to freedom of peaceful assembly and association.

(2) No one may be compelled to belong to an association.

Article 21. (1) Everyone has the right to take part in the government of his country, directly or through freely chosen representatives.

(2) Everyone has the right of equal access to public service in his country.

(3) The will of the people shall be the basis of the authority of government; this will shall be expressed in periodic and genuine elections which shall be by universal and equal suffrage and shall be held by secret vote or by equivalent free voting procedures.

Article 22. Everyone, as a member of society, has the right to social security and is entitled to realisation, through national effort and international co-operation and in accordance with the organisation and resources of each State, of the economic, social and cultural rights indispensable for his dignity and the free development of his personality.

Article 23. (1) Everyone has the right to work, to free choice of employment, to just and favourable conditions of work and to protection against unemployment.

(2) Everyone, without any discrimination, has the right to equal pay for equal work.

(3) Everyone who works has the right to just and favourable remuneration insuring for himself and his family an existence worthy of human dignity, and supplemented, if necessary, by other means of social protection.

(4) Everyone has the right to form and to join trade unions for the protection of his interests.

Article 24. Everyone has the right to rest and leisure, including reasonable limitation of working hours and periodic holidays with pay.

Article 25. (1) Everyone has the right to a standard of living adequate for the health and well-being of himself and of his family, including food, clothing, housing and medical care and necessary social services, and the right to security in the event of unemployment, sickness, disability, widowhood, old age or other lack of livelihood in circumstances beyond his control.

(2) Motherhood and childhood are entitled to special care and assistance. All children, whether born in or out of wedlock, shall enjoy the same social protection.

Article 26. (1) Everyone has the right to education. Education shall be free, at least in the elementary and fundamental stages. Elementary education shall be compulsory. Technical and professional education shall be made generally available and higher education shall be equally accessible to all on the basis of merit.

(2) Education shall be directed to the full development of the human personality and to the strengthening of respect for human rights and fundamental freedoms. It shall promote understanding, tolerance and friendship among all nations, racial or religious groups, and shall further the activities of the United Nations for the maintenance of peace.

(3) Parents have a prior right to choose the kind of education that shall be given to their children.

Article 27. (1) Everyone has the right freely to participate in the cultural life of the community, to enjoy the arts and to share in scientific advancement and its benefits.

(2) Everyone has the right to the protection of the moral and material interests resulting from any scientific, literary or artistic production of which he is the author.

Article 28. Everyone is entitled to a social and international order in which the rights and freedoms set forth in this Declaration can be fully realized.

Article 29. (1) Everyone has duties to the community in which alone the free and full development of his personality is possible.

(2) In the exercise of his rights and freedoms, everyone shall be subject only to such limitations as are determined by law solely for the purpose of securing due recognition and respect for the rights and freedoms of others and of meeting the just requirements of morality, public order and the general welfare in a democratic society.

(3) These rights and freedoms may in no case be exercised contrary to the purposes and principles of the United Nations.

Article 30. Nothing in this Declaration may be interpreted as implying for any State, group or person any right to engage in any activity or to perform any act aimed at the destruction of any of the rights and freedoms set forth herein.

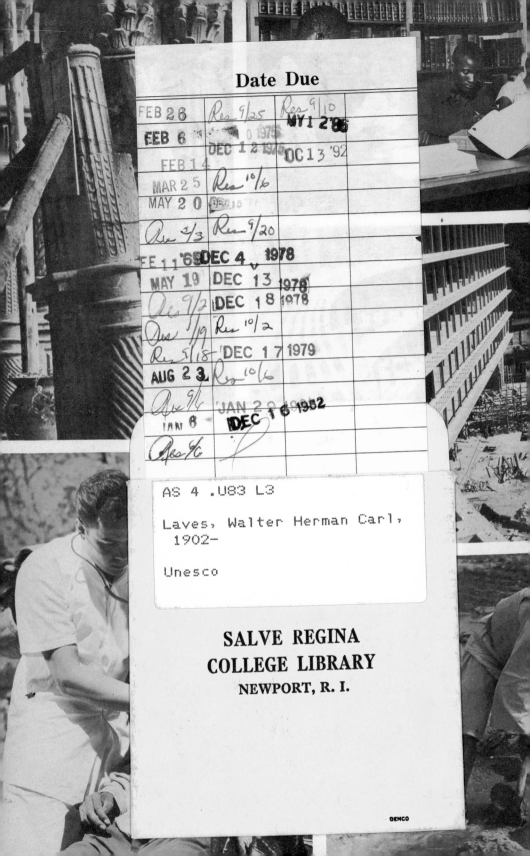